D0075744

Critical
Perspectives
on
Harry Potter

Critical Perspectives on Harry Potter

2nd edition

Edited by
Elizabeth E. Heilman

Routledge
Taylor & Francis Group

NEW YORK AND LONDON

First published 2003 by
RoutledgeFalmer

This edition published 2009
by Routledge
711 Third Avenue, NY 10017

Simultaneously published in the UK
by Routledge
2 Park Square, Milton Park, Abingdon, Oxfordshire OX14 4RN

First issued in hardback 2015

Routledge is an imprint of the Taylor & Francis Group, an informa business
© 2003; 2009 Taylor & Francis

Typeset in Minion by Wearset Ltd, Boldon, Tyne and Wear

All rights reserved. No part of this book may be reprinted or reproduced or utilized in
any form or by any electronic, mechanical, or other means, now known or hereafter
invented, including photocopying and recording, or in any information storage or
retrieval system, without permission in writing from the publishers.

Trademark Notice: Product or corporate names may be trademarks or registered
trademarks, and are used only for identification and explanation without intent to
infringe.

Library of Congress Cataloging in Publication Data
Critical Perspectives on Harry Potter / edited by Elizabeth E. Heilman.—2nd ed.
p. cm.
Rev. ed. of: Harry Potter's World, 2003.
Includes bibliographical references and index.
1. Rowling, J. K.—Criticism and interpretation. 2. Children—Books and reading—
English-speaking countries. 3. Children's stories, English—History and criticism. 4.
Fantasy fiction, English—History and criticism. 5. Rowling, J. K.—Characters—Harry
Potter. 6. Potter, Harry (Fictitious character) 7. Wizards in literature. 8. Magic in
literature. I. Harry Potter's World.
PR6068.O93273 2008
823´.914—dc22   2008005439

ISBN 13: 978-1-138-12887-3 (hbk)
ISBN 13: 978-0-415-96484-5 (pbk)

To Alex, my amazing son

To my spirit filled daughters,
Anneliese, Kathleen, and Maryrose

To book reading sons and daughters everywhere
and the parents and teachers who guide them

Contents

Contents   ix

Acknowledgments

I would like to express my appreciation for the talented cast of scholars who have contributed to this book. I am grateful for their wisdom and insight as they often worked through several drafts. Contributors Maria Nikolajeva, Philip Nel, Trevor Donaldson, and Kate Behr, each read and commented on a colleague's chapter in the collection as well. I thank my research assistants, Won Pyo and Alexander Wang for their typing up notes, and eye for detail, and Ellen Ott, Morgan Ott, Marcia Ratliff, Katie Gjerpen, and Ellen Ratliff who assisted with proofreading. I especially thank Alexander (my son) with whom I began this project nearly ten years ago when we presented a paper together on the books. Alex discussed many of the chapters with me and provided critical feedback. I thank my dear partner, Ken Waltzer for reading and editing my portions of the manuscript and for taking the kids out of the house when the book was in the final stages during Winter Break. This was a collective effort.

I am grateful to Barbara Bobbitt for 20 years of friendship and our many conversations about gender, race, media, capitalism, power, and culture. I would also like to thank Joanne Braxton and Robert Fehrenbach of the Department of English, and Roger Smith of the Department Government, at the College of William and Mary for the inspiration they provided when I first began the academic study of literature, democracy, and culture; and Jesse Goodman and Robert Arnove of Indiana University, for honoring and helping to hone my critical perspectives. I owe you all my sincerest thanks.

Introduction

Fostering Insight Through Multiple Critical Perspectives

ELIZABETH E. HEILMAN

Harry Potter has become more than just a book; it has become an icon, a Michael Jordan, a Coca-Cola, a Pop-Tart, in modern pop culture. The Potter books are now ubiquitous early texts for children, and are also a popular choice for many adults. As the most commercialized books in recollection, the phenomenon deserves multidisciplinary analysis. While the first edition of this volume addressed cultural themes, literary analysis, and critical perspectives, this second edition book speaks as well towards the phenomenon that Harry Potter has become, including the expansion into film, internet, and computer games, and also the increasingly wide array of theory that can be productively engaged to explore the texts.

The latest Harry Potter book sold nine million copies within the first 24 hours of release. There are now seven books, and multiple video games and movies (each ranking in the top 20 of all time highest grossing films), the Harry Potter iPod has recently been licensed, as well as more than 400 other Potter products. The Harry Potter brand is worth an estimated four billion dollars, which makes J. K. Rowling, by some reports, more wealthy than Queen Elizabeth II. While the first edition examined the first novels as an emerging cultural phenomenon, we can now examine Harry Potter and Pottermania as a whole. With more than 420 million copies of Rowling's books in print worldwide in some 60 languages, Harry Potter is present in most of the public and cultural spaces in which we live. In 1998, there were no spin-off products; by 2001, I was already able to find an entire aisle of toys in a major department store devoted to a mind boggling array of Harry Potter paraphernalia, and as the decade has progressed, there are spin-off products that go well beyond toys and include expensive jewelry, special vacations, a wall clock, tiffany lamps, and more. You can even get a Harry Potter cell phone cover and ring tone.

This phenomenon has grown into the biggest children's publishing and merchandising phenomenon of modern times. It has also been credited for a renaissance in reading for children all over the world—but this is largely a folk legend. Though indeed many children read the Harry Potter series, an extensive analysis of research on reading trends supported by the National Endowment for the Arts shows that most of these children do not go on to read many other books outside of school or become teens and young adults who read. Others will remain reading strictly in fantasy/mystery genres. More than half of American adults won't read a single novel in a year according to the National Endowment for the Arts and, in the last decade, as millions of Harry Potter books have sold, the decline of reading has almost tripled. The Harry Potter series hasn't spawned a new generation of readers, and many literary critics find the series comparatively unimpressive. As Ron Charles (2007) observed, "Philip Pullman's 'His Dark Materials' is a dazzling fantasy series that explores philosophical themes [including a scathing assault on organized religion] that make[s] Rowling's little world of good vs. evil look, well, childish." Still, there is no question that the Harry Potter series is important.

The narrative story, images, and lessons of the books are infiltrating the lives and imaginations of readers and consumers of related products. We encounter Harry Potter in all sorts of places—the bookstore, the software dealer, the library, the card shop, and the local schools. Harry Potter is discussed in coffee shops and on public radio. We encounter the face of the Harry Potter actor peering out from prosaic magazines such as the American *TV Guide, Ladies Home Journal,* and *Vanity Fair* and many similar publications around the world. There are references to Harry Potter in the more cerebral offerings of the *New Yorker, Atlantic Monthly,* and *Salon* as well. When narrative text and images become such a pervasive part of the cultural environment, they also become part of the identity of the people who read and consume the images and narratives. Harry Potter then is not just books we read or movies we see or things that we buy. The text and images of Harry Potter become part of who we are. This is true of individuals and it is true of "us" as a global culture. Harry Potter books have been read, discussed, celebrated, and vilified in Taiwan, Mexico, Mozambique, and Russia. They are read by children in Harlem, children on Indian reservations, and children in Siberia. To a large degree (as Jorge Luis Borges has famously suggested) we are what we read. So, what does the popularity of Harry Potter suggest about who we are? What do the books themselves have to say and how do they say it?

These works contain powerful, thought-provoking literary themes as well as portrayals of social and cultural normalcy. They cumulatively serve as a powerful form of social text and deserve serious critical attention. The view that literature and cultural products can simultaneously represent, reproduce, and transform cultural, political, and institutional norms has become an increasingly important perspective in literary theory, cultural studies, curriculum theory, art, and aesthetics. This book brings together scholars from a diverse set of academic specialties to provide literary, cultural, sociological, and psychological examinations of the Harry Potter books as both cultural products and literary texts. Our new edition is more international, featuring five non-American scholars—Alice Mills from Australia, Peter Ciaccio from Italy, Maria Nikolajeva and Anna Gunder from Sweden, and Taija Piippo from Finland—and draws on a wider range of intellectual traditions by including a moral–theological analysis, psychoanalytic perspectives, and philosophy of technology. Authors make use of formal and structural analysis, archetypal criticism, psychological analysis, genre criticism, historical criticism, and critical theory. Since these novels engage the social, cultural, and psychological preoccupations of our times, we examine worlds of consciousness and the construction of cultural worlds, and how modern anxieties about subjectivity and individuality are reflected in these texts. Such an interdisciplinary presentation is emblematic of the ways in which approaches to literary discourse and other cultural discourses have become increasingly rich and entwined. The book is divided into four inter-related parts, yet these theories and the chapters organized accordingly are not mutually exclusive nor competing interpretations.

Perspectives on Identity and Morality

While most readers see the books as engaging fantasy, Christian censors around the world see the books as diabolic stories encouraging occult practice, magic, and witchcraft. Some parents, who may not be concerned about magic and witchcraft, see the books as yet another example of overly scary and violent media that children should not be exposed to. These matters are important not only for cultural theorists to ponder, but are of concern to psychologists, and teachers as well. Exactly how are children influenced (or not) by what they read? In Chapter One, "Controversial Content," Taub and Servaty-Seib explore these issues. They explain that children's responses to literature varies a great deal according to the developmental and psychological contexts in which they are reading.

Most Christians do not seek censorship, however. In "Harry Potter and Christian Theology," Chapter Two, Rev. Peter Ciaccio writes from the perspective of a Southern European Protestant theologian and details the role of magic, charisma and identity, overcoming dualisms, the notion of treasures, death, curses, sin, and the temptations of power—a panoply of Christian themes. Nicholas Sheltrown also reads the series as a morality tale. In Chapter Three, "Harry Potter's World as a Morality Tale of Technology and Media" he reveals Rowling's critical engagement with the role of technology in shaping personal lives and collective destinies. Personal lives are also examined through Sigmund Freud's psychoanalytic theory and Gilles Deleuze and Félix Guattari's poststructuralist theory in Chapter Four, "Is Desire Beneficial or Harmful in the Harry Potter Series?" where Taija Piippo explores the connection between desire and identity development, and more broadly as a driving narrative theme.

Peter Appelbaum, writing in Chapter Five, locates another narrative theme related to identity development. The Harry Potter books belong to the genre, *Bildungsroman*: a young man is led by a collection of hands higher than he is aware of toward his destiny. The surface story is the main character's maturation, but the underlying themes address his apprenticeship and the decisions that are made in the crafting of it. The character of Snape is the under story in the Harry Potter books and raises the notion of the "good teacher" in terms of pedagogical techniques, the creation of the perfect society, and of individual moral character. These are explored in "The Great Snape Debate."

Each author writes convincingly from very different standpoints. The psychoanalytic view that responses to literature are highly variable and that meaning is a product of individual psychic response to a work is consistent with a broad body of literary theory in which literature is understood as that which is received by the reader rather than that which is created by the author. Reader response theory, introduced by Stanley Fish (1980) focuses on "an analysis of the developing responses of the reader in relation to the words as they succeed one another in time" (p. 27). At its most extreme, this theory suggests that the reader is really the author. This idea is consistent with philosophical postmodernism, which emphasizes "local knowledge" and questions the truth of any collective authoritative interpretation or "meta narrative."

Reader response theories suggest that each reader creates a text as they read. Yet, the texts certainly seem to exist on their own. Readers cannot read in a void. Readers' and authors' interpretations are intimately tied up with all previous experiences, including experience with other texts. Anytime we understand something, it is because we relate it to an idea, a text, or category we have already seen. Thus, each text and each reading of text is actually intertextual. A book, and even a paragraph, is chock full of direct and indirect references to these other texts, media, and experiences. There is nothing new under the sun. The debts of texts to other texts seems endless. As Barthes (1977) describes this:

> The text is a tissue of quotations drawn from the innumerable centers of culture ... the writer can only imitate a gesture that is always interior, never original. His only power is to mix writings, to counter the ones with the others, in such a way as never to rest on any one of them.
>
> (pp. 146–147)

From this point of view, a literary work is no longer the product of an author's original thoughts. Instead, the author is a recycler who is limited by the availability of a pre-existing language system with words, signs, and symbols, and a pre-existing literary system with conventions for things like plot, genre, characterization, images, and narrative voice. These ideas about literature fall within the broad category "poststructural," which is not a single theory but a group of theories that share similar ideas and a rejection of earlier "structural" approaches to literature. In its most narrow sense, structuralism assumes that a work has intrinsic meaning that pre-exists the realization of any meaning. If nobody is around to hear a tree falling in a forest a structuralist would say that there is still a sound, but a poststructuralist would not. Furthermore, a structuralist believes that the individual, the unconscious, and the social and cultural world are all composed of the same signs, codes, and conventions, all working according to similar principles. Literary texts are also structured according to these same signs, codes, and conventions. Literature then is best understood as a complete system of reference. Individual works can be studied according to the ways in which they participate in this complete system and possess identifiable literary conventions.

Critical and Sociological Perspectives

Chapters Six through Ten of this book examine the treatment of particular themes: schooling (Six), home and family (Seven), gender (Eight), animals (Nine), and public culture (Ten). These chapters are written in ways that combine elements of both structuralism and cultural studies. Structuralism tends to be a comparative methodology in that a close reading of the text reveals the use of literary themes, patterns, systems, and structures. A critic then compares the use of these elements in one text with other texts. Cultural Studies, however, also consider texts in terms of their social, political, economic, and cultural influence rather than their literariness or comparative use of theme alone. Texts inevitably contain ideological messages about who has power and why, what is of value, and commentary on normalcy and success. Ideological critique aims to show how ideology functions within texts and, also, around texts, since texts are also produced in the midst of certain social, economic, and political contexts. What is allowed to be in print and what is collectively considered to be literature at any given historical point is related to these ideological and power-driven contexts.

Ideological critique encourages critical reading, which enables the reader to understand the subtle and overt ideologies of the text. Ideology can be hard to see because the most compelling ideology comes in the form of the more subtly suggestive and pleasurable reading. Readers can be ideologically influenced without being aware of it. As Foucault describes, in modern society, power can be hard to recognize because "a relationship of power is that mode of action that does not act directly and immediately on others. Instead it acts upon their actions" (1983, p. 229). Yet, readers also respond to ideological messages in different ways. Ideological texts, like other texts, are multivalent. They can be read in multiple ways and in multiple contexts. Also, there are multiple ideologies, not just one ideology.

A postmodern critique of ideology aims to reveal systems of thinking that legitimate particular worldviews and enable oppression, but, at the same time, acknowledges that there is no ideologically free reality to compare it to. In addition, post-Marxist cultural studies of literature attempt to recognize that literature and cultural products can simultaneously represent, reproduce, and transform cultural, political, and institutional norms. They can be both literary and ideological and text can promote both liberation and oppression.

In Chapter Six, "Schooling Harry Potter," Megan L. Birch details the series' mockery of schools and teachers and the suggestion that teachers have very little power to shape instruction or the institution of schooling. She questions the implicit claim that being a good teacher is about who you are as a person rather than what you know and that who you know is profoundly more valuable than what you know. In "Comedy, Quest, and Community: Home and Family in Harry Potter," Kornfeld and Prothro examine home, family, and leaving home. Harry's quest of self-discovery, which parallels his quest to defeat Voldemort, forms the basis of all young adult coming-of-age literature, in which protagonists create their own version of home out of the strangeness they encounter when they are in exile.

In Chapter Eight, Trevor Donaldson and I examine gender identity conventions and hierarchies in the Harry Potter books and reveal that the Harry Potter books often feature females in secondary positions of power and authority and replicate some of the most demeaning, yet familiar, cultural stereotypes even though the later books feature comparatively less sexism. The girls still often giggle, cry, and gossip and are obsessed with, and even crippled by, their relationships. The strong, adventurous, independent boy serves as a heroic expression of masculinity, while the weak, non-successful male is mocked and sometimes despised. Peter Dendle, writing in Chapter Nine "Monsters, Creatures, and Pets at Hogwarts" shows how the responsibilities of stewardship over the realm of subordinate creatures of Rowling's making is a continuous anxiety in the Harry Potter series, and one that maps shrewdly—in capturing many of the same successes and hypocrisies alike—onto the actual human relationship with animals at the turn of the third millennium. In Chapter Ten, "Harry Potter, the War against Evil, and the Melodramatization of Public Culture" the Harry Potter series is examined by Marc Bousquet as a significant artifact in the contemporary resurgence of the melodramatic in mass-mediated public culture including the conviction that evildoers are less than human, that they can and should be tortured to clarify the plot, and that there can be no relief to good until the evil other is destroyed.

Literary Perspectives: the Hero, Myth, and Genre

Structuralist literary critics believe they can dissect, evaluate, and describe a text's literariness and importance. What seems tricky here is that this often requires an analysis of the ways in which the text is intertextual or related to other texts. These chapters are critiques that fall, to some extent, within the structuralist tradition. As Genette (1988) describes in *Structuralism and Literary Criticism*, the structuralist critic analyzes the "themes, motifs, key words" that create the text.

In Chapter Eleven, "Playing the Genre Game," Anne Alton reviews "Rowling's incorporation of a vast number of genres in the books in the tradition of genre criticism." She explains that genres often dismissed as "despised" genres—including pulp fiction, mystery, gothic and horror stories, detective fiction, the school story, the closely related sports story, and series books—appear throughout the Harry Potter books, along with more "mainstream" genres (at least in children's literature) such as fantasy, adventure, quest, romance, and myth" and concludes that ultimately, "Rowling has fused a number of genres to create something new: a generic mosaic which is a composite, made up of numerous smaller pieces combined in a way that allows them to keep their original shape and structure and yet changes their individual significance, and thus the meaning of the whole. In Chapter Twelve, "Harry Potter and the Secrets of Children's Literature," Maria Nikolajeva considers the tremendous success of Harry Potter and suggests that in contemporary Western children's fiction, most of the child characters seem to appear on low mimetic and ironic levels and these books are a fortunate attempt to reintroduce the romantic character into children's fiction. She also makes use of carnival theory to examine how the novels empower children and have a subversive effect, showing that the rules imposed on the child by the adults are arbitrary. Alice Mills provides a critical analysis of classical allusions in Chapter Thirteen, "Harry Potter and the Horrors of the *Oresteia*," and details what she effectively argues is Rowling's profoundly anti-Oresteian view of human life. Chapter Fourteen, "Philosopher's Stone to Resurrection Stone: Narrative Transformations and Intersecting Cultures across the Harry Potter Series," by Kate Behr reviews transformation on the surface level, in the details of the wizarding world, in its language and customs, and, at a deeper level, in Harry Potter's character as he moves through adolescence to adulthood, making more and more difficult choices. She argues that transformation is at the heart of the series itself.

Cultural Studies and Media Perspectives

In the final part of this book, authors explore Harry Potter as a cultural phenomenon. Their work is a form of "cultural studies," a critical tradition that draws from the fields of anthropology, communications, history, literary criticism, political theory, sociology, and psychoanalysis in order to explore relationships among texts, media, and cultural practices. The cultural studies movement has redirected literary criticism more broadly into cultural criticism, which considers a wide range of texts in terms of their social, political, economic, and cultural influence rather than their literariness alone, and encourages the study of mass culture and popular forms in addition to elite genres and canonical works. These chapters are not focused so much on looking inside of the books. Instead, they are looking at the ways in which the books and the Harry Potter phenomenon fit into contemporary culture and the ways in which Harry Potter has been interpreted in various new and different media beyond the novels. When I watched the films I was struck by how novels with slowly developing mystery, suspense, and a feel of everyday school life occurring over a year were transformed into action movies.

Books that didn't seem horrific became scary movies not suitable for many elementary schoolers. Philip Nel describes what is "Lost in Translation" in Chapter Fifteen. Anna Gunder, in Chapter Sixteen, provides a fascinating comparison of the books and video games, exploring how the Harry Potter series is particularly well suited for ludolization, i.e., transposition into game form. In Chapter Seventeen, Ernest L. Bond and Nancy L. Michelson explore the theoretical underpinnings for the participatory authoring of literary worlds and then examine a vast array of student writing, blogs, vlogs, song fic, video trailers, bands, and more in response to the Harry Potter series. Finally, Turner-Vorbeck's chapter, "Pottermania: Good, Clean Fun or Cultural Hegemony?," critically examines the intensive marketing efforts related to the Harry Potter books, and product spin-offs, and considers issues of imagination, power, and control. Reading, along with other aspects of child culture, is increasingly becoming an opportunity for marketing and consumerism instead of a private, relatively low cost pleasure.

Conclusion

I have assembled this collection as a curriculum theorist dedicated to the notion that democracy and social justice must rely on the critical intellectual insights, civic courage, and imaginative power of communities, rather than the best ideas of any authority. The critical study of literature and culture is essential to such a vision. In the postmodern context in which we live, cultural products promoted by multinational corporations can serve as a powerful form of authority promoting unequal relations of power and a dreary aesthetic. Yet, literature and culture can be read in many ways, particularly with assistance from critical works such as this. We can talk back to Harry Potter. In order to have rich conversations and develop critical insight and imagination, I contend that the engagement of popular and literary texts should draw from multiple paradigms and employ multiple theoretical lenses.

In this collection, I have tried to provide a multidisciplinary framework that can bring interesting and potent theories to readers and students of literature, to children, their parents, and their teachers. I hope this text helps to bridge the gap between critical theory and critical pedagogy. Though literary theory has moved away from structuralism and New Criticism to include psychoanalytic, poststructuralist, and cultural studies analyses, these approaches have had little effect on the ways in which literature is taught in undergraduate studies and even less in K-12. Similarly, though there is an increasing body of scholarship on critical pedagogy, critical literacy, multiculturalism, and critical and reflective social studies, things have changed very little across the curriculum.

Thus, in addition to the literary and cultural studies significance of this collection, this book is important because it can help parents and teachers to make school curriculum and conversations about books more meaningful. Exploring critical and liberating ways of reading is certainly a valuable goal, but it is hard to do, even with support.

Chapters providing psychoanalytic perspectives can help teachers think about the complexity of readers' motivations and responses. Chapters on hero, myth, and genre can help children understand literary structures and allusions. The "Critical and Sociological Perspectives" chapters can help parents and teachers stimulate powerful discussions and integrate powerful curricular themes to consider who has power in society. These chapters can give support for discussions about the construction of identity, the meaning of home, the difference between schooling and learning, and what it means to be a leader.

Curriculum—especially Social Studies and English—can potentially serve as a vehicle for deconstructing these complex issues. Without support, teachers developing curriculum around these books sometimes focus on trivia, for example, having students create models of Hogwarts School or invent their own flavor of Every Flavor Bean. Much critical scholarship asks teachers to use powerful critical themes, address popular culture, and make meaningful connections to students' interests. This book gives teachers a tool to do so on a range of levels, examining the relationship among cultural products and power at the macro level of political and economic structures—but also at the micro level, considering cultural and aesthetic nuances in language, texts, and personal responses.

References

Barthes, R. (1977). The death of the author. in R. Barthes (ed.), *Image, music, text* (S. Heath, trans.) (pp. 142–148). New York: Hill & Wang.

Charles, R. (2007, July 15). Harry Potter and the death of reading. *Washington Post Sunday*, p. B01.

Fish, S. (1980). *Is there a text in this class? The authority of interpretive communities.* Cambridge, MA: Harvard University Press.

Foucault, M. (1983). The subject and power. In *Michel Foucault: Beyond hermeneutics and structuralism* (pp. 208–226). Chicago, IL: University of Chicago Press.

Genette, G. (1988). Structuralism and literary criticism. In David Lodge (ed.), *Modern criticism and theory*. London: Longman.

National Endowment for the Arts (NEA). (2007). *To read or not to read: a question of national consequence.* Retrieved January 18, 2008, from http://www.nea.gov/research/ToRead.pdf.

Perspectives on Identity and Morality

Part I

Perspectives on
Identity and
Morality

Chapter One

Controversial Content
Is Harry Potter Harmful to Children?

DEBORAH J. TAUB AND
HEATHER L. SERVATY-SEIB

The publication of the seventh and final Harry Potter book, *Harry Potter and the Deathly Hallows*, set publishing records, selling 8.3 million copies in its first day of release (Blais and DeBarros, 2007). Even as the Harry Potter books have been heralded as a publishing and cultural phenomenon, they also have been the subject of challenge and controversy from the publication of the first book through the last. The Harry Potter books were the seventh most frequently challenged books of 1990–2000 (up from forty-eighth on the 1990–1999 list) according to the American Library Association (ALA, 2007a). Objections to the books stem from their controversial content—from the centrality of magic to the topic of death to scenes that some believe are too violent, intense, or scary for children.

Controversy over children's books is not new. According to Shannon (1989), "The history of the struggle over the content of children's and adolescents' reading material is nearly as long as the history of schooling in America" (p. 97). One of the bases for this struggle is the view of "children-as-innocent-and-in-need-of-protection" (Dresang, 2003, p. 21). In this view children need to be "protected from certain kinds of literature" (Stevenson, 1996, p. 305) that could be harmful to their innocence. Challenges to children's books center on "what knowledge they [the challengers] think is valid, valuable, and virtuous for school curricula and library shelves" (Shannon, 1989, p. 97); those who challenge books "may believe that the materials will corrupt children and adolescents, offend the sensitive or unwary reader, or undermine basic values and beliefs" (American Library Association, 2006).

This chapter explores the controversial content of the Harry Potter series and whether the books might be harmful to children. Focusing particularly on the themes of magic, religion, violence and scariness, and death, the chapter concludes with guidelines for teachers and parents.

Challenges to Harry Potter: the Religious Argument

In his book about censorship in schools and public libraries, Foerstel (1994) states "there is no hotter topic among today's bookbanners than the devil and witchcraft ... materials about witchcraft and the occult account for the largest number of challenges to resources in libraries today" (p. 109). During the period 2001–2005, witchcraft was a major concern in challenges to books (American Library Association, 2007b). This is reflected in the many challenges to Harry Potter based on religious objections.

Most religious objections to the magic in Harry Potter are based on various passages of scripture, most commonly Deuteronomy 18:9–12:

> When you come into the land which the Lord your God gives you, you shall not learn to follow the abominable practices of those nations. There shall not be found among you any one who burns his son or his daughter as an offering, any one who practices divination, a soothsayer, or an augur, or a sorcerer, or a charmer, or a medium, or a wizard, or a necromancer. For whoever does these things is an abomination to the Lord; and because of these abominable practices the Lord your God is driving them out before you.
>
> (Revised Standard Version)

The dangers of Harry Potter from a Christian perspective can be found on the Internet under such titles as "The Harry Potter Series: A Vision of the Antichrist" (Chambers, 2007); "Bewitched by Harry Potter" (Kjos, 1999); "Harry Potter Lures Kids to Witchcraft—with Praise from Christian Leaders" (Kjos, n.d.); "Harry Potter: A New Twist to Witchcraft" ("Harry Potter: A New Twist," n.d.); and "Harry Potter and DandD—Like Two Peas in a Pod?" (Kjos, 2000). The religious concerns include assertions that the books portray magic as harmless, fun, or good and that they may encourage children to dabble in the occult. Similar arguments have been made about the role-playing game "Dungeons and Dragons" ("D and D") and certain rock music (Blimling, 1990; Hicks, 1991; Hunter, 1998; Kjos, 2000, 2003).

The rhetoric of many of these websites is extreme, and both the reasoning and the interpretation of scripture frequently is convoluted. For instance, Joseph Chambers (2007) wrote, "Without question I believe the Harry Potter series is a creation of hell helping prepare the younger generation to welcome the Biblical prophecies of demons and devils led by Lucifer himself." He continued by suggesting that the source of the inspiration for the Harry Potter books, which are widely reported to have just popped into author J. K. Rowling's head fully formed, is Satan. He concluded with his certainty that "the Harry Potter books are just another means [of Satan] of blinding millions to the truth."

Many may find it difficult to take such extreme ideas seriously or to believe that others might. To many it will appear ridiculous that so many are taking a fantasy seriously. To understand this perspective, it is essential to understand religious views on fantasy, magic, and the occult.

Religion is a critical factor influencing parental attitudes about children's fantasy behavior in that there are stark differences between what is considered real and what is considered fantasy from one religion to the next (Taylor and Carlson, 2000). They continue by describing how specific religious orientations (e.g. Hinduism, fundamental Christianity, and Mennonite) affect parents' views of childhood fantasy-related behavior. Taylor and Carlson address two primary objections to fantasy offered by parents with fundamental Christian beliefs. First, those with fundamental beliefs appear to equate fantasy with deceit and express concerns that fantastical activity and storytelling will lead to lying and other deceitful behavior. In addition, members of fundamentalist groups who are focused on issues of "spiritual warfare" believe that it is necessary to protect their children from evil forces in the spiritual world. Some in this latter group have even expressed concern about public elementary schools, stating that they expose children to dangerous ideas about witchcraft, occult practices, and Halloween.

In their research on the imaginary companions of children, Taylor and Carlson found a qualitative difference between the responses of parents with fundamental Christian beliefs and the other parent participants. In general, most parents who expressed concern regarding the behavior usually did so in relation to the inconvenience of including the imaginary companion in family activities and worries that the behavior was developmentally inappropriate and/or that it might indicate that the child was struggling with distinguishing fantasy from reality. In contrast, parents with fundamental Christian beliefs associated imaginary companions with the devil. Taylor and Carlson argue that these disparate views of the same behavior "reflect a divergent perception on the part of the adults of what is real and what is fantasy" (p. 248).

This divergence of viewpoints can be seen in the reactions to Harry Potter by members of various Christian groups and denominations. While some Christian leaders support and admire the Harry Potter books (Granger, 2006; Olsen, 1999), others condemn them as dangerous.

For fundamentalist Christians "witchcraft is as real to us as any other religion" (Gish, 2000, p. 263). This belief—that witchcraft is real and is necessarily evil—lies at the heart of the religious objections. To those who believe in the reality of witchcraft, the threat of the Harry Potter books is that they might desensitize children to the sinfulness of magic and that "children may learn to see them [occult or Satanic practices] as acceptable" (p. 264). (Those interested in a detailed and excellent description of the religious objections to the Harry Potter books and other popular children's fantasy books are directed to Gish's article.) "Once again: when you believe that witches and occult practices are real, and contrary to God's laws, those books are quite different from what the authors probably intended" (p. 264). Gish provides a useful gloss of Deuteronomy 18:9–12 as those verses are applied to Harry Potter. She points, for example, to the Divination course offered by Hogwarts and, obviously, the fact that Harry and his friends are learning to be wizards.

Several Christian leaders who support and admire the Harry Potter books find the books promoting values such as courage, love, friendship, and loyalty, with a moral approach of good vs. evil. Granger, in his book *Looking for God in Harry Potter* (2006), asserted that "the Harry Potter stories 'sing along' with the Great Story of Christ [which] is a significant key to understanding their compelling richness" (p. 2). Although many writers have commented on the near total lack of the mention of any religion in the first six Harry Potter books, in *Harry Potter and the Deathly Hallows* the reader encounters "whispers" of Christianity (Smietana, 2007). In the cemetery in Godric's Hollow on Christmas Eve, Harry and Hermione read the inscriptions on the graves of Kendra and Ariana Dumbledore and of James and Lily Potter—both passages from the New Testament. Shortly after the publication of *Deathly Hallows*, Rowling, in a press conference, explained that she has always seen her series as based extensively on Christian themes, including questions about the afterlife and the power of love over death (Adler, 2007). According to Rowling, she hesitated to make the religious parallels too explicit as the series developed to keep readers from anticipating too early where the story was going.

Just before the release of *Harry Potter and the Deathly Hallows*, the Church of England published a guide to teach youth leaders in the church how to use the Harry Potter books to teach Christian messages to young people (*Use Harry Potter*, 2007). The author of the guide, Owen Smith, stated,

> To say, as some have, that these books draw younger readers towards the occult seems to me both to malign JK Rowling and to vastly underestimate the ability of children and young people to separate the real from the imaginary.

The Occult

What about the concerns that exposure to magical ideas such as spells, wizards, and potions tempts young people to dabble in the occult or become members of a cult? On her website in her discussion of the dangers of Harry Potter, Kjos (2000) asserts,

> For most children tutored in paganism by popular authors and computer programmers, there will be no turning back.... A little dabbling

in the occult usually fuels urges to explore other practices.... Packaged for our youth as D and D [Dungeons and Dragons] or as Hogwart's School of Witchcraft and Wizardry, they desensitize their captive fans to the dangers of occult forces. They can become irresistible.

Hunter (1998) also cites the progression from fantasy role-playing games to dabbling in satanic rituals to cult membership. Some people even assert that satanists use Dungeons and Dragons to recruit members (Foerstel, 1994).

Hicks (1991), a law enforcement expert whose book, *In Pursuit of Satan*, addresses alleged satanic crime, debunks this notion of a causal link between fantasy games such as Dungeons and Dragons and occult dabbling. In a study of a stratified random matched sample of fantasy role-playing gamers, satanic "dabblers," and students who were neither game-players nor dabblers, Leeds (1995) found the gamers and the uninvolved comparison group to be similar to one another in terms of their beliefs in the paranormal and personal stability and the satanic dabblers to be different from the other two groups in both of those areas. Based on his study, Leeds concluded, "the occult and satanism are two distinctly different realms, and ... one does not necessarily lead to the next" (p. 158). He continued: "These results do not support popular media suggestions that involvement in fantasy role-playing games are the direct antecedents to satanic practices, beliefs in magical spells, and demon-summoning in impressionable youth" (p. 158). Hicks (1991) deplores the notion, suggested by the popular media, "that teens have so little judgment where fantasy is concerned that parents must absolutely control all that they read and hear" (p. 271). Can children and adolescents exercise judgment about fantasy?

Fantasy and Reality

Beyond the religiously based concerns expressed well by Gish (2000) are those of parents who do not believe that magic, of the type presented in the Harry Potter series, is real. These parents may express concerns that their child(ren), however, could begin to view such practices as real. Their concerns are grounded in the idea that reading books like the Harry Potter series, which include fantastical and magical content, could foster confusion regarding the distinction between fantasy and reality.

Although the subject of fantasy is still an emerging area within developmental psychology, there is valuable information to be gleaned from the research that has been done. The scholarly work reviewed here addresses developmental and methodological issues related to the fantasy–reality distinction, factors that appear to affect children's ability to distinguish fantasy from reality, and potential benefits of fantastical thinking and play.

In her thorough review of the fantasy/reality literature, Woolley (1997) indicates clearly that the ability to distinguish fantasy from reality, at a very basic level, is in place by three years of age. She and her colleagues have found that around the age of three years children express differences between reality and pictures, reality and pretense, and reality and toys in their everyday conversations (Woolley and Wellman, 1990). Skolnick and Bloom (2006) found that not only can children (aged three to six) distinguish between real and fantasy figures, they separate fantasy worlds as adults do (e.g., Batman does not believe that SpongeBob is real). Sharon and Woolley (2004) found that the three to five year olds in their study had some difficulty correctly categorizing real vs. fantastical entities, but that five year olds (closely followed by four year olds) were strikingly similar to adults in their attributions of the properties (i.e., physical, biological, social, and mental) of real and fantastical entities. Five year olds were much more likely to attribute human-like properties to real entities (e.g., a child of the same sex) than they were to fantastical entities (e.g., monster, fairy, Santa Claus).

The approach used to challenge and assess children's ability to distinguish fantasy from reality is a significant issue (Bourchier and Davis, 2000; Sharon and Woolley, 2004). It is evident from reviewing the literature that researchers are continually fine-tuning their approach to assessment in an attempt to understand best what is occurring cognitively for children as they engage in the experimental procedures. Questions arise about numerous potential confounding factors (e.g., inclusion or exclusion of response choices, language used). For example, Sharon and Woolley (2004) provided children with the option to place entities in an "unsure" pile if they were not confident that an entity was either real or fantastical—an option that children used quite frequently. They reasonably argued that the failure to offer this option in previous research likely affected findings as children who were unsure were required to choose. Deák (2006) contends that current methods of investigation offer more information about children's "failure to understand the unfamiliar discourse format of the standard test" (p. 546) than they provide insight regarding children's confusion between fantasy and reality.

Keeping in mind the developmental and methodological issues noted above, there are factors that seem to affect children's ability to distinguish fantasy from reality and their beliefs about magic. More specifically, the factors we discuss, primarily noted by Woolley (1997), include exposure to or engagement with fantastical material, the emotional tenor of the object/entity being considered, the interpersonal context within which objects/entities are considered, and children's knowledge of the physical world.

To begin, no evidence was located to suggest that the reading of the Harry Potter series or any other book with fantastical content disrupts children's basic ability to distinguish fantasy from reality. Confirming Taylor, Cartwright, and Carlson's (1993) earlier work, Carrick and Quas (2006) recently found that children's report of enjoyment of engaging in fantasy play was not related to their ability to distinguish fantasy from reality. Sharon and

Woolley (2004) actually found that children who were more interested and involved in fantasy content and play were *better* able to distinguish between fantastical and real entities. They suggest, as do others (Taylor, 1999) that exposure to and engagement with fantastical material allows children to learn more about the fantasy world and, therefore, strengthens their understanding of the boundaries of imagination.

The emotional tenor of objects/entities appears to affect whether or not children will make accurate judgments regarding fantasy vs. reality (Woolley, 1997). In general, children tend to believe erroneously, regardless of the actual status of the entity, that positively charged entities are real and negatively charged entities are unreal (Samuels and Taylor, 1994; Phelps and Woolley, 1994) and that happy fantasy events are more possible to occur than frightening or angry fantasy events (Carrick and Quas, 2006). Woolley (1997) states the possibility "that children's judgments about imagined entities may reflect whether or not they *want* the entity to appear" (p. 995). In relation to the Harry Potter series, children may be more likely to believe in the existence of the Marauder's Map or the Patronus than they are to believe in Lord Voldemort or the Dementors.

Research also suggests that the interpersonal context within which fantasy or magical objects/entities are considered affects children's ability to distinguish accurately fantasy from reality. Bateson (1972) described fantasy as a "communicational mode" and contends that it is actually the metacommunication (verbal and nonverbal) that accompanies an event that affects how that event will be interpreted. Vanderburg (1998) stated that "it is crucial that children know what is serious and what is not, and that they understand and trust the regularities and particularities of communication that are essential for appropriate participation in intersubjective mutuality" (p. 298). Golomb and Galasso (1995) found that when children were clearly informed in the midst of a pretending that "they had to end the game," few made errors with regard to believing that fantasy could create reality.

Parents have a powerful role to play in influencing how children perceive fantastical or magical material and/or entities. Children are more likely to make errors about fantasy figures being real when they are figures for which parental and societal support is most common (e.g., Santa Claus, Easter Bunny) (Sharon and Woolley, 2004). Subbotsky's (1993 as cited in Woolley, 1997) research suggests that children are more likely to espouse magical beliefs when they have first been exposed to another individual who endorses such beliefs. Rosengren, Hickling, Jurist, and Burger (in preparation, as cited in Rosengren and Hickling, 2000) asked parents to keep a record of their child's questions and parental responses to these questions during the week following attendance at a magic show. They found that parents of preschoolers generally provided magical explanations and affirmed the existence of magic, while parents of older children tended to respond to children's questions by describing the events as tricks or by providing physical/natural explanations. Parents and other concerned adults need to become more aware of the informal messages they send to children regarding the actual existence of magical phenomena (Rosengren and Hickling, 2000). Subbotsky (1993, cited by Woolley, 1997) found that the presence of an adult can often inhibit children's use of magical thinking and subsequent behavior. This finding suggests that concerned adults might want to read the Harry Potter books to their children or at least be present during the child's reading of the books to be available for any questions that the child may wish to ask.

Phelps and Woolley (1994; as cited in Woolley, 1997) found that children's knowledge of the physical world greatly influenced their tendency to use magical explanations of events. The less information children had about a certain phenomenon, the more likely they were to incorporate magical concepts. Children with an understanding of principles and scientific facts such as gravity are, therefore, likely to recognize that the flying broomsticks and game of Quidditch in Harry Potter are imaginary.

The focus thus far has been on the distinction between fantasy and reality and has addressed concerns parents may have about fantastical thinking and variables that may be considered if one wished to minimize the level of fantastical thinking in which children engage. The flip side of this issue is presented by Johnson (1997) and Vanderburg (1998) who spoke to the *benefits* of fantastical thinking and play, respectively. They both addressed how these processes allow humans to think beyond the constraints of their culture in order to think more abstractly and theoretically. Johnson (1997) argued the need to acknowledge the positive and productive nature of fantastical thinking and the fact that it is not just mistaken thought processes gone awry, but is actually something that we as humans have the capacity to engage in and utilize intentionally as a tool. He offered Einstein as an example of his understanding of one who used fantastical thinking in its most productive sense.

In addition, Vanderburg (1998) noted that in play "real experiences are rendered 'not real,' and the serious made playful, thus allowing for it to be seriously reconsidered" (p. 300). Speaking in a similar tone about fantastical literature, Johnson (personal communication, April 26, 2001) offers that "it is a mistake to think that this genre is an escape from reality. Fiction/fantasy can vividly portray very real issues. In fact, it may amplify these issues, making them more vividly real." Perhaps the realistic issues faced by Harry (e.g., isolation, grief, conflicts with friends, difficulty with authority) could provide catalysts for discussion about issues that would be too difficult for children to discuss in a direct and personal manner (Taylor, 1999). It may be that the fantastical presentation of these topics can make such discussions more safe and possible for children. In fact, the books have been used to explore grief issues with bereaved children and teens (Markell and Markell, 2004).

Scary

It is common to refer to certain movies, television programs, and books as "too scary for children" or too scary for children *of a certain age*. However, adult perceptions of what is "too scary" for children may be inaccurate and may be based on flawed reasoning (Stevenson, 1996).

Adults label books as too scary based on an adult understanding of what is frightening to children; they also make the assumption that children need special protection from the content of such books. Often, adults make the argument that a given book or scene would have frightened them as children but, as Stevenson (1996) argues,

> we can never really re-experience the children we were without bringing along the adults we've become; our adult-imagined children often do not judge or respond to books as would real contemporary children or even as our younger selves would have.
>
> (p. 310)

As noted earlier, there is, in fact, no research on the effects of given books on children. Research on movies and television suggests that *visual images* have a much greater capacity to frighten children than do the word portrayals in books (Cantor, 1998).

Books are different from TV and movies because, for young children, an adult is present as the reader and provides a reassuring presence (Cantor, 1998). (This is similar to the findings reported earlier about the effects of the presence of an adult on magical thinking.) When reading aloud, the adult can edit and interpret as s/he reads. The child who is reading independently has the ability to control the pace of the story rather than being at the mercy of the pacing of the movie or TV show—pacing that often is designed to heighten the tension and suspense of scenes and is accompanied by a sound-track designed to further intensify the experience. The child has a number of options including putting the book down, skipping over the scary paragraphs or pictures, reading more quickly or more slowly, peeking ahead at the ending to reassure him/herself that everything comes out OK, and so on. (Stevenson (1996) gives the example of Ramona in *Ramona the Brave* opening and closing her book in which there is a frightening picture.) Furthermore, the images in movies and TV are larger than book illustrations and have the added power of movement and sound (Cantor, 1998).

What is specifically frightening to children appears to depend on their developmental level. According to Cantor (Cantor, 1998), young children (aged two to seven) are frightened of both realistic and fantastic visual images of frightening things, of physical transformations of characters, of the depiction of a parent's death, and of vividly presented natural disasters. Children ages 7–12 (more the age range of Harry Potter readers) find realistic threats and dangers, violence, and child victims frightening. Children ages 13 and older are frightened by realistic physical harm, sexual assault, and threats from aliens and occult forces.

There is no debate over the fact that the Harry Potter series includes numerous and horrendous instances of violence. Because violence, physical harm, and child victims are particularly frightening to children in the Harry Potter reader age range, the question is whether exposure to such depictions is harmful. Although research does suggest a positive relationship between exposure to violent acts in visual forms of media (e.g., TV, movies) and engagement in aggressive behaviors and positive attitudes toward violence, there is a lack of empirical evidence to suggest any connection between reading violent material and similar negative outcomes (Kirsh, 2006). It is important to note, however, that there is likewise no research support for recent anecdotal claims (Jones, 2002) that exposure to violent forms of media is somehow cathartic and/or beneficial to children and adolescents (Kirsh, 2006). Although scholars focused on examining the effects of violent media on children have varied opinions about its effects, they appear aligned in their emphasis on the powerful role that parents and other significant adults have in influencing the manner in which exposure to violence is processed by children (Eron, 2001; Jones, 2002; Kirsh, 2006).

It has been suggested that "scary" books intended for children can help them learn mastery and control of fear (Stevenson, 1996). (Similar results have been found with some movies and TV programs (Cantor, 1998).) These books typically portray protagonists who learn or demonstrate mastery over the threat present in the book. These protagonists can serve as models for children about controlling fear. As Johnson (personal communication, April 26, 2001) observed about the utility of fantasy literature, the ability to deal with issues of fear through books is an example of an opportunity for children to confront real issues in the safe venue of a book.

Death and Grief

Particularly powerful examples of the portrayal of real issues in fantasy literature are the representations of death in the Harry Potter books. In a number of media interviews, Rowling has emphasized death as a central theme within the series (Grieg, 2006; Jones et al., 2000; Vieira, 2007). This has raised concerns for both parents and teachers. Is death—particularly the vivid portrayal of death—too sad, too frightening, or appropriate for children's books? Gray (1999) noted that Rowling indicated that the books become "darker" as the series progresses, noting particularly that "there will be deaths" (p. 72). Rowling has argued that "if you are writing about evil, which I am, and if you are writing about someone who's essentially a psychopath—you have a duty to show the real evil of taking human life" (BBC, 2001).

A critical issue that must be addressed is the necessity to separate the topic of death from issues of violence and evil. It is potentially problematic that nearly all of the deaths in the Harry Potter series do occur as the result of violence/evil, in that death cannot and should not be equated with these concepts. Death is not "dark" in and of itself. The inappropriate representation in Western society of these ideas as consistently merged has and is likely to continue to perpetuate the mistaken notion that death is some kind of abnormality of our existence: an evil force. In reality, death is the inevitable end for all living beings. It is a natural stage in development. Society's continuing tendency to link the experience of death with evil fosters difficulties such as death denial (Becker, 1973), the avoidance of dying individuals (Kalish, 1966; Sweeting and Gilhooly, 1991–1992), and the isolation of grieving persons (Corr, Nabe, and Corr, 2000; Kastenbaum, 1998).

With this criticism of Rowling's representation of death duly noted, the fact that she does address issues of death, dying, and bereavement is to be commended. The growing body of literature focused on the childhood experience of death is virtually unanimous in its recommendation for straightforward discussions about death at an early age, prior to the occurrence of a death-loss crisis (DeSpelder and Strickland, 1995; Fitzgerald, 1992; Silverman, 2000). In fact, Grollman (1990) contended that "death education begins when life begins" (p. 3).

Despite this call for openness and candor, adults continue to struggle with addressing the topic of death with children. This hesitancy is likely due to a number of factors including a desire to protect children from the pain of grief, an underlying philosophy of "let kids be kids," and the fear associated with the direct death-related questions children are likely to ask (Schaefer and Lyons, 1993; Silverman, 2000). The paradox that arises when death-focused conversations do not occur is that children are left to make sense of death from the wide array of examples they are exposed to on a daily basis through media, such as cartoons, video games, and TV news programs. In reality, children are receiving education about death from multiple sources, the question, according to Grollman (1990), is "whether the education they are receiving is helpful and reliable" (p. 1). When children are isolated from the truth of death, they are likely to create "a wild fantasy, much worse than the facts" (Schaefer and Lyons, 1993, p. 5).

It is highly unlikely that the Harry Potter books will be children's first exposure to the idea of death. Children are quite aware of and frequently experience death and dying within their own lives (Corr, 1996; Schaefer and Lyons, 1993). In their overview of the major research findings on children's understanding of death, Speece and Brent (1996) concluded that despite considerable variability among studies, most children have a mature understanding of death by the age of seven years. The notion of a mature understanding of death hinges upon the idea that the concept of death is most accurately represented as incorporating the distinct sub-components of universality, irreversibility, nonfunctionality, and causality.

It is possible that death due to magical causes could be confusing for some children. They are in the midst of learning about the abstract and realistic internal (e.g., loss of blood) and external (e.g., visible cut) causes of death (Corr, 1996). Children often struggle with "magical thinking" when faced with death experiences, believing that their thoughts or actions actually produced the death (Grollman, 1990; Schaefer and Lyons, 1993; Webb, 2005). Although there are no clear cases of reversible deaths in the Harry Potter series, there are some elements that may be confusing for children. A vast number of ghosts roam the halls of Hogwarts. Rowling makes attempts throughout the series to clarify this issue with numerous statements about the finality of death and most explicitly at the end of *Order of the Phoenix* when Harry talks with Nearly Headless Nick about ghosts being imprints of departed souls. Nick stresses that Sirius will not return and will not choose the path of being a ghost. The scenes late in *Deathly Hallows* where Harry initially appears to die and speaks with Dumbledore may be confusing for children as well. Rowling has Harry directly ask Dumbledore whether Dumbledore is dead (yes) and whether he himself is dead (no). As with the distinction between fantasy and reality, parents have a significant role to play in children's understanding of the causes of death, and these books could serve as catalysts for such conversations.

Rowling's representation of child and adolescent grief experiences are accurate and insightful. There are a number of deaths throughout the series; some that are most personal and central for Harry (e.g., his parents, Sirius, Dobby) and others that affect Harry, but also have a broader impact on many characters (e.g., Cedric, Dumbledore). Rowling's own experience of parental death seems to have informed and strengthened her portrayal of Harry's experience, including his continuing connection with his parents and his regrieving process over time (Oltjenbruns, 2007). In addition, as Harry and his friends work through their grief, their experiences highlight many contemporary issues in the field of thanatology including uniquely adolescent aspects of grief, distinct manifestations of grief (e.g., instrumental vs. expressive grievers), and the importance of mourning rituals.

The first death losses the reader is confronted with are those of Harry's parents. Lily and James Potter are murdered by the evil Lord Voldemort. These deaths occur when Harry is just an infant, and he has no actual memories of his parents. It is realistic that Harry grieves the deaths of his parents even though they died before he knew them. Although not directly addressed within the parental death literature, Davies (2001) found that siblings who experienced the death of a sibling prior to their own birth grieved in similar ways to those experiencing the death of a sibling subsequent to their own birth. Harry cannot grieve actual, physical relationships with his parents, but he can and does grieve the relationships he was never able to establish with them.

Related to this idea is the continuing relationship Harry *is* able to maintain with his deceased parents. Harry makes frequent references to his parents and actually interacts with them in book one through the use of the Mirror of Erised (*Sorcerer's Stone*, p. 207), in book three (*Prisoner of Azkaban*) during Harry's production of the Patronus, in book four when he and Lord Voldemort's spells become connected (*Goblet of Fire*, p. 667), and as he faces death in book seven (*Deathly Hallows*, pp. 699–703). He gains glimpses of them through photos, dreams, visions, and conversations throughout the whole series. Harry also visits their graves in Godric's Hollow. Although some of these are instances when magical forces facilitated Harry's contact with his parents, his relationships with his deceased parents are examples of "continuing bonds," a significant concept within the grief and bereavement literature (Klass, Silverman, and Nickman, 1996). In contrast to the traditional Freudian (1919) notion that ties to the deceased must be severed for healthy adjustment to take place, the continuing bonds movement within the field acknowledges the human need to maintain, albeit in an altered state, a connection with deceased loved ones who are no longer physically present. More specifically, Silverman, Nickman, and Worden (1992) found that children with a continuing, though altered, relationship with their deceased parent appeared better able to cope with the death loss as well as other accompanying life changes. Silverman (2001) directly connected Harry's experience with her understanding of continuing bonds as she referenced the following statement made to Harry by Dumbledore at the end of book three: "You think the dead we loved ever truly leave us? You think that we don't recall them more clearly than ever in times of great trouble? Your father is alive in you, Harry, and shows himself most plainly when you need him" (*Prisoner of Azkaban*, pp. 427–428). Also consistent with the literature (Oltjenbruns, 2007), Harry's relationship and grief for his parents shifts and transforms over time as he learns more about the depth of his mother's love and goodness and the rather mixed character of his father. He must adjust his ideal representation of his father to include the cruelty that he learns his father inflicted on others, particularly upon Snape. A similar adjustment occurs in Harry's experience of grief following Dumbledore's death. He works in *Deathly Hallows* to reconcile his rather idealized view of his beloved mentor with the controversial information he learns about Dumbledore's life as a young man.

Beyond Harry's grief for his parents are the portrayals of grief following the deaths of many other characters. Harry grieves these death losses in a manner that is quite consistent with the general adolescent bereavement literature. His grief also differs from that of others highlighting distinct patterns of grief that often can and do emerge. Finally, the books suggest the importance of ritual and other acts of remembrance in the lives of those grieving significant death losses.

Harry expresses and exhibits symptoms and behaviors common for bereaved teenagers. His responses are often multifaceted and include shock, numbness, blame and guilt, sadness, and rage. More specific to being a teenager, Harry is actively reluctant to discuss his grief, particularly following the deaths of Cedric and Sirius. He appears to camouflage his grief, which is common for bereaved teenagers who are working to fit in and minimize any differences that may exist between them and their peers (Oltjenbruns, 2007). Although this behavior is motivated by a desire to belong, it often results in young people not having opportunities to process their experiences with others (Lenhart and McCourt, 2000). Harry also seems to struggle with the idea that anyone could understand his feelings—another common experience for teenagers in general (Samuel-Traisman, 1992). In particular, when Dumbledore attempts to normalize Harry's pain following Sirius' death by indicating that he knows how Harry feels (*Order of the Phoenix*, p. 823), Harry explodes in rage. Harry describes his experience as "white-hot anger like his insides, blazing in the terrible emptiness, filling him with the desire to hurt Dumbledore for his calmness and his empty words" (*Order of the Phoenix*, p. 823). This description is clearly in line with a frequently used journal for bereaved teens entitled *Fire in my Heart: Ice in my Veins* (Samuel-Traisman, 1992). Such intense and unpredictable emotions, particularly anger, can be troubling for bereaved teens and for those around them. Also consistent with what is known about grieving teens, it is actually Luna Lovegood, speaking from her own experience of parental death at the end of *Order of the Phoenix*, who seems to reach Harry in his grief; emphasizing the power that exists when bereaved teens are given the opportunity to connect with one another.

In addition to a development lens, the grief experiences of Harry and other characters in the books can also be examined with regard to dominant patterns of grief (Martin and Doka, 2000). Harry appears to display the instrumental pattern of grief. Instrumental grievers are more likely to use active, problem-solving, and cognitive approaches to processing their grief. Although Harry does avoid talking about his grief, his active pursuit of Voldemort, work with both the Order of the Phoenix and with Dumbledore's Army, and eventual caretaking for his godson Teddy are ways to problem solve, to master his environment, and to commemorate the lives of those who died—all instrumental expressions of grief (Martin and Doka, 2000). In contrast to Harry, in the aftermath of Cedric's death Cho exhibits many elements of the intuitive pattern of grief. More specifically, she cries frequently, seeks and appears to benefit from opportunities to talk about her grief, and at times is overwhelmed by her emotions. The differences in the ways that they grieve create tension between Harry and Cho. Although the intuitive pattern is often associated with women whereas the instrument is associated with men, it is important to note that this is not always the case (Martin and Doka, 2000). Rowling highlights this point by portraying Hagrid, the rugged half-giant, as more of an intuitive rather than instrumental griever (see *Half-Blood Prince* following Dumbledore's death and *Deathly Hallows* as he weeps believing Harry dead).

Rowling effectively describes different mourning rituals in which Harry and his friends take part. Rituals such as funerals prove helpful by offering a way to acknowledge the death, remember the deceased, or understand and openly express feelings about the deceased (Rando, 1993) and "their power comes from the faith that the individual has in their ability to provide meaning" (Rando, 1985, p. 402). Research suggests that adolescents perceive traditional funeral services as less satisfying and less helpful in the process of coping than do adults (Servaty-Seib and Hayslip, 2002). This finding holds true for Harry's experience. Although he found that Dumbledore's funeral made the death more real for him, overall "it did not mean much to him. It had little to do with Dumbledore as Harry had known him" (p. 644). The service included important elements of remembrance displayed by Hagrid, the merpeople, the centaurs, and others, but the fact that Harry observed rather than actually took part in those acts of remembrance left him feeling separated from the ritual. It held little meaning for him. In contrast, when Dobby died in *Deathly Hallows* (pp. 477–481), Harry had the opportunity to take the lead in acknowledging and commemorating his death. More specifically, Harry physically dug Dobby's grave, dressed the elf, and personally marked his grave with a fitting epitaph that Harry wrote. The contrast between these experiences is quite striking and consistent with the focus in the literature on the need to personalize rituals.

Guidelines

Given the convergence of the popularity of the Harry Potter series and the concerns that it raises for many, how can parents and teachers best approach these books? Because the books have become part of American popular culture, children will be exposed to them. The publicity that will attend the release of films based on the remaining books and the inevitable related merchandising will continue to make Harry Potter part of child and adolescent culture.

1. *Forbidding the books is not the answer.* Gish (2000) cautions even religiously concerned parents against forbidding children to read the Harry Potter books, recognizing the temptation of the forbidden fruit.
2. *Know your child.* Although some age-related developmental generalizations can be made, most research suggests that age is not the primary determining factor in what content children find frightening, in children's ability to make sense of fantasy, or in children's understandings of death. A specific child may be "old enough" to read Harry Potter and possess the reading skills to tackle such long chapter books but may be particularly sensitive or easily frightened. The recommendations of experts about age appropriateness should not substitute for parents' judgment.

3. *Recognize that the books change as the series progresses.* It also is important to keep in mind that, as the series progresses, Harry and his friends grow older and the questions and problems they confront in the books become more complex (as appropriate to their ages). Likewise, parents and teachers should bear in mind that the books become less light-hearted and more frightening as the series progresses.

4. *Discuss the topics raised in the books.* Gish (2000) suggests that parents with religious concerns about the content of the Harry Potter books should take this as an opportunity to discuss their beliefs and concerns with their children. The later books in the series offer numerous opportunities to discuss beliefs related to the soul and the afterlife. Likewise, the theme of death in the books presents readily "teachable moments" (Ryan, 1988) for discussions of death (DeSpelder and Strickland, 1995; Fitzgerald, 1992; Wass, 1991). Discussing death with children prior to an immediate and personal loss experience allows adults, unencumbered by their own grief, the ability to provide reasonable and deliberate responses to questions and concerns. In addition, children are likely to gain knowledge and a sense of control, empowering them for when the inevitable does occur. The Harry Potter books also present opportunities for parents and teachers to discuss topics such as isolation and loneliness, conflicts with friends, and difficulty with authority—problems that many children experience in their own lives—in the safer context of the books.

5. *Help children distinguish fantasy from reality.* Adults should discuss with children their understanding of what is real and what is imaginary in the books. Further, adults should overtly and covertly reinforce with children that the content of the books is fantasy and not real. Because an understanding of the laws of science and the natural world contribute to a child's ability to distinguish fantasy from reality, concerned parents and adults should expose children to information about the physical world such as would be present at science museums, but also can be understood through home experiments and through watching educational television programs.

6. *Provide an adult presence.* The presence of an adult, whether as reader at home or in a classroom read-aloud or merely as a companion in the room with an independently reading child, can reduce the likelihood that fantasy and reality will be confused and the likelihood that the scariness of the books will be overwhelming.

7. *Distinguish between the books and the movies.* The fact that a child was "old enough" to read the Harry Potter books and found them

fun and entertaining does not necessarily mean that he or she will not be overwhelmed or frightened by the movies. The power of movies to frighten is much greater than that of books (Cantor, 1998). Hollywood's depiction of Lord Voldemort, the Dementors, and Aragog, the enormous spider, all may be much more frightening than the depictions in the child's imagination—and they have the added power of size, movement, and sound. Furthermore, the child is unable to control exposure and pacing as a member of the movie audience the way he or she is as a reader.

8. *Respect others' beliefs and viewpoints.* Some families may wish for their children to "opt out" of Harry Potter read-alouds. This is an opportunity to model understanding and respect.

9. *Teach about grief.* Use the issues arising from these portrayals of death and grieving to help children understand their own grief and the grief of others.

References

Adler, S. (2007). *"Harry Potter" author J. K. Rowling opens up about books' Christian imagery.* Retrieved October 17, 2007, from http://www.mtv.com/news/articles/1572107/20071017/index.jhtml.

American Library Association. (2006). *Dealing with challenges.* Retrieved November 6, 2007, from http://www.ala.org/Template.cfm?Section=dealingandTemplate=/ContentManagement/ContentDisplay.cfm.

American Library Association. (2007a). *The 100 most frequently challenged books of 1990–2000.* Retrieved November 6, 2007, from http://www.ala.org/ala/oif/bannedbooksweek/bbwlinks/100mostfrequently.htm.

American Library Association. (2007b). *The state of America's libraries, April, 2007.* Retrieved November 6, 2007, from http://www.ala.org/ala/pressreleases2007/march2007/statechallenges.htm.

Bateson, G. (1972). *Steps to an ecology of mind: A revolutionary approach to man's understanding of himself.* New York: Chandler Publishing Company.

Becker, E. (1973). *The denial of death.* New York: The Free Press.

Blais, J., and DeBarros, A. (2007, July 24). "Deathly Hallows" records lively sales. *USA Today* (Online version). Retrieved October 17, 2007, from http://www.usatoday.com/life/books/news/2007-07-24-potter-sales_N.htm.

Blimling, G. S. (1990). The involvement of college students in totalist groups: Causes, concerns, legal issues, and policy considerations. *Cultic Studies Journal, 7,* 41–68.

Bourchier, A., and Davis, A. (2000). Individual and developmental differences in children's understanding of the fantasy–reality distinction. *British Journal of Developmental Psychology, 18,* 353–368.

British Broadcasting Company. (2001, December 28). *Harry Potter and me.* (BBC Christmas Special). British Broadcasting Company.

Cantor, J. (1998). *"Mommy, I'm scared": How TV and movies frighten children and what we can do to protect them.* San Diego, CA: Harcourt Brace.

Carrick, N., and Quas, J. A. (2006). Effects of discrete emotions on young children's ability to discern fantasy and reality. *Developmental Psychology, 42,* 1278–1288.

Chambers, J. (2007). *The Harry Potter series: A vision of the antichrist.* Retrieved November 6, 2007, from http://www.pawcreek.org/articles_pcm/end_times/harry_potter_antichrist.htm.

Corr, C. A. (1996). Children, development, and encounters with death and bereavement. In C. A. Corr and D. M. Corr (eds.), *Handbook of childhood death and bereavement* (pp. 3–28). New York: Springer.

Corr, C. A., Nabe, C. M., and Corr, D. M. (2000). *Death and dying: Life and living* (3rd edn.). Belmont, CA: Wadsworth.

Davies (2001, May). When a child is dying: Fathers' experiences. Paper presented at the King's College International Conference on Death and Bereavement, London, ON, Canada.

Deák, G. O. (2006). Do children really confuse appearance and reality? *TRENDS in Cognitive Sciences, 10,* 546–550.

DeSpelder, L. A., and Strickland, A. L. (1995). Using life experiences as a way of helping children understand death. In D. A. Adams and E. J. Deveau (ed.), *Beyond the innocence of childhood: Vol. 1. Factors influencing children and adolescents' perceptions and attitudes toward death* (pp. 45–54). Amityville, NY: Baywood.

Dresang, E. T. (2003). Controversial books and contemporary children. *Journal of Children's Literature, 29,* 20–31.

Eron, L. D. (2001). Seeing is believing: How viewing violence alters attitudes and aggressive behavior. In A. Bohart and D. Stipek (eds.), *Constructive and destructive behavior: Implications for family, school, and society* (pp. 49–60). Washington, DC: American Psychological Association.

Fitzgerald, H. (1992). *The grieving child: A parents' guide.* New York: Fireside.

Foerstel, H. N. (1994). *Banned in the U.S.A.: A reference guide to book censorship in schools and public libraries.* Westport, CT: Greenwood.

Freud, S. (1919/1957). Mourning and melancholia. *Collected papers,* vol. 4. New York: Basic Books.

Gish, K. W. (2000). Hunting down Harry Potter: An exploration of religious concerns about children's literature. *Horn Book Magazine, 76,* 262–271.

Golomb, C., and Galasso, L. (1995). Make believe and reality: Explorations of the imaginary realm. *Developmental Psychology, 31,* 800–810.

Granger, J. (2006). *Looking for God in Harry Potter.* Carol Spring, IL: Tyndale House.

Gray, P. (1999, September 20). Wild about Harry. *Time* (Online version). Retrieved November 8, 2007, from http://www.time.com/time/magazine/article/0,9171,992017–1,00.html.

Grieg, G. (2006, January 10). There would be so much to tell her…. *Tatler Magazine.* Retrieved March 19, 2008, from http://www.accio-quote.org/articles/2006/0110-tatler-greig.html.

Grollman, E. A. (1990). *Talking about death: A dialogue between parent and child.* Boston, MA: Beacon.

Harry Potter: A new twist to witchcraft. (n.d.) Retrieved November 8, 2007, from http://www.exposingsatanism.org/harrypotter.htm.

Hicks, R. D. (1991). *In pursuit of Satan: The police and the occult.* Buffalo, NY: Prometheus.

Hunter, E. (1998). Adolescent attraction to cults. *Adolescence, 33,* 709–714.

Johnson, C. N. (1997). Crazy children, fantastical theories, and the many uses of metaphysics. *Child Development, 68,* 1024–1026.

Jones, G. (2002). *Killing monsters: Why children need fantasy, super heroes, and make-believe violence.* New York: Basic Books.

Jones, M., Sawhill, R., Power, C., Springer, K., Cooper, A., and Scott, H. W. (2000, July 17). Why Harry's hot. *Newsweek,* pp. 54–56.

Kalish, R. A. (1966). A continuum of subjectively perceived death. *Gerontologist, 6,* 73–76.

Kastenbaum, R. J. (1998). *Death, society, and human experience* (6th edn.). Needham Heights, MA: Allyn and Bacon.

Kirsh, S. J. (2006). *Children, adolescents and media violence: A critical look at the research.* Thousand Oaks, CA: Sage.

Kjos, B. (n.d.) *Harry Potter lures kids to witchcraft—with praise from Christian leaders.* Retrieved November 8, 2007, from http://www.crossroad.to/text/articles/HarryandWitchcraft.htm

Kjos, B. (1999). *Bewitched by Harry Potter.* Retrieved November 8, 2007, from http://www.crossroad.to/text/articles/Harry9–99.html.

Kjos, B. (2000, June 28). *Harry Potter and DandD—Like two peas in a pod?* Retrieved November 6, 2007 from http://www.crossroad.to/text/articles/DandDandHarry.htm.

Kjos, B. (2003, February). *Role-playing games and popular occultism.* Retrieved November 7, 2007, from http://www.crossroad.to/articles2/2003/occult-rpg.htm.

Klass, D., Silverman, P. R., and Nickman, S. L. (eds.). (1996). *Continuing bonds: New understandings of grief.* Philadelphia, PA: Taylor & Francis.

Leeds, S. M. (1995). Personality, belief in the paranormal, and involvement with satanic practices among young adult males: Dabblers versus gamers. *Cultic Studies Journal, 12,* 148–165.

Lenhart, A. M., and McCourt, C. (2000). Adolescent unresolved grief in response to the death of a mother. *Professional School Counseling, 3,* 189–196.

Markell, K. A., and Markell, M. A. (2004, April). The boy who lived: Exploring Harry Potter to help grieving children. Paper presented at the annual meeting of the Association for Death Education and Counseling, Pittsburgh, PA.

Martin, T. L., and Doka, K. J. (2000). *Men don't cry … women do: Transcending gender stereotypes of grief.* Philadelphia, PA: Taylor & Francis.

Olsen, T. (1999, December 13). Opinion roundup: Positive about Potter. *Christianity Today.* Retrieved October 17, 2007, from http://www.christianitytoday.com/ct/1999/150/12.0.html.

Oltjenbruns, K. A. (2007). Lifespan issues and loss, grief, and mourning. Part 1: The importance of a developmental context: Childhood and adolescence as an example. In D. Balk (ed.), *Handbook of thanatology* (pp. 143–149). Northbrook, IL: Association for Death Education and Counseling.

Phelps, K. E., and Woolley, J. D. (1994). The form and function of young children's magical beliefs. *Developmental Psychology, 30,* 385–394.

Rando, T. A. (1985). Creating therapeutic rituals in the psychotherapy of the bereaved. *Psychotherapy, 22,* 236–240.

Rando, T. A. (1993). *Treatment of complicated mourning.* Champaign, IL: Research Press.

Rosengren, K. S., and Hickling, A. K. (2000). Metamorphosis and magic: The development of children's thinking about possible events and plausible mechanisms. In K. S. Rosengren, C. N. Johnson, and P. L. Harris (eds.), *Imagining the impossible: Magical, scientific, and religious thinking in children* (pp. 75–98). New York: Cambridge University Press.

Rowling, J. K. (1999). *Harry Potter and the prisoner of Azkaban.* New York: Scholastic.

Rowling, J. K. (2000). *Harry Potter and the goblet of fire.* New York: Scholastic.

Rowling, J. K. (2003). *Harry Potter and the order of the phoenix.* New York: Scholastic.

Rowling, J. K. (2005). *Harry Potter and the half-blood prince.* New York: Scholastic.

Rowling, J. K. (2007). *Harry Potter and the deathly hallows.* New York: Scholastic.

Ryan, M. (1988). The teachable moment: The Washington Center Internship Program. *New Directions for Teaching and Learning, 35,* 39–47.

Samuels, A., and Taylor, M. (1994). Children's ability to distinguish fantasy events from real-life events. *British Journal of Developmental Psychology, 12,* 417–427.

Samuel-Traisman, E. (1992). *Fire in my heart: Ice in my veins.* Omaha, NE: Centering Corporation.

Schaefer, D., and Lyons, C. (1993). *How do we tell the children?* New York: Newmarket Press.

Servaty-Seib, H. L., and Hayslip, B. (2002). Post-loss adjustment and funeral perceptions of parentally bereaved adolescents and adults. *Omega, 46,* 251–261.

Shannon, P. (1989). Overt and covert censorship of children's books. *New Advocate, 2,* 97–104.

Sharon, T., and Woolley, J. D. (2004). Do monsters dream? Young children's understanding of the fantasy/reality distinction. *British Journal of Developmental Psychology, 22,* 293–310.

Silverman, P. R. (2000). *Never too young to know: Death in children's lives.* New York: Oxford University Press.

Silverman, P. R. (2001). Bereaved children and adolescents: When do gender differences matter? Paper presented at the King's College International Conference on Death and Bereavement, London, ON, Canada.

Silverman, P. R., Nickman, S., and Worden, J. W. (1992). Detachment revisited: The child's reconstruction of a dead parent. *American Journal of Orthopsychiatry, 62,* 494–503.

Skolnick, D., and Bloom, P. (2006). What does Batman think about SpongeBob? Children's understanding of the fantasy/fantasy distinction. *Cognition, 101,* B9–B18.

Smietana, B. (2007, July). The Gospel according to J. K. Rowling. *Christianity Today* (web only). Retrieved October 17, 2007, from http://www.christianitytoday.com/2007/julywebonly/130-12.0.html.

Speece, M. W., and Brent, S. B. (1996). The development of children's understanding of death. In C. A. Corr and D. M. Corr (eds.), *Handbook of childhood death and bereavement* (pp. 29–50). New York: Springer.

Stevenson, D. (1996, May/June). Frightening the children? Kids, grown-ups, and scary picture books. *Horn Book Magazine, 72,* 305–314.

Subbotsky, E. V. (1993). *Foundations of the mind: Children's understanding of reality.* Cambridge, MA: Harvard University Press.

Sweeting, H. N., and Gilhooly, M. L. (1991–1992). Doctor, am I dead? A review of social death in modern societies. *Omega, 24,* 251–269.

Taylor, M. (1999). *Imaginary companions and the children who create them.* New York: Oxford University Press.

Taylor, M., and Carlson, S. M. (2000). The influence of religious beliefs on parental attitudes about children's fantasy behavior. In K. S. Rosengren, C. N. Johnson, and P. L. Harris (eds.), *Imagining the impossible: Magical, scientific, and religious thinking in children* (pp. 247–268). New York: Cambridge University Press.

Taylor, M., Cartwright, B. S., and Carlson, S. M. (1993). A developmental investigation of children's imaginary companions. *Developmental Psychology, 29,* 276–285.

Use Harry Potter to spread Christian message. (2007, July 18). Retrieved November 8, 2007, from http://www.telegraph.co.uk/news/main.jhtml?xml=/news/2007/07/17/npotter217.xml.

Vanderburg, B. (1998). Real and not real: A vital developmental dichotomy. In O. N. Saracho and B. Spodek (eds.), *Multiple perspectives on play in early childhood education* (pp. 295–305). Albany, NY: State University of New York Press.

Vieira, M. (Interviewer). (2007, July 30). *Harry Potter author J. K. Rowling gets personal* (Television broadcast). New York: MSNBC.com.

Wass, H. (1991). Helping children cope with death. In D. Papadatou and C. Papadatos (eds.), *Children and death* (pp. 11–32). New York: Hemisphere Publishing Corporation.

Webb, N. (ed.). (2005). *Helping bereaved children, second edition: A handbook for practitioners.* New York: Guildford Press.

Woolley, J. D. (1997). Thinking about fantasy: Are children fundamentally different thinkers and believers from adults? *Child Development, 68,* 991–1011.

Woolley, J. D., and Wellman, H. M. (1990). Young children's understanding of realities, nonrealities, and appearances. *Child Development, 61,* 946–961.

Chapter Two

Harry Potter and Christian Theology

PETER CIACCIO

A theological analysis of the Harry Potter series can be quite a controversial endeavor, yet it is a fascinating challenge leading to interesting results. It is important to state, to begin with, that my analysis of Harry Potter is not *the* Christian analysis, but just *a* Christian one. This chapter will focus on the spiritual, religious, and moral messages in the books from the perspective of a Southern European Protestant theologian, who considers Harry Potter an outstanding children's story and not a theological treatise. Thus, I believe it is not fair simply to *judge* the text, but it is appropriate to *engage* with it. It is important to bear in mind that, as Christians, we have very different perspectives on many subjects, even if we are united by the name of Jesus Christ, and that not even members of the same Christian denomination share the same understanding on many issues.

Having a positive Christian understanding of Harry Potter, nevertheless, carries the risk of asserting the opposite of what anti-Rowling Christians state: that Joanne K. Rowling is a Christian author and her work, Christian books. This would not be a fair characterization. Even if Rowling is indeed a member of the Church of Scotland, it is important to bear in mind that being a Christian is not equivalent to writing Christian books or to being a Christian author. She is an author of children's books and it is her contribution to this broad genre that I will explore in relation to the Christian message.

Children's books are generally morality tales explaining many real issues and unpleasant realities in a symbolic or metaphorical way, so that children may better understand them. The confusion of these morality tales with Christian symbolic morals lies in the fact that Jesus taught by parables following a similar narrative pattern. When Jesus is asked about the Kingdom of God, He does not answer straightforwardly, but tells a tale, for example, "The Kingdom of God is like yeast that a woman took and mixed in with three measures of flour until it was all leavened" (Matt. 13.33). Jesus Himself explains why He answers in this way: "The reason I speak to them in parables is that seeing they do not perceive, and hearing they do not listen, nor do they understand" (Matt. 13.13).

In this chapter I will compare the morals presented in the series with traditional Christian ones. In particular, I will detail the role of magic, charisma and identity, overcoming dualisms, the notion of richness, death, curses, sin, and the temptations of power—a panoply of Christian themes. In conclusion, I will suggest that Harry Potter offers a complex understanding of life: death and grief play an important part; loyal and critical friends are preferable to noncritical servants; and love, trust, and honesty are always preferable, even if they bring danger.

The Role of Magic and the Supernatural

In the Christian tradition, magic has always had a negative connotation. This led to the persecution and execution of people considered to deal with magic. Such actions unfortunately cast a bloody shadow on the reputations of Christians. Furthermore, in today's generally scientific culture, there is no place for magic; so the murder of people accused of performing magic seems even crueller, given the absurdity of the accusation. Nowadays, as a matter of fact, those who believe that magic exists are considered to be fools or superstitious. It is interesting to see how Italian semiologist, Umberto Eco, in defending Harry Potter, compares people who are afraid of magic with those who consider it a suitable way of life.

> Do we really believe that children who read stories of magic, once they become adult, will believe in witches? [...] All of us have felt a healthy fear of ogres and werewolves, but, as grown-ups, learned to fear not poisoned apples, but the hole in the ozone-layer. [...] The real problem lies in those people who, as children, never read stories of magic and, as adults, believe whatever TV tells them, e.g. seeking help from those who read the leaves or the tarots, from those who celebrate black Sabbaths, from healers and seers, believing those who reveal the secrets of Tutankhamun.
>
> (Eco 266)

As Servaty and Taub detail in Chapter Three, children perceive the difference between fiction and reality surprisingly well: children do not normally try to fly from a window with a broom!

According to the Bible, on the other hand, nature has a supernatural origin: God. God creates the world from nothingness (Gen. 1.1–2) and, from then on, events are divided between those coming from nature and those coming from God. The Lord's promises are mainly actions that will overcome nature. For example, Abraham and Sarah are too old to bear a child naturally, but the Lord says, "Why did Sarah laugh, and say, 'Shall I indeed bear a child, now that I am old?' Is there anything too wonderful for the Lord?" (Gen. 18.13–14). In the books following Genesis, it is clear that there are events that do not come from God, yet are inexplicable. This is the reason that we find magicians, wizards, and seers, who perform supernatural wonders, while it is not clear where they get their powers. On the other hand, it is indeed clear that God's prophets and priests may perform miracles in the name of the Lord. So the question is not whether supernatural actions exist or not, but in whose name they are performed. "By what authority are you doing these things?" (Matt. 21.23) is in fact the Pharisees' question to Jesus as he enters in Jerusalem.

According to Christian apologetics of the first centuries, the Christian faith was "the religion of pure reason and moral firmness" (Harnack 196). This was not historically true, however, since the Christian message had to come to terms with Greek philosophy, superstitions, and pagan rites. Through the historical process of resolving the Greek tradition, the question of authority shifted slightly: it became no longer important in whose name wonders were performed, but wonders became per se evidence of divine authority.

In the Middle Ages, the Church became the bearer of God's authority, thus declaring saints those who were thought to have performed miracles in the name of the Church, while condemning those who were suspected of having performed supernatural actions outside the Church. The rule of law was discretionary and people were tried for more supernatural offenses than were actually committed. This means that heretics were treated like witches and vice versa. The Church's opposition to scientific progress and to activities outside of its control are still reflected in the present radical separation of faith and science.

Rowling's depiction of magic in the Harry Potter series is quite original: in fact, in Harry's world, magic is an element of nature, rather than a supernatural trick. It is so hard to master magic that one needs to go through a tough and thoroughly comprehensive curriculum at a special school. Yet, magical people are naturally magical, likewise Muggles are quite as naturally non-magic people. The last book of the series is quite clear on the natural quality of magic. Persecution against Muggle-born wizards and witches is based on the apparently unfair question of from whom they stole their magical powers (*Deathly Hallows* 214). How could Muggle-born wizards and witches defend themselves from such an absurd allegation? In a less dramatic way, the natural character of magic is confirmed, as even magic has to comply with precise laws of physics. When Ron Weasley is hungry and wishes to have food by simple magic, Hermione reminds him that food cannot be created out of nothing as stated in one of the "five principal exceptions of Gamp's Law on Elementary Transfiguration" (*Deathly Hallows* 241).

Charisma, Identity, and the Sorting Hat

The Greek word *charisma* (pl. *charismata*) is mainly used in the New Testament to describe a "gift"; its root *charis* ("grace"). Thus *charismata* are related to grace as particular attributes that humans receive from God. Incidentally, Charismatic Churches emphasize more than others the event of Pentecost (Acts 2), when the Holy Spirit descended on the Apostle, giving them the words and the courage to go into the streets to preach the Gospel of the Jesus Christ. In his first letter to the Christians in Corinth, the Apostle Paul describes the relationship between *charismata*, Christians, and God.

> Now there are varieties of gifts, but the same Spirit; and there are varieties of services, but the same Lord; and there are varieties of activities, but it is the same God who activates all of them in everyone. To each is given the manifestation of the Spirit for the common good. To one is given [...] the utterance of wisdom, and to another the utterance of knowledge [...], to another faith [...], to another gifts of healing [...], to another the working of miracles [...], to another prophecy, to another the discernment of spirits, to another various kinds of tongues, to another the interpretation of tongues. All these are activated by the one and the same Spirit, who allots to each one individually just as the Spirit chooses.
>
> (1 Cor. 12.4–11)

Harry Potter is also about *charismata*. The four Hogwarts' founders Godric Gryffindor, Rowena Ravenclaw, Helga Hufflepuff, and Salazar Slytherin acknowledged four main *charismata* for a witch or a wizard: courage, cleverness, diligence, and ambition. This is the criterion used by the Sorting Hat to place students in the four Hogwarts Houses. To sort a schoolboy or a schoolgirl in a particular House is not merely an organizational matter: there is a deeply intense bond to the House, a strong identity that creates a high spirit of competition, together with, however, a high risk of divisiveness. Faithfulness to one's House identity becomes the main influence on students' behavior: the clearest example is the Gryffindors' loyalty to Albus Dumbledore and the Slytherins' to Lord Voldemort. Moreover, such radically diverse behavior is expected by others, thus creating a reciprocal lack of trust. The Harry Potter series, mostly written from the perspective of a member of Gryffindor House, transmits to the reader this sense of competition and thus most readers would rather prefer to be sorted into Harry's House than Draco's. The degeneration of House competition into House division is highly challenged by the extreme situation of Lord Voldemort's siege of the school in the seventh book. "The time has come for Slytherin House to decide upon its loyalties," says Minerva McGonagall to Horace Slughorn (*Deathly Hallows* 484). Conflict between Houses was not in the intention of those who discerned the four *charismata*, as the Sorting Hat says at the beginning of Harry's fifth year at Hogwarts:

The founders of our noble school
Thought never to be parted:
United by a common goal
They had the selfsame yearning,
To make the world's best magic school
And pass along their learning.
            (*Order of the Phoenix* 184)

In Christian theology, gifts are strictly linked with the concept of call: vocation according to charisma is one of the main pivots of the Church. Thus,
conflict between *charismata* is one of the sources of division and, consequently of ineffectiveness in the Church's engagement in society. One can
say the same for the secular society: a well governed community needs at least
a good educational system in cooperation with a good government. This need
is well reflected in Harry Potter, as the relationship between the school and
the Ministry is quite crucial, and often is not friendly and smooth, but rather
is characterized by a lack of mutual trust. Since the books are written from the
point of view of the schoolchildren, it is the Ministry that seems provocative,
negligent, and sometimes obsessed by the strong reputation of Albus Dumbledore. At the end of the fourth book this relationship degenerates into one of
direct conflict, with serious consequences at all levels. At a general level Lord
Voldemort begins his silent rise, at a more private level, Percy Weasley cuts
off any communication from his family, as he considers them disloyal to the
Ministry.

> Your loyalty, Ron, should not be to [Dumbledore], but to the school
> and the Ministry. [...] It pains me to criticise our parents, but I am
> afraid I can no longer live under their roof while they remain mixed up
> with the dangerous crowd around Dumbledore.
>   (*Order of the Phoenix* 267)

It is difficult for the Ministry and the school to work together for the
common good. Conflict between those involved in politics and those involved
in education brings the risk of the destruction of society. The message arising
from Harry Potter is that diverse groups should aim for the common good,
and not at being only a fanatic devotee of a certain "political" group. This is a
very similar moral message to the one above quoted from the Apostle Paul:
"There are varieties of services, but the same Lord" (1 Cor. 12.5).

The Kingdom of God and the Realm of Magic

"You will have a treasure in heaven" (Mark 10.21). The Christian message is
eschatological: the rise of the Kingdom of God will be the ultimate implementation of all His promises to His people. According to Matthew, Jesus'

ministry begins with the so-called Sermon on the Mount, where God's promises for the poor, the weak, the persecuted, are retold by Christ. The first Beat-
itude is "Blessed are the poor in spirit, for theirs is the kingdom of heaven"
(Matt. 5.3).

Harry Potter grows up as an extremely poor boy. He became an orphan at
the age of one and, since then, has been hosted by his only living relatives, the
Dursleys. He is not a welcomed guest. He is mistreated, is underfed, and is
dressed in ill-fitting hand-me-downs. The way his relatives treat him reminds
the reader how Fagin treated Oliver Twist, with some key differences: Harry
lives in contemporary times and not in Victorian England, and the Dursleys
are wealthier than Fagin, being a well-to-do average middle-class family.
Moreover, the more Aunt Petunia and Uncle Vernon spoil their son Dudley,
the more they mistreat Harry, and with their example in mind, Dudley feels
that he is authorized to punch and bully his poor cousin.

When Harry reaches his eleventh birthday, he receives unexpected good
news (in Greek, "euangelion" = "Gospel"). That is, he is not poor and
unwanted anymore. He is rich, very rich, not in the world where he has lived
until now with his family, but in the wizarding society. His wealth is not
limited to the material richness found in his vault at Gringotts Bank; he is
socially and spiritually rich, indeed, he is happy. When he enters the world his
parents belonged to, everybody has heard of him already and many people
wish to befriend him (even Draco Malfoy!). His material wealth grows during
the seven books: he receives expensive gifts and inherits substantial property.

Harry's relationship with the magicians' society is eschatological: it is the
place where he gets his reward. The epitaph on the tomb of Kendra and
Ariana Dumbledore seems to confirm this eschatology: "Where your treasure
is there your heart will also be" (*Deathly Hallows* 266; Luke 12.34). An even
more interesting aspect of Harry's eschatological wealth is his reaction to it.
Harry could become arrogant, he could abuse his wealth in both worlds, but
he does not. Harry does not take vengeance on the Muggles who bully him,
and his false threats to his cousin Dudley are just a way to survive during
summer holidays. Harry's humble reaction to the good news seems like a very
Christian way of relating to eschatology, "Blessed are the meek, for they will
inherit the earth" (Matt. 5.5). On the other hand, for self-righteous Christians
it may seem that Harry does not act or think in a Christian way. He does not
have Hagrid's instinctive childish love for dangerous creatures nor
Hermione's drive for social justice. Moreover, Harry does not always have a
selfless attitude: he likes to bend rules, he disobeys Arthur Weasley's advice to
"Never trust anything that can think for itself if you can't see where it keeps
its brain" (*Chamber of Secrets* 242) as he generally tends to disobey adults,
putting himself and others at great risk. Anyway, Harry Potter is not a "saint"
in a restricted meaning of the word, but he is a teenager like others who has to
face situations that many grown-up adults would not be able to face. Harry is

able to respond radically to his call, and at the end he resolves to die in order to destroy death. "The last enemy that shall be destroyed is death" (1 Cor. 15.26, quoted in *Deathly Hallows* 269).

Death and Life

Death casts a shadow on the whole of Harry Potter's life, from the very beginning. He is born in a time of death, during the first war with Lord Voldemort. He lost his parents when he was one year old. Sirius Black and Albus Dumbledore are just two of the many friends that Harry loses during the second war with Lord Voldemort. Harry Potter's life is characterized by his yearning to defeat death. When he is first given the right of life or death over another person, Peter Pettigrew, Harry spares his life. Sirius Black and Remus Lupin ask him if they may kill him or if Harry would rather send him to prison. "'You're the only person who has the right to decide, Harry,' said Black ... 'He can go to Azkaban,' Harry repeated" (*Prisoner of Azkaban* 275). In *Deathly Hallows*, Harry not only spares but rescues his rival Draco.

In the final book, at Godric's Hollow graveyard, there are the first two explicit Bible quotations of the entire series. The first one, the eschatological one, has just been mentioned (Mk. 10.21); the second one is on James and Lily Potter's tombstone and reads, "The last enemy that shall be destroyed is death" (*Deathly Hallows* 269; 1 Cor. 15.26). In front of this epitaph, Harry and Hermione engage in an interesting exegetical debate on Death and Resurrection. Harry sees a grave and the word "death" on it. It is an ultimate sight, there is no hope in the face of his parents' tomb. Hermione suggests to Harry that the epitaph talks of life beyond death. Their brief exegetical discussion ends with no apparent conclusion. There cannot be a clear conclusion, since in the face of the beloved departed there can only be flowers and grief. Death is the boundary where faith stands or falls: to believe or not to believe.

In Christian theology, death plays an important part. According to Paul, it is the consequence of Adam's sin (Rom. 5.12), and this is why Jesus delivered humankind from sin *and* death. 1 Cor. 15.26, quoted on Harry's parents' grave, is the ultimate effect of Jesus' sacrifice. In the first centuries, the Church considered the sacrifice of Christian martyrs as a proof of Christ's defeat of death. Gnostic and Docetist heretics believed it impossible that Christ actually died, as Christ was a being of Godly nature who only *seemed* a man ("Docetism" comes from the Greek word "dokeis" = "it seems"). The consequence of this theological understanding was the underestimation of the body and bodily matters, thus looking at death as the moment in which the soul is finally granted freedom: *this* is a culture of death.

Harry Potter can be considered a serious story about death, as many fairy tales are as well. The way Rowling deals with death is quite in contrast with how it is treated in contemporary Western culture. Nowadays, we tend to forget that death is a shadow on all of our lives. Thus, in our "civilized" society, real death is mostly confined to hospitals, hospices and old people's homes. Virtual death is obsessively present in movies, videogames, and, most of all, on television. Celebrities' funerals become worldwide TV events. Tsunamis, wars, and murders are part of the dinner menu for many Western families. In other words, death is either hidden in safe places or presented as a virtual event. The flawlessness and incorruptibility of the body is a modern idol. For people who wish to be successful, it is important to look young. This paradoxically creates a culture of death, as if one cannot die, life loses its value. The way Rowling deals with death in Harry Potter brings instead a healthy message: one cannot remove death from life, but one should live taking death into serious consideration. People can overcome their grief and survive only by seriously accepting it and fully living through it.

The Unforgivable Curses and the Unforgivable Sin

Grief and mourning affect one's life because they affect human relationships. Rowling deals with the dark side of relationships by marking some rules and limits pertaining human behavior toward the others. In the magical world of Harry Potter, where everything seems allowed or amendable, there are three unforgivable curses: *Imperius*, *Cruciatus*, and *Avada Kedavra*, the killing curse. It is interesting to explore the criterion Rowling used for choosing these particular curses as unforgivable ones. The relationship between the three curses suggests their unforgivable nature. With the *Imperius Curse* the perpetrator controls the actions of the victim, who can be forced even to perform illegal actions. The *Imperius Curse* breaks the rule of individual responsibility and steals what is most precious and unique to a person: freedom to act according to one's own will. The *Cruciatus Curse* tortures the victim, making him or her stay alive in tremendous pain and suffering, until they go mad: this was the fate of Neville Longbottom's parents. During the exploits of Dumbledore's Army in the Ministry of Magic, Harry attempts to use the *Cruciatus Curse* on Bellatrix Lestrange, who has just killed his godfather Sirius. Harry is furious, but, when he sees the effects of the torture, he stops immediately. Bellatrix then mocks him,

> Never used an Unforgivable Curse before, have you boy? ... You need to *mean* them, Potter! You need to really want to cause pain—to enjoy it—righteous anger won't hurt me for long—I'll show you how it is done, shall I?
>
> (*Order of the Phoenix* 715)

The killing curse needs no explanation. Yet it is interesting that the effects of it can rebound on the perpetrator. In Horace Slughorn's most hidden memory, as he tells Tom Riddle about making Horcruxes, he reveals that "killing rips the soul apart" (*Half-Blood Prince* 465).

Why should a theologian be interested in all this? The reason lies in the fact that in Christian Theology there is also something which is unforgivable: the blasphemy against the Holy Spirit. "Therefore, I tell you, people will be forgiven for every sin and blasphemy, but blasphemy against the Holy Spirit will not be forgiven ... either in this age or in the age to come" (Matt. 12.31.32; see also Mark 3.28–30 and Luke 12.10). The unforgivable sin is a puzzling subject as it seems to contradict the infinity of God's love and as it is quite unclear why something that is just said is particularly unforgivable, if compared with apparently graver actions. In the synoptic Gospels (Matthew, Mark, and Luke) this subject reads more like a quotation of what Jesus once accidentally or offhandedly said, rather than a thought-out issue, such as the Kingdom, repentance, discipleship etc.

To understand what makes *Imperius*, *Cruciatus*, and *Avada Kedavra* particularly unforgivable, one may compare this with the concept of unforgivable sin and, in a hermeneutic process, see if Rowling offers a possible contribution to the comprehension of the biblical understanding of what is not forgivable. In Harry Potter these curses are unforgivable not only for what they mean to others, but mostly for the consequences suffered by the offender. To be forgiven means to come back to prelapsarian state, when humans could stand whole before their creator as sin had not yet corrupted them. This is the sense of the Hebrew word *teshuvà*, translated in modern languages as "conversion." In *Secrets of the Darkest Arts*, Hermione reads that it is nearly impossible to put one's soul back together once it is ripped. Lord Voldemort cannot reunite his Horcruxes to rebuild his soul: by killing he arrived at a point of no return (*Deathly Hallows* 89). A confirmation of this is that the punishment for using the Killing Curse is to have one's soul sucked by a Dementor. If we apply Harry Potter's understanding of the unforgivable to Theology and, particularly, to the blasphemy against the Holy Spirit, we can say that a sin is unforgivable not on God's part but on a human's part. God's love is and remains infinite, but the unforgivable sin changes a human soul in an irreversible way. "You need to mean them" implies that the unforgivable curse (or sin) is already part of the offender's soul. It is something set deep inside the person. This understanding seems in harmony with the new concept of sin presented by Jesus in his so-called Sermon on the Mount, in opposition to the Pharisees' legalistic view: to sin is not simply performing an illegal action, but also just wishing to do it (Matt. 5–7).

Hermione tells Harry and Ron that there is, in any case, the possibility of restoring the wholeness of the soul. It is something "excruciatingly painful" and potentially fatal: remorse. "You've got to really feel what you have done ... The pain of it can destroy you" (*Deathly Hallows* 89). Incidentally, here we find one of the many interesting links to the *Star Wars* saga. In *Episode VI: The Return of the Jedi*, the consequence of Darth Vader's ultimate remorse is his death. And, according to the Apostle Paul, in order to be saved from sin one must be "dead in sin" (Rom. 6.1–14).

Overcoming Dualism

Even if there is a relationship between *Star Wars* and Harry Potter, an important difference emerges in that the former presents a dualistic vision of life (e.g., Darth Vader, the "Dark Father," dressed in black, and Luke Skywalker dressed in white) while the main moral teaching in the Harry Potter series is rooted in its strong anti-dualistic attitude. Even the eternal struggle between Good and Evil, which is at the basis of Rowling's books and, indeed, of most children's literature, is not presented in a black-and-white way. In Harry Potter, people are not divided between absolutely good or absolutely bad: the question is not about *who* is good and *who* is bad, it is rather about *what* is good and *what* is bad.

Even if it is clear that Lord Voldemort is the villain of the story, it is important for Harry to know how his nemesis became so evil. In *Half-Blood Prince* Albus Dumbledore strives to force Harry to understand everything about Tom Riddle. At first, Harry does not agree with this "intellectual exercise." Rather, he would prefer to fight Voldemort immediately. Then, he discovers something that he would have never liked to know. That is, there are many similarities relating him to the Dark Lord. Tom's childhood is very similar to Harry's. Just like Harry, Tom lived as an orphan in a hostile Muggle context, he was poor and lonely, and, at the same time, mysteriously gifted. Just like Harry, Tom received the unexpected good news of being a wizard at the age of 11 and entered Hogwarts, which is the place where both felt happier than ever in their lives. These similarities are a great narrative theme in the books. This case study of the genesis of a Dark Lord does not hide the fact that Harry and Tom become two radically different persons at the end.

Dumbledore presses Harry to do something that humans usually do not like to do: going deeply into the mind of the "monster," as criminologists do. The reason people do not like it is that, just like Harry, they may discover that they share some features with the criminal mind. The German-American philosopher Hannah Arendt wrote about this while reporting for the *New Yorker* on the trial of Adolf Eichmann, the supervisor of the Nazi genocide of Jews. In observing this "monster," Arendt stated that his most shocking characteristic is that he seems "normal." Thus, she talks of the "banality of evil." If one looks at the offender as a monster, simply ignoring his human features, one will not necessarily avoid behaving in a similar way. Dumbledore wants Harry to understand what he experienced himself a long time before at the expense of his sister Ariana: the evil potentials of *any* human being.

Christianity is largely the result of the encounter between a radically monotheistic culture such as Judaism and a generally dualistic one such as Hellenism. Dualism has always played an important part in Western thinking.

It is still a flourishing concept today and a clear sign of this is, for example, the widespread success and appeal of popular films like *The Matrix,* which show precisely a false world as opposed to an authentic one. The plot of *The Matrix* was, in fact, first conceptualized by Plato, the Greek philosopher who best represents dualistic thinking. He theorized the "hyperuranion" (= "above the sky"), the authentic world of ideas, as opposed to the false world in which we live. According to Plato, everything we experience in our lives is a copy of the perfect model existing in the "hyperuranion." This is dualist metaphysics, comparing something fake opposed to something authentic.

Dualism radically allocates opposites (e.g., body and spirit, female and male, black and white, impure and pure, profane and sacred) into two spheres: a positive one and a negative one. This allocation creates false and subjective analogies between negatives or positives. Consequently, spiritual, male, white, pure, and sacred are traditionally considered positive while bodily, female, black, impure, and profane are considered negative. The worst consequence of such an implementation of dualism is that the power of the "positive one" over the "negative one" is thus conceived as justified. Thanks to such dualistic thinking, in many cultures (and even in many Churches!) women are kept in a lower position than men.

In Harry Potter dualism is continually challenged. The project "For the Greater Good" of young Albus Dumbledore is very similar to what Lord Voldemort and his Death Eaters put into practice. Harry considers his father James a hero since he died in the fight against evil, as someone who paid with his life the choice of being on the right side; but then Harry discovers that his father was arrogant and rather a bully. Dolores Umbridge is the character most resembling Adolf Eichmann according to Arendt's description; she is no more than a normal bureaucrat following the orders of the Ministry of Magic regardless of who is in charge. The consequences of her carrying out superior orders are brutally evil.

People with a dualistic understanding are the real "bad ones" of the story. Some so-called "pure-blood" witches and wizards (the reader then discovers that being "pure-blood" is generally a false claim) hate Muggles, as they are non-magical people, and consider them less than human. Their hatred intensifies when it comes to wizards and witches who descend from Muggles, whom they call "mudbloods," as if non-magical blood were dirty. The consequence of this dualistic thinking is that Muggles and mudbloods deserve to die. Apart from the obvious analogies with persecutions made by Nazi Germany and by the Apartheid regime in South Africa, the Death Eaters' hooded outfits are a clear reference to the Ku Klux Klan.

Blood is not the only criterion for dualistic thinking in Harry Potter. Class and money are another one, the reason why the Malfoys hate a pure-blood family such as the Weasleys. A comparison of the two families is quite interesting. The Weasleys are a large family, with seven children, and all of them have red hair, like Irish people, according to a general stereotype. The Malfoys have only one spoiled child and are all blond: their name tells the reader of the aristocratic status, as French surnames in England are traditionally aristocratic (and, incidentally, "mal-foy" means "bad faith"). The way the Malfoys treat the Weasleys resembles the dualistic behavior that England commonly had toward Ireland, the poor country where people bear more children than they can afford to feed. Harry Potter overcomes this pattern. Even if he is surprisingly rich, he respects the Weasleys: he loves them for who they *are*, not for what they *have*. Moreover, he is very careful not to offend Ron's pride by offering him money as to a beggar. The episode of Harry's sponsoring Fred and George's *Weasley Wizard Whizzes* (*Goblet of Fire* 635) is more of a confirmation than of an exception to his behavior towards the poor family. The twins unfairly lost money to Ludo Bagman and Harry felt that he himself did not deserve to receive the prize for winning the Triwizard Tournament: so Harry does not give money from his own possessions. Another example of Rowling's anti-dualistic thinking is that Albus Dumbledore, the leader of the Order of the Phoenix, tends to seek the good in everyone. Moreover, in the seventh book, not only can readers finally learn what they suspected for a long time, i.e., that Severus Snape was the most faithful ally of Dumbledore, but also that there was a time in his life when the champion of Good was not so good, but was following a rather evil aim: Dumbledore had a plan to become the most powerful of all wizards, with the illusion that, through this project, "The Greater Good" would have been achieved.

The Temptation of Power

Before Emperor Constantine granted religious freedom to Christians (Edict of Milan, AD 313), the Church was persecuted in the Roman Empire. There was a legal reason for this persecution. That is, Rome had an official religion (which we usually, if incorrectly, call "pagan"), yet there were some beliefs that were given the status of *religio licita* ("legitimate religion"). These were usually traditional religions of the peoples that the Romans conquered. Thus, Christianity had two difficulties: not only was it not the traditional religion of the province of Palestine, but it conflicted with the *religio licita* of the area: Judaism. Moreover, Christians had a critical approach towards the state, since, if Jesus is the one and only Lord, the Emperor is just a human being like others. Since Constantine, Christian political thought experienced an interesting shift: the Church reached an accord with political power. The spreading of the new faith all around the Empire together with the Church's political acceptability, led to the declaration of Christianity as the established religion. It was not easy for Christians to accept this new status and many people foresaw the risks of meddling with "state interests," as a Church protected by political power is not independent in its actions. Yet most of the Church leaders thought that, by gaining freedom and by becoming more and more powerful in the establishment, they would really be able to change people's lives for the better. History teaches us that this dream of goodwill became a dark nightmare for many, as those who disagreed with the Church's decisions suffered violent persecution.

The temptation of the Fourth Century Church leaders is very similar to those of the young Albus Dumbledore in his dangerous project "For the Greater Good." His and Grindelwald's plan was to be in charge of inferior non-magical people, as magical people could better take care of them. In human history no dictator has come to power without presenting himself as someone who would bring order and good. A similar temptation grabs the young Severus Snape at a more private level. His deepest and noblest feeling is his love for Lily Potter, but, instead of courting her, he decides to stand with the most powerful and determined wizard (who happens to be Lord Voldemort) and to ask him for his rival's life, in exchange for his loyalty. As we know, things did not go as he foolishly expected, for the Dark Lord, numb to love, murdered Lily also in the attempt to kill Harry. The terrible experience they had meddling with power led both Dumbledore and Snape to a conversion experience. They live this conversion together while being two very different people. Dumbledore is publicly a good guy, but his remorse and shame deeply erode him, while Snape is publicly a bad guy, even if he is secretly working to amend his mistakes and to honor his love for Lily, that he was not able to honor while she was alive. Not only do they reject power in favor of service, but they also give their life for the benefit of the good cause. Two radically different people, such as Dumbledore and Snape, share the same vocation, and are bonded by it. Harry Potter understands this and calls one of his children Albus Severus, "You were named for two headmasters of Hogwarts. One of them was a Slytherin and he was probably the bravest man I ever knew" (*Deathly Hallows* 607).

As explored above, Christians (like all other human beings) are and have always been tempted by power, even though Jesus Christ was crucified by those in power. Yet Rowling's critical approach to dualistic thinking and to power is not only an interesting challenge and critique of a consistent part of Church history and its present behavior. It also challenges the aggressive and divisive ways taught by our society and media, where competition among people (and young people in particular) is confused with progress, and where the rule of law is mostly in the hands of those who can afford better lawyers. In Rowling's world, the hero is a poor orphan, who becomes a prince through the love of his parents and his friends. Love is a means of redemption and ultimate victory.

References

The Bible, New Revised Standard Version: Anglicized Edition, Cross-Reference Edition. Oxford: Oxford University Press, 2003.

Arendt, Hannah. *Eichmann in Jerusalem; a report on the banality of evil.* New York, Viking Press, 1963.

Eco, Umberto. *A passo di gambero. Guerre calde e populismo mediatico.* Milano: Bompiani, 2006. My translation in English.

Harnack, Adolf von. *Storia del Dogma.* Torino: Claudiana, 2006. Italian edition of *Dogmengeschichte.* 1893. My translation in English.

Rowling, J. K. *Harry Potter and the Chamber of Secrets.* New York: Scholastic, 1998.

Rowling, J. K. *Harry Potter and the Prisoner of Azkaban.* New York: Scholastic, 1999.

Rowling, J. K. *Harry Potter and the Goblet of Fire.* New York: Scholastic, 2000.

Rowling, J. K. *Harry Potter and the Order of the Phoenix.* New York: Scholastic, 2003.

Rowling, J. K. *Harry Potter and the Half-Blood Prince.* New York: Scholastic, 2005.

Rowling, J. K. *Harry Potter and the Deathly Hallows.* New York: Scholastic, 2007.

Star Wars: Episode VI—Return of the Jedi. Dir. Richard Marquand. USA, 1983.

The Matrix. Dir. Andy Wachowski, Larry Wachowski. USA, 1999.

Chapter Three

Harry Potter's World as a Morality Tale of Technology and Media

NICHOLAS SHELTROWN

Never trust anything that can think for itself, if you can't see where it keeps its brain.

Arthur Weasley, Office of the Misuse of Muggle Artifacts

Harry Potter's world is a fascinating land of wonderment, magic, imagination, and exploration. Like good fantasy stories, the Harry Potter series draws its readers in and allows them to imagine and experience unfamiliar places, through the eyes of people they do not know, facing dangers they cannot imagine, and for this, the stories of Harry and his friends are loved. Through her detailed descriptions, J. K. Rowling vividly creates an immersive, persistent, alternate world through which we can explore possibilities that the natural laws of our non-magical world do not allow. More than entertainment, the adventures of Harry Potter give the critical reader opportunities to reexamine old problems in new ways. By creating a rich world for her readers to enjoy, Rowling's work speaks directly to a number of problems we face in the non-magical world. This chapter examines Rowling's treatment of technology and media, technology's marriage to magic, and the relationship between technology and identity in these books. I begin by describing the thoroughly technological nature of Harry Potter's world, arguing that technology is at the center of the storyline.

Harry Potter as a Tale of Technologies

While the principal story line of Harry Potter is a classic tale of good versus evil, the stories are thoroughly technological in character. Harry's adventures, beginning with his first trip to Diagon Alley and ending with his arduous journey to defeat Lord Voldemort, are necessarily technological. Technology is not simply a popular fixture in these stories, reduced to the description of silly but fantastic gadgets; rather, technology is deeply embedded in the character of Harry Potter. One of the ways Rowling manufactures her magical world is through her rich description and invention of magical technologies. Sometimes these technologies are essential to the story line—such as Harry's use of the Marauder's Map, his Invisibility Cloak, broom, and various wands to carry forth the adventures that lie before him. Other times, the technologies just expand Rowling's fog of fantasy for her readers. Technological elements such as the Weasley's magical joke devices, the wizard and witch trading cards, self-sorting cards, and Howlers (letters that contain audio tirades) add not only to the character of the story, but also communicate to young readers that in Harry Potter's world, magical technologies are everywhere.

Rowling's stories thoroughly, persistently, and consistently blur the line between technology and magic, making it difficult for the reader to know where one ends and the other begins. The marriage of technology and magic in Harry Potter are of two kinds. First, there is *magic-tech*. This includes ordinary items from our Muggle world that have been magically modified, such as flying cars, Omnioculars (which allow a viewer of a Quidditch match to pause, slow down, or rewind a live match), flying broomsticks, and photographs featuring moving subjects. These objects exist in some form in our world—as regular automobiles, binoculars, brooms, and photographs— however they lack the special properties that Rowling imbues on them. The other division of technology in Harry's world I call *tech-magic*. Tech-magic are those items that have no Muggle world counterpart and are still used as technologies in the wizarding world. The most common and best example of tech-magic is the wand. For Rowling's wizards and witches, the wand is the primary medium of magic. Without a wand in hand, few of the charms, curses, or counter-curses young Hogwarts students learn in their lessons are possible. Other examples of tech-magic are less prominent, but still important in influencing the character and atmosphere of Harry's world. In the *Prisoner of Azkaban*, Ron gives Harry a pocket Sneakoscope, which lights up and spins when someone untrustworthy is around. Mrs. Weasley tracks the location of her family members with a large clock that has nine golden hands (one for each Weasley). The clock's hands point not to times, but descriptions like "home," "school," "work," and even "lost," "prison," and "mortal peril." Hermione uses a Time-Turner, a device that allows for time travel, extensively in the *Prisoner of Azkaban* to attend concurrent courses and help Harry save Sirius Black and the Hippogriff Buckbeak. Most of the materials used in Quidditch, specifically the Bludgers and the Golden Snitch, are examples of tech-magic.

Between magic-tech and tech-magic, Rowling creates a thoroughly magical/technological world. The goal for most fantasy writers is to create an immersive world for readers to probe, and Rowling peppers her world with technology and magic to add to the depth of the world we experience. Strip the tech-magic or magic-tech from Harry Potter and you have a much different and less interesting story. To paraphrase Marshall McLuhan (1964): if the medium is the message, and magic is the medium, then what's the message of magic? What should we make of a world so thoroughly dependent on the technology/magic marriage?

There are at least three important implications of Rowling's technology/ magic hybrid. First, there is the matter of technology as expressive of identity in the wizarding world. This collection of stories often emphasizes a close relationship between technology and identity, particularly as we consider the role of the wand as a passport into and out of the world of witches and wizards. A second important question that rises up out of the pervasive nature of technology/magic in Harry Potter is the nature of the existence engendered by technology/magic. Is a thoroughly magic/technological world presented as a positive outcome in these stories? Third, for readers young and old, is the question of how these stories may shape our attitudes and beliefs toward technology. This part of the chapter presents the paradoxical nature of the Harry Potter stories, which while being wholly magical/ technological, are also oddly insulated from technological development in the Muggle world. Such insulation may introduce the possibility for further critical reading.

Technology as Identity

Simply put, one's identity is the answer to the question, who am I? Cultural theorist Stuart Hall (1997) suggests that identity development is about who we are and with whom we belong. Questions surrounding individual identity are answered in a social context, making identity development processes cultural as well as psychological. Hall identifies personal and social interactions as the principal location for defining identity, but he also recognizes the importance of technology and media in this process—"especially, these days, in the modern mass media, the means of global communication, by complex technologies, which circulate meanings between different cultures on a scale and with a speed hitherto unknown in history" (p. 3). In fact, many informed observers of technology and media have recognized the increasingly visible role of technology and media in shaping individuals and influencing Hall's "circuit of culture." Critic Neil Postman (1993) writes, "Tools bid to *become* the culture" (p. 28), while Thoman and Jolls (2004) observe that "media no longer just shape our culture—they are our culture" (p. 18). Tracing the circuit of culture seems a world away from Harry Potter, but one of the most important implications of Rowling's thoroughly technological world is that technology processes and tools are an integral part of the identity closure in the wizarding world.

Magical Objects that Reveal Identity

It is hard to overestimate the importance of the wand in the Harry Potter series. On the surface of the story, wands are tools wielded by wizards and witches to do everything from the benign (cleaning dishes or moving trunks) to the horrific (killing or torturing another person). Wands are a regular fixture of wizarding life, the principal instrument for conducting one's magical activities. However, wands are far more than mere tools like shovels or toothpicks. Rowling presents wands as technical instruments of identity development, as well as passports to a qualified status in a wizarding society. Harry's trip to Diagon Alley to purchase school supplies for his first year at Hogwarts culminates with Harry's procurement of a wand. "A magic wand ... this was what Harry had been really looking forward to," writes Rowling (*Sorcerer's Stone*, p. 81). Harry learns from the famous wand-maker, Mr. Ollivander, that wands are a technology unlike anything he has experienced in his years growing up with the Muggles. Wands, according to Ollivander, form a special relationship with their witch or wizard. Mr. Ollivander recounts for Harry, "Your father, on the other hand, favored a mahogany wand. Eleven inches. Pliable. A little more powerful and excellent for transfiguration. Well, I say your father favored it—it's really the wand that chooses the wizard, of course" (*Sorcerer's Stone*, p. 82). The wand that chooses Harry has the same core as the wand that chose Tom Riddle before he assumed the identity, Lord Voldemort.

The significance of the wand choosing the wizard is played out throughout the series, as Harry struggles to understand himself and his identity. Is he good or evil? What is the meaning of this connection he seems to have to Lord Voldemort? Harry's identity crisis is further complicated by his interaction with the Sorting Hat, a device that places Hogwarts students into their various houses, and in doing so, says something about the defining characteristic of the individual—Hufflepuff, the accepting; Ravenclaw, the intelligent; Gryffindor, the brave; and Slytherin, the opportunistic and cunning. Perhaps shaken from his interaction with Mr. Ollivander, Harry fears being placed in Slytherin, the same house as Lord Voldemort. As Harry sits in front of the entire school with the Sorting Hat on his head, a debate rages internally. The Sorting Hat recognizes that Harry is a complex case full of courage, a good mind, and talent and it pauses to consider where to put Harry.

> Harry gripped the edges of the stool and thought, *Not Slytherin, not Slytherin.* "Not Slytherin, eh?" said a small voice. "Are you sure? You could be great, you know, it's all here in your head, and Slytherin will help you on your way to greatness, no doubt about that—no? Well, if you are sure—better be GRYFFINDOR!"
>
> (*Sorcerer's Stone*, p. 121)

Harry wins his struggle with the Sorting Hat and finds his way to the Gryffindor House for his years at Hogwarts; yet, he wonders in his coming adventures if the Sorting Hat's first inclination was not the correct one. In the years that follow, Harry struggles to understand himself, wrestling with a doubt that he might be pragmatic and self-serving like many of the Slytherins.

In these two examples, we can see that in Harry Potter's world, technology is instrumental in revealing identity. Wands also represent membership in wizarding society. Thus, when Rubeus Hagrid is expelled from Hogwarts, his wand is taken and destroyed. Hagrid remains magical, but loses the status and privilege of being a wizard and performing magic. He must seek permission from Dumbledore for the magic he performs as the grounds and gamekeeper at Hogwarts. In the *Chamber of Secrets*, Draco Malfoy sneers that Ron Weasley's dad "loves Muggles so much he should snap his wand in half and go and join them" (*Chamber of Secrets*, p. 222). Losing one's wand represents a loss of status and ability, which may explain why Lord Voldemort takes Lucius Malfoy's wand away from him. When Lord Voldemort needed a wand different from his own to attack Harry, he required Lucius to surrender his wand to punish him for past failures and a lack of loyalty to the Dark Lord. Second class creatures such as house-elves and goblins, though self-aware and intelligent, are not allowed to possess or use wands. Such a policy represents the sharp status differences between wizards and witches and other magical creatures, which the goblins find quite objectionable.

It is also no accident that one of the darkest, most desperate moments of the *Deathly Hallows*—when Hermione and Harry narrowly escape Voldemort's trap in Godric's Hollow—leads to even greater despair when it is discovered that Harry's wand was broken during the flight. The relationship Harry built with his wand during his years at Hogwarts, in which both he and his wand learned magic together could not be easily replicated by another's wand. Having won Draco Malfoy's wand from him, he asks Mr. Ollivander if it is safe to use. "A person can still use a wand that hasn't chosen them, though?" asked Harry. Mr. Ollivander answers,

> Oh yes, if you are any wizard at all you will be able to channel your magic through almost any instrument. The best results, however, must always come where there is the strongest affinity between wizard and wand. These connections are complex. An initial attraction, and then a mutual quest for experience, the wand learning from the wizard, the wizard learning from the wand.
>
> (*Deathly Hallows*, p. 493)

Wandlore is a complex branch of magic in the Harry Potter series, but what is clear is that the wand is a technology with tremendous implications for identity in the wizarding world. Wands are semi-autonomous instruments with the power to select their master or bow to a new master, if conquered. Wands have memories, just like wizards and witches. Wands also represent the key credential for being a witch or wizard, and those that must turn over their wands do more than give up their most important device—they also surrender who they are and with whom they belong.

A final magical object in Harry Potter that is closely tied to identity is the mysterious Mirror of Erised. At first glance, the Mirror of Erised does not appear very different from mirrors in our Muggle world, but as its name implies (Erised is "Desire" spelled backwards), the mirror provides a glimpse into the deepest desires of those that gaze into it. The inscription engraved at the top of the mirror reads "Erised stra ehru oyt ube cafru oyt on wohsi," which is translated, "I show not your face but your heart's desire." Harry discovers the mirror during one of his night-time excursions in the *Sorcerer's Stone*, and when he gazes into it, he sees dead members of his family he has never known, most notably his mother and father. Dumbledore finds Harry in front of the mirror one night and explains to him the danger of such a device:

> [The Mirror of Erised] shows us nothing more or less than the deepest, most desperate desire of our hearts. You, who have never known your family, see them standing around you. Ronald Weasley, who has always been overshadowed by his brothers, sees himself standing alone, the best of all of them. However, this mirror will give us neither knowledge or truth. Men have wasted away before it, entranced by what they have seen, or been driven mad, not knowing if what it shows is real or even possible.
>
> (*Sorcerer's Stone*, p. 213)

By revealing the deepest desires of one's heart, the Mirror of Erised gives tremendous insight into the viewer's identity and character. Through the Mirror of Erised, Rowling is reaffirming the Christian teaching, "where your treasure is, there your heart will be also" (Matthew 6:20). The lessons of the Mirror of Erised are revisited throughout the series, as Rowling also includes this Biblical passage in the *Deathly Hallows* as inscriptions on the tombstones of Dumbledore's mother and sister.

Through the wand, the Sorting Hat, and the Mirror of Erised, Rowling paints a vivid picture of technology's role in identity development. While her devices are magical, the relationship between technology and identity is quite evident in the non-magical world. Regularly, individuals define themselves through their material possessions. Society includes "mac people," Jeep enthusiasts (captured by the slogan, "You wouldn't understand—it's a Jeep thing"), and even foodies (a nickname for food connoisseurs). Such examples reaffirm technology's role in identity development, as articulated by Hall (1997) and others.

The Existence Engendered by Magic

Whether through tech-magic or magic-tech, fans of Harry Potter see how fantastic a world of magic through technology can be. But the critical reader may wonder, is the presentation of technology in Harry Potter too optimistic in its promises and too positive in its outcomes? As Carl Mitcham (2003) observes,

> In any serious discussion of issues associated with technology and humanity there readily arises a general question about the primary member in this relationship. On the one hand, it is difficult to deny that we exercise some choice over the kinds of technics with which we live— that is, that we control technology. On the other hand, it is equally difficult to deny that technics exert profound influences on the ways we live—that is, structure our existence.
>
> (p. 490)

The relationship between humans and their technologies (or technologies and their humans) in children's literature is one that bears discussion. Often, J. K. Rowling's work is compared to other famous British children's authors, including J. R. R. Tolkien and C. S. Lewis. On some level, one can see the influence of these two authors on Rowling. Knowingly or not, Rowling employs many of the strategies Tolkien and Lewis used when writing for children. Tolkien enjoyed creating immersive, internally consistent worlds (much like Harry's world) and Lewis was a master at examining the stories he told from the perspective of a child, which is why he so prominently featured delicious foods in *The Chronicles of Narnia*. Similar features are found in the Harry Potter series, particularly in Rowling's description of the food in the Great Hall and the sweets featured at Honeydukes. But in the matter of the presentation of technology, do these authors provide a unified criticality toward technology, one reflective of the tension Mitcham describes?

It is easy to see that both Tolkien and Lewis express their reservations about technology and modernization through their stories. J. R. R. Tolkien's *The Lord of the Rings* contains strong admonitions against the failings of modernity, technology, and science through his characterization of evil. In Tolkien's tale, the enemies of the human race, the Orc, destroy the natural beauty of Middle Earth through their pursuit of weapon development. The central evil of his trilogy is a magic ring, a weapon developed by the sinister Sauron, which must be destroyed to save Middle Earth. The ring represents the allure and misfortune of humanity's technology. Tolkien's friend and fellow fantasy author, C. S. Lewis (1956), also frames his most influential work, *The Chronicles of Narnia*, around a struggle against evil that would sub-jugate Narnia through a technological industrialization. In the final book of the series, *The Last Battle*, an unlikeable, greedy ape named Shift sells his fellow Narnians into forced labor. In his explanation to the newly enslaved talking beasts of Narnia, Shift delivers a cold, paternalistic vision for a new Narnia:

> "There! You see!" said the Ape. "It's all arranged. And all for your own good. We'll be able, with the money you earn, to make Narnia a country worth living in. There'll be oranges and bananas pouring in—and roads and big cities and schools and offices and whips and muzzles and saddles and cages and prisons—oh everything."
>
> (p. 685)

Shift exchanged the animals' freedom for an industrial makeover of Narnia, a type of "progress" for which Lewis held particular disdain. The cantankerous Ape's cruel vision for Narnia's industrial reshaping led to the downfall of this bucolic world, and also served as Lewis' warning against the dangers of modern alienation and mechanization in post-World War II industrial devel-opment.

In their two most famous works, Tolkien and Lewis leave little ambiguity as to their anti-technology, anti-industrial dispositions (for further explo-ration of these themes, see Rossi, 1984). What is less clear is how to evaluate Rowling's depiction of technology in Harry Potter. The easy conclusion is that this series is primarily utopian in its presentation of technology, embracing technology without any consideration of its implications, impact, or influence on the lives of those within its sphere of influences. Rarely are the unintended consequences of technology emphasized in these stories, and the solution to many of the stories' problems are found in tech-magic or magic-tech. Harry's wand, the Sorting Hat, the sword of Gryffindor, and the Time-Turner all influence the outcome of key events and resolve important conflicts of the series.

Expressing a utopian vision about technology may be expected for a series like this. Part of the fun of Harry Potter is the tech-magic and magic-tech that permeates the characters' daily activities. The enjoyment of Harry Potter is leaving the world of the Muggles, the control of the Dursleys, and the tyranny of the ordinary to experience something extraordinary. So in that regard, it is not surprising if Rowling does not question technology, as technology/magic is the drive-train for her stories. But is this a fair conclusion? I argue that like her predecessors Tolkien and Lewis, Rowling critically engages technology, albeit in a much more subdued fashion. Such a criticality is evidenced by the reaction regular wizards have to Muggle technology, the oddly non-technological character of the wizarding world, and the lessons Harry learned during his journey to defeat Lord Voldemort.

Arthur C. Clarke once quipped, "Any sufficiently advanced technology is indistinguishable from magic." While true at the outset, one of the realities of technology is that it can quickly fade into the background of human existence. Regular contact with the technology breeds a relaxed familiarity for the technology and with it, a number of hidden biases, assumptions, and practices. The more prevalent a technology, the less conspicuous it becomes. As Steve Johnson (1997) once observed:

> Technology. The word has become so commonplace in our culture that we take it for granted, unless, of course, technology doesn't do what we expect it to do (like when the soda machine takes our last quarter or the electricity in our house goes off).
>
> (p. 75)

When users take a technology for granted, the values built into or produced by the technology through its use often become assumed, expected, or perceived as "natural." Lost is our critical distance and our sense of surprise or imagination for the tool's effects. Lost is technology's magic. When technologies become assumed, we also lose sight of the implicit values "frozen in the code" (Bowker & Leigh-Star, 1999). Rowling addresses the issue of familiarity with technology in how she depicts the wizarding community's reaction to Muggle technologies. This is best seen through the Weasley family's response to technology.

The Weasleys are a true wizarding family. As "pure-bloods" (both Arthur and Molly Weasley come from wizarding families), they have spent their entire lives immersed in a magical life and away from Muggle society. Arthur Weasley, whose work at the Ministry of Magic focuses on the "misuse of Muggle artifacts," expresses a keen interest in the technological practices of the Muggle world. Throughout the series, Arthur Weasley consistently offers genuine admiration for Muggle technology: "'*Fascinating!*' [Arthur] would say as Harry talked him through using a telephone. '*Ingenious,* really, how many ways Muggles have found of getting along without magic'" (*Chamber of Secrets*, p. 43). Later on in the series, Arthur tries to impress the Dursleys (Harry's Muggle relatives) with his understanding of Muggle technology:

> Mr. Weasley was looking around. He loved everything to do with Muggles. Harry could see him itching to go and examine the television and video recorder.
>
> "They run off eckeltricity, do they?" he said knowledgeably. "Ah yes, I can see the plugs. I collect plugs," he added to Uncle Vernon. "And batteries. Got a very large collection of batteries. My wife thinks I'm mad, but there you are."
>
> (*Goblet of Fire*, p. 46)

The actions of the other Weasleys reveal the presence of extraordinary technologies in the Muggle world. In the *Prisoner of Azkaban*, Ron tries to use the telephone to speak with Harry during their summer holiday. Ron fails to realize that he doesn't need to shout into the device for someone to hear him on the other end. In *Goblet of Fire*, Molly Weasley sends Harry a letter via the Post, and "hope[s] we've put enough stamps on." Rowling describes the humorous outcome of Mrs. Weasley's ignorance of the Muggle mail system:

> [Uncle Vernon] held up the envelope in which Mrs. Weasley's letter had come, and Harry had to fight down a laugh. Every bit of it was covered in stamps except for a square inch on the front, into which Mrs. Weasley had squeezed the Dursley's address in minute writing.
>
> (*Goblet of Fire*, p. 30)

These actions of the Weasleys, while humorous, do more than merely entertain the reader. By responding to the novelty of everyday technologies, the Weasleys highlight what is truly magical about our world and confirm Arthur Clarke's insight that advanced technologies are indeed magical. Before we can consider our relationship with technology, we must first recognize its artificiality. The Weasleys help us do this: what is magical to them is mundane to us. This, I believe, is one of the real strengths of Rowling's stories. She helps us appreciate the strangeness of our modern existence. This is best revealed in a conversation between Ron Weasley and Harry on their first trip on the Hogwarts Express. The subject of their conversation is the nature of photographs in their respective worlds. The boys are enjoying "chocolate frogs," which come with trading cards of famous witches and wizards. After reading the back of Dumbledore's card, Harry makes a shocking discovery:

> Harry turned the card back over and saw, to his astonishment, that Dumbledore's face had disappeared.
> "He's gone!"
> "Well, you can't expect him to hang around all day," said Ron. "He'll be back. No, I've got Morgana again and I've got about six of her ... do you want it? You can start collecting."
> Ron's eyes dropped to a pile of Chocolate Frogs waiting to be unwrapped.
> "Help yourself," said Harry. "But in, you know, the Muggle world, people just stay put in photos."
> "Do they? What, they don't move at all?" Ron sounded amazed. "*Weird!*"
>
> (*Sorcerer's Stone*, p. 103)

Both boys marvel at the technical novelty of the other's world. As we read the story, we certainly can identify with Harry's shock and amazement. Rowling could have ended the exchange there and still have kept the reader's attention rapt, but she presses forward, forcing Harry Potter fans to confront the technical "magic" of our own world—one in which changing, digital photographs that hang on the wall are increasingly common. Such scenes remind us of the novelty and artificiality of our own technologies. There is nothing natural about them, and in many ways, they are "weird." A question that follows is, "what are the implications of 'weird' technology?" No matter our answer, the Harry Potter series creates opportunities to reconsider our own technologies, an important first step in the critical consideration of technology.

Rowling also reduces the transparency of technology by creating a wizarding world that lacks many of the common technologies of our world. Though the wizarding world is saturated with tech-magic and magic-tech, it is also strangely non-technological. Students at Hogwarts write with quills, parchment, and ink. Their photographs, though moving, are in black-and-white. They lack electricity, phones, and other regular fixtures of the Muggle world. Of course, much of what they do with magic replaces the need for clever technologies; however, some of the difficulties Harry and his friends faced could have been more easily remedied with basic Muggle technologies. How much easier would Harry's fight against the Ministry of Magic's misinformation campaign have been had he been able to blog about his encounter with Lord Voldemort at the end of the Triwizard Tournament? Or in researching the Horcruxes, objects embedded with fragments of Voldemort's soul, Hermione would have likely enjoyed a few minutes in front of Google. Instead of lugging books in her magical beaded bag, she could have carried a loaded Blackberry. Perhaps Harry's communication with his godfather Sirius Black would have been a little easier had he used a cell phone on a Hogsmeade weekend, rather than relying on owls and the Floo Network. One wonders if Harry would have felt similarly isolated at the Dursleys had he been able to use Dudley's computer to email Hogwarts friends. Rowling's segregation of the wizarding world from regular technologies is critical in that it throws our dependency on these technologies into sharp relief. If one has a hard time remembering life before the Internet, texting, GPS systems, and cell phones, pick up one of the Harry Potter books and enjoy how the characters solve problems and develop relationships outside the context of many technologies basic to the Muggle world.

Rowling also complicates her presentation of technology by creating a world that ignores many important aspects of material life in both Muggle and magical worlds. A careful reading of Harry Potter introduces a number of questions regarding the technological and material consistency of Rowling's world. For example, what is the wizarding economy based on? How do wizards and witches earn money, obtain food (which cannot be created magically), or acquire other goods? Often, we find that the clothes, furniture, and housing of the wizarding world are old, shabby, or run-down. First, we should question how they come to obtain such possessions. Is it by magic, manual labor, or through commerce with the Muggles? Wizarding dwellings and villages are often integrated with or near Muggles (Hogsmeade is the only all-wizarding town in Great Britain). Who builds these magical dwellings? Second, one may question why some magic is not applied more consistently to make material life for wizards and witches better. For example, why wouldn't the houses of wizards and witches be immaculate and well-maintained, given the availability of the scouring charm and Reparo spell? Why does the wizarding community rely on the indentured servitude of house-elves rather than leveraging labor by magic? Perhaps the answer to such questions may be that the over-application of any magical technology or spell will complicate the lives of wizards and witches in unforeseen ways. This is the reason Professor Slughorn gives in the *Half-Blood Prince* as to why one would not want to use the potion Felix Felicis (which produces luck) too often. He tells his students, "If taken in excess, [Felix Felicis] causes giddiness, recklessness, and dangerous overconfidence … too much of a good thing, you know … highly toxic in large quantities" (*Half-Blood Prince*, p. 187).

The examples presented thus far show how Rowling subtly challenges unforeseen technologies. This is not to say that Rowling does not directly speak to the critical considerations of technology, as Tolkien and Lewis did in their principal works. In fact, one may argue that at the center of the Harry Potter story is the question of the value of technology and its impact on human life. Perhaps Harry Potter is, at its core, a morality tale about technology. Consider where the series begins, in the first book with Harry narrowly keeping Lord Voldemort from gaining access to the Sorcerer's Stone, a magical object that produces endless days and money for those who possess it. At the end of the book, Harry is in the hospital wing recovering from his ordeal with Voldemort and his vessel Professor Quirrell, and has a very revealing conversation with Dumbledore about the problems of technology. Dumbledore reveals that he has destroyed the Sorcerer's Stone, as the prospect of Voldemort with such a tool is too grave a threat for Dumbledore to ignore. Harry balks at Dumbledore's actions, and in response, Dumbledore gives Harry his first lesson on technology:

> You know, the Stone was really not such a wonderful thing. As much money and life as you want! The two things most human beings would choose above all—the trouble is, humans do have a knack of choosing precisely those things that are worst for them.
>
> (*Sorcerer's Stone*, p. 297)

With these words, Dumbledore is providing Harry with a lesson about the revenge effects of altering nature—outcomes of technology we do not antici-pate. Yes, the benefits of the Sorcerer's Stone are quite attractive to the human heart; yet, as Dumbledore has realized over the course of his life, trouble is the traveling companion of well-intentioned magical technologies. Over the next six years, as Harry comes to grip with his impending confrontation of Lord Voldemort, he struggles to learn this lesson. Without Hermione's inter-vention in the *Prisoner of Azkaban*, Harry would have changed the past by killing Peter Pettigrew and thus alter history unpredictably. In the *Half-Blood Prince*, Harry places enormous faith in the unknown prince's potions book, which results in his careless use of the Sectumsempra curse on Draco Malfoy (Harry creates a gaping gash across Malfoy's chest). It is not until the final installment of the series, the *Deathly Hallows*, that Harry finally works out the lesson Dumbledore was teaching at the end of his first year at Hogwarts.

The *Deathly Hallows* is a book marked by a dark atmosphere of confusion and indecision for Harry, Hermione, and Ron. They understand that the now-deceased Dumbledore wished them to seek the five remaining hidden Horcruxes that contain fragments of Voldemort's fractured soul (in the process, Harry learns that he is actually the final Horcrux, and must also be destroyed). The trio's problem is that they lack clarity as to where to find these Horcruxes and how to destroy them once they find them. This creates some dissension among the three friends, particularly as they wander aim-lessly, narrowly avoiding Lord Voldemort and his Death Eaters. In the course of their fugitive life, they discover clues revealing the legend of the Deathly Hallows, a collection of powerful magical objects that may help them in their fight against Voldemort. The legend of the Deathly Hallows says that when the three Hallows are united, the possessor will conquer death itself. Harry, Hermione, and Ron all question whether they should seek the Deathly Hallows—the Invisibility Cloak, the Resurrection Stone, and the Elder Wand—rather than trying to locate Voldemort's hidden Horcruxes. Ulti-mately, Harry decides to let Voldemort gain the Elder Wand, and that he, Ron, and Hermione must pursue "Horcruxes not Hallows," and finish the quest as originally conceived. However, in completing the quest and defeating Voldemort, Harry gains possession of all three Hallows. Near the conclusion of the book, Harry is granted one final conversation with Dumbledore, this time through his hanging portrait among the other dead headmasters in the headmaster's office of Hogwarts.

> Exhausted and bleary eyed though [Harry] was, he must make one last effort, seeking one last piece of advice.
>
> "[The Resurrection Stone] that was hidden in the Snitch," he began, "I dropped it in the forest. I don't know exactly where, but I'm not going to go looking for it again. Do you agree?"

"My dear boy, I do," said Dumbledore, while his fellow pictures looked confused and curious. "A wise and courageous decision, but no less than I would have expected of you. Does anyone else know where it fell?"

"No one," said Harry, and Dumbledore nodded in satisfaction.

"I'm going to keep Ignotus's present, though," said Harry, and Dumbledore beamed.

"But of course, Harry, it is yours forever, until you pass it on!"

"And then there's this."

Harry held up the Elder Wand, and Ron and Hermione looked at it with a reverence that, even in his befuddled and sleep deprived state, Harry did not like to see.

"I don't want it," said Harry.

"What?" said Ron loudly. "Are you mental?"

"I know it's powerful," said Harry wearily. "But I was happier with mine.... The wand's more trouble than it's worth ... and quite frankly, I've had enough trouble for a lifetime."

(*Deathly Hallows*, pp. 748–749)

At last, Harry has mastered a lesson that Dumbledore presented at the end of book one, a lesson that Dumbledore had to learn the hard way (as his own pursuit of the Hallows led to his death). Harry understands that even a technology as great as the Elder Wand, the unbeatable wand, comes with a price—a continual worry of those that may come to kill the master of the wand, so that they may possess it. He learns that technologies present intended and unintended effects, and it's the unintended effects that are so easily overlooked and often problematic. In this way, Harry's success as the hero of the story is contingent on his critical disposition toward technology, making Harry Potter a morality tale of technology. It was not that Harry mastered technology (such as a special spell) to defeat Lord Voldemort; rather, he mastered human use of technology by recognizing its problems and limits. Ultimately, Lord Voldemort's error and downfall were not different from Dumbledore's; the men had the same ends (to conquer death) but different means. Dumbledore confesses this to Harry in their meeting at the spiritual King's Cross station after Harry absorbed Voldemort's killing curse for a second time: "Master of death, Harry, master of Death! Was I better, ultimately, than Voldemort?" (*Deathly Hallows*, p. 713). Both Voldemort and Dumbledore blindly accepted the value they placed on their preferred technologies—Horcruxes and Hallows, respectively—without considering the full implications of these magic objects. In this way, these two powerful wizards were bested by Harry Potter, a far less talented wizard.

Media

According to the *OED*, media are "the main means of mass communication, esp. newspapers, radio, and television, regarded collectively; the reporters, journalists, etc., working for organizations engaged in such communication." In critical studies of technology, media occupy a special position, as many scholars have identified media as uniquely influential on the social, economic, and political development of a society.

Media in Harry Potter are best represented by the most popular newspaper of the wizarding world, the *Daily Prophet*. Like the mainstream media of the Muggle world, the *Daily Prophet* is enormously influential in shaping public opinion in wizarding communities. Through the example of the *Daily Prophet*, Rowling presents the many faces of media: political watchdog, sensational tabloid, entertainer, educator, and propaganda machine. I begin with the role of the *Daily Prophet* as political watchdog.

In Potter's world, the Ministry of Magic is a humorous, if not sometimes sadly accurate, caricature of modern government. While the Ministry faces a number of daunting challenges including the escape of Sirius Black, the breakout of the Death Eaters from Azkaban, not to mention the return of Lord Voldemort, Ministry officials seem more concerned with preserving their power and maintaining a polished public image. Those that can help the Ministry with its public perception are friends of the Ministry. At times, the *Daily Prophet* is such a friend, but early in the series, it is more likely to expose incompetence at the Ministry. On numerous occasions, Fudge worries about what the *Prophet* will report, particularly as his incompetence leads to so many problems for the Ministry. When Sirius Black escapes from Azkaban, the inept Minister of Magic worries that "the *Daily Prophet* is going to have a field day with this." After the security debacle at the Quidditch World Cup, the Ministry of Magic has its feet held to the fire by the *Daily Prophet*. Arthur Weasley notes that *Prophet* reporters have been "ferreting around all week, looking for more Ministry mess-ups to report" (*Goblet of Fire*, p. 153). The *Prophet*'s reporting on Fudge's many mistakes ultimately leads to his dismissal as Minister of Magic.

While the *Prophet* functioned as a political watchdog on occasion, it was more likely to act as a tabloid or lap dog of the Ministry of Magic. More than anyone, the *Prophet* reporter Rita Skeeter engages in fast and loose reporting. Her work is usually a small mix of fact with a large dose of creative license and exaggeration to create the most sensational story she can. She reports on "Dumbledore's Giant Mistake" in the *Goblet of Fire*, outing Rubeus Hagrid as a half-giant, an association that carries no small level of scorn from the wizarding community. She refers to venerable Hogwarts headmaster Albus Dumbledore as an "obsolete dingbat" in her article on the International Confederation of Wizards' Conference, and portrays Hermione as "a plain but ambitious girl" who was toying with the emotions of famous Harry Potter and the Bulgarian wizard, Viktor Krum. Rita Skeeter's treatment of Harry Potter is particularly exploitive. In her article covering the Triwizard Tournament, Skeeter (with help from her Quick-Quotes Quill) produces a sensational piece about Harry's life story, reporting "an awful lot of things that [Harry] couldn't remember saying in his life" (*Goblet of Fire*, p. 314). Later on, Rita takes a different angle on Harry, and casts him not as a sympathetic orphan, but a disturbed menace. She publishes an article entitled, "Harry Potter 'Disturbed and Dangerous'" in which she describes Harry's pain from his scar as either a mental illness or a desperate plea for attention (*Goblet of Fire*, p. 611).

Media critics may be concerned that the base and exploitative nature of media reflects a public desire for tabloid sensationalism (Paddy Chayevsky once noted, "Television is democracy at its ugliest."); however, the most troubling aspect of media for many commentators is its potential to limit how consumers think about their government, economy, society, and fellow citizens. Herbert Marcuse (1964) cautions that "in the medium of technology, culture, politics, and the economy merge into an omnipresent system which swallows up or repulses all alternatives." As such, Marcuse anticipated the "one-dimensional man," where personal interests are collapsed into a public, corporate agenda through the technologies of mass media. Central to the critical perspective is a broad suspicion of technology, particularly the tendency of technology to homogenize societies through the centralization of media. Often philosophers view technology as in an implicit power relationship with their users, or more accurately over their users. We are cogs in a large machine, trapped by technology's deterministic effects. Emblematic of this position, Theodor Adorno and Max Horkheimer (1944) cast media and technology as "aesthetic activities" that bind us to "the rhythm of an iron system." In what has become a common argument in the sociology of technology, Adorno and Horkheimer see hegemony, control, and monolithic power in technology and media, a system that makes subjects of its users.

The most disturbing presentation of the *Daily Prophet* by Rowling resonates with Marcuse and others' critique of media as a powerful juggernaut. For the second half of the series, the *Daily Prophet* protects the interests of Cornelius Fudge and other Ministers of Magic. Specifically, the *Prophet* long denies the return of Lord Voldemort and presents Harry as a disturbed, attention-hungry boy. In these instances, the *Daily Prophet* was clearly working against the public interest. While Rita Skeeter is a thoroughly unlikeable character and the principal example of media acting as tabloid, she also provides the most penetrating analysis of the motives that drive big media in Harry Potter. In a conversation with Hermione, Rita Skeeter speaks candidly about the activities at the *Daily Prophet*:

"We don't need another story about how Harry's lost his marbles!" said Hermione angrily. "We've had plenty of those already, thank you! I want him given the opportunity to tell the truth!"

"There's no market for a story like that," said Rita coldly.

"You mean the *Prophet* won't print it because Fudge won't let them," said Hermione irritably.

Rita gave Hermione a long, hard look. Then, leaning forward across the table toward her, she said in a businesslike tone, "All right, Fudge is leaning on the *Prophet*, but it comes to the same thing. They won't print a story that shows Harry in a good light. Nobody wants to read it. It's against the public mood. This last Azkaban breakout has got people worried enough. People just don't want to believe You-Know-Who's back."

"So the *Daily Prophet* exists to tell people what they want to hear, does it?" said Hermione scathingly.

Rita sat up straight again, eyebrows raised, and drained her glass of firewhisky.

"The *Prophet* exists to sell itself, you silly girl," she said coldly.

(*Order of the Phoenix*, p. 567)

Through Rita Skeeter, Rowling presents the worst of media in a way that would likely satisfy Marcuse, Adorno, and Horkheimer. She reveals the dubious influence that profit motive and government can exert on media outlets. Rowling contrasts the self-serving activities of the *Daily Prophet* with the bandit radio station produced by Lee Jordan and others as a way to get the truth out about Voldemort. Even the magazine *The Quibbler*, which publishes wild conspiracy theories and stories about non-existent animals, can be viewed as an alternative to big media, particularly as it printed Harry's true account of his encounter with Lord Voldemort at the end of the Triwizard Tournament. The important point here is that through her treatment of big media, Rowling provides young readers further opportunity to think critically about the role of media in the economy of ideas.

As a text, Harry Potter provides an effective platform for dialogue about technology and media. At first glance, this series could be viewed as evidence of Rowling's infatuation with technology and the magic it may add to our lives. However, as we carefully examine Rowling's work by reading these texts as a morality tale about technology, readers will find that Rowling recognizes the dilemmas of technology and media. From Harry's first year at Hogwarts to his demanding journey to defeat Lord Voldemort in the final installment of the series, Rowling frames the story around the potential pitfalls of technology and technology's tendency to amplify the moral shortcomings of humanity. Victory for Harry is realized once he recognizes this perspective. While Rowling's technological critique is more subtle than that of C. S. Lewis or J. R. R. Tolkien, it is compelling nonetheless.

References

Adorno, T., & Horkheimer, M. (1944). The culture industry: Enlightenment as mass deception [electronic version]. *Dialectic of enlightenment.* Retrieved February 5, 2005 from http://www.marxists.org/reference/subject/philosophy/works/ge/adorno.htm.

Bowker, G., & Leigh-Star, S. (1999). *Sorting things out: Classification and its consequences.* Cambridge, MA: MIT Press.

Chayevesky, P. (Writer) & Lummet, S. (Director). (1976). *Network* [Motion Picture]. Los Angeles, CA: MGM Studies.

Clarke, A. C. (1962). *Profiles of the future: An inquiry into the limits of the possible.* Gollancz: London.

Hall, S. (1997). The work of representation. In S. Hall (ed.), *Representation: Cultural representations and signifying practices.* London: Sage.

Johnson, S. (1997). *Interface culture: How new technology transforms the way we create and communicate.* New York: Basic Books.

Lewis, C. S. (1956). The last battle. In *The chronicles of Narnia.* New York: HarperCollins.

Marcuse, H. (1964). *One-dimensional man: Studies in the ideology of advanced industrial society.* Boston, MA: Beacon Press.

McLuhan, H. M. (1964). *Understanding media: The extensions of man.* New York: McGraw-Hill.

Mitcham, C. (2003). Three ways of being-with technology. In R. C. Scharff & V. Dusek (eds.), *Philosophy of technology: The technological condition* (Vol. 18, pp. 490–506). Malden, MA: Blackwell Publishing.

Oxford English Dictionary (Online Edition). Online, available at: dictionary.oed.com/cgi/findword? query_type=word&queryword=media

Postman, N. (1993). *Technopoly: The surrender of culture to technology.* New York: Knopf; distributed by Random House.

Rossi, L. D. (1984). *The politics of fantasy, C.S. Lewis and J.R.R. Tolkien.* Ann Arbor, MI: UMI Research Press.

Rowling, J. K. (1999a). *Harry Potter and the chamber of secrets.* New York: Arthur A. Levine Books.

Rowling, J. K. (1999b). *Harry Potter and the prisoner of Azkaban.* New York: Arthur A. Levine Books.

Rowling, J. K. (1999c). *Harry Potter and the sorcerer's stone.* New York: Scholastic.

Rowling, J. K. (2000). *Harry Potter and the goblet of fire.* New York: Arthur A. Levine Books.

Rowling, J. K. (2003). *Harry Potter and the order of the phoenix.* New York: Scholastic.

Rowling, J. K. (2005). *Harry Potter and the half-blood prince.* New York: Arthur A. Levine Books.

Rowling, J. K. (2007). *Harry Potter and the deathly hallows* (1st edn.). New York: Arthur A. Levine Books.

Thoman, E., & Jolls, T. (2004). Media literacy—A national priority for a changing world. *American Behavioral Scientist, 48*(1), 18–29.

Tolkien, J. R. R. (1954). *The lord of the rings.* Boston, MA: Houghton Mifflin.

Chapter Four

Is Desire Beneficial or Harmful in the Harry Potter Series?

TAIJA PIIPPO

J. K. Rowling's Harry Potter novels, like many children's books, include a good deal of moral and ethical, even philosophical thematic. One such topic especially labels the first novel, *Sorcerer's Stone*, but also comes forth in the whole series: desire. This novel ends the first stage of Harry's personal growth and development with a discussion between him and Dumbledore, which specifically sums up the novel's teaching about desire,

> [Dumbledore tells Harry] You know, the Stone was really not such a wonderful thing. As much money and life as you could want! The two things most human beings would choose above all—the trouble is, humans do have a knack of choosing precisely those things which are worst for them.
>
> (*Sorcerer's Stone*, 215)

Desire in the Harry Potter novels is often rather implicitly expressed but can be observed in many things the characters do, as a base for specific actions and even for their whole existence. Central aspects of Harry's desire are how it is presented, what it reveals about him, and how it contributes to the development of his identity. Other characters' desires bring out several points that could not be otherwise illustrated, and contribute to the whole by giving new insights into interpreting the deeper meaning behind a desire, in other words, what lies behind its outward manifestation. Rowling seems to continually question the effect of desires on the characters' lives: the most often posed situation resulting from desire is dysfunctional, threatening, or even fatal. It is of special interest for me to look into the harmfulness and usefulness of desire and to explore the reasons for presenting it as either. The most central theories I use in this exploration are Sigmund Freud, Gilles Deleuze, and Félix

Guattari's theories of desire, the former being more oriented to desire in a familial context, the latter to collectively constructed desire.

Freud's account of desire concentrates on an individual's inner dynamics, emphasizing the importance of childhood experiences, such as the Oedipus complex, in the family surroundings (42). It is mainly concerned with sexual desire, but the concept of desire also includes drives, instincts, and passions that naturally determine a person's behaviors and beliefs (200–202), even as they are continually repressed (524). It would not be entirely exaggerated to say that all of Freud's work is based on research on human psychosexual development and its disorders, but in the context of this chapter we need to give up those overtly sexual associations connected to the word "desire," as sexuality is hardly the most vital desire in the Harry Potter series. I start with a very basic definition: a desire is a "feeling or emotion which is directed to the attainment or possession of some object from which pleasure or satisfaction is expected" or "an object of desire; that which one desires or longs for" (*Oxford English Dictionary*).

Social Pressures as Desires

In Harry Potter's world, the forefront representant of Oedipus and its effects is Harry's foster family, the Dursleys. There are also occasions where Harry's and even Lord Voldemort's, or his former self Tom Riddle's, actions and thoughts conform to the Freudian mode of thinking. The Dursleys are "proud to say that they were perfectly normal, thank you very much" (*Sorcerer's Stone*, 7), and go to extremes in their frantic attempts to assure themselves of the fact that the world is a rational, causally explicable place. They lose their peace of mind at the slightest implication that it could be otherwise and rather pretend not to understand if there is a chance of seeing something out of the ordinary. "[Mr. Dursley]'d forgotten all about the people in cloaks until he passed a group of them next to the baker's. He eyed them angrily as he passed. He didn't know why, but they made him uneasy" (*Sorcerer's Stone*, 9). The Dursleys' desire to live in a logical, normal world also comes out as an intense fear and anxiety of all things inexplicable or extraordinary, and Suman Gupta sees this as a consequence of their knowledge that magic, in fact, does exist: their rigid opinions are so unpleasant and oppressive precisely because they do not fit into the Muggle world (87). Thus, even though the Dursleys start from the assumption that Harry's magical abilities are abnormal and must be forced into a mold of normality, the more abnormal thing in their world is to believe in magic at all, as is often inversely stated in the wizarding community, "[N]o Muggle would admit their key keeps shrinking ... they'll go to any lengths to ignore magic" (*Chamber of Secrets*, 34). Despite all their trying, the Dursleys cannot avoid this contradiction and live in constant fear that someone will find out about their freak relatives, building their life on lies, secrecy, and fakeness in order not to be labeled odd themselves.

The greatest desire of the Dursley family is to be respected full members of the society surrounding them, preferably on a slightly higher level in the hierarchy than most of the others, and to be on good terms with those that undeniably surpass them in that hierarchy. They feel a strong need to mix into the conservative, wealthier, upper middle class community and on the surface they succeed excellently, being able to provide the outward material signs of success and wealth, which are considerably valued. Additionally, in the pursuit of status especially important to him, Mr. Dursley aims at success at work, effectively reaching the common goal of the family as well.

The Dursleys' identities depend on their society, on other people's opinion of them, and the most important thing for them is to keep up the façade of an honorable, typical family flawless. Their commitment and attitude towards society is hierarchical, the whole immediate environment is characterized by competition and envy, and the largest uniform unit in this community is the psychoanalytic nuclear family, inside which identities are inflexible and fossilized—at least the Dursleys strive for that preferable condition. They do not even want to understand the multiple and changing nature of things, but find the feeling of security in stability.

Only in *Order of the Phoenix* do the Dursleys admit the existence of the magical world so much as to discuss it with Harry, "The arrival of the Dementors in Little Whinging seemed to have breached the great, invisible wall that divided the relentlessly non-magical world of Privet Drive and the world beyond" (*Order of the Phoenix*, 39). This is clearly in line with the former argument about the nuclear family: Dudley has been attacked on the way home with Harry, and his parents are beside themselves questioning the boys. As Gupta puts it, "Magic is apparent as magic because it defeats the desires and sharpens the explanatory failures of Muggles" (87). When compelled against the threat of the total shattering of the familial idyll, even the most hard-boiled Muggles give in and listen to the one that can give them answers, wizard or not. However, when they manage to restore the familial trichotomy and balance, their identities are soon back to where they were; indicatively, Mr. Dursley informs Harry, "We—that is to say, your aunt, Dudley and I— are going out" (*Order of the Phoenix*, 45). They are ready again to mingle with society to prove their normality.

The Dursleys will never be happy with only what they are or have, but constantly need affirmation and accumulation. It creates a vicious circle: the more they pursue the consolidation of material goods in the attempt to define their identity, the weaker that identity becomes and consequently it needs even more cementing. In contradiction, for Deleuze and Guattari, desire is rather a primary psychic force or process, which is separated from need, want, or drive which are seen as products of social institutions or entirely biological instincts (Deleuze and Guattari, 25–29). Deliberately contradicting Jacques Lacan's psychoanalytic theory on desire as lack, they describe desire as production, a free-floating, essentially nomadic energy (Deleuze and Guattari, 26). Deleuze and Guattari's concept of deterritorialization refers to ideas that have been separated from their original context or relation and applied to others; thus, although they admit the libidinal nature of desire, they criticize Freud's view by defining it as a concept deterritorialized from adult sexuality applicable in any context or relation: it emerges spontaneously, generating relationships by fusing multiplicities together (Deleuze and Guattari, 350–355).

Some remarkable instances of the deterritorialization of desire take place between Harry and Professor Dumbledore in *Sorcerer's Stone* and *Chamber of Secrets*. In the former, Dumbledore helps Harry to break his fixated conception of the relation between the Mirror of Erised and his parents, so that his future desire may be invested more diffusely and practically in the social field. By explaining the way the Mirror works, Dumbledore shows Harry the deterritorialization inherent in it and makes him realize that everyone looking into it sees different things, "It shows us nothing more or less than the deepest, most desperate desire of our hearts" (*Sorcerer's Stone*, 157). With this information, Harry is a step ahead in applying his knowledge to acquire the Sorcerer's Stone when he faces Professor Quirrell and Lord Voldemort in front of the Mirror. This illustrates the process of deterritorialization from another standpoint: if the Mirror can show a desire in one situation, it can show another desire in another situation, even for the same individual. It is inarguable that Lacan's theory of desire as lack presents a possible explanation here. Both Harry and Ron see what they lack in the Mirror of Erised: parental love and success over others. Lack can change over time, so that desires change, although we later see Harry reverting back to his original desire.

The Burden of Heritage and the Desire for Identity

In *Chamber of Secrets*, Harry is battling with suspicions of being the heir of Salazar Slytherin, "'There's not a single witch or wizard who went bad who wasn't in Slytherin'" (*Sorcerer's Stone*, 62). He is in the middle of an identity crisis, which matches the type Robyn McCallum depicts: marginalization undermining a developing identity (68–69, 100–101). Harry has suffered such a great deal of marginalization in the form of unfair accusations that he caused recent disasters, (purely on account of being misfortunate enough to be in the wrong place at the wrong time too often) that he is having misgivings about his unknown heritage and his supposed tendencies and loyalties. He also faces the problem of being different from other people, to which his first reactions somewhat childishly (after all, he is only 12) are denial and an intense desire to be like others. As Rosemary Jackson (1981) points out, difference is often labeled as evil or otherness (52–53), which naturally are not preferable characteristics to be identified with, as is seen when others first discover that Harry can talk to snakes,

"I'm a what?" said Harry.

"*A Parselmouth!*" said Ron. "You can talk to snakes!"

[...]

"It matters," said Hermione, speaking at last in a hushed voice, "because being able to talk to snakes was what Salazar Slytherin was famous for." [...]

"But I'm in *Gryffindor*," Harry thought. "The Sorting Hat wouldn't have put me in here if I had Slytherin blood..."

"*Ah*," said a nasty little voice in his brain, "But the Sorting Hat *wanted* to put you in Slytherin, don't you remember?"

(Chamber of Secrets, 146–147)

Harry is driven by the desire to find out his real heritage and his chances of influencing his involuntary condemnation to the allegedly evil Slytherin house. This is primarily in order to fasten his identity on a certain point in society, the Gryffindor house, where his parents and friends also belong. His doppelgänger, Tom Riddle, is quite an obvious manifestation of his darker side, the heir of Slytherin, who possesses all those unwanted characteristics by which Harry fatalistically fears to have been tied down. McCallum describes the situation in which the doppelgänger fragments and destabilizes the character's sense of self by pointing out an unwanted direction of development (75–77). The idea of a doppelgänger is often used in crime or detective fiction, where a detective needs to step inside a criminal's mind and construct the logical course of action that is to follow. It is a disturbing thought that an upright officer has to mime and identify with an immoral, possibly violent criminal; it does not give a very flattering picture of the detective to succeed in this task. The doppelgänger relation between Tom Riddle and Harry along these lines can be seen as complementing. Tom as Voldemort completes Harry, having given him a set of traits that he has not acknowledged or even noticed in himself so far. There is enough similarity that Harry begins to believe in a one-to-one matching possibility, until Dumbledore points out that not all their common features need to be negatively seen.

"You happen to have many qualities Salazar Slytherin prized in his hand-picked students. His own very rare gift, Parseltongue ... resourcefulness ... determination ... a certain disregard for rules," he [Dumbledore] added, his moustache quivering again. "Yet the Sorting Hat placed you in Gryffindor."

(Chamber of Secrets, 245)

From the psychoanalytic point of view this could be seen as evidence that so far, Harry has neither been able to understand nor cope with his darker side that includes the more questionable characteristics of his personality, nor is he able to combine it with his more appreciated features. This psychology is usually typical of very small children and might even be taken as some sort of disability in Harry at the age of 12, since, moreover, he does not have very developed means to deal with this conflict. However, with a little help, he is able to deterritorialize and reterritorialize aspects of his life and personality when he learns to see the parallel nature and multiplicity of qualities that can be used in many diverse ways, and at the same time realizes that external signs or internal abilities cannot, by themselves, decide where a person is located on the axis of good and evil.

Desire for Power brings Common or Personal Good … or Bad?

A central feature in Deleuze and Guattari's (*Anti-Oedipus*, 36, 315) theory is a continual material flow, a decoded flow of desire. However, Julian Wolfreys (51) points out that they believe there is no organizing or generative center or origin, not even a self that would produce desire. Neither does desire take persons or things as its objects, but rather the entire surroundings, its flows and vibrations, adding breaks and captures. It is characteristically an anonymous and migrant desire (291). This is something of a hindrance, as it is virtually impossible to generalize so much as to handle this topic completely without concrete examples of subjects and objects of desire, so I have used objects from the lives of Harry and other characters and applied Deleuze and Guattari's concepts and theory structures to them.

Stripped down to the very atomic level, many of the characters' desires illustrate similar things, being most frequently associated with social goals, hopes, and ambitions; this general underlying current could be called the flow of desire after Deleuze and Guattari. Basically, everyone wants to be respected and valued in society and strives for this by various means, whether it is by exerting power and spreading fear, protecting the individuals in the society, maintaining and preserving the existing institutions, or surrounding themselves with impressive material. Their motivations are also multiple, at the most elementary level focusing somewhere between the selfish and selfless.

Deleuze and Guattari explain that the social field is a historical product of desire and is also immediately invested by desire, and indeed that "[t]here is only desire and the social, and nothing else" (*Anti-Oedipus*, 29). From this even the most repressive and fatal forms of social reproduction are created by desire, and here fascism is introduced in the theory with Wilhelm Reich's remark about people wanting humiliation and slavery. Reich will not accept ignorance or illusion as an explanation, only an explanation that takes desire into account (29).

Deleuze and Guattari explore fascism, not in its historical meaning, but the fascism in everyone's everyday behavior, which Michel Foucault characterizes as "the fascism that causes us to love power, to desire the very thing that dominates and exploits us" (xiii). The most central principle is to place de-individualization above the rights of an individual. Rather than bonding individuals in a hierarchy, the group must fuse them together. This is because individuals are produced by power and must not, for their own as much as for the sake of society, love or crave power (Foucault, xiv).

Examples in the Harry Potter novels are ample. There are those who grab power, never stopping to wonder whether it is actually beneficial even for themselves, but also those who accept and even desire their own subjection for different reasons, rarely wondering at the benefits of their choice of self-subjection.

Tom Riddle, later as Lord Voldemort, desires unrestricted power in a fascist (cf. Gupta, 101) society, which he will lead uncompromisingly. What he does not realize is that the "desire for mastery and power results in destruction when it is not based on self-knowledge and self-mastery," and that in order to survive personal turmoil everyone has to know their limits, that is, themselves (Goodheart, 35). Tom/Voldemort is as lost as the day his mother left him, when he unknowingly became unable ever to understand love, as Dumbledore repeatedly tells Harry (for example, *Sorcerer's Stone*, 216; *Half-Blood Prince*, 477–478).

This lack of knowledge is also demonstrated by the way Tom's desire has such a strong control of him that his identity has intertwined in a crooked way with it, aiming at the subjection and destruction of the dominating class. He is attacking his own people as he admits he is half-blood, but he has identified with the pure-blood identity so strongly that it loses importance. It is remarkable that Tom has created this new identity, almost a whole new person, through a change of name and severe metamorphoses, all for the powerful character he desires and aims to be. It is as if he needs a mythical or even a supernatural alter ego to hold him up and to emphasize the traits he deems necessary for the leadership of the wizarding world.

Besides fascism, Deleuze and Guattari might accuse both Dudley and Voldemort of a severely enslaving Oedipus complex. Dudley Dursley comes close to Voldemort in the means he takes as he strives to fulfill his desire: both are keen on terror and violence and like to exercise their will through other people. Dudley needs his gang even when he is beating up ten year olds; Voldemort calls for his Death Eaters to do his bidding whether it is keeping him alive or finding out information. There is no evidence of Dudley punishing his friends, whereas Voldemort does not have such inhibitions towards his supporters. Dudley, however, orders his parents around. This seems like a classic representant of oedipal desire. He is seeking to overtake his father in material possessions and is also very jealous of his mother's love—a feature of the Oedipus complex that Voldemort has taken even further and ultimately has concretized by murdering his father in bitter revenge for taking his mother from him. Dudley is a model example of a child who has always got what he wants and will most probably use this experience through the later stages of his life as a justification to have what he thinks is rightfully—or forcefully—his.

Dudley's parents shower him with expensive gifts without noticing they only make him want more external evidence of his power, and encourage him to exert the same kind of power that he has over them to others as well. His first victim is Harry, later other children, later yet, maybe his co-workers, employees, or his own family. Voldemort has already gone further down that path; only the souvenirs he used to take have changed to burned marks on the arms of his followers. The main psychological impact is the need to show power: to gain it and keep it hanging above others' heads. More importantly, nevertheless, both Dudley and Voldemort are slaves themselves. They are equally crushed under their own desire for power that takes them away from real friends, emotions, and society at large. They are as much incapable as they are unwilling to form close relationships or to feel empathy, pity, or love. Both could be classified as victims of Oedipus: Dudley in his nuclear family spoiling him with all of its might and thus fulfilling his oedipal fantasies, Tom or Lord Voldemort in his overflowing rage against his traitorous father and the mother who dared die and leave him alone. Even Dudley's reformation in *Deathly Hallows* is somewhat dubious. Does he really value Harry for who and what he is, or is it only a desire for protection from further attacks?

Professor Quirrell's desire in *Sorcerer's Stone*, as well as his commitment to the Dark Side, originates from Voldemort's mind, judging from the self-depreciating words sounding as if issued from outside, "A foolish young man I was then, full of ridiculous ideas about good and evil. Lord Voldemort showed me how wrong I was" (*Sorcerer's Stone*, 211). Because their master–servant relationship is based on fear and an inferior's servitude, neither is properly on the receiving side. Quirrell is ready to go to any lengths to keep Voldemort alive and well, and is destroyed because of his desperate desire to be led—in his own words, weakness. It could also be seen as a desire to be approved of, which labels him so intently that his identity begins to crack and fall apart. He truly desires his enslavement, which ends in agony and death. Even then he does not dare question the orders he is receiving, proving his internalized fascism by acknowledging Voldemort's power.

Desires for Different Kinds of Enslavement

Deleuze and Guattari reproach psychoanalysis for having stifled the order of production, shunting it into representation instead. They accuse the agency of family of distorting and disfiguring social desiring-production by reducing social manifestations of desire to itself, and representation of inflating itself with all the power of legend and tragedy to keep a rein on production (175). As Deleuze and Guattari point out, instead of allowing the child to communicate with the father, Freud insists that the father is inflated with all of the "forces of myth and religion" and with phylogenesis (296–298). Deleuze and Guattari want to draw attention to the immense historical status Freud has gained and the way his thoughts still prevail. In particular, in his theories of the Oedipus complex, unconscious and repression hold their ground; "our society is the stronghold of Oedipus" (175) and "[t]he unconscious believes in Oedipus" (296), they complain, seeing that when repression starts its pervasion from home, it is more difficult to cut away later. Mark Seem adds that Deleuze and Guattari aim at freeing the multiplicity of desire from the oedipal neurosis and neuroticism, and coin the term "oedipalization" to illustrate Oedipus as a figure of power injected into the unconscious, teaching us to desire our own repression, surrounding us everywhere (xx).

A particularly acute instance is described in *Prisoner of Azkaban*. Harry's urgent desire becomes to fight back his memories, to fight back the fear that incapacitates him when confronting a Dementor, but he soon realizes he might not be all that eager to get rid of his memories, "Terrible though it was to hear his parents' last moments replayed inside his head, these were the only times Harry had heard their voices since he was a very small child" (*Prisoner of Azkaban*, 180). Harry is captured by the voices of his parents just as effectively as he was by their reflections in the Mirror of Erised. His underlying desire has not changed as much as could have been assumed but is as continuous a flow as ever, and despite his socially acceptable reason (winning a team sport cup) for wanting to abolish his parents from his mind, he still has very personal reasons for wanting both to keep them in and banish them. Harry is again enslaved by his desire, again desiring his enslavement, and this time there are several desires clashing with each other, which altogether makes it considerably more difficult to concentrate on practicing the method with which he could resist the influence of the Dementors. Despite the realization that his desire and fear originate from the same source, which should facilitate the rationalization of the trauma (Chetwynd, 1982), Harry finds it increasingly hard to conjure a Patronus magically, and feels angry and guilty about his secret.

Besides its name, which is Latin for "guardian" and of the same origin as the Latin *pater*, "father," Harry's Patronus is interesting especially to a psychoanalyst. In a desperate situation against a horde of Dementors, Harry thinks he sees his father sending a Patronus from some distance. Its form is a stag, which was also Harry's father's Animagus (animal) form, his nickname at school correspondingly being Prongs. In the end, Harry finds out it was he, not his father, who sent out the Patronus, and, despite the original joy of being capable of advanced magic and a fully able protector, he feels sorely disappointed and again needs Dumbledore's explanation, "I expect you're tired of hearing it, but you do look *extraordinarily* like James. [...] Your father is alive in you, Harry, and shows himself most plainly when you have need of him" (*Prisoner of Azkaban*, 312). Significantly, it is the sense of self that the Dementors take, and it surely is no coincidence that Harry is saved from losing his identity by his father, whatever shape he acts in—Harry's outward appearance or his Patronus. It appears that exactly the "inflating of the father with myth and phylogenesis" is at work here, the idea about which Deleuze and Guattari so criticize Freud. They would probably be of the opinion that Harry's parents, or rather his longing for his parents, is obstructing the continuous flow of his desire. Adding to that theory, especially considering his attachment to Sirius—a father figure or parent substitute—they might consider Harry a lost case to Oedipus.

There is a certain connection between what Freud calls repression and Deleuze and Guattari call fascism. Repression creates an uninterrupted striving towards the fulfillment of a desire and creates unconscious symbols that attract the conscious, finding their way out not only through dreams but also by forming the basis of human endeavors and values. The repressed drive will always aim at full satisfaction by repeating a primal satisfying experience; this is a perpetual process because there is an eternal difference between the desired and the actual satisfaction (Furth, 62).

Harry's repressions are revealed early on in the encounter with the Mirror of Erised in *Sorcerer's Stone*. The analogy between dreams and the Mirror's function illustrates Freud's dream theory in revealing repressed thoughts and emotions despite Harry being awake. There are, after all, slight similarities between the dream state and Harry's state. He is accused of "dwell[ing] on dreams and forget[ting] to live" (*Sorcerer's Stone*, 157). The Mirror puts him in a trance-like state, "How long he stood there, he didn't know" (*Sorcerer's Stone*, 153). Moreover, the concept of a mirror is often used to show a person's inner self, feelings, or memories (de Vries). We also use other people as mirrors to get to know ourselves (Chetwynd). This thought is further explored on a general level by Sabine Melchior-Bonnet, who points out that before the mirror became a means for self-reflection or self-knowledge, it estimated the degree of commitment a person may have to social norms when it made people self-conscious of their reflection. It created an identity based on the experience of being publicly seen, and it was thus an aid in achieving social status and adjustment to society (p. 146).

Professor Dumbledore states that what the Mirror of Erised shows is not even a reflection of reality—in fact, anything we see in a mirror is always a reverse image, and, as such, it already is to a certain extent disconnected from reality. The Mirror of Erised, however, has the special power of capturing people with the fantastic pictures that they produce out of their deepest desires. Deleuze and Guattari's ironic comment about psychoanalysis explaining only fantasy seems the more valid theory here, because there is a certain contradiction between their insistence on the realness of what is desired and the operational principle of the Mirror.

Harry's underlying desire for parental love is clear. He lost his parents at the age of one and cannot remember them. He never felt loved in his dreadful foster family, the Dursleys. A peculiar Christmas gift, an Invisibility Cloak having allegedly belonged to his father, stirred his heart and awakened a need to get closer to his parents, "his father's Cloak—he felt that this time—the first time—he wanted to use it alone" (*Sorcerer's Stone*, 151). As both conscious activity and unconscious desire are connected to latent dream thought, this might be seen as the Mirror's concrete function. It works similarly to the psychological occasion for the dream, giving unconscious wishes a possibility to come into sight of the consciousness. It could thus even be termed as "the Mirror of the Preconscious."

Usually, dream work helps the dreamer to avoid anxiety by disguising desire through symbols (Furth, 45), but the viewers of the Mirror face a threat in this aspect. As their desires come concretely into focus in the Mirror, there is no possibility for repression, and the (day)dream of Harry's parents being alive results in them being "alive" in the Mirror of Erised. The danger is that the Mirror shows the "most desperate desire of our hearts" but still "will give us neither knowledge or truth," and there is no knowing whether what it shows will ever come true (*Sorcerer's Stone*, 157). The viewer keeps feeding an unconscious desire with conscious activity, receiving nothing in return, "[Harry] had a powerful kind of ache inside him, half joy, half terrible sadness" (*Sorcerer's Stone*, 153). When Harry is separated from the Mirror, he finds out that "[a]ll is counterbalanced, and extremes (even of love and calm restraint) tend to build up an opposite unconscious reaction" (Chetwynd). He then starts having nightmares.

Personal and Collective Identity Desires

The *Concise Encyclopedia of Psychology* defines "identity formation" as follows:

> *Personal identity* refers to a sense of sameness or continuity of the self despite environmental changes and individual growth. Personal memories of the past as well as hopes and aspirations for the future provide evidence in the present of this sense of identity.

This concept is enriched by taking into account the theory of the psychoanalyst Erik H. Erikson (1968), who explains identity formation in adolescence as an integration or a restructuring of previous self-images and identifications, in a process that is dependent on society (159) and is only complete when the adolescent has identified him/herself in a new way and achieved sociability and a competitive status among peers (155).

McCallum emphasizes the social impact on identity even more. Identity to her is a sense of a personal identity an individual has of her/his self as distinct from other selves, as occupying a position within society and in relation to other selves, and as being capable of deliberate thought and action. Concepts of personal identity and selfhood are formed in dialogue with society, with language, and with other people (3).

In fact, she prefers the wider term of "subjectivity," emphasizing the complex intertwining of personal, physical, and mental growth and one's relationships between society and other individuals (3–4). However, McCallum wants to keep the relationship between an individual and society even, one not privileged over the other, which is a central problem for a theory of subjectivity (6).

According to Brian Massumi (1980/1987), Deleuze and Guattari emphasize multiplicity generally and specifically in their discussions about identity (1980/1987 xi–xiii). Seem has further depicted how singularity and collectivity reach an agreement and collective expressions of desire become possible by forming and connecting new, collective arrangements that de-normalize and de-individualize, urging everyone to work against the power subjugating them (xxi). The goal is to forge a collective subjectivity, "a nonfascist subject—anti-Oedipus" that destroys the neurotic individual dependencies created through oedipalization (xxiii).

Deleuze and Guattari further develop the concept of multiplicity in their theoretical structure of rhizomes. The rhizome cannot be reduced either to the one or the multiple. Instead, a rhizome is composed of linear multiplicities laid out on a plane of consistency, and whenever a multiplicity changes dimension, it changes profoundly as in a metamorphosis (p. 9). A more concrete way of understanding a rhizome derives from its biological structure. Plants that have rhizomes seem to be both individual and separate. They have vast and multiple connections underground, forming a wide network of similar units, an entire community. Each part of the rhizome is able to function alone, but no part is above others and all are equal in the operation of the whole. In fact, even though it might appear that only one individual in the rhizome is working, or that several or all of them are doing the same thing independently, they are actually sharing (7–8, 36–37).

The *Order of the Phoenix* offers straightforward examples of a rhizome identity. The idea of identicalness is, of course, unrealistic to apply to humans, but can be loosely applied to inward qualities. In the *Order of the Phoenix*, different people are working to reach the same target; they are separate people with different life experiences but support the same ideology and share the same desires to a certain extent. There are also smaller groups that can be considered rhizomes. Harry forms one with Ron and Hermione, and another with his father James.

In the first three novels, Harry forms the basis of his identity rhizome on different levels or perhaps branches. In *Sorcerer's Stone*, he (in psychoanalytic terms) successfully faces the positive regress, going back towards infancy in order to move on towards maturity—one of a mirror's symbolic functions (Chetwynd, 1982). Harry becomes aware of where he stands and what he fights for, and even though his parents cannot be brought back, his situation is relieved by the rhizomatic connections he has formed, the line of close friends and his (extended) family. His newly found wizard's identity is slowly beginning to flourish; he already makes fun of Muggles.

In *Chamber of Secrets*, Harry deepens his slowly accumulating understanding of the social effects of his actions and the rhizome he belongs to, and, in the end, he forges an even stronger commitment on a larger scale than before to his society. In *Prisoner of Azkaban*, he is only beginning to form the greater network of the many connections that will crisscross the society, first in smaller entities and then linking to each other in different ways and for different purposes. Harry is in the continuous process of building his own rhizome, making a network of connections that is both a source of happiness and is also of practical use in varying contexts to him.

Harry also gains more knowledge about himself and his father in *Prisoner of Azkaban* and is able to gradually assimilate it into his existing scenario. The sudden realization that he is to save both himself and Sirius from the Dementor's Kiss is a jubilant one. Harry is finally able to put some distance between himself and his father while at the same time coming closer to him. They become one and multiple at the same time, clearly separate but sharing common features, the smallest unit for a rhizome, two connected.

Harry, Ron, and Hermione's friendship begins the rhizome of which they will be equal parts, and this particular rhizome widens and deepens throughout the Harry Potter series. They take their places as members of the community and also achieve confidence in their own personal skills, which they use not only for themselves but also for others. As the three of them gradually become able to connect to a larger construction (such as Dumbledore's Army) and understand their own part and meaning in it, they become more de-individualized and at the same time more flexible in their endeavors so that they can fully direct themselves towards social desiring-production.

Deleuze and Guattari (1980/1987) admit that "a rhizome may be broken, shattered at a given spot" (p. 9), but hasten to add that it will reformulate either on some of its old lines or on new ones. Groups and individuals comprise microfascisms that may crystallize at any given time. Even good and evil are "only the products of an active and temporary selection, which must be renewed" (9–10).

The rhizome of the *Order of the Phoenix* is not entirely without ruptures. The most prominent one is between Sirius and Snape, an intense enmity and hatred maintained over a long period of time. The fundamental problem between these two seems to be on Sirius' part that he does not recognize

Snape as a member of the Order; on Snape's part it might be that he does not sufficiently contribute to behaving as a typical member so that he could be recognized as one. In other words, Sirius fails to reterritorialize Snape in his unexpected role as a member of the Order, or Snape fails to deterritorialize from his alleged image of a Death Eater in hiding. Most probably both hold prejudicial shortcomings in equal measure which consolidate each other cyclically.

Here the rhizome is not so much fracturing as being left completely unformed. The flow of desire is blocked when neither unit is willing to allow the desire, which is the very same circulating in and through both of them. A certain degree of concretization is appropriate, since in a human rhizome it is essential that the capacity for thought be taken into account. If Sirius and Snape's case is briefly considered from the angle of desire and identity, it could be said that both miss the universal nature of desire as a continuous flow and attempt to chain it for themselves to use for their own purposes. Sirius does this by excluding Snape from the rhizome he feels he but not Snape is part of. Snape does this by jealously placing his desire out of Sirius' reach, perhaps afraid of otherwise being forced to relive the trials he has gone through in the past, his broken relationship with Lily not the least important among them. (Peter Appelbaum explores this subject further in Chapter 5). Their individual identities push to the fore, leaving unfulfilled the expectation of de-individualization and making them vulnerable to attacks of Oedipus. The impression is of two little boys arguing about the favor of the father and not two adult men working for the same cause.

Achieving the Heart's Desire

Is it good or beneficial in the long run to achieve the heart's desire? The Harry Potter series does not give an explicit answer but Rowling indirectly brings out details that appear to discourage the irrational, and even irrelevant desire. This tactic is the most pronounced with Professor Dumbledore, who is almost completely detached from personal desires or at least keeps them tightly under control. The contrast to anyone else is stark. It is of course remarkable that not many of the characters are able to conquer their desires. Throughout the novels, even the more healthy, typical, or innocent-appearing desires enchain and restrict personal life and the development of identity. Ron, for example, is hampered by his desire for Hermione, and for status and power. When is he going to accept, respect, and trust himself without doubtful comparisons to his successful brothers or to Harry Potter? The desire for fame has only deepened his insecurity throughout his life, from his first encounter with the Mirror of Erised to the dramatic destruction of the locket Horcrux in *Deathly Hallows*.

Dumbledore has seen what desire can do to a human being and realizes its dangers; he has profound understanding of the ways desire bends people away from, instead of towards, their ideal life, as is deducible from his words about the Mirror of Erised: "Men have wasted away before it, entranced by what they have seen, or been driven mad, not knowing if what it shows is real or even possible" (*Sorcerer's Stone*, 157). He even gives an entirely opposite opinion of the Sorcerer's Stone from what most people would hold in his perhaps most illuminating remark, quoted at the beginning of the chapter, which shows the selflessness that he has reached and also seeks in Harry.

Dumbledore's desire for power in his youth, as depicted in *Deathly Hallows*, shows that even the best of us can be blinded by desire, and perhaps that it can only be cured with a loss so overwhelming that everything in life needs to be rethought and rearranged from the initial point. Maybe Rowling even wants to make such a strong statement as to say that desire is always predisposed to bring tragedy along, because people desire wrong things for themselves. This is in Dumbledore's words to Harry, "I had proven, as a young man, that power was my weakness and my temptation. It is a curious thing, Harry, but perhaps those who are best suited to power are those who have never sought it" (*Deathly Hallows*, 575). It is naturally a tragedy to realize, as Ron perhaps does in getting "a bad feeling" about the Mirror, that a desire might never turn into reality. For Dumbledore, the most concrete effect of the desire for power is that innocent people die. Power is Voldemort's ultimate quest as well, so it is no wonder that Dumbledore is so keen on stopping him when all power turns out to be harmful.

Several theorists have agreed on the subjecting effects of desire along the same lines as Deleuze and Guattari: René Girard points out that although enslavement is at first distant and unnoticed, it is always the final result of desire (180). It is naturally very human not to be willing to admit, sometimes even to yourself, an obsession for something possibly or definitely unattainable, such as dead parents or the lordship of the world. Linda Ruth Williams maintains that a key channel for desire is pleasure in pain, which may culminate in the destruction of the ego where masochism takes over (172), but Girard intensifies this with the opinion that metaphysical desire naturally tends towards masochism (180). The dramatic results of this process are seen in Quirrell's fate. Tom Chetwynd (1982) explains the conflict between wish and fear as the positive and negative sides of the same impulse, and nowhere else than in *Prisoner of Azkaban* is this better illustrated. It is as much a question of being able to stand against one's own desire as being able to strive to reach it. This theme is reinforced in almost every desire in the Harry Potter series. Harry's understandably compulsive desire for parental love leads him into hardships; Sirius is ready to lose his sense of self over a desire for revenge without a second thought; ambition and desire intertwine together blurring the borders between civilized behavior and brutality, humanity, and calculation, as happens with Dolores Umbridge or Bartemius Crouch Senior in *Goblet of Fire*, even with the young Dumbledore, among others.

The example of Sirius offers an interesting angle for this discussion. The triggering factor of his escape from the notorious Prison of Azkaban is a suddenly flamed obsessive desire, "It was as if someone had lit a fire in my head, and the Dementors couldn't destroy it … it wasn't a happy feeling … it was an obsession … but it gave me strength, it cleared my mind" (*Prisoner of Azkaban*, 272–273). What the desire aims at or whether it is, so to speak, a positive or a negative force, is less significant than the fact that it reconstructs Sirius' feeling of responsibility and independence, an important part of which is "knowing who I am" (*Prisoner of Azkaban*, 272). He becomes a fully acting agent again. Taking the shape of a dog is no longer a passive way of escaping unbearable conditions but is an active means to run away from them. The compelled deprivation of human relationships with the outer world is exchanged to a limited but voluntarily controlled freedom. In McCallum's terms (7) it could be said that Sirius regains full subjectivity, having at least a slight chance of interaction with the environment, along with the full scope of human psychological states. In this case, desire could be seen as a positive force, contrary to most other examples.

Sirius' contact with the social world, though, needs transgression described by McCallum: briefly put, it is resistance against social norms (118–119). Sirius is still in conflict with society and is going to deliberately violate its rules by killing Peter Pettigrew; thus, his desire is more powerful than the fear of consequences. Even though Sirius may feel he has nothing to lose even if he received the Dementor's Kiss, the loss of his identity would still be due to an all-encompassing desire that led him to full conflict with the society and transgression of its norms in the first place.

One theme is clearly recognizable throughout. Social desires are accepted if for the general good, and the benefit of the society. Dumbledore distinctly announces this,

> "How did I get the Stone out of the Mirror?"
> "…You see, only one who wanted to *find* the Stone—find it, but not use it—would be able to get it, otherwise they'd just see themselves making gold or drinking Elixir of Life."
> (*Sorcerer's Stone*, 217)

In his hope to overcome Voldemort, Harry's principal aim is to free the wizarding community from a selfish tyrant whose desire is not directed towards the communal well-being but to personal advantage. However, there is also desire in the gray area of morality, and it is emphasized that as long as Harry retains his anxious desire for personal revenge and fails to put his own special strength (love) into use for the whole society, he will not be able to defeat Voldemort. Individual suffering makes way for a vaster experience of solidarity in Harry, a superior level of thought that enables him to redirect his individual desire for the sake of his society,

> "Yes, Harry, you can love," said Dumbledore. [...] "In spite of all the temptation you have endured, all the suffering, you remain pure of heart, just as pure as you were at the age of eleven, when you stared into a mirror that reflected your heart's desire, and it showed you only the way to thwart Lord Voldemort, and not immortality and riches."
>
> (*Half-Blood Prince*, 476–478)

It seems occasionally that Harry might jeopardize his quest by giving in to the fascism that resurfaces in him from time to time; not only the fascism in surrendering to his obsessive longing for his parents, but also in exerting power over his enemies, "Harry shouted, '*Crucio!* [...] 'I see what Bellatrix meant,' said Harry, the blood thundering through his brain, 'you need to really mean it'" (*Deathly Hallows*, 477). This scene is very different from the one in *Prisoner of Azkaban*, where Harry spares Wormtail's life—it is more significant here that he does it at all than the reasons why he does it. In the end, Harry yields himself to Voldemort and this ultimate act of love, facing death for his society, proves to be the one that saves them all.

References

Chetwynd, Tom. "Mirror" and "Wish" in *A Dictionary of Symbols*. London: Paladin, 1982.

Corsini, Raymond J. and Alan J. Auerbach, eds. "Identity formation" in *Concise Encyclopedia of Psychology*. New York: John Wiley, 1998.

Deleuze, Gilles and Félix Guattari. *Anti-Oedipus. Capitalism and Schizophrenia*. Trans. Robert Hurley, Mark Seem, and Helen R. Lane. London: Athlone Press, 1972/1984.

———. *A Thousand Plateaus. Capitalism and Schizophrenia*. Trans. Brian Massumi. Minneapolis, MN: University of Minnesota Press, 1980/1987.

de Vries, Ad. "Mirror" in *Dictionary of Symbols and Imagery*. Amsterdam: North-Holland Publishing Company, 1974.

Erikson, Erik H. *Identity. Youth and Crisis*. London: Faber and Faber, 1968.

Foucault, Michel. "Preface" to Deleuze, Gilles and Félix Guattari. *Anti-Oedipus. Capitalism and Schizophrenia*. Trans. Robert Hurley, Mark Seem, and Helen R. Lane. London: The Athlone Press, 1972/1984.

Freud, Sigmund. *The Essentials of Psycho-Analysis. The Definitive Collection of Sigmund Freud's Writing*. Ed. Anna Freud. Trans. James Strachey. London: Penguin Books, 1991.

Furth, Hans G. *Knowledge As Desire. An Essay on Freud and Piaget*. New York: Columbia University Press, 1987.

Girard, René. *Deceit, Desire and the Novel. Self and Other in Literary Structure*. Trans. Yvonne Freccero. Baltimore, MD: Johns Hopkins University Press, 1961.

Goodheart, Eugene. *Desire and Its Discontents*. New York: Columbia University Press, 1991.

Gupta, Suman. *Re-reading Harry Potter*. New York: Palgrave Macmillan, 2003.

Jackson, Rosemary. *Fantasy. The Literature of Subversion*. London: Routledge, 1981.

McCallum, Robyn. *Ideologies of Identity in Adolescent Fiction. The Dialogic Construction of Subjectivity*. New York: Garland, 1999.

Massumi, Brian. "Foreword" to Deleuze, Gilles and Félix Guattari. *A Thousand Plateaus. Capitalism and Schizophrenia*. Trans. Brian Massumi. Minneapolis, MN: University of Minnesota Press, 1980/1987.

Melchior-Bonnet, Sabine. *Histoire du Miroir*. Paris: Imago, 1994.

Oxford English Dictionary Online. "Desire." Oxford University Press. Retrieved January 17, 2008, from http://dictionary.oed.com/entrance.dtl.

Rowling, J. K. *Harry Potter and the Sorcerer's Stone*. London: Bloomsbury, 1997.

———. *Harry Potter and the Chamber of Secrets*. London: Bloomsbury, 1998.

———. *Harry Potter and the Prisoner of Azkaban*. London: Bloomsbury, 1999.

———. *Harry Potter and the Goblet of Fire*. London: Bloomsbury, 2000.

———. *Harry Potter and the Order of the Phoenix*. London: Bloomsbury, 2003.

———. *Harry Potter and the Half-Blood Prince*. London: Bloomsbury, 2005.

———. *Harry Potter and the Deathly Hallows*. London: Bloomsbury, 2007.

Seem, Mark. "Introduction" to Deleuze, Gilles and Félix Guattari. *Anti-Oedipus. Capitalism and Schizophrenia*. Trans. Robert Hurley, Mark Seem, and Helen R. Lane. London: The Athlone Press, 1984.

Williams, Linda Ruth. *Critical Desire. Psychoanalysis and the Literary Subject*. London: Edward Arnold, 1995.

Wolfreys, Julian. "Desire" in *Critical Keywords in Literary and Cultural Theory*. New York: Palgrave Macmillan, 2004.

Chapter Five

The Great Snape Debate[1]

PETER APPELBAUM

Do you think Snape is a hero?

J.K. Rowling: Yes, I do; though a very flawed hero. An anti-hero, perhaps. He is not a particularly likeable man in many ways. He remains rather cruel, a bully, riddled with bitterness and insecurity—and yet he loved, and showed loyalty to that love and, ultimately, laid down his life because of it. That's pretty heroic!

(Bloomsbury, 2007)

People say John Nettleship, of Five Lanes, near Caerwent, resembles the dastardly Severus Snape, Professor of Potions at Hogwarts School of Witchcraft and Wizardry. As reported in the *South Wales Argus* (Lombard, 2007), that may not be the most flattering comparison—ruling his class with a rod of iron, Snape is not well-liked by the apprentice wizards. Far from taking offense, Mr. Nettleship is proud to have been an inspiration to a series that has sold 350 million copies around the world.

> The first I knew was when a reporter from a national newspaper knocked on the door seven years ago and said: "You're Professor Snape aren't you?"
>
> I suppose I was quite strict as a teacher, but I said to my wife, "she thinks I'm Professor Snape." She said, "of course you are, but I didn't want to tell you."

J. K. Rowling does not like to discuss inspirations for her characters, and has not publicly stated that Mr. Nettleship was an inspiration (Wikipedia, 2006). Yet, Mr. Nettleship is pleased to be associated with one of her characters.

"Fortunately for me, quite a lot of people like Alan Rickman, who plays Snape in the films." Mr. Nettleship described his teaching as

> filled with lots of "bang and smells" using chemistry kits but Joanne did not appear interested. I knew something was going on in her head but she would never say what. Her friends later said she was inventing stories, and the Harry Potter stories must have come from these. Her mind was working on wizards all the time.

Eighth-grade teacher Strausser (2007) blogged about reserving her personal copy of the final book six months early. At the counter was a choice of two bumper stickers.

> I quickly snagged "Snape is a very bad man." But when I left the store I sat in my car and thought about it (yes I know, I really need a life) and then quickly went back in and traded it in for "Trust Snape."

Julia Lipman of *flakmagazine* intoned, "I've had a crush on Rickman's character, the invariably-described-as-sinister Potions teacher Severus Snape, ever since he first glared at the boy wizard on page 126 of 'Harry Potter and the Sorcerer's Stone'" (Lipman, 2007).

> There are many other wackos like me. *Yahoo Groups* alone hosts six Snape discussion groups, the largest of which comprises 398 members. Snape fan sites abound on the Web. But try finding a site devoted to, say, Hogwarts' eccentric elderly headmaster Albus Dumbledore. Not a one. That's because Snape is sexy.

Like Strausser, I prepared for the seventh book by dwelling in *The Great Snape Debate* (Berner, Card, and Millman 2007), in my case a "Border's exclusive" perfectly timed for impatient Potterfanatics. On one side, "The Case for Snape's Innocence," is a collection of essays that support Snape as a good guy; the flip side flips the argument: the same authors pen "The Case for Snape's Guilt." Is Snape Harry Potter's Friend? Is Snape Harry Potter's Foe? Unlike my daughter, who prepared for each new book in the series by rereading them all, I used *The Great Snape Debate* as a quick-prep "cliff's notes" version of the whole series. By the seventh book's unveiling, I had reduced the point of the series, like many others, to the question of Snape's morality.

But aren't the books about Harry Potter? They all have *his* name in the title. On the surface, the books are about Harry. But, is Snape friend or foe? Rowling would not be the first author to use the literary technique of naming books after one character while using the narrative to explore another. We can go back to Johann Wolfgang Goethe's Wilhelm Meister, often touted as originating the genre of a series that tells the tale of a young man's formative learning experiences. Wilhelm's *Lehrjahre*, his years of apprenticeship (1796/1980), and the *Wanderjahre* (years of travel, 1821/1980), have Wilhelm in the titles. By the end, we see that Wilhelm is the main character for the plot, but the story is really about the role that a team of adults plays in carefully orchestrating his apprenticeship into adulthood. The Harry Potter books belong to this same genre, *Bildungsroman*: a young man is led by a collection of hands higher than he is aware of toward his destiny. I will refer to a few *Bildungsroman* novels to make the link with the tradition; if you have not yet read them, the details I provide should be enough to help you see the underlying themes that the Harry Potter series shares.

Harry Has Good Adventures, as a Good Puppet Should

Like Goethe's classic, the surface story in the Harry Potter series is the main character's maturation, but the underlying themes address his apprenticeship and the decisions that are made in the crafting of this apprenticeship behind the scenes. I believe the "Great Snape Debate" was so much a part of fan and media hype because it directed us to these underlying themes. Snape is above all a teacher and later Headmaster. He is also a former or present follower of Voldemort. What is most important, however, are his motivations. Rowling addresses this in my opening quote: he acts because of love, and is therefore a hero. How this love unfolds is initially the counterpoint to Harry's apprenticeship. I claim that the kind of apprenticeship Snape orchestrates, or to which he contributes, can only be understood once we work our way through the great debate. I maintain that his actions do not establish a philosophy of education, but instead help us to understand more fully the limitations of our ability to determine the ideal apprenticeship of young adults.

At first, we believe Headmaster Dumbledore directs the education at Hogwarts. Officially he does, until his death, other than a short period when he is displaced. Yet I claim Snape steers Harry's actual apprenticeship throughout: he looks like the bad guy, but is the real teacher. I claim further that a liberating apprenticeship requires a student to disobey his teacher, a paradox given that the teacher must orchestrate this so that it feels to the student as if they are making all of the decisions. As others have pointed out in their analysis of the *Bildungsroman* literary tradition, this liberating pedagogy is even more paradoxical in that it leads the apprentice to accept their fate in life through a series of independent forms of disobedience; hence, the disobedience is a curious tool of ultimate obedience to authority. Snape absorbed our attention because the debate about whether he is good or bad helped us to focus on these paradoxes. In the end, we cannot really know what a best form of education would be, but we are more fully aware of the issues; we appreciate that the paradoxical liberating pedagogy depends more on the moral character of the teacher than on his or her methods. Dumbledore is ultimately revealed as a victim of greed in his final failed grasp at the power of the Deathly Hallows. Snape, in contrast, acts consistently on more noble motivations, sacrificing his life for the good of all humankind. This is the critical model for Harry, who must make a similar decision.

These books do not definitively answer any pedagogical questions, but do something more important. Specifically in reference to the Great Snape Debate, they evoke a "politics of aesthetics" that binds the apprenticeship of the individual with conceptions of the fairest and best community. While Rowling has never once claimed to be a philosopher of education or an advocate of a particular form of social organization, her books are at least representations of the culture of which they are a part, a possible key to unlocking the mysteries of our cultural assumptions and dreams. Other books in this tradition, such as Goethe's Wilhelm Meister series and Herman Hesse's *The Glass Bead Game*, have been located in the cultural history of European fascism. Jean-Jacques Rousseau's *Emile* was an overt philosophical treatise. Even if Rowling herself might one day disclaim any such motivation, there is no reason not to use her work to think through our own personal commitments and assumptions (Appelbaum, 2007).

I begin with the patriarchal apprenticeship, and return to its links with politics at the end of the chapter. One aspect of the patriarchy common to this genre is the need for education to occur outside of the regular social sphere. Rousseau's *Emile* (1762/1979) blames society for corrupting the naturally good human being. For Goethe, Wilhelm leaves his family and bourgeois society in order to learn from the land. Harry is initially whisked away from misery into a magical, wonderful world, the perfect society, where people can do what they want (magic), and every fantasy can be fulfilled—or is this really so? For one thing, the teachers are pretty bad. They are arbitrary, whimsical, and prone to teach more by example of character than through effective instructional methods. (This is my own normative judgment; yet part of my argument is that they need to be rather bad teachers in order for the students to do what the teachers do not teach, to seek out knowledge and skills on their own, and thus to have educational adventures.) On the one hand, it seems like we simply should think diagonally to break out of our current materialism (Harry's cousin's surfeit of toys and grotesque weight might be a symbol of such spiritual death) and live outside the lines. (We enter through "Diagon Alley.") As we read further, we quickly realize that jumping out of the nonmagical, "Muggle" world is not enough: underlying moral uncertainties still exist, rumbling uncannily beyond our ability to know.

In Hermann Hesse's *Glass Bead Game* (*Die Glassperlenspiel*, 1943/1970), we encounter another utopian pedagogical province. In this one, as in Goethe's and Rowling's, students learn more from teachers as moral actors than they do from instruction. Hesse yearns for teachers like the music master, with superior intellect, deep comprehension of the interconnections of knowledge and emotion, and a mystical universal enlightenment. Like the Professors of Hogwarts, who cannot help but participate in serious battles between good and evil, Hesse's Joseph Knecht slowly understands that the cultivation of young minds cannot continue as if the outside world does not exist. This is the classic crisis of the *Bildungsroman*, and the paradox of a liberating pedagogy (Roosevelt, 1980). At the heart of the matter is an age-old question about whether our lives are shaped primarily by external influences or by inner dispositions. We get mired in debates between nature and nurture, instinct and pedagogy, self and circumstance, not realizing that these debates circumscribe the possible ideas that we can muster for thinking about how a person becomes an adult through years of schooling, apprenticeship, and other learning experiences.

In Goethe's version, Wilhelm creates his own adventures, kept secret from his parents, writing his own script for a life in which he himself is both director and star. His father thinks he is learning how to conduct business. These business trips are his education. But it's more complicated. Wilhelm imagines his life to be like the puppet shows he created and obsessed about as a boy; by the end of the first book he learns that a secret "Society of the Tower" has been behind the scenes all along. He has been *their* puppet in a grander show, although each action felt as if it was carried out by his own free will, and specifically counter to the wishes of those who would oversee his life. In Hesse's version, Knecht slowly realizes the fate that awaits him, as a member of the elite, despite years of pursuing purely independent intellectual goals. Like Wilhelm, he only later understands that the music master had already recognized his fate when he met him as a small boy. Knecht seems to pursue adventures counter to this fate, writing poetry, debating with a guest student from the outside world, apprenticing with a Chinese hermit, and forming diplomatic ties with outsiders. Ironically, this is what makes him best suited to assume the most "inside role" of them all, the Master of the Glass Bead Game. Knecht's teachers, like Wilhelm's puppet masters, carefully groom Knecht to make independent decisions uniquely appropriate as preparation for serving the Order; what an ironic twist, given that the Order demands subservience of the individual to the good of the community, seemingly in tension with Knecht's consistently independent choices.

In Rowling's version, Harry and his friends consistently seek adventures parallel to the Hogwarts curriculum. I always imagined that each Hogwarts clique had equivalent experiences. I suspected we only knew of Harry, Ron, and Hermione's adventures because the books were written from their perspective. Surely there were innumerable unwritten Wizarding books, where each child receives a letter telling them they are special and should go to Hogwarts; once there, each would suffer unbearable and comical teachers while carrying out concurrent world-saving adventures comprising their education. The classes are like the business experiences Wilhelm Meister thinks he is expected to be having. The adventures are the real curriculum, observed and gently manipulated by a cadre of wise puppet masters. Otherwise, the education at Hogwarts seems fairly empty to me.

Retroactive Prediction

By the end of the series, widespread educational adventuring seems less than likely. Only Harry, Ron, and Hermione, and maybe a few others such as Neville Longbottom, are lucky enough to live the *Bildungsroman* apprenticeship. The rest of the Hogwarts students merely suffer the mostly poor teaching. Yet this is a series of novels, not an educational utopia. In fact, the *Bildungsroman* genre typically has only one lead character who serves the purpose of demonstrating educational possibility. In Rousseau's *Emile*, the child is removed from society so that his natural self can emerge unscathed. Rousseau meant this as a plea for a kind of education, and in turn for a society of honest and talented people. The same with Wilhelm: Goethe does not mean for the apprenticeship and journey years to be superficial fables. They raise riddle-like questions about the nature and purposes of the puppet masters behind the scenes, enabling a young adult to make independent choices, experience risk and adventure, but also to assume eventually the role that fate has in store for him.

A pedagogy that enables a person to choose well contains the paradox of a pedagogue who is disobeyed. The teachers must be disobeyed in order to emphasize the autonomous choices of the apprentice. Hesse has Knecht violate the Order; he leaves the highly esteemed post of Glass Bead Game Master. His last independent decision is paradoxically the purest subjection to the Order he can provide: he risks his own life in order to guarantee the safety of the Order itself. Harry, like his teacher Snape, makes the same sacrifice: he accepts his own death in order for his life to serve the Wizarding world. Luckily for Harry, only the Voldemort Horcrux within him dies.

This is why I was disappointed in the neat and tidy final installment and its implications that other students are not disobeying Hogwarts' rules in order to pursue an adventure-education. Cultivation of self-will and self-sacrifice for a greater good demand that the apprentice dismiss the wisdom of the teacher (Roosevelt, 1980). Trainers of teachers and educational policy-makers may not want to think about this. We resort like the puppet masters of the *Bildungsroman* to manipulating the experience of free will from behind the "scenes." In each *Bildungsroman* novel, the students' choices in disobeying the directions of the teachers are the "right" choices. Goethe's Wilhelm is healthier, taller, stronger, and straighter than his friend Werner who has followed the "correct" incorrect choices. Hesse's Knecht is best-prepared to be the Glass Bead Game Master thanks to his "incorrect" choices, and can only commit his final act of disobedience because it is the "naturally" right decision, and thus, the final test of the correctness of his life-long apprenticeship. Looking back on the Harry Potter series from Snape's perspective, we see how hard Snape's job was: no matter how hard he tried to keep Potter safe, Harry kept making those "wrong" decisions that put him in the midst of the most serious dangers. The paradox is, of course, that these were the "right" decisions, and Harry made them thinking they were of his own free will. A teacher's job is hard indeed.

Snape's actions are at the heart of the pedagogical paradoxes. Media blitz and fan hype were manifestations of "retroactive prediction," a rhetorical term common in geology and archaeology, where one projects into the past possible explanations for a present that would have then been the future. This is a modernist reduction or displacement of rumination to explanation. Causes for what would be later developments presumably explain the how and why of events. They remove the possibility of other kinds of action, such as imagining alternatives. In the paradox of an education for autonomy, the pedagogy contains within itself its own negation, which means that explanation and retroactive prediction cannot take place. We need something other than prescribed methods based on cause and effect if we hope for a "good enough" education. Snape represents this "something."

So What's a Teacher to Do?

Harry and his friends are always in and out of school, saving all humanity from Voldemort. Where and when do they receive their apprenticeship for entry into the adult community? Without Voldemort, they would not have any of the essential life-threatening adventures. One could say the same thing for Goethe's Wilhelm, who almost dies in a Napoleonic battle. Or of Hesse's Knecht, who does die for the sake of one spoiled rich kid. The comparison of Wilhelm and Knecht helps us understand Harry Potter, and the role Snape plays in Harry's *Bildungsroman*. Knecht appears at first passive, accepting his fate, while Wilhelm appears at first active, master of his own fate (Halpert, 1961). By the end of each story, we learn that active and passive do not adequately illustrate the complexity of the relationships among pedagogy, apprenticeship, authority, autonomy, and duty. Harry is hardly passive: he chooses Gryffindor House, despite a clear indication that he belongs in Slytherin. He chooses, time after time, that he is not like Voldemort, even as there are so many reasons to worry that he is. Because there is a piece of Voldemort within him, he chooses to die in order to have lived as Harry. Like his predecessor Knecht, he "chooses" to sacrifice himself to the causes to which those behind the scenes have committed him all along. The underlying message seems to be, "to abdicate one's free will to the larger whole is the key to individual freedom," as the ultimate form of self-will.

What does this have to do with Snape? It is the choices *he* made in contrast with his destiny that teach Harry how to act. Rowling called Snape "a child conceived outside of love" (Bloomsbury, 2007), and suggested he could never understand that power and trust cannot replace love. But he does decide to override his insatiable passion for the Dark Arts in order to act on his love for Harry's mother. Each of Snape's actions, however terrible they may have originally seemed, are transformed in meaning by the childhood scenes Harry sees in the Pensieve after Snape's death. Like Hesse's Knecht, Snape dies so that his student can be transformed by the relationship that this action creates. In contrast, Dumbledore appeared so "good," but has fought his own personal battle with self-interest and power. He doomed himself—even when the world was fighting Voldemort in an ultimate war for survival—risking everything for one last attempt at uniting the Deathly Hallows and personally reaping the benefits. Snape made his moral commitment when he approached Dumbledore to help against Voldemort, a dedication that ran counter to that implied by his own childhood and apprenticeship. Snape constantly and actively reaffirmed his allegiances with each act of support for those united against Voldemort. So in the end, it is Snape who turns out to be the self-determined teacher, and Dumbledore the shallow cad.

When we first meet Snape, he is tyrannical and unpredictable, with a talent for potions, few social skills, and hardly any more pedagogical skills. By the end of the series, if teachers in these pedagogical provinces teach not by method but by example, then it is Snape who is the only teacher Harry has truly had the honor to have studied with, as he is the only teacher who has sacrificed his life specifically to make it possible for Harry to make the same choice. The hours of Occlumency training helped with some fundamental skills. But sacrificing one's life to save others is the one act that Harry must emulate if he is to save the world and himself from Voldemort. It is not his clearly superior talent with spells and the invention of new ones that makes Snape someone to be admired, but his choices to act in the name of love, even if, and especially if, no one but he knows this. True, his hatred of Harry's father is real, and his cruelty to Harry is definitely a theme; but perhaps they were used by Snape to hide his fundamental loyalty to Harry and the Wizarding world? One might suggest that only unselfish love is heroic. Snape appears to act on his love for one single woman; he appears more like a stalker than a hero. I believe Snape's first act in switching alliances from Voldemort to Dumbledore originated less admirably; however, I maintain that his later actions are more carefully designed to enable Harry's apprenticeship than to perpetuate the relationship with Harry's mother.

Any reader of the *Bildungsroman* already understands this need for the best teachers to sacrifice themselves for the larger society: those from whom Goethe's Wilhelm learns the most are those who are no longer alive at the end of the book; the ostensible teachers, the members of the society, have merely compiled memories for an archive of apprenticeships to be stored in the tower. The music master, Knecht's greatest teacher in the book by Hesse, lives out the end of his life in silent mystical bliss; his choice of death is what makes the strongest educational impact on Knecht. In Harry's case, from the moment he learned of the Wizarding world and his place within it, the question of his choices versus his destiny was directly at hand. Because Snape took hold of destiny through his choices, rather than merely rising to the occasion like Harry, he seems to be the greater man, or should I say wizard. Perhaps this is why Snape was a teacher, and why it appears that Harry, in the final epilogue, is not: he simply is not up to the job.

Why Were People So Concerned with Snape's Allegiances?

We see Snape first through the eyes of new students, as a nasty and suspicious teacher. He seems vindictive when it comes to Harry, seemingly using him to retaliate for the humiliation that Harry's father had forced him to suffer when they themselves were students. Hints that Snape is simultaneously rescuing Harry from life-threatening situations can be read either as attempts to serve Voldemort by saving the final death-wielding blow for his master, or perhaps as working for Dumbledore and the Order of the Phoenix. By the end of the last book, we know a great deal more. We begin to see that Snape's complicated relationship with Harry represents his intricate triple-agent status, working for both Voldemort and the Order, in order ultimately to work for the Order—although we do not know this for certain until very late.

The changing image of Snape might represent Harry's development over time, or it might indicate the changing understanding of motivations and life choices that matter for the narrator. The education of the narrator is also a common element of the *Bildungsroman* (Miles, 1974). The narrator might be Rowling herself, figuring out what she wants to say, or it may represent the reader, as our understanding develops over time. By the end of the fifth book, *Order of the Phoenix*, and into the sixth, the *Half-Blood Prince*, Snape matters more than he seemed to at first. Why?

This may be due to the portrayal of Snape by Alan Rickman in the films. Snape in the books seems confusingly one-dimensional, but Rickman–Snape seems bewilderingly complicated. This may be a historical first: when have films and popular fan fiction influenced later volumes in literature? It is also the case that Rowling needed to establish the ambiguity of Snape in order to dramatize the role of love, commitments, and self-determination that emerge as central themes of her larger story. Rickman discussed the character with Rowling; he was one of the few actors to provide input (Lady Claudia, n.d.). People noticed a transition in the character. The good-guy/bad-guy balance seemed to shift through Rickman toward the good. Some viewers suggested this was because the books are told from Harry's point of view, whereas the films delivered a perspective outside of any one character. It may be that Rickman's discussions with Rowling gave him insight into the character that readers did not yet have, leading him to play Snape in a more nuanced way.

Snape is also a symbol of the permeability of apparent boundaries between the real world and the utopian, pedagogical province. He flows between and through both Hogwarts and the world of Voldemort as a double and triple agent. The ambiguity of his character places the paradox of pedagogy within another dilemma regarding education of the apprentice, that of engagement with the real world. If schooling is an oasis away from the spoils of society, an important question is, how does one prepare the student for this world if he or she is not experiencing this world? Rousseau answered the question axiomatically in *Emile*: he declared that human beings are naturally good and will follow a natural pattern of growth and development that is the best preparation for acting in the "real world" if they are apprenticed in an unadulterated oasis. Goethe problematized this: Wilhelm can only apprentice through real-world risks, free from perceived authorities. Hesse confronted the question more crassly: he made the pedagogical province have a long and storied history, a utopia distinct from the rest of society. And we learn that Knecht, the servant who made it possible for the Rousseauian oasis to remain, did so by recognizing the inappropriateness of this separation. What a conundrum.

Snape is at the heart of the conundrum. Hogwarts is removed from the rest of the world, protected from danger by powerful spells. Students needing to escape the claustrophobic atmosphere are occasionally released in their third and later years, in carefully supervised trips to a small village nearby. But the oasis is shattered by goings-on related to Voldemort. The early rumblings are not enough to scare people. Later, parents are not even sure it is safe enough to send kids to school, as Hogwarts becomes a site of particular contestation. Snape, in his unique multiple-agent role, is both in and out, the only Hogwarts teacher who maintains links to the real world. And, he is on the edge; he seemingly can go either way. He is liminal. He is the Potions master, a standard part of the curriculum. But he also teaches Harry Occlumency and Legilimency, skills for the outside world, not for graduation. While most of the teachers are caricatures whom we rarely see outside of their teacher role, Snape is clearly busy in the world as well.

David Miles' (1974) discussion of twentieth century *Bildungsroman* form suggests that the hero in this form is shattered by authors such as Franz Kafka and Gunter Grass, with the implication that this genre is somewhat dead, signifying that we must begin anew. Interestingly, the Harry Potter books have more in common with earlier works in this tradition, which lead the main character back into bourgeois society, as if nothing needs to change in the world. The epilogue, in fact, suggests that everything is as it was pre-Voldemort, with no need to think differently about one's life choices or commitments. Despite the allusions to social structure, the need to rethink the status of magical creatures and half-bloods within the Wizarding world, we are left with a fairly conservative message that all has been set aright. Snape and Harry, as Wilhelm, Knecht and others before them, accept their place in the existing world rather than transform it. So the message of Snape's allegiances is finally clear: it mattered where he stood because it made a difference in whether the world could go on as before. Snape is a tool of an author who pretty much likes society as it is.

Foils and Pedagogy

Snape is important as teacher to both Harry and Draco Malfoy. Whereas Harry is our hero, Draco seems to be our anti-hero. Snape is the only adult who serves as a teacher through example for both characters. The *Bildungsroman* typically portrays a comparative "friend" whose education differs and who therefore serves as a foil for the educational philosophy that is presented. Wilhelm's foil, Werner, is apprenticed simply by working with his father, as opposed to being sent off to find his own adventures. He seems to always make the "correct" choices. But when Werner and Wilhelm meet later, the comparative descriptions of their physical appearance tell us "once again that health and growth come, not from obedience to external pressures, but from living according to one's natural tendencies and convictions" (Roosevelt, 1980, p. 117). Werner is struck by how much taller, stronger, and straighter Wilhelm looks; the impression Werner made on Wilhelm was less favorable: "The honest man seemed to have retrograded than advanced." The same sort of distinction can be made between Hesse's Knecht and his foil, Plinio, a guest student from a wealthy family. Plinio's years of apprenticeship in the family business likewise turn him into a sadder and weaker man. This is in sharp contrast to his vibrant adolescence, where his very disobedience to the Order in publicly debating its wisdom establishes the kind of successful apprenticeship that a utopian pedagogical province promises. It is only through reacquaintance with and tutoring from Knecht that he can slowly gain control over both his life and his well-being.

Draco is a different foil because of the special role that Snape plays in his life, enabling him, like Harry, to experience the essential adventures of self-determination that allow him to maintain a healthy and happy life. Like Wilhelm's puppet masters, and Knecht's elite authorities, Snape works behind the scenes to orchestrate Draco's free choices as well as Harry's. Only after Draco does not kill Dumbledore as directed does Snape carry out his own vow to take the Headmaster's life. He stays true to the role of the paradoxical teacher. He needed to be the person who killed Dumbledore; but he arrives at exactly the appropriate time to do this deed for Draco, making it possible for the young man to choose his own destiny. This very act of disobedience to Voldemort, whether carried out by moral strength or lack of courage, is crucial for Draco's real education outside the classroom. His nod to Harry in the epilogue signals their common destinies; they are forever linked through Snape's actions. Hesse's Knecht died for only one child. Snape died for two, and thus becomes the teacher of both the apprentice and the foil.

In the fifth book, Harry looks in the Pensieve and learns that his father was not the hero he had imagined. James Potter is teasing Snape, and it is clear that this is not the only time. Snape gets angry and tells Harry to leave and never come back. Was Snape embarrassed? It seems more plausible that additional Occlumency lessons would enable Harry to learn too many secrets too soon in his apprenticeship. The anger could have been a mask. Harry demonstrates the ability to bounce Snape's spell back, an indicator that the lessons have been successful. He was able both to bounce the spell successfully, and to do so in a moment of defiance; both were likely Snape's objectives as the teacher. Meanwhile, Harry is allowed to learn that Snape has always had a genuine talent for Potions, setting the stage for Harry to trust Snape in the future as a talented wizard. The sixth book is an entire allegory of Snape the secret hero. Was it really by chance that Harry was able to use Snape's old copy of the Potions textbook? This seems doubtful. The textbook is one more special gift in a line of secret treasures, from the Invisibility Cloak to the Marauder's Map to the sword of Gryffindor, and finally the Deathly Hallows. Snape was a skilled teacher outside the classroom for both Draco and Harry.

Politics of Aesthetics

My final perspective is that the Great Snape Debate helps readers and viewers recognize how the acculturation or *Bildung* of an individual models a political process. In this sense, the pairing shifts from Harry and Draco to Harry and the Wizarding world. Snape claimed our attention precisely because of his parallel roles in both. He established this relationship and hence preserved the existence of Hogwarts into the future through his self-sacrifice, in the same way that Hesse's Knecht saved Castalia. This connection is not so far-fetched. Since at least Plato's *Republic* and Homer's *Iliad*, people have been linking the education of an individual with the evolution of a community, and using one as the metaphor for the other. Politics as theater provided a model for public rhetoric (Chytry, 1989).

Movement from the internal and theory to practice and political utopia is a narrative of *Bildung*, which Redfield describes as "the elaboration of a notion of art as *techne*, in the course of which aesthetics emerges as a highly effective, and profoundly unstable, political force" (Redfield, 1996, p. 17). More to the point, this thematic investigation of the *Bildungsroman* makes sense when we think about Rowling's interest in exploring fascism and racist ideologies in the Harry Potter books. Nazi Germany is a clear model for the interest of many wizards in preserving the "pure-blood" character of the Wizarding world. It is surely no accident that Harry carries the thunderbolt symbol on his forehead, the same symbol worn by Nazi SS soldiers, or that Hermione introduces a movement to challenge the existing second-class, racialized status of "magical creatures." Given that the aesthetic politics of the *Bildungsroman* has been identified repeatedly by scholars as critical to the evolving German consciousness of nationhood and history (Lacoue-Labarthe, 1990), any parable that evokes similar themes is bound to connect in some way to the literature of such a consciousness. A novel of apprenticeship to adulthood that explores themes of fascism and racism will undoubtedly share common motifs with those early works upon which fascist and racist ideologies have been crafted. I claim Snape focuses our attention on these issues by requiring us to debate his allegiances. Snape's moral character determines whether the world is fundamentally good or bad, welcoming of diversity or fascist in its racist ideologies.

When Redfield refers to *techne*, he notes that the political, the crafting of a community, is a plastic art. The struggle for the kind of Wizarding world that will emerge in Harry Potter's world requires statesmanship, just as an artist or craftsman can only do his or her job by using appropriate skills and crafts. Voldemort and Dumbledore are sculpting the fate of the world through Snape as a tool; but at the same time, Dumbledore and Voldemort are Snape's tools. Snape was the better artist. He placed himself in a position to influence the new order regardless of who ended up in charge. He knew better than to destroy Voldemort himself; he made it possible for Voldemort to be crushed by a collection of youth, the future of the community, rising up against him. In arranging his own death, Snape secures a more lasting and satisfying outcome.

Lacoue-Labarthe (1990) defines *techne* more precisely as the surplus of nature, through which nature "deciphers" and presents itself. The implication is that art has a political function of deciphering the organic emergence of the community, making it possible for the community to recognize itself *as* a community. We can apply this to Harry Potter; as a work of art, this series represents society to itself, so that we within this society can better know what we accept as true and natural. I worked within this form of criticism in my contribution to the first edition of this book (Appelbaum, 2002). I suggested the popularity of the books was consistent with their role as cultural products reflecting a postmodern era of emerging sociopolitical realities and the provisional nature of knowledge. Hence the idea that these books "belong" to us because we live in "Harry Potter's world." More relevant to the current discussion is Snape as political artist. As the only character to win the trust of both Dumbledore and Voldemort, both the Order of the Phoenix and the Death Eaters, he sculpts the outcome. Snape looks suspicious to Harry. Yet he is watching over him and protecting him as early as a Quidditch match in the first year. It is Snape who kills Dumbledore, at the Headmaster's own request, making it possible for Snape himself to seem to be the rightful owner of the Elder Wand; this directs Voldemort's attention to Snape, away from Harry and Draco. It is Snape who artfully waits to kill Dumbledore after Draco has already disarmed Dumbledore, so that Draco can in fact be the true secret owner of the wand, and also appear to have tried to kill Dumbledore as directed. This critical staging of the owner of the Elder Wand makes it probable that Harry will be able to disarm Draco later, becoming the owner of the wand. Snape also waits for Draco to choose *not* to kill Dumbledore, so that Draco's apprenticeship can take the correct turn. Finally, Snape artfully releases his memories to Harry at just the right time, so that Harry can know his true motivations, understand that Snape sent the doe Patronus, and fully comprehend that he himself is a Horcrux. Looking back, who could believe that Harry would be able to steal a peek at Snape's worst memory when they were involved in the occulemency lessons? Surely Snape, who can deceive a wizard as powerful as Voldemort, would only intentionally let Harry learn this first lesson, more important than the Occlumency, about his parents and their relationship to Snape. It is Snape who has orchestrated almost everything that makes a difference in the ultimate unraveling of Voldemort.

The struggle of the Death Eaters is based on the identification of the nation with a single member of that nation. Voldemort and Voldemort's life are made synonymous with the life of the Wizarding world. Comparisons with Fascist Germany and the identification of the nation with a single leader are overt here. The claims of the Death Eaters (and the fears of all others) that Voldemort's ascendency is fated grow out of this common slippage from politics as organic to politics as biologic. Lacoue-Labarthe's point—that racism is "primarily, fundamentally, an aestheticism" (1990, p. 69)—helps us appreciate the degree to which aesthetics, in the most general sense, shaped both the official culture and the ideological energy of Nazism. Rowling recreates this historical moment as allegory. The political becomes the production of itself as the total work of art, and thus also becomes, as Lacoue-Labarthe and Redfield have argued, a violent ideologization of the absolute, self-creating Subject of the metaphysical tradition, a subject that purports to embody itself in "an immediate and absolutely 'natural' essence: that of blood and race" (Redfield, 1996, pp. 16–17). In Harry Potter's world, the racial issue is pure versus mixed blood, human versus creature. The self-creating subject is Voldemort. The aesthetic politics of the *Bildungsroman* can thus be understood as necessarily embedded in Harry Potter's world as well. Hitler's defeat took an alliance of nations; Voldemort's required a single Snape.

Little Box, Political Bigwig

Placing Rowling in the context of the German *Bildungsroman* genre helps us see how the Harry Potter stories have become a prominent feature of a transnational *Bildung* of our own. They enable a global community to use these stories for understanding connections between education and the polis. We can also use our readings of these books to craft our own theories of apprenticeship and aesthetics (Appelbaum, 2007). *Bildungsroman* novels suggest teaching methods are less critical to the *Bildung* enterprise than the ways that "teachers," in and out of school, teach by moral example. Most crucial are the opportunities given our youth to disobey their authorities and to experience educational adventures. Rowling's series might have a significantly conservative message, aiming to reproduce a culture rather than transform it, as if we already live in a present utopia. In this worldview, all is set aright in the end, if we follow our instincts rather than our authority figures—but only if these authority figures are manipulating our free will from behind the scenes, like Goethe's puppet masters. Otherwise, the only liberating pedagogy that can be conceived appears to us as arbitrary and uncontrollable, given that the best chance of success is when our youth do not heed our advice. The key moment is when we reveal our own motives to our youth, establishing in this act the meaning of our relationships with them. (The pivotal scenes of resolution in each *Bildungsroman* convey this point. The timing of initiation into the secret society for Wilhelm, Knecht's confrontation with the Order, Snape's memories released at his death—each validates the free agency of the youth but purposefully guarantees that the motivations of the masters are in the long term more powerful educationally than the disobedience of the apprentices.)

Training of educators currently focuses worldwide on scientifically predetermined methods for producing facility with skills. School tends to reduce *techne* to recipe. Roosevelt's point in writing about Goethe was that we might be better served by allowing youth to act on their earnest openness to experience than in training teachers: "For without openness to experience, without the ability to take life and those around one seriously; above all, without the capacity to embrace that which is important to one's *self*—is any education possible?" (Roosevelt, 1980, p. 121). To redirect our attention towards the opportunities that youth have for adventure outside of classrooms would be a massive cultural shift. What we have instead is the passive acceptance that such opportunities cannot be created by those adults who work with our youth. Read this way, works like Harry Potter reinforce stereotypes of bad teachers aloof to what youth do on their own. Such readings miss the careful oversight behind the scenes that enables adventure to be both dangerous and important, both life-threatening and adventurous enough. At the same time, the paradox remains: if we embrace the message, our culture does not change, because this kind of apprenticeship returns each apprentice to the place for which they were destined rather than transforming our community into a utopian *polis*. In other words, this reading opens us to the limits of our own consciousness: to heed the message would require a significant cultural transformation of which we are not able to conceive; at the same time, even if we did heed this message, the newly enacted pedagogy would be fundamentally conservative anyway, returning us to the constant reproduction of our culture rather than a truly revolutionary *techne*.

The Great Snape Debate leads us to the centrality of these issues in the light of aesthetic politics. It is not that Rowling necessarily advocates a conservative aesthetic politics of social reproduction, but that the conflation of the political with key political figures, such as a mass revolutionary movement with Voldemort as its figurehead, manifests itself in such a politics of aesthetics. From this perspective, the Great Snape Debate is an opportunity for opening ourselves to these complex issues, rather than a tool for making decisions about the right pedagogy that can move society in the perfect direction. The link between the fantasy of such a rhetorical tool and the fascist ideologies of aestheticism is made more tangible: Voldemort's apprentices are true fanatics.

We run the risk of applying moral lessons from literature, as if they are a technology for decision-making. Characters and artifacts are turned into symbols with deeper meanings. We demand retroactive prediction. Here we can learn another lesson from Goethe. In his *Wanderjahre*, there is an amusing fable of a small box missing its key. The box is an overt symbol for the concept of symbol itself. Thinking through this fable might help us consider Snape as well, who through most of the Harry Potter series was himself a box missing its key. We could never see inside. In the *Wanderjahre*, the value of the box lies in the very fact that the key is missing. Of course, the key is found; but in his rush to solve the mystery, Wilhelm's son breaks the key into pieces trying to open the box. The box represents the concept of symbol as a gathering of little pieces, and as something that can never truly be opened. The power of Snape lies in his equally symbolic role. Despite the obvious allegorical narrative of Voldemort as the fragmented key, unable to be pieced together, Voldemort is more the foil in this case. It is Snape whom we never see inside of and who remains the enigma forever. Like the little box in the *Wanderjahre*, Snape enframes what we can't know, both about him personally as a character, and about pedagogy, the unfolding and results of which we also cannot know.

In Goethe's story, Redfield (1996) explains, the contents of the little box remain a mystery, but we do learn more: a skilled craftsman can in fact unlock a symbol; also, one of the secrets to being a skilled craftsman is a talent for keeping secrets secret. In the wake of the misguided attempt to unlock the secrets of the little box, to possess its meaning, a jeweler demonstrates that the two pieces of the key are magnetic; he quickly opens the box, but then swiftly shuts it again, intoning the dictum that such a mystery should never be stirred. How many readers continue to use the first descriptions of Snape, the narrator's and Harry's perspectives, as a mean and scary teacher, like the *South Wales Argus* did (before the seventh and final book)? The Great Snape Debate was about the *confusion of this description*. All the outward signs of bad guy were doubly readable as cover for his status as good guy—which, in the debate, might have been a further cover for his tasks as a bad guy. Only the best teacher teaching by example rather than method could have orchestrated such a complexity. The Harry Potter Filks website (Marcius, n.d.) splits its Snape pages Horcrux-wise into two parts: "The (Relatively) Benign Years

(Books One–Five)," and "The (Arguably) Malignant Years (Book Six and Beyond)." I am very fond of the appropriately ambiguous and permeable, parenthetic titles.

Snape, I claim, is both the mysterious box and the jeweler. He is the box because of his remaining a mystery despite the key he provided, the memories in the Pensieve. They gave us a peek but did not let us stir. And he is the jeweler, because he summoned forth the magic that became *techne*, fundamentally linked to the unknowability of the symbol. Following the politics of aesthetics, a symbol's *mélange* of secrecy, *techne*, and formal totalization acquires political clout through the valorization of a pragmatic aesthetic. Yet Snape was also a master craftsman of the *polis*. He could not have been trusted unless he was also a very bad man. The fundamental question is whether he could be the bad guy he needed to be due to basic character traits, or whether he crafted himself like an actor on the stage. The debate enframes a mystery we can't answer. By sacrificing his life he enables the mystery to live forever, opening us to the unanswerable. As Heidegger once said regarding *techne*, the recognition of the ineffectuality of a political or social response leads both to move away from the call for a violent recapturing of a primordial *techne*, and to suggest instead that within the enframing lies an opportunity to once again experience the disclosure of a sense of limitation (Tabachnick, 2006). The power of "The Great Snape Debate" is that it allows us to understand how neither bumper sticker gets it right, how both sides of the Snape Debate book need to be there: the existence of the debate itself represents the important questions of apprenticeship and their relation to the artful vision of the fairest and best community.

Acknowledgment

A previous version of this chapter was pubished in Volume IV of *The Journal of the American Association for the Advancement of Curriculum Studies*.

Note

1. I would like to thank Noah Appelbaum, Sophia Appelbaum, Belinda Davis, Alan Block, and especially Elizabeth Heilman, for numerous insights and critical readings of early drafts.

References

Appelbaum, P. (2002). Harry Potter's world: Magic, technoculture, and becoming human. In E. Heilman (ed.), *Critical perspectives on Harry Potter* (pp. 25–52). New York: Routledge.

Appelbaum, P. (2007). *Children's books for grown-up teachers: Reading and writing curriculum theory.* New York: Routledge.

Berner, A., Card, O. S., and Millman, J. (2007). *The great Snape debate.* Chicago, IL: BenBella Books, Independent Publishers Group.

Bloomsbury. (2007). Web chat with J. K. Rowling July 30, 2007. On Bloomsbury.com. Retrieved March 12, 2008, from http://www.raincoast.com/harrypotter/pdfs/webchat-jkr.pdf.

Chytry, J. (1989). *The aesthetic state: A quest in modern German thought.* Berkeley, CA: University of California Press.

Goethe, J. W. (1796/1980). *Wilhelm Meisters Lehrjahre.* Frankfurt am Main: Insel Verlag.
Goethe, J. W. (1821/1980). *Wilhelm Meisters Wanderjahre.* Frankfurt am Main: Insel Verlag.
Halpert, I. (1961). Wilhelm Meister and Josef Knecht. *German Quarterly, 34*(1), 11–20.
Hesse, H. (1943). *Die Glasperlenspiel.* Zürich: Fretz & Wasmuth.
Hesse, H. (1970). *The glass bead game.* New York: Bantam Books.
Lacoue-Labarthe, P. (1990). *Heidegger, art, and politics: The fiction of the political.* London: Basil Blackwell.
Lady Claudia. (n.d.). Alan Rickman interviews. Transcripts about Snape. Retrieved March 12, 2008, from http://whysnape.tripod.com/rickman.htm.
Lipman, J. (2007). Professor Severus Snape. *flakmagazine.* Undated. Retrieved March 12, 2008, from http://www.flakmag.com/film/snape.html.
Lombard, D. (2007). JK Rowling's inspirational teacher. *South Wales Argus,* Friday, July 20, 2007. Retrieved March 12, 2008, from www.southwalesargus.co.uk/news/swanews/display. var.1559519.0.jk_rowlings_inspirational_teacher.php.
Marcius, C. (n.d.). Harry Potter filks. Retrieved March 12, 2008, from http://home.att.net/~coriolan/.
Miles, D. (1974). The picaro's journey to the confessional: The changing image of the hero in the German *Bildungsroman. PMLA, 89*(5), 980–992.
Redfield, M. (1996). The dissection of the state: Wilhelm Meister's *Wanderjahre* and the politics of aesthetics. *German Quarterly, 69*(1), 15–31.
Roosevelt, J. (1980). Wilhelm Meister's apprenticeship: The paradox of a liberating pedagogy. *Journal of Aesthetic Education, 14*(1), 105–122.
Rousseau, J.-J. (1762/1979). *Emile: Or, on education.* Translation, introduction and notes by Allan Bloom. New York: Basic Books.
Rowling, J. K. (1997). *Harry Potter and the sorcerer's stone.* New York: Scholastic Press.
Rowling, J. K. (2003). *Harry Potter and the order of the phoenix.* New York: Scholastic Press.
Rowling, J. K. (2005). *Harry Potter and the half-blood prince.* New York: Scholastic Press.
Rowling, J. K. (2007). *Harry Potter and the deathly hallows.* New York: Scholastic Press.
Strausser. (2007). A teacher's perspective. February 4, 2007. Retrieved March 12, 2008, from http://strausser.blogspot.com/2007/02/trust-snape.html.
Tabachnick, D. (2006). The tragic double bind of Heidegger's techne. *Phaenex, 1*(2), 94–112.
Wikipedia, (2006). Usertalk archive 4, March–December 2006. Retrieved March 12, 2008, from http://en.wikipedia.org/wiki/User_talk:JHMM13/Archive4.

Part II

Critical and Sociological Perspectives

Chapter Six

Schooling Harry Potter
Teachers and Learning, Power and Knowledge

MEGAN L. BIRCH

School permeated my girlhood and adolescence, captivating my adoration and foreshadowing my future in teaching and teacher education. Like all children I knew, I spent a great deal of time in school and studied the usual core subjects; yet, my school experiences and significant lessons extended beyond the bounds of the school day and the formal curriculum. I was not only a student *in* school but also a student *of* school. Searching for a desirable identity as a student and a way of being in relationship with my teachers and the other adults at school, one of my favorite "subjects" in school was the teachers themselves. Most compelled by benevolent women with a fondness for books and rule-following girls with inquisitive imaginations, I analyzed my favorite teachers' behaviors and dress. I emulated a ponytail using a barrette instead of an elastic band and adopted a particular style of penmanship for signing my own name. My curiosity about school and teachers affected my time spent outside of school too. In play, I enacted teaching personas with real and imaginary friends, interpreting versions of my own teachers, and I often relied on strict dichotomies: compassionate or mean, creatively informative or tediously boring. Further, young adult novels and television shows often offered me additional images of teachers. Among my favorites were Miss Edmunds, the unconventional and gentle music teacher in Katherine Patterson's *Bridge to Terabithia*, and Laura Ingalls Wilder both in the *Little House on the Prairie* books and television series. They further fed my understanding of what, who, and how students and teachers could be.

Today, I am a teacher educator and along with my students, I still analyze teachers, both real and imagined. Many times, my students recall an early attraction to and fascination with school and teachers similar to my girlhood experiences. Theorist-educators, such as Sandra Weber and Claudia Mitchell, drawing on cultural and media studies, literary theory, and curriculum studies, help me to understand the experiences my students and I share as our engagement with part of a larger "cumulative cultural text" about teachers, in which conceptions of teachers and schools are socially and dialectally constructed in personal biography, children's and young adult literature, childhood, and popular culture (19). Thinking of text broadly like this, as Weber and Mitchell do, calls for a kind of reading, a critical examination of an ongoing and reflexive sense-making process, of the weaving together of images and lived-experiences that point to what is and is not possible in school or to what and who teachers can be. Critically reading images of teachers as text raises important questions, particularly useful for pre-service teachers: how do texts afford or conceal particular versions of teachers and students, or particular attitudes, beliefs, and values about teaching and learning? How did images of teachers and students shape us, as a student and a teacher? How do they shape our students? These questions came to guide my interest in and reading of J. K. Rowling's Harry Potter series and they serve to focus the purpose of this chapter. How does Harry Potter contribute to the "cumulative cultural text" about teachers, schools, and learning?

My delayed reading of the Harry Potter series in 2007 had not sheltered me from the enormous popularity, critiques, or the basic plotlines of the books. I had witnessed both high school students and college students of all majors anticipate the arrival of new books in the series. When I was at Penn State University, a group of first year students excitedly planned a dorm-wide read aloud of their favorite passages before and after *Harry Potter and the Half-Blood Prince* debuted in bookstores. Their enthusiasm compelled me. Intrigued by the series' popularity and eager to engage critically in the numerous conversations about the series, I began reading. Quickly, I found myself engrossed in a seemingly familiar school story with hackneyed images of teachers and school administrators, both positive and negative portraits. Depicting a highly ritualized school structured around competition and book learning, the series holds strong to the idea that "real" learning occurs through progressive "hands-on" experiences and mostly outside of the classroom. In this chapter, I share my observations about the representation of teachers, curriculum, and learning in the Harry Potter series.

The Teachers

Most teachers at Hogwarts are stock caricatures. Their behaviors, their dress and appearance, the subjects they teach, and their instruction fit neatly into shallow and conventional stereotypes. As such, the cast of teachers in the Harry Potter series mirror clichéd portraits of teachers in other examples of youth culture, literature, and the media, as explored in numerous scholarly works (Bolotin & Burnaford; Bulman; Dalton; Mitchell & Weber; Weber &

Mitchell). In their analysis of school teachers of the twentieth century, Pamela Joseph Bolotin and Gail E. Burnaford suggest that we can best understand the images of teachers in terms of "polarities," "paragons," and "complexities." That is, teachers are often represented as essentialized types, types that frequently stand in opposition to other distinct types; sometimes certain types are portrayed as exemplars; less often teachers are represented with complexity. Bolotin and Burnaford's interpretation reflect the teachers in the Harry Potter series well.

Polarities

Images of teachers at Hogwarts can be divided or easily categorized: morally good or evil; wise or incompetent in their area of expertise; lenient or strict in terms of school discipline; and capable or inept pedagogically. Professor Binns, History of Magic teacher, is one such teacher. A stereotypical bore, he is dull and fact-driven, and focused on spewing information to the point that he "hadn't let his own death get in the way of continuing to teach" (*Goblet of Fire* 392).

> The most boring class was History of Magic, which was the only one taught by a ghost. Professor Binns had been very old indeed when he had fallen asleep in front of the staff room fire and got up the next morning to teach, leaving his body behind him. Binns droned on and on while they scribbled down names and dates, and got Emeric the Evil and Uric the Oddball mixed up.
>
> (*Sorcerer's Stone* 133)

To teach, Rowling describes, Binns simply

> opened his notes and began to read in a flat drone like an old vacuum cleaner until nearly everyone in the class was in a deep stupor, occasionally coming to long enough to copy down a name or date, and then falling asleep again.
>
> (*Chamber of Secrets* 148)

The professor, like his subject, is history—a relic, old, outdated, out of touch with the students, literally a ghost.

In contrast to Binns stands Divination professor, Sybill Trelawney. Both Binns and Professor Trelawney are seemingly ineffective teachers who are not closely tuned in to their students, Binns forgetting students' names and Trelawney making seemingly false and random predictions about unfortunate events in students' lives. Unlike Binns, however, Professor Trelawney's reclusive and aloof behaviors and personality, not age and death, distance her from students. "Draped in a gauzy spangled shawl" and "seated in a winged chair in front of the fire" she introduces herself to students, explaining her lack of presence at Hogwarts. She says, "You may not have seen me before, I find that descending too often into the hustle and bustle of the main school clouds my Inner-Eye" (*Prisoner of Azkaban* 102–103). Trelawney's distance, thus, is explained as necessary to her abilities and expertise. Trelawney's classroom, in contrast to the cold of that which could be associated with death and ghosts like Professor Binns, is "stiflingly warm, and the fire that was burning under the crowded mantelpiece was giving off a heavy, sickly sort of perfume as it heated a large copper kettle" (*Prisoner of Azkaban* 102). Unlike Binns' reliance on facts, confidence in evidence, and study of history, Trelawney studies the future and believes in auras, magic, premonitions, crystal-gazing, and clair-voyance. As such, she typifies the new-age, alternative, free-spirited teacher who is gentle and kind, though ineffective.

Rubeus Hagrid, as Care of Magical Creatures teacher, fulfills yet another teacher stereotype. Hagrid is literally a gentle giant, an oaf of an instructor whose genuine compassion is often misjudged because of his appearance, his past, his displays of emotion, and his "unfortunate liking for large and mon-strous beasts" (*Chamber of Secrets* 249). Rowling first introduces Hagrid in *The Sorcerer's Stone*.

> He was almost twice as tall as a normal man and at least five times as wide. He looked simply too big to be allowed, and so *wild*—long tangles of bushy black and his beard hid most of his face, he had hands the size of trash can lids, and his feet in their leather boots were like baby dol-phins. [He had] vast, muscular arms.
>
> (14)

Holding classes in or near his hut on the edge of the Forbidden Forest, Hagrid's respect and intuitive knowledge for magical creatures and his enthu-siasm for his lessons blind him from practical concerns, such as the safety of his students. For example, his first lesson, a lesson in which students stroke and ride real Hippogriffs, ends disastrously as Draco Malfoy is thrown to the ground and injured. Though his teaching is not always successful and he suffers from low self-esteem and drinks to assuage his troubles, teaching is a position he values greatly. Harry, Hermione, and Ron "knew how much being a teacher would mean to Hagrid. He wasn't a fully qualified wizard; he had been expelled from Hogwarts in his third year for a crime that he had not committed" (*Prisoner of Azkaban* 94). In other words, Hagrid cares a great deal about his position as he cares for magical creatures. Further, Hagrid has deep allegiance to and is deeply trusted by both Harry and Dumbledore. It is Hagrid that helps Harry prepare to face the Triwizard Tournament in *Goblet of Fire* and Hagrid who carries Dumbledore after his death in *Half-Blood Prince*, and carries Harry after his seeming death in *Deathly Hallows*. In these examples, we understand that deeply emotional Hagrid, like Professor Binns and Trelawney, Hagrid embodies his subject, Care, even if it is at the expense of his effective instruction.

In these three characters, several common motifs emerge: the blur of person and profession, ineffective and disconnected teachers, and passion without practical application. Through these characters, the Harry Potter series attributes and equates most teachers' professional knowledge and abilities to their personality, sense of individuality, and overall being. The person makes the teacher. The teacher embodies the subject matter. Magic and wizardry, unique to the school stories of Harry Potter, dramatize the characters even further because the stereotypical ways of being are also literal. We understand that Hagrid *is* a giant, and Binns *is* a ghost, for example. This is true, as I will explicate in more detail later in this chapter, for Professor McGonagall too; as a witch who can take the form of a cat, she *is* "witchy" and "on the prowl." Further blurring personal and professional personas, most of what we learn about each teacher's life story takes place in, relates to, or impacts the school of Hogwarts, or involves the area of expertise for which he or she has been hired to teach or perform. Therefore, we do not see teachers and administrators outside their professional role as a teacher or as an expert of a particular discipline. We rarely see teachers at home, and we do not see, for example, teachers as parents, lovers, as friends of people outside of Hogwarts, or as people with interests unrelated to their work. As narrowly defined caricatures fail to present a complex, conflicted, or multidimensional way of being a teacher, there is little possibility, one may even wonder if there is any role, for individuals who are not fully "teachers"—mind, spirit, and body, in and out of the classroom. Not only is the notion of who can be a teacher unhelpful, limiting, and potentially unhealthy and impossible if attempted by real teachers, with regard to the second two emergent motifs, the integration and envelopment of individual and professional identities constructs particular pedagogies.

The Harry Potter series relates a teacher's pedagogy to the qualities that define that teacher's identity. Within the confines of narrowly defined images of teachers, teachers must embody their subject matter. In the case of the teachers at Hogwarts, passion and expertise, in part, serve as markers of this embodiment. The series often suggests that the most passionate expert of a subject makes the best teacher for that subject. As we cannot easily separate one's individuality and personal and professional identity, we can not separate curriculum and instruction from course content, the teacher's passion and expertise, or his or her identity; therefore, a pedagogical flaw of sorts, a teacher's identity, and content expertise assumes some instructional limitations. That is, we must accept History of Magic as boring and irrelevant, or Divination as "out there," or Care of Magical Creatures as risky because history itself is past and seemingly distant, and auras by definition are mystical, and caring requires being open to one's emotions and vulnerable to being hurt. This vision, built on the essentialized representations of teachers, not only serves to limit further what and how teachers can be, but it also polarizes teaching and learning as well. The implicit message is that teachers cannot be passionate and effective teachers, experts in their field and connected to students; real learning, as I will discuss in detail later in this chapter, is separate from classroom teaching.

Minerva McGonagall: Complexity?

There are other teachers at Hogwarts, notably more prominent characters in the series, who provide additional and more in-depth portraits of how and what teachers can be. Professor Minerva McGonagall is one example. Professor McGonagall—Head of Gryffindor, Acting and Deputy Headmistress, and the Transfiguration teacher at Hogwarts—is highly intelligent, prudent, and rational. She is also quite strict. Initially, Professor McGonagall's appearance, her personality, and her pedagogy conjure images of a stereotypical schoolmarm: a strict woman teacher with a keen sense of discipline, a regard for school protocol, and a strong appeal for diligent studying and hard work. In this image, her character supports some of the same assumptions and limiting ideas about teachers that Binns, Trelawney, and Hagrid do. For example, McGonagall's physical appearance blends with her strict and no-nonsense expectations for students to suggest, that she, as Harry quickly surmises, "is not someone to cross" (*Sorcerer's Stone* 113). Rowling first describes Professor McGonagall's appearance early in *Harry Potter and the Sorcerer's Stone* as a "rather severe-looking woman" with "glasses exactly the shape [that her Animagus cat form has] around its eyes ... her black hair was drawn into a tight bun." (9). As previously mentioned, she is literally both a cat and a witch, which further serves to qualify her persona as "on the prowl" and "witchy." A demanding teacher, known for "complicated notes" (*Sorcerer's Stone* 134) and a lot of homework, her expectations, like her bun, are tight. Her "severe" look mirrors her pedagogical stance. She says about her subject, "Transfiguration is some of the most complex and dangerous magic you will learn at Hogwarts. Anyone messing around in my class will leave and not come back. You have been warned" (*Sorcerer's Stone* 134). She implies that success in her course will require both self-control and intellectual capacity, and she clouds the distinction between a student's good behavior and her success in school, which in turn clouds the distinction between McGonagall's presence as a teacher and her presence as a powerful disciplinarian.

Yet, the portrait of Professor McGonagall is more detailed and complicated than portraits of more minor characters. As her subject matter might predict, she does metaphorically transfigure her schoolmarm caricature from time to time, revealing a more complex, temperate, and compassionate way of being. One website suggests that McGonagall shows a "softer side," citing that she blushes from a kiss from Hagrid at the Christmas party in *Sorcerer's Stone*. She wears dress robes and a wreath, and dances with Ludo Bagman at the Yule Ball in *Goblet of Fire*, and even occasionally sheds a tear.[1] Further, she has interests outside of Transfiguration, as she is an ardent Quidditch fan. She apparently diverges from her rule-following ways when she permits Hermione to enroll in several courses at once through the use of the Time-Turner. Finally, McGonagall voices contentious opinions, which extend beyond the bounds of her course and role as disciplinarian, such as her dismissal of Trelawney and Divination: "Divination is one of the most imprecise branches of magic. I shall not conceal from you that I have very little patience with it. True Seers are very rare, and Professor Trelawney..." (*Prisoner of Azkaban* 109). Through McGonagall, Rowling constructs a more dynamic and complex character, but she does not necessarily present a more complex image of a teacher.

McGonagall's apparent divergences, interests and opinions certainly qualify her as a schoolmarm but ultimately fail to challenge the image because both the stereotype and divergences can be explained by her loyalty to Hogwarts, Dumbledore, and to her students. That is, she represents a schoolmarm with strict discipline, but she is not evil, random, or vindictive towards students. In fact, her pedagogy and interactions with students emerge through and not in spite of her strict disciplinary stance. She equates discipline with learning and knowing, even outside the classroom. For example, her reprimands ask "what were you thinking?" and accuse students of being "foolish." McGonagall respects and seeks to treat students equally, if not fairly. Glimpses into her class, such as her gruff encouragement to Neville Longbottom in *Order of the Phoenix*, demonstrate her belief in all students' ability to learn.

> "You cannot pass an OWL" said Professor McGonagall grimly, "without serious application, practice and study. I see no reasons why everybody in this class should not achieve an OWL in Transfiguration as long as they put in the work." Neville made a sad little disbelieving noise. "Yes, you too, Longbottom" said Professor McDonagall. "There's nothing wrong with your work except lack of confidence."
>
> (257)

Readers come to believe that she is deeply concerned about her students, though this is in the context in her code of ethics—following the rules and working hard. Importantly, in terms of who, what, and how teachers can be, the texts suggest that teachers care for their students and that strict discipline is necessary to this care and to learning. This qualification, rather than expanding or exploding teacher stereotypes, simply affirms conventional images in more detail.

If we consider her apparent complexities as part of her uncompromising devotion to the institution of Hogwarts and her concern for students, her image as a teacher and an administrator is not anomalous to the images previously presented. As a more fully developed character with a dual role at the school, she embodies the entire institution rather than just one class. She follows rules and protocols of the school. For example, she distributes severe reprimands to *all* students who do not follow the school rules, including harsh penalties toward students of her own Gryffindor House. In the few instances in which we do see her break a rule, we come to believe she does so thoughtfully, in high regard for the school as an institution, and for the better of Hogwarts or her students and their learning. She seeks permission from Dumbledore for Harry to play as Seeker on the Quidditch team despite being only a first year student. She not only follows protocol to obtain permission, but she also reaffirms her high expectations for Harry: "'I want to hear that you're training hard, Potter, or I might change my mind about punishing you'. Then she suddenly smiled" (*Sorcerer's Stone* 152). Another example is of Professor McGonagall's willingness to pursue permission from the Ministry of Magic, in *Prisoner of Azkaban,* for Hermione to employ the Time-Turner to take multiple courses at the same time. We learn that teachers can be rule-breakers, can present disagreements, and can even show compassion for students within the context of school as an institution.

Perhaps the best example of McGonagall as a teacher and as an embodiment of Hogwarts as an institution surfaces in the *Order of the Phoenix,* through her response to Dolores Umbridge. The contrast between the two characters is important to a reader's construction of teachers. Though we might read Umbridge, who is described as "someone's maiden aunt," as a schoolmarm, the two "schoolmarms" contrast greatly (*Order of the Phoenix* 203). A polarity to McGonagall, a Hogwarts insider, Umbridge is an outsider; McGonagall's discipline is well-intended and Umbridge's discipline is mal-intended. Further, though not necessarily a complex image of a teacher, McGonagall mediates Umbridge's threats to her students and to her institution in nuanced ways. For example, she warns Harry to keep his temper with Umbridge to avoid detentions and further reprimand, but she also openly challenges Umbridge during her observation, "I wonder how you expect to gain an idea of my usual teaching methods if you continue to interrupt me. You see, I usually do not permit people to talk when I am talking" (*Order of the Phoenix* 320). She is a complex character with unified goals and allegiances, still a detailed but hackneyed image of a teacher.

Severus Snape: Complexity

Professor Severus Snape, Potions instructor, Head of the Slytherin House and eventual Defense Against the Dark Arts instructor, is arguably one of the more complex and multifaceted teachers portrayed in the Harry Potter series.

In part, this complexity stems from the continuous question of whether Snape supports Dumbledore or Lord Voldemort and the Death Eaters; however, the lack of clarity about Snape's position in the wizarding world does not preclude most readers from constructing an initial and lasting image of Snape as an undesirable, exploitative, evil, and malevolent teacher.

With the combination of his dress, his attitudes and behaviors, and even his classroom decor, Snape employs pedagogy of fear and intimidation. His appearance serves this fear. Rowling describes, "His eyes were black like Hagrid, but with none of Hagrid's warmth. They were cold and empty, and made you think of dark tunnels" (*Sorcerer's Stone* 136). His "sallow skin, a hooked nose and greasy, shoulder-length black hair" (*Chamber of Secrets* 78), a seemingly unpleasant appearance augurs his unpleasant and implacable presence with students, a presence that centers negative perceptions of student ability and other prejudgments. As he introduces his Potions course, for example, he discourages rather than encourages students.

> "You are here to learn the subtle science and exact art of potionmaking," he began. He spoke in barely more than a whisper, but they caught every word—like Professor McGonagall, Snape had the gift of keeping a class silent without effort. "...I don't expect you will really understand the beauty of the softly simmering cauldron with its shimmering fumes, the delicate power of liquids that creep through human veins, bewitching the mind, ensnaring the senses.... I can teach you how to bottle fame, brew glory, even stopper death—if you aren't as big a bunch of dunderheads as I usually have to teach."
>
> (*Chamber of Secrets* 137)

He deflects his responsibility for effective instruction onto the difficulty of the subject matter and the inherent lack of capacity of students, which one can only imagine must chip away at student confidence and imbue more fear and intimidation. His reliance on fixed, and usually hopeless or powerless notions about students (with the exception of students in his own House) is divisive and intimidating. To and about Harry, in *Goblet of Fire*, he reveals, "You might be laboring under the delusion that the entire wizarding world is impressed with you.... To me, Potter, you are nothing but a nasty little boy who considers rules beneath him" (516). In *Prisoner of Azkaban*, Snape connects Harry to his father, James:

> How extraordinarily like your father you are, Potter.... He too was exceedingly arrogant. A small amount of talent on the Quidditch field made him think that he was a cut above the rest of us too. Strutting around the place with friends and admirers.... The resemblance is uncanny.
>
> (284)

Additionally, in contrast to Professor McGonagall, who encourages struggling Neville Longbottom, Snape publicly belittles him. "Perhaps no one's warned you, Lupin, but this class contains Neville Longbottom. I would advise you not to entrust him with anything difficult. Not unless Miss Granger is hissing instructions in his ear" (*Prisoner of Azkaban* 132). A final source of fear is Snape's classroom. Upon entering his Defense Against the Dark Arts classroom in the *Half-Blood Prince*, students noted changes: "Snape had imposed his personality onto the room already; it was gloomier than usual.... New pictures adorned the walls, many of them showing people who appeared to be in pain, sporting grisly injuries, or strangely contorted body parts" (177). Eerily, we learn that Snape not only teaches Defense Against Dark Arts for a short time but he also spoke of Dark forces with "a loving caress in his voice" (*Half-Blood Prince* 178).

What makes Snape complex and multifaceted, and how does this matter to our construction of what, who, and how teachers can be? Consider two distinguishing qualities of Snape's persona. First, while other images of teachers presented in Harry Potter mock schools and teachers, as well as book learning, the magnitude of iniquity represented in Snape offers a more overt critique, almost a prescription or a warning of who, what, and how not to be a teacher. While other images signify ineffective instruction, which is also problematic or potentially harmful to students, ineffective teaching is not morally wrong. Yet, through Snape, we learn that some "bad" teachers abuse and enjoy power, hurt children, and play favorites at high costs. We learn to be skeptical of teachers, surmising that some discipline—perhaps the version McGonagall utilizes—fosters learning but other kinds are just plain mean. Because of Snape, we hold open the possibility that some teachers stand against, rather than for or with students and their learning. Yet, fleeting moments in which Snape acts in unexpected ways and actually helps Harry cause us to question if he is really as "bad" as he appears and presents himself to be. Thus, through Snape, we learn to be suspicious even accusatory of "bad" teachers and at the same time we learn to search for doubt and suspend our judgments of bad behaviors.

The question of Snape's loyalty and allegiance is the second distinguishing aspect of Rowling's characterization. Though wavering over Snape's true allegiance does not necessarily influence or change a reader's identification of Snape as an evil, malevolent teacher with an inexcusable fear-induced pedagogy. My tentative beliefs about his devotion did shape my interpretation of that identity, however. That is, as readers vacillate between believing Snape was loyal to Dumbledore and believing that he was faithful to Voldemort, we make sense of Snape's attitudes and behaviors differently. Believing that Snape was committed to Voldemort strengthens and reifies Snape as morally bad. He embodies evil. He behaves the way he does because he is evil, naturally. Yet, believing that Snape is faithful to Dumbledore challenges us to explain why and how Snape came to be evil and vindictive. Accordingly, we piece together bits of Snape's personal history to learn that as a student at Hogwarts Snape was always fascinated and known for his talent in the subject; to learn that he loved Harry's mother and hated his father; to learn that schoolmates picked on Snape; to learn that Snape is a reformed Death Eater; and to learn that Dumbledore has defended Snape on numerous occasions, forgiving him for leaking Trelawney's first prophecy announcing Harry's birth to Voldemort. Whether readers choose to forgive or excuse is independent of the portrait that Rowling offers about why he came to be the teacher and the person that he is. Rowling offers images of individual heartaches, individual relationships, good and bad, and individual decisions that led to tragedies, of individual suffering. We do not see stories of opportunities afforded or denied based on social, political, or cultural structures. A teacher's personal biography, the texts suggest, shape the kind of teacher they can become.

Albus Dumbledore: Paragon

> Professor Dumbledore, though very old, always gave the impression of great energy. He had several feet of long silver hair and beard, half-moon spectacles, and an extremely crooked nose. He was often described as the greatest wizard of the age, but that wasn't why Harry respected him. You couldn't help trusting Albus Dumbledore.
>
> (*Prisoner of Azkaban* 91)

Kind and gentle, energetic and wise, trusting and trusted, experienced and patient, Albus Dumbledore is a paragon, a quintessential "great" teacher. Like his Patronus form, the Phoenix, Dumbledore continues to "rise up" to assist Harry and ward off danger. Furthermore, he does so, as Harry notes, with "great energy" (*Prisoner of Azkaban* 91). Dumbledore defies age, unlike Binns, to remain a vibrant and contributing member of the Hogwarts faculty. His trust defies commonly held suspicions, as he consistently supports Hagrid, defends Harry's transgressions, and supports Snape's questionable morality. He is courageous. For example, it is Dumbledore who teaches Harry to say Voldemort's name because "fear of a name creates fear of the thing itself" (*Sorcerer's Stone* 298). He fights off Death Eaters. He is protective and comforting. About Dumbledore, Hagrid admired, "Great Man, Dumbledore. 'S long as we got him, I'm not too worried" (*Goblet of Fire* 719). Moreover, he serves in leadership positions: he is not only the Headmaster of Hogwarts, but he also plays a pivotal role in the Order of the Phoenix. Finally, in one of the few examples of learning, which will be discussed later in the chapter, Dumbledore is a great mentor to Harry and his peers. He stages learning opportunities and instills confidence. As Harry states, in *Sorcerer's Stone*:

> I think he sort of wanted to give me a chance. I think he knows more or less everything that goes on here, you know. I reckon he had a pretty

good idea we were going to try, and instead of stopping us, he just taught us enough to help. I don't think it was an accident he let me find out how the mirror worked.

(302)

The image of Dumbledore as a teacher is not a mockery of the teaching profession, though it is not unproblematic. Dumbledore's greatness is made even more visible as he stands in opposition to other teachers, all of whom have some imperfections. Dumbledore is not vain like Professor Lockhart is, nor needs to be as strict as Professor McGonagall does. He is not "two-faced" as Professor Quirrell is, nor seeking to be a well-liked friend as Professor Lupin. He cares but he is not overly emotional, as Hagrid is, nor evil like Professor Snape is. Instead, he offers a very alluring, larger-than-life, positive—even heroic—representation of a teacher. As a hero, he sticks up for his students, as he did when Umbridge discovers the Defense Association (D.A.). He took full responsibility for the group's existence and stepped down from his position. Of course, his death is the ultimate embodiment of heroics. His ambitious and impressive persona tells us that great teachers must be epic and superhuman. This message is unhelpful and problematic to a reader's understanding of the real work of a teacher. That is, like the other teachers in the series, we are to believe that Dumbledore is the kind of teacher he is because of the kind of person he is, in this case superhuman. To be a great teacher you simply must be super. As such, the message that teachers must be epic hides the real work of teachers—the planning, the collaboration, the intellectual demands, the challenges, the instructional strategies, as well as the institutional constraints on what should be possible, for example.

The Curriculum and the Institution

To understand more fully the "cumulative cultural text" about teachers, it helps to consider the contexts in which they work. Teachers teach within institutions that have particular curricular visions and that limit and permit how teachers can be. Many readers will relate to the conventions of Hogwarts, an institution structured around competition and imbued with a legacy of conflicts. Students are positioned for competition in their first year when the Sorting Hat selects which House will become home to each student. A student's disposition and family legacy determine which House they will be sorted into, though a powerful student can sometimes sway the Hat's decision, as Harry does. The division of Houses is significant, as it affects students' experiences in and out of classrooms, and it affects the social order and learning at the school. Students earn or lose points for their House based on behavior, clever problem solving, as well as intramural Quidditch games. School dances and all school meetings are also a regular occurrence at Hogwarts. We learn that part of a teacher's job is to maintain the rituals and routines of the school. Teachers at Hogwarts are preservationists; that is, they do not challenge or disrupt but rather reify the institution of school. The organization, rituals, and routines at Hogwarts are presented as if it is the way it has always been, and because many of the teachers at Hogwarts were former students, we can assume that these rituals and routines are not only their job but reflect their conceptions of what it means to be in school. Traditions overshadow learning and we learn that the most important aspects of school do not occur during class instruction.

The curriculum at Hogwarts is also highly ritualized: tests mark time and accomplishment. The ritual of testing drives learning and signifies what it means to get an education. In *Goblet of Fire*, for example, Professor McGonagall and students discuss the most important tests at Hogwarts.

> "You are now entering the most important phase of your magical education!" she told them, her eyes glinting dangerously behind her square spectacles. "Your Ordinary Wizarding Levels are drawing closer—"
>
> "We don't take O.W.L.s till fifth year!" said Dean Thomas indignantly.
>
> "Maybe not, Thomas, but believe me, you need all the preparation you can get."
>
> (255)

The curriculum *is* the preparation for the test. Instruction is ineffective in meeting student needs and desires. In a few examples when learning is interesting and "hands-on" as in Hagrid's lesson about Hippogriffs or Lupin's Defense Against the Dark Arts lessons, teachers are made out to be foolish and careless. Harry and his friends frequently need knowledge about particular subjects in order to face very real problems, but subject learning they get from their teacher is either just fun or is overly theoretical, and is thus rarely useful. In fact, even when students ask for subjects to address their needs teachers sometimes cannot do this. Professor Lupin explains to Harry when he asks for help with the Dementors, "I'll try and help. But it'll have to wait until next term, I'm afraid, I have a lot to do before the holiday" (*Prisoner of Azkaban* 189). Though students are successful in overcoming many obstacles they learn to do so outside of formal classroom instruction.

With regard to curriculum and the institution, the *Order of the Phoenix* stands out as a critique of both institutional constraints that schools face today, such as increased accountability, standardization, and high-stake testing, as well as a critique of common curriculum practices. When the Ministry of Magic interferes with the Hogwarts curriculum, the instruction becomes even more divorced from student needs and desires, positioning the lives of students against the curriculum, and the practical against theoretical. This is best depicted when Dolores Umbridge takes over as Defense Against the Dark Arts teacher. She employs a textbook about the theory of Dark Arts, aims to "return to basic principles," and as Hermione points out, she does not teach them anything about "*using* defensive spells" (*Order of the Phoenix* 239–241). Dolores Umbridge explains, "As long as you've studied the theory hard enough, there is no reason why you should not be able to perform the spells under carefully controlled examination conditions" (*Order of the Phoenix* 244). Umbridge's teaching is particularly alarming because she has displaced existing teachers and because she refuses to admit to and teach to the real possibility of an attack by Lord Voldemort. While readers opposed to current educational policies may laud the book's critique, as I do, the critique falls short.

Though the series presents Umbridge and the Ministry of Magic as an intrusion to the school, as evil forces that disrupt and stand to ruin the school and endanger the students, it does not provide a substantial alternative vision of how school can be. That is, instruction and curriculum depicted in the earlier books when the Hogwarts teachers were in charge do not suggest another way. The challenge from the Ministry is read mostly as a personal attack on the teachers and the institution rooted in politics. Readers may feel badly that the teachers and the students are being wronged by the Ministry because we develop a fondness for Harry and even his teachers by Year Five. Yet, the series' ability to stand in critique of such attacks, are weakened by the lack of thought, philosophical stance, pedagogical knowledge, and instructional capacity depicted in the images of teachers. Most of what we learn about what it means to be a teacher relates to the person the teacher is, and therefore, the attacks on the school and the teachers can only be personal and not about differing intellectual, philosophical, or professional perspectives on how best to educate.

Real Learning

Hogwarts, Hogwarts, Hoggy Warty Hogwarts,
Teach us something please,
Whether we be old and bald
Or young with scabby knees,
Our heads could do with filling
With some interesting stuff,
For now they're bare and full of air,
Dead flies and bits of fluff,
So teach us things worth knowing,
Bring back what we've forgot,
Just do your best, we'll do the rest,
And learn until our brains all rot.

(*Sorcerer's Stone* 128)

In the Harry Potter series, real learning occurs outside the classroom and with little influence from a teacher's instructional style and ability or their knowledge. As the school chant suggests to the teachers, "Just do your best, we'll do the rest." Students "do the rest" as they solve mysteries and face dark forces, befriend and meet with teachers outside of class. Only a few, like Hermione, read books outside of class. Harry and Ron are repeatedly depicted becoming sleepy and distracted when they try to read. But studying does not often matter. Despite doing very poorly in Umbridge's Defense Against the Dark Arts course, Harry forms Dumbledore's Army (D.A.) in which he *teaches* his peers about the Dark Arts. Sometimes Harry and his friends learn important lessons from their teachers, but it happens privately and outside of the class and formal curriculum, such as Hagrid's lessons that help Harry win the Triwizard Tournament or when Dumbledore teaches Harry the history of Hogwarts by introducing him to the Pensieve, or when Snape agrees to teach Harry private Occlumency lessons, or Lupin's lessons about the Patronus Charm. Real learning, however, rarely happens in the classroom. One way to understand how the series constructs and privileges real learning is to consider how learning is connected to conceptions of power and knowledge.

Power, Knowledge, and Anti-intellectualism

A strong theme in the series is that book learning is very much less important than who one knows, how brave one is, how strong one is, and what one's moral directives are. In terms of the importance of intellectual capacities, readers might think of Dumbledore's adage from *Chamber of Secrets*, to understand that "it is our choices ... that show what we truly are, far more than our abilities" (333). Intellectuals, in particular teachers as intellectuals, are overtly mocked even as Harry and his peers need to know certain things to solve real problems. Because readers are not privy to scenes of teachers working collaboratively to plan lessons or to understand students better, and we are instead overwhelmed with hackneyed images of ineffective teachers whose teaching is directly related to their personality rather than what they know, because the curriculum rarely serves Harry well, we come to understand Harry's major triumphs and achievements as separate from school or book learning. Further, even outside of class, the intellectual and academic work of students is not as important to their success as other qualities. Harry is braver than he is smart. Though Hermione's studiousness and her knowledge often rescue Harry and his friends, her tendency to study and read is mocked. The wise Ravenclaws are marginalized compared to the brave and chivalrous Gryffindors. Harry often does things based on inspiration and impulse not through thinking things out. At Hogwarts, bravery and magic powers, friends and connections, physical prowess on the broom, and sheer luck matter much more than intellectual and academic achievement.

One way to think about the anti-intellectual ideas presented in the Harry Potter series is to analyze the kinds of power that matter most in terms of Harry's accomplishments over his school years. French and Raven (*The Bases of Social Power*) identify five types of power, which are useful when looking at a particular person's sources of power and the examples of what matters and how one learns at Hogwarts. These include legitimate, reward, coercive, expert, and referent power. These five power bases were expanded by Hershey and Blanchard (*Management of Organizational Behaviour*) who added two more bases of power: connection and information. Legitimate power (sometimes called authority or formal power) derives from one's position in an organization. Reward and coercive power stems from legitimate power. Expert power is based on having special knowledge while referent power is based on being liked, respected, and trusted. Connection power comes through networks and is like social capital, while information power comes from having access to information that others lack.

The Harry Potter series suggests that connection and referent power matter more and are more useful than other kinds of power, and in doing so, the series dismisses the importance of teachers, classroom instruction, and intellectual engagement. Readers can locate examples of many forms of power at Hogwarts. A super-hero teacher, Dumbledore possess all types of power. Dumbledore and McGonagall, as school leaders, exert legitimate power. Teachers, especially prominent teachers, like Snape hold legitimate power too. Umbridge legitimizes her own power and takes away the legitimate power of the regular faculty when she takes over the school and through her numerous educational decrees. The entire structure of the institution, through the awarding of House points, is built of reward and coercive power. Many of the instructors hold expert power in their wizardry. Dumbledore, because of his long history and kind disposition holds a lot of referent, connection, and information power too. Lupin and Hagrid possess a good degree of referent power because students generally like them.

Rowling reveals an anti-intellectual stance by deprivileging expert power. In terms of learning and knowledge, the expert knowledge of the teacher is not so helpful or impressive at least as it is presented in the formal curriculum. Rowling expresses this as she describes Harry's respect for Dumbledore: "[Dumbledore] was often described as the greatest wizard of the age, but that wasn't why Harry respected him. You couldn't help trusting Albus Dumbledore" (*Prisoner of Azkaban* 91). Further, readers do not see any examples of expert power that grows from expert teaching. Harry enjoys a lot of referent power, however, each time he goes somewhere he is not supposed to or uses magic when he is not supposed to. On these journeys, he often gathers information that he later uses to fight off serious threats to the school or himself. He achieves this kind of learning because people, especially Dumbledore, like him. He is given the benefit of the doubt. He also uses connective power. Because of his long legacy and the respect it spawns, more referent power, he is looked after by many adults in the book. Sirius Black and the Weasleys provide him with information and a protective environment that he needs to learn. In winning Triwizard Tournament tests, Harry relied on a great deal of advice from friends. More broadly, because he is thought to be in direct danger from Lord Voldemort's return, he is often privileged with administrative and historical views on Hogwarts that provide him with special information. Both his connection and referent power afford him private lessons with Dumbledore, in which he gathers information through the expert power of a mentor. Once again, readers learn that who you know, how brave you are, how strong you are, and what your moral directives are, are much more powerful and matter more than book learning and intellectual pursuits.

Implications

As a teacher educator, I read the Harry Potter series thinking about students and teachers. Like Deborah Britzman, I am concerned about the socialization of teachers and "what [pre-service teachers] make happen because of what happens to them" (56). Britzman outlines several cultural myths related to learning to teach and suggests that part of the task of teacher education is to examine "how we become entangled in and can become disentangled from the dynamics of cultural reproduction" (233). As part of the larger "cumulative cultural text" about teachers, I imagine what my students and my students' students might do with what they take from reading Harry Potter. I am struck by the series' mockery of schools and teachers and the suggestion that teachers have very little power to shape instruction or the institution of schooling. Also, I am disturbed by the limiting idea that being a good teacher is about who you are as a person rather than what you know or who you have the capacity to become. Further, the series suggests that in order for teachers to have any kind of impact on students, personality and personal relationships between teachers and students matter most. I am mindful of the absence of intellectual work by teachers as well as the singular and completely school-based identities of the teachers. Last, I worry about the message that who you know is profoundly more valuable than what you know. Readers must critically examine the images of teachers, schools, and of valuable knowledge in popular culture. With this chapter, I hope to have sparked such an examination of the Harry Potter series.

Note

1. *The Harry Potter Lexicon.* Retrieved December 26, 2007, from www.hp-lexicon.org/wizards/mcgonagall.html

References

Bolotin, Pamela Joseph and Gail E. Burnaford, eds. *Images of Schoolteachers in Twentieth-Century America.* New York: St. Martin's Press, 1994.

Britzman, Deborah. *Practice Makes Practice: A Critical Study of Learning to Teach.* Albany, New York: State University of New York, 1991.

Bulman, Robert C. *Hollywood Goes to High School: Cinema, Schools, and American Culture.* NY: Worth Publishers, 2004.

Dalton, Mary M. *The Hollywood Curriculum: Teachers and Teaching the Movies.* New York: Peter Lang, 1999.

French, John R. P. and Bertram Raven. *The Bases of Social Power. Studies in Social Power.* Ann Arbor, MI: Institution for Social Research, 1959.

Hersey, Paul and Kenneth Blanchard. *Management of Organizational Behaviour* 4th edn. Englewood Cliffs, NJ: Prentice-Hall, 1982.

Mitchell, Claudia and Sandra Weber. *Reinventing Ourselves as Teachers: Beyond Nostalgia.* London: Falmer Press, 1999.

Rowling, J. K. *Harry Potter and the Sorcerer's Stone.* New York: Scholastic, 1997.

—— *Harry Potter and the Chamber of Secrets.* New York: Scholastic, 1998.

—— *Harry Potter and the Prisoner of Azkaban.* New York: Scholastic, 1999.

—— *Harry Potter and the Goblet of Fire.* New York: Scholastic, 2000.

—— *Harry Potter and the Order of the Phoenix.* New York: Scholastic, 2003.

—— *Harry Potter and the Half-Blood Prince.* New York: Scholastic, 2005.

—— *Harry Potter and the Deathly Hallows.* New York: Scholastic, 2007.

Weber, Sandra and Claudia Mitchell. *That's Funny, You Don't Look Like a Teacher: Interrogating Images and Identities in Popular Culture.* London: RoutledgeFalmer, 1995.

Chapter Seven

Comedy, Quest, and Community
Home and Family in Harry Potter

JOHN KORNFELD AND LAURIE PROTHRO

When A. Bartlett Giamatti (1989)—who after leaving his job as President of Yale in the 1980s became, briefly, Commissioner of Major League Baseball—talked about baseball as a metaphor for life, he pointed out that in life, just as in baseball, you leave home, then spend all the game trying to get back home: back to a place where you know what the score is, you know where you stand, you are safe. This transformational journey—which all young people must take to discover who they are and where they fit in the world, to create their own version of home out of the strangeness they encounter when they are "away"—forms the basis of much young adult, coming-of-age literature. And unless they leave, they cannot know what it is they seek. As Rochman and McCampbell (1997, p. vii) write, "We leave home to find home."

The concept of home is inextricably entangled with that of family—individuals who together "create worlds of their own, with particular kinds of boundaries separating them from the larger world" (Handel, 1994, p. xxiv). Ideally, within these worlds, members offer one another security, support, and other assets that can become "protective factors" (Gilgun, 1999) for young people leaving home and struggling with the inevitable challenges of life. But family is not always (or only) a team clustered in the dugout, urging you on with hope and faith as you set out on your quest, waiting to welcome you with wild cheers when you return home, safe. The various cross-relationships among individuals within a family group can be welcoming or isolating; for the young adult feeling alone in the world, images of home and family can provide sustenance, or a motivation to escape. We see the effects of such family dynamics in young adult novels as the protagonists move forward purposefully in their quests. And even if the family is a harmonious, loving community, the journey demands separation from it, a "necessary abyss" (Rochman, 1993, p. 13) as a young person comes of age. Ultimately, however, it is the protective factors that young people can draw on during their journey toward self-discovery and meaning in the world; and in the Harry Potter series, we see what can happen when the family unit both succeeds and fails to provide them.

Family Dynamics in the non-Hogwarts World

Like so many protagonists in coming-of-age novels, the Harry Potter we meet in Book 1 is essentially alone in the world. His parents, we learn, were killed when he was an infant and, because his aunt and uncle are his only relatives, they have become Harry's unwilling guardians who treat Harry "like a dog that had rolled in something smelly" (*Chamber of Secrets*, p. 5). Throughout the first 11 years of Harry's life, they exclude him from family activities, lock him in his cupboard for prolonged periods of time, and, worst of all, withhold from Harry the truth about his parents and himself. The Dursleys remind us of Aunt Sponge and Aunt Spiker, the malignant guardians in Roald Dahl's *James and the Giant Peach* (1961/1988) who routinely abuse and imprison James Trotter after his parents' sudden deaths (they were eaten by a rhinoceros that had escaped from the London Zoo) when he was four years old. Yet, as horrible as Trotter's and Potter's guardians may be, it is difficult to take them terribly seriously. As one-dimensional characters, their treatment of the boys reads more like farce than tragedy. Early in the story, Dahl (1961/1988, p. 40) unceremoniously disposes of James' aunts in comic book fashion by rolling a giant peach over them: "Aunt Sponge and Aunt Spiker lay ironed out upon the grass as flat and thin and life-less as a couple of paper dolls cut out of a picture book." The Dursley family members suffer equally cartoonish (although less dire) fates: Dudley first sprouts a tail (*Sorcerer's Stone*), then later a four-foot long tongue (*Goblet of Fire*), and his Aunt Marge balloons to an enormous size and floats to the ceiling (*Prisoner of Azkaban*). How can we fail to laugh at characters who send Harry a toothpick (*Chamber of Secrets*) and a tissue (*Goblet of Fire*) as Christmas gifts?

Rowling devotes considerable attention in each of the first four books to family dynamics in the non-Hogwarts world. Much of that attention revolves around the antics of the Dursleys and another family, the Weasleys—the wizarding family whose son Ron becomes Harry's best friend at Hogwarts. The scenes at both Harry's and Ron's homes read like theater of the absurd, reducing family life to slapstick comedy. In the Dursley house, Uncle Vernon goes to increasingly ridiculous (and futile) extremes in his role as head and protector of the family to prevent Harry from getting mail from Hogwarts, ultimately rowing the family in a violent storm to a broken-down shack on a remote island. Meanwhile, Molly Weasley, like Samantha in the old television show *Bewitched*, keeps her family and house in order through cute and funny magical means—making the dishes wash themselves in the sink, and using enchanted clocks to keep track of her children's schedules and her husband's whereabouts.

As in many situation comedies about family relationships, the struggle between parents and sons is constant. Compared to their clever, mischievous sons, the parents seem dull-witted and obtuse. The Dursley and Weasley parents are often unaware of their sons' pranks (and equally oblivious to the deeper struggles that their children undergo in the magical world); they barely manage to contain the damage the kids create and to maintain their tenuous image of normalcy in their respective communities. The sons embody the ubiquitous cultural phenomenon that Steinberg and Kincheloe (1998) call "young males with an attitude"—"smart-ass kids" depicted in popular movies who run circles around their clueless parents while garnering audience sympathy. The mildly adversarial parent/son relationships seem designed primarily for the humor they engender; families in Rowling's non-Hogwarts world, at least in the first four books, are comical, conventional, superficial, and stereotypical.

From the Mundane to the Magical

Fortunately, when the protagonists (and the readers) in those early Harry Potter books enter the magical world of Hogwarts, the characters, events, families, and relationships take on depth and dimension. The difference between the Muggle and magical worlds is as striking as the difference between the black-and-white plains of Kansas and the technicolor world of Oz. Muggle football pales when compared with the pace and competition of Quidditch; no Muggle photograph can compete with the kinetic excitement of a magical picture; and any Muggle prison guard would seem positively benevolent compared to the terrifying Dementors of Azkaban. The contrast between the Muggle and magical worlds recalls Plato's allegory of the cave, in which the prisoners see only their pale shadows that the fire casts on the wall. Unable to turn around and see the objects themselves in the sunlight, the prisoners "in every way believe that the truth is nothing other than the shadows of those artifacts" (Plato, 1997, p. 1133). Similarly, Muggles remain unaware of the magical world all around them. As the Knight Bus conductor explains, "Them! ... Don' listen properly, do they? Don' look properly either. Never notice nuffink, they don'" (*Prisoner of Azkaban*, p. 36).[1]

This inability to recognize (or refusal to acknowledge) magic in the world is common in classic British children's fantasy literature. In C. S. Lewis' Narnian chronicles, Susan can no longer get into Narnia when she starts caring about "nylons and lipstick and invitations" (Lewis, 1956/1988, p. 128); in J. M. Barrie's *Peter Pan* (1911/1987), Wendy can no longer fly with Peter when the "real" world becomes more important than the magical world. The division between believers and non-believers highlights the disparity between the two worlds. In *Peter Pan*, the dull and one-dimensional world of the Darlings is juxtaposed with the gloriously exciting magical world of Neverland; in E. Nesbit's *The House of Arden* (1908/1958), the children leave their "ordinary life … where nothing particularly thrilling had ever happened" (p. 58) when they inherit a castle with a magical mole-like creature who sends them on all sorts of exciting time travels. In these and other British books of magic, it seems that a major purpose of the 'real' world is to show how much more real the magical world is: a place where all important events occur, a place where someone alienated and alone might find a home. As Cart (2001, p. 1546) suggests, this alternative world can offer "reassurance that magic could intrude into a recognizably 'real' world whose ugly vicissitudes might otherwise have been intolerable." The young Harry, like Peter Pan or James in *James and the Giant Peach*, yearns to escape the real world, because only in the world of magic does the vision of home and family take on any meaning or permanence.

Home and Family at Hogwarts

At Hogwarts, the notions of home and family are far more complex and multidimensional than in the 'real' world. Family connections and loyalties are bound not by birth and genetics, but by more enduring factors; the roles family members assume are determined less by age or gender than by actions and relationships forged among individuals.

When he first arrives at Hogwarts, Harry learns that he will join one of four houses. Says Professor McGonagall, "Your house will be something like your family within Hogwarts … each [with] its own noble history" (*Sorcerer's Stone*, p. 114). As the Sorting Hat explains, the members of each house share certain key personality traits and perspectives—Gryffindors are brave, Hufflepuffs loyal and hardworking, and so on. Hess and Handel (1994) write that a "family theme" characterizes the unique worldview of every family. At Hogwarts, members of each house, connected by common attributes that they bring to Hogwarts, as well as by the history of the house to which they belong, unite around their family theme,

> a pattern of feeling, motives, fantasies, and conventionalized understandings grouped about some locus of concern which has a particular form in the personalities of the individual members. The pattern comprises some fundamental view of reality and some way or ways of dealing with it. In the family themes are to be found the family's implicit direction, its notion of "who we are" and "what we do about it."
>
> (Hess and Handel, 1994, pp. 10–11)

While at first Harry's fellow Gryffindors comprise his only family at Hogwarts, over the course of the series, Harry becomes part of several groups that exhibit the qualities to which Hess and Handel refer. Most important to Harry is the triumvirate he forms with Ron and Hermione, a sort of mini-family unit within the extended family of Gryffindor. Their commitment to one another begins to emerge in the first book when Harry and Ron risk their lives to save Hermione from a troll, and then Hermione lies to Professor McGonagall to save Harry and Ron from punishment. Rowling writes (*Sorcerer's Stone*, p. 179), "There are some things you can't share without ending up liking each other, and knocking out a twelve-foot mountain troll is one of them"; but what is perhaps more significant about the encounter is that each of the three friends, in turn, recognizes each other's needs and sublimates his/her own immediate interests and needs in order to help that person. This is the essence of Noddings' (1992) notion of caring, in which an individual is "seized by the needs of another" (p. 16) and, for a time, becomes the carer.

This shared purpose and emphasis on caring characterizes the other groups of which Harry becomes a part throughout the series: the Weasley family, Dumbledore's Army, and the Order of the Phoenix. No matter what the danger, no matter what obligations may hinder them, each member can count on the others to provide the "protective factors" that Gilgun (1999) says are key to resilient families. Presumably, such relationships exist among other student groups as well, both in Gryffindor and in other houses. Moreover, we learn that years ago Sirius Black, Remus Lupin, Peter Pettigrew, and Harry's father James Potter enjoyed such a relationship until Peter betrayed the Potters. The three surviving members' strange encounter in the Shrieking Shack after years of separation (*Prisoner of Azkaban*), with each knowing the others so well, has the feel of a somewhat strained family reunion.

In moving from the Muggle to the magical world, Harry also moves emotionally from a place of isolation and loneliness to a sense of community and belonging. After one year at Hogwarts, Harry knows what home can mean, and back at the Dursleys for the summer holidays, he longs for it:

> He missed Hogwarts so much it was like having a constant stomach ache. He missed the castle, with its secret passageways and ghosts, his classes (though perhaps not Snape, the Potions master), the mail arriving by owl, eating banquets in the Great Hall, sleeping in his four-poster bed in the tower dormitory, visiting the gamekeeper, Hagrid, in his cabin next to the Forbidden Forest in the grounds, and, especially, Quidditch, the most popular sport in the wizarding world.
>
> (*Chamber of Secrets*, p. 3)

Clearly, home for Harry represents connection, shared meals, the bonding of a team sport, even a specific place within the Gryffindor quarters respected by others as his own individual, private space. For the first time in his life, Harry knows what it means to belong.

But Harry's sense of belonging does not mean that relationships at Hogwarts are entirely harmonious. In fact, Hogwarts is rife with disagreements, mistrust, and intrigue. While members within each house generally support one another and espouse similar worldviews, competition among houses fuels deceit, anger, and conflict. The world of Hogwarts recalls the classic sociological dichotomy of *Gemeinschaft* and *Gesellschaft* (Tönnies, 1887/1957). According to Tönnies, social entities can be characterized by two antithetical concepts, community and society. *Gemeinschaft* (community) consists of people bound together by physical proximity and intellectual affinity:[2]

> They speak together and think along similar lines.... There is understanding between people who love each other. Those who love and understand each other remain and dwell together and organize their common life. A mixed or complex form of common determinative will, which has become as natural as language itself and which consists of a multitude of feelings of understanding which are measured by its norm, we call concord (*Eintracht*) or family spirit.
>
> (p. 48)

In direct opposition to *Gemeinschaft* is the notion of *Gesellschaft* (society):

> In the *Gemeinschaft* [individuals] remain essentially united in spite of all separating factors, whereas in the *Gesellschaft* they are essentially separated in spite of all uniting factors.... Their spheres of activity and power are sharply separated, so that everybody refuses to everyone else contact with and admittance to his sphere; i.e., intrusions are regarded as hostile acts.
>
> (p. 65)

In the classic vision of *Gesellschaft*, the individual is essentially alone: there is no Gryffindor-type microcosm to support him or her. Harry occasionally feels that, even at Hogwarts, he is completely alone in a hostile world: in *Chamber of Secrets*, when his classmates believe that he has been attacking students; in *Goblet of Fire*, when even his closest friend believes that he secretly put his name into the goblet; in *Order of the Phoenix*, when virtually everybody doubts his claim that Voldemort has returned; and in *Deathly Hallows*, during which he is in hiding for most of the book and his very presence jeopardizes the safety of anyone with him. For the most part, though, the alienation that characterizes the *Gesellschaft* in the world of Hogwarts occurs among houses rather than within them. This estrangement is particularly disturbing because the teachers and the headmaster himself cultivate and encourage it.

From the day that students arrive at Hogwarts, they learn that competition among houses is a time-honored tradition, that at the end of each year the house with the most points will win the house cup. Rather than merely motivating students to do their very best in school, these "family feuds" undermine any chance of camaraderie among houses and intensify their antipathy toward one another. Thus, for example, to an outsider, members of Slytherin are not merely cunning, they are devious; rather than respecting Hufflepuffs for their stolid dependability, "everyone says Hufflepuff are a lot o' duffers" (*Sorcerer's Stone*, p. 80). The secret location of each house's common room and sleeping quarters fosters a sense of security and community among house members, but it also magnifies the houses' sense of separateness from one another: they are sanctuaries in an otherwise perilous environment.

The most troubling instance in which competition undermines community and cooperation is the Triwizard Tournament (*Goblet of Fire*), in which one champion from each of three wizarding schools competes (although, as it turns out, Hogwarts fields two champions: Harry from Gryffindor and Cedric Diggory from Hufflepuff). Headmaster Dumbledore explains that a major purpose of this tournament is to foster goodwill among the different schools; but instead of encouraging communication, the competition merely feeds animosity and mistrust among the students from each school. In fact, as Professor Moody tells Harry (*Goblet of Fire*, p. 343), "Cheating's a traditional part of the Triwizard Tournament and always has been." Worse still is the way Harry and Cedric are pitted against each other. Amazingly, the two of them actually manage to transcend the competitive atmosphere and help one another solve clues to accomplish the required tasks. In an exhilarating moment of friendship and cooperation, the two decide to grasp the Triwizard Cup simultaneously and share the victory. The immediate result of this rare instance of inter-house cooperation is that Cedric is murdered, suggesting the disquieting notion that there is little value in working together to extend one's family beyond its usual boundaries. And while the competition in Hogwarts causes alienation, conflict, and dissolution of potential understanding within the Hogwarts community, Rowling, like her characters, never questions or challenges this aspect of community interaction throughout Books 1–4, but rather accepts it as an integral part of life. Nor does Rowling ever seriously entertain the possibility of British wizards collaborating with other wizarding communities around the world. A Department of International Magical Cooperation supposedly exists at the Ministry of Magic, but that department is run by incompetent, ineffectual, and ultimately untrustworthy wizards. In Book 5, Charlie Weasley is in Romania making contacts for the Order of the Phoenix because "Dumbledore wants as many foreign wizards brought in as possible" (*Order of the Phoenix*, p. 70), but this indication of magical cooperation on a global scale to fight the Death Eaters never comes up again.

The Family Covenant

In spite of her uncritical acceptance of destructive competition among houses, Rowling offers a compelling vision of the vital role that home and family play in the lives of young people coming of age. In the early books, Harry's growing bond with Hermione and Ron, as well as his membership in the *Gemeinschaft* of Gryffindor, allows him to break away physically and emotionally from the prison of the Dursley household. From the day the Dursleys grudgingly take Harry into their home, they abuse him, lie to him, and ignore his needs: they deny him those essential protective factors that caring family members provide one another. Leibowitz (1978) writes that family memberships are defined by publicly acknowledged contractual agreements, usually marriage contracts and the like. But for Rowling, the contract that holds a family together involves much more than a legal obligation; it is an inviolable covenant among family members to provide care and support for one another, whatever the cost. In breaking that covenant, the Dursleys relinquish any right to Harry's loyalty, and compel him to seek home and family elsewhere.

When family members in Rowling's magical world break this covenant, the consequences are serious and potentially permanent. After Dolores Umbridge becomes Hogwarts High Inquisitor in Book 5, she breaks the Hogwarts family covenant by turning the school from a refuge into a repressive regime. That action—and her refusal to teach her students how to defend themselves—gives her students the right to resist Umbridge's authority and form Dumbledore's Army. Peter Pettigrew betrayed the trust of his friends James and Sirius, causing the deaths of James and Lily Potter and Sirius' unjust imprisonment, and, in so doing, doomed himself to enslavement to Voldemort. Mr. Crouch "should have spent a bit more time at home with his family, shouldn't he? Ought to have left the office early once in a while … gotten to know his own son" (*Goblet of Fire*, p. 528). Instead, when the young Crouch got in trouble with the Ministry of Magic, the elder Crouch put personal ambition over the welfare of his own son and sent him to Azkaban. Because Crouch failed to respect the family covenant, his family is destroyed, and his son leaves home to find a new family—with Voldemort serving as surrogate father: "I will be his dearest, his closest supporter … closer than a son" (*Goblet of Fire*, p. 678).

Voldemort's descent into evil, like Crouch's, provides an object lesson in the destructive consequences of a father's (and grandfather's) broken covenant with his family. Voldemort's father abandons his pregnant wife before Voldemort's birth, thus consigning him to a lonely childhood in an orphanage when his mother dies in childbirth, and neither his father nor his father's parents want anything to do with him when he later seeks them out. In light of his Muggle father's desertion and his paternal family's rejection of him, Voldemort's hatred of Muggles and murderous obsession with the purity of wizard families is not surprising—nor is the fact that, like the younger Crouch, Voldemort later kills his father and both his grandparents, then seeks a new family in the Death Eaters, united in their concern about wizard bloodlines, to whom he refers as "my *true* family" (*Goblet of Fire*, p. 646).

Fortunately, Rowling furnishes us with numerous examples of parents and guardians who have provided the support their children needed. The Weasley family may get caught up in frequent family squabbles, but when the children need help, they can count on parents and siblings alike to be there. (Even Percy, the Weasley son whose pride and ambition leads him to support the Ministry and its increasingly harmful response to Voldemort's rise to power, returns to the family in its time of greatest need (*Deathly Hallows*).) In a very different family, Harry's huge friend Hagrid, the product of a giantess mother and wizard father, has overcome his mother's desertion and the consequent break-up of his family, thanks to the steadfast support of his diminutive father. And in the later books, Hagrid shows he understands the importance of family covenants by bringing his half-brother Grawp into his home and nurturing him as if he were his own son. Even the despicable Narcissa Malfoy places the safety of her son Draco above all else (including her loyalty to Voldemort), lying to Voldemort about Harry because doing so will make it possible for her to find and protect her son (*Deathly Hallows*, p. 726).

Harry himself has benefited from the support of parents and loved ones. Unbeknownst to Harry, Dumbledore's magic has protected him from Voldemort throughout his life at the Dursleys. Sirius Black, after his escape from Azkaban, risks recapture in order to help Harry, thereby "fulfilling [his] duty as a godfather" (*Goblet of Fire*, p. 522). And Harry's parents even reach from beyond the grave to give him the advice and protection he needs to survive his confrontations with Voldemort and the Death Eaters in *Goblet of Fire* and *Deathly Hallows*. When he first holds the Invisibility Cloak, he thinks: "His father's ... this had been his father's. He let the material flow over his hands, smoother than silk, light as air" (*Sorcerer's Stone*, p. 205). And the first time he uses the Cloak, he stumbles upon the Mirror of Erised and sees his dead mother and father waving and smiling at him: "Harry was looking at his family, for the first time in his life" (*Sorcerer's Stone*, p. 209). Three years later, when he has been forcibly transported hundreds of miles away (*Goblet of Fire*), his parents' images emerge from Voldemort's wand and guide him back to the safety of Hogwarts.

Constant reminders of his heritage—the fact that he has his mother's eyes, or his father's athletic skills—from the Hogwarts community give Harry insight into the parents he never knew, while reinforcing his connection to them and the covenant they share. "Your father would have been proud. He was an excellent Quidditch player himself"(*Sorcerer's Stone*, p. 152), Professor McGonagall tells Harry when she picks him to be Seeker for Gryffindor. Later, Hagrid gives him an album full of wizard photographs of his parents, "smiling and waving at him from every page" (*Sorcerer's Stone*, p. 304). Perhaps most important for Harry is the protection that his mother gave him just before Voldemort killed her. The scar on his forehead serves as an emblem not only of Voldemort's failure to kill him, but also of his mother's love, which saved him from Voldemort's death curse. As Dumbledore tells Harry, "If there is one thing Voldemort cannot understand, it is love ... to have been loved so deeply, even though the person who loved us is gone, will give us some protection forever" (*Sorcerer's Stone*, p. 299).

To Harry, then, the family covenant is absolute and sacrosanct. When Lupin leaves his pregnant wife, Tonks, to join the fight against the Death Eaters, Harry attacks him with a vengeance. "So you're just going to dump her and the kid and run off with us?" he asks viciously. The idea that Lupin could abandon his family, just as Crouch's and Voldemort's fathers did, is an unforgivable sin: "Parents ... shouldn't leave their kids—unless they've got to" (*Deathly Hallows*, p. 215). Tom Riddle lives according to no such covenant. The product of a union based on deception rather than love, deprived of the protective factors imbued in Harry during the first year of his life and reinforced over time, Tom would never be able to associate home and family with the kind of love that Harry found after leaving the Dursleys.

Tom does become part of a family, as Harry does years later, when he arrives at Hogwarts, "his first real home, the place that meant he was special; it meant everything to him" (*Deathly Hallows*, p. 289). But there are key differences between the communities that Voldemort and Harry each create. Compare, for example, the two groups surrounding their leaders, at the climax of the series in *Deathly Hollows*. As the news of Harry's return to Hogwarts spreads, his supporters come from all over England to rally around him. Neville declares, "We're [Dumbledore's Army]. We were all in it together ... everyone in here's proven they're loyal to Dumbledore—loyal to you [...] Let us help!" (*Deathly Hallows*, pp. 580, 582). The intersecting, overlapping, and expanding circles of family that surround Harry—the Ron, Hermione, and Harry triumvirate, Dumbledore's Army, the Order of the Phoenix, the Hogwarts community—all share a spirit of caring for one another, the hallmark of Tönnies' *Gemeinschaft*. This bond connects them even when they disagree, and even when Harry is unaware of their support (such as the ongoing student resistance at Hogwarts and the broadcast of "Potterwatch" taking place while he is in hiding in *Deathly Hallows*). Even the dead, who sustain Harry as he walks toward his own death, ensure that he is never alone.

This kind of support differs markedly from the Death Eaters' loyalty to Voldemort. Like the members of the Order of the Phoenix, the Death Eaters rush to join their leader, but only out of fear of what violent consequences may result if they don't respond when called by the Dark Mark—itself a violent act, burned on their skin. Voldemort's chosen "family," responsive only to his orders, reflects the separation and alienation of Tönnies' *Gesellschaft*:

Some of them were masked and hooded; others showed their faces. Two giants sat on the outskirts of the group, casting massive shadows over the scene, their faces cruel, rough-hewn like rock. Harry saw Fenrir, skulking, chewing his long nails; the great blond Rowle was dabbing at his bleeding lip. He saw Lucius Malfoy, who looked defeated and terrified, and Narcissa, whose eyes were sunken and full of apprehension.

(*Deathly Hallows*, p. 702)

Even when they are together, bound by a common purpose, Voldemort and the members of his family are isolated in their own private spheres—watchful, afraid, and alone.

From Comedy to Quest: Leaving Home to Find Home

The protective factors that a family offers its members are key to holding that family together and supporting its young people when they head off on their own. In the Harry Potter series, we see not only what can happen when the family breaks this covenant, but also how home and family can sustain young adults trying to find their place in the world.

The scar on Harry's forehead reminds us of his mother's love; but at the same time it acts as a brand, forever marking Harry as different from the rest of the students, so that despite his growing sense of connection at Hogwarts, he remains an outsider. When Hogwarts residents are mysteriously attacked (*Chamber of Secrets*), many of the students suspect Harry, and he experiences once again the feeling of alienation that dominated his years with the Dursleys. Even when he is representing Hogwarts in the Triwizard Tournament, he feels "as separate from the crowd as though they were a different species" (*Goblet of Fire*, p. 349). The Invisibility Cloak, which he dons to go places that have been forbidden to him, epitomizes this sense of isolation.

This idea of being an outsider in your own home appears repeatedly in both contemporary and classic young adult coming-of-age literature. In Nancy Farmer's *A Girl Named Disaster* (1996), Nhamo feels like she doesn't belong in the home she has shared with her relatives ever since her father had run away and her mother had been killed by a leopard. "The [women] sat comfortably together, like kernels on a mealie cob. There was no space where Nhamo might fit herself in, so she waited patiently in the doorway" (Farmer, 1996, p. 13). Similarly, in Monica Hughes' *The Keeper of the Isis Light* (1981), 16-year-old Olwen Pendennis has lived alone on the planet Isis all her life with a robot Guardian. But when settlers from Earth come, she learns that the Guardian has genetically altered her to keep her alive in the Isis atmosphere. The settlers are repulsed by her lizard-like skin, and she becomes an alien in her own home.

This sense of alienation eventually gives these characters, including Harry, the resolve to leave what had been familiar and seemingly safe, and embark on their journey of self-discovery. Harry still seeks the family that he lost when he was an infant (he even plays the position of "Seeker" on the

Gryffindor Quidditch team), and he gets closer to that goal only when he leaves behind the protection of his Hogwarts family.

Harry's role as outsider becomes even more central beginning in Book 5, when the established order of Rowling's two parallel worlds abruptly disintegrates: Dementors, hitherto confined to the magical world, inexplicably appear on Privet Drive and attack Harry's Muggle cousin Dudley. Suddenly and without warning, we have left the comfort of the British magical novel, where the reader can always count on returning from exciting, even terrifying, adventures to the mundane calm of the ordinary world. As Rowling explains,

> The arrival of the Dementors in Little Whinging seemed to have caused a breach in the great, invisible wall that divided the relentlessly non-magical world of Privet Drive and the world beyond. Harry's two lives had somehow become fused and everything had been turned upside down.
>
> (*Order of the Phoenix*, p. 37)

The Dementors' terrifying foray into a Muggle neighborhood spreading icy despair over its inhabitants is reminiscent of Tolkien's (1954/1974) Black Riders' first appearance in Hobbiton. Up until their arrival, the hobbits we grew to love in *The Hobbit, or, There and Back Again* (Tolkien, 1937/1987) could expect to live simple, ordinary lives, untouched by events or strangers from the world beyond their borders. With the weakening of safeguards provided by powerful protectors in the outside world, the "ordinary" heroes of tales like *Lord of the Rings* (Tolkien, 1954/1974) or *His Dark Materials* (Pullman's epic trilogy comprising *The Golden Compass* (1996), *The Subtle Knife* (1997), and *The Amber Spyglass* (2000)) are drawn, willing or not, into a struggle against forces of evil spreading into places that had once seemed safe—that is to say, into the very sanctuary of home.

The shift in the established order that begins in Book 5 mirrors a restructuring of family dynamics, as previously type-cast characters take on new dimensions. Ginny Weasley emerges as a strong, independent, popular girl quite capable of acting on her own, even spearheading the secret resistance to Voldemort when, in the final book, Hogwarts is taken over by the Death Eaters. Percy Weasley moves from privileged position of honored son, held up by his parents as an example to the others, to a "ministry-loving, family-disowning, power-hungry moron" (*Deathly Hallows*, p. 606) at the Ministry of Magic (although he eventually sees the error in his ways). At the same time, the "smart-ass" twins who seemed like they would never amount to anything become, first, savvy businessmen, and, later, powerful resistance fighters whose frivolous inventions become essential weapons against the dark forces. Hermione—whose own Muggle parents are presented as caring and supportive, though never an active part of the tale—becomes the de facto parent when she arranges a new life for them in Australia. In an ultimate gesture of self-sacrifice of a parent for a child, she erases all memories of herself from their minds, to keep them safe. And even Harry's Aunt Petunia, upon learning that the evil forces that killed her sister Lily now threaten her son, takes over the role of decision-making head of family from Uncle Vernon—with the encouragement of a Howler reminding her of her unwilling connection to the magical world (*Order of the Phoenix*, p. 40). Through her actions, Harry realizes that Petunia is more connected to the magical world than he had previously thought: "All of a sudden for the very first time in his life, Harry fully appreciated that Aunt Petunia was his mother's sister" (*Order of the Phoenix*, p. 38)—and even the Howler indicates that there is more to Petunia than the slapstick character offered in the first four books.

In fact, what was once simply comic material for Rowling often becomes weighted with dark portent in the last three books. The hands of the enchanted clock that Mrs. Weasley watched to keep track of her family now point permanently to "Mortal Peril" (*Half-Blood Prince*, p. 85). The twins still joke all the time, but it is black humor; and in the last book the always-cheerful Fred dies in battle, "the ghost of his last laugh still etched upon his face" (*Deathly Hallows*, p. 637). The sweaters that Mrs. Weasley knits each Christmas, a source of humor in the first four books, become instead symbols of home and loving family connections. And Mrs. Weasley herself emerges as a fierce protector (in addition to loving caretaker), rather than the stereotypical bemused (albeit magical) housewife of the first four books, ultimately dueling Bellatrix Lestrange to the death when Bellatrix threatens her daughter (*Deathly Hallows*, p. 736).

Hogwarts is not immune to this shift in the established order of Harry Potter's world. After the evil Professor Umbridge takes over as Head of Hogwarts in *Order of the Phoenix*, school becomes increasingly less relevant, and certainly less safe. Hogwarts no longer provides the nurture and protection the students feel they need in an increasingly dangerous world, so the children take both their education and their defense upon themselves, creating Dumbledore's Army. In *Half-Blood Prince*, with Dumbledore greatly weakened and frequently absent, the Death Eaters breach Hogwarts' hitherto impregnable defenses; and by the final book, with Snape at the helm and the Death Eaters in charge, Hogwarts has become perilous for all but supporters of Voldemort.

The gradual collapse of the stability and structure of Hogwarts, upon which Harry and other students depended, generates widespread fear and discomfort; but at the same time it also leads to an unexpected—and exhilarating—coalescing of new family units. To resist the powers of evil and establish Dumbledore's Army, the students have no choice but to break down the traditional divisions among three of the four Hogwarts houses (Slytherin still supports Umbridge and the dark forces she represents), to put aside their differences and unite according to the shared goal of defeating Voldemort. With students motivated by this newfound "family spirit" (Tönnies, 1887/1957, p. 48), the competition, enmity, and alienation that ordinarily characterized the *Gesellschaft* of Hogwarts inter-house relationships gives way to a sense of community never before seen at the school.

In spite of this evolving *Gemeinschaft* among Hogwarts houses, Harry's alienation from those he loves steadily increases over the course of the final three books. As he learns of the prophecy that it must be he who kills Voldemort (*Order of the Phoenix*), he leaves Hogwarts in search of the Horcruxes (*Half-Blood Prince*), and becomes ever more in tune with Voldemort's thoughts and actions (*Deathly Hallows*), Harry—like Frodo in *Lord of the Rings* (Tolkien, 1954/1974) and Lyra in *His Dark Materials* (Pullman, 1996, 1997, 2000)—is drawn into events much greater than himself. The only way to return home is across Rochman's "necessary abyss," a tortuous path that leads him into ever greater danger; and along this journey, many of the places that he associates most closely with home turn out to be the most dangerous of all. The disastrous trip to Godric's Hollow, the village where he lived as a baby with his mother and father, results not only in a horrifying encounter with Voldemort and his snake, but also in the destruction of his wand. He does find occasional refuges, but often, ironically, in unlikely places: The "gloomy and oppressive" Grimmauld Place, for example, where he, Ron, and Hermione set up housekeeping, for a brief period becomes "their one safe refuge: even ... a kind of home" (*Deathly Hallows*, p. 271).

Eventually, of course, the quest leads him back home to Hogwarts, "the first and best home he had known" (*Deathly Hallows*, p. 697). But, as with Godric's Hollow, this home is not the same one that Harry left. "Your time's up," says one of the Death Eaters to Professor McGonagall. "It's us what's in charge here now, and you'll back me up or you'll pay the price" (*Deathly Hallows*, p. 597). His insolence to the venerable professor vividly reminds us of the ruffians' takeover of the hobbits' beloved Shire, or Toad Hall in *The Wind and the Willows* (1908/1961) overrun by weasels and stoats: the safety and sanctuary that Hogwarts once provided for Harry exists no longer. Happily, just as in *Lord of the Rings*, this common enemy has engendered a new, united, and more powerful community, without which Harry's victory over Voldemort would be impossible: "All were jumbled together, teachers and pupils, ghosts and parents, centaurs and house-elves, and Firenze lay recovering in a corner, and Grawp peered in through a smashed window" (*Deathly Hallows*, p. 745).

The allies' victory, ironically, also brings about the demise of their alliance. Nineteen years later, the barrier dividing the "real" and the magical worlds—epitomized by the invisible barrier separating platform nine and three-quarters from the rest of King's Cross station—is firmly back in place. As once again wizarding families send their children off to school, Harry's son frets that he won't get into Gryffindor; Malfoy and Harry don't talk to each other; and Ron encourages his daughter to "beat [Malfoy's son] in every test" (*Deathly Hallows*, p. 756). Without the common enemy to unite the houses, the camaraderie that reached its zenith at the Battle of Hogwarts has disappeared. Enmity among the houses has become once again an accepted part of life, and even though Harry saved Malfoy's life more than once, and Malfoy's mother saved Harry's life, there is no friendship between the two men, only an uneasy truce.

But at least there is a truce, with the hint of possible community among the houses suggested by Harry's choice of names (Albus Severus) for his younger son. Light-hearted humor abounds once again, the concept of pure bloodlines reduced to a casual joke—"Granddad Weasley would never forgive you if you married a pure-blood" (*Deathly Hallows*, p. 756)—and most of the conversation on the station platform revolves around love: Teddy caught "snogging" Victoire, Ginny sending her love to Neville Longbottom (now a Hogwarts professor), the final kisses of a family parting, but only temporarily. With his defeat of Voldemort, Harry truly has found home again—not the disordered, tumultuous, unpredictable community that enveloped and nearly smothered him after he killed Voldemort ("Harry could not hear a word that anyone was shouting, nor tell whose hands were seizing him, pulling him, trying to hug some part of him, hundreds of them pressing in" (*Deathly Hallows*, p. 744)), but the safe, predictable, loving unit that he had been seeking ever since his parents died.

Harry's solitary search for his true family is a search for his own identity; his quest for home and family is the journey all young people take trying to find their place in the world. They can move, as Harry does, "from innocence (and ignorance) to the truth about themselves and the world" (Rochman, 1993, p. 32) only by breaking free of home and creating their own. In Rodman Philbrick's *The Last Book in the Universe* (2000), Spaz leaves what is to him familiar and relatively safe to go to his sick sister, who represents all he has ever known of love or family connection. It is a terrifying journey through alien territory, but he undertakes it out of love and ultimately finds hope for a new and better home. Similarly, in Cynthia Voigt's *A Solitary Blue* (1983), Jeff leaves the emotionless home he shares with his father in search of the home where he feels "wrapped in love" (p. 40) by his mother. But when her promises prove false, he realizes what his father has provided—a safe haven from the destructive manipulation of his mother—and returns to make a better home with his father. There are no set formulas for finding home; like Harry, the characters in these and countless other coming-of-age books—and the young people reading them—must find their own way. Although they frequently feel isolated and alone, both Spaz and Jeff, like Harry, find help and support along the way.

Without the protective factors that the infant Harry received from his parents, he might have turned out more like Tom Riddle, loveless and cruel;

he might not have become the center of the ever-expanding spheres of "family" that encircled him; he might not have learned he needed first to make a home in Hogwarts and then to break away, "to go the long way around, to stray and separate in the hope of finding completeness in reunion, freedom in reintegration with those left behind" (Giamatti, 1989, p. 93). In the end, Harry finds that completeness in the distillation of all his family circles into one small, close-knit community. After all, Harry only ever wanted to be ordinary: he easily rejects the opportunities for power and control that the Elder Wand offers him, telling Ron and Hermione, "I've had enough trouble for a lifetime" (*Deathly Hallows*, p. 749). And while he will always bear the scar, it no longer hurts and it no longer identifies him as an outsider; it simply identifies him, and reminds him of the importance of home. In the end, he gets exactly what he wanted.

Notes

1. Of course, Muggle ignorance regarding the magical world is not entirely a result of Muggle obtuseness. The magical world has established a complex bureaucracy to ensure that Muggles do not learn about the existence of witches and wizards. Like the prisoners in Plato's cave, their Muggle heads are kept pointing away from the light.
2. In addition to the importance of neighborhood and friendship, Tönnies' *Gemeinschaft* also involves "closeness of blood relationship" (1887/1957, p. 48) among some adults and their children. At Hogwarts, blood connections often exist within communities (parents and siblings usually belonging to the same house), but, for the most part, *Gemeinschaft* at Hogwarts is defined more by physical and intellectual proximity—and a shared worldview—than by blood relationships. As Dumbledore explains in *Chamber of Secrets*, the Sorting Hat placed Harry in Gryffindor because Harry asked it not to put him in Slytherin. "It is our choices, Harry, that show us what we truly are" (*Chamber of Secrets*, p. 333), he tells Harry.

References

Barrie, J. M. (1987). *Peter Pan*. New York: Henry Holt and Co. (Original work published 1911.)

Cart, M. (2001). Fantasy is flourishing. *Booklist, 97*(16), 1546.

Dahl, R. (1988). *James and the giant peach*. New York: Puffin Books. (Original work published 1961.)

Farmer, N. (1996). *A girl named disaster*. New York: Orchard Books.

Giamatti, A. B. (1989). *Take time for paradise: Americans and their games*. New York: Summit Books.

Gilgun, J. F. (1999). Mapping resilience as process among adults with childhood adversities. In H. I. McCubbin, E. A. Thompson, A. I. Thompson, & J. A. Futrell (eds.), *The dynamics of resilient families* (pp. 41–70). Thousand Oaks, CA: Sage Publications.

Graham, K. (1961). *The wind in the willows*. New York: Scribner. (Original work published 1908.)

Handel, G. (1994). Introduction to the first edition, 1967. In G. Handel & G. G. Whitchurch (eds.), *The psychosocial interior of the family* (pp. xxiii–xxx). New York: Aldine de Gruyter.

Hess, R. D., & Handel, G. (1994). The family as a psychosocial organization. In G. Handel & G. G. Whitchurch (eds.), *The psychosocial interior of the family* (pp. 3–17). New York: Aldine de Gruyter.

Hughes, M. (1981). *The keeper of the Isis light*. New York: Atheneum.

Leibowitz, L. (1978). *Females, males, families: A biosocial approach*. Belmont, CA: Wadsworth Publishing.

Lewis, C. S. (1988). *The last battle*. London: Lions. (Original work published 1956.)

Nesbit, E. (1958). *The house of Arden*. London: Ernest Benn, Ltd. (Original work published 1908.)

Noddings, N. (1992). *The challenge to care in schools*. New York: Teachers College Press.

Philbrick, R. (2000). *The last book in the universe.* New York: Blue Sky Press.

Plato (1997). *Complete works* (J. M. Cooper, ed.). Indianapolis, IN: Hackett Publishing.

Pullman, P. (1996). *The golden compass.* New York: Alfred A. Knopf.

Pullman, P. (1997). *The subtle knife.* New York: Alfred A. Knopf.

Pullman, P. (2000). *The amber spyglass.* New York: Alfred A. Knopf.

Rochman, H. (1993). *Against borders: Promoting books for a multicultural world.* Chicago, IL: American Library Association.

Rochman, H., & McCampbell, D. Z. (1997). Introduction. In H. Rochman & D. Z. McCampbell (eds.), *Leaving home: Stories* (p. vii). New York: HarperCollins.

Rowling, J. K. (1997). *Harry Potter and the sorcerer's stone.* New York: Scholastic Press.

Rowling, J. K. (1998). *Harry Potter and the chamber of secrets.* New York: Scholastic Press.

Rowling, J. K. (1999). *Harry Potter and the prisoner of Azkaban.* New York: Scholastic Press.

Rowling, J. K. (2000). *Harry Potter and the goblet of fire.* New York: Scholastic Press.

Rowling, J. K. (2003). *Harry Potter and the order of the phoenix.* New York: Scholastic Press.

Rowling, J. K. (2005). *Harry Potter and the half-blood prince.* New York: Scholastic Press.

Rowling, J. K. (2007). *Harry Potter and the deathly hallows.* New York: Scholastic Press.

Steinberg, S. R., & Kincheloe, J. L. (1998). Privileged and getting away with it: The cultural studies of white, middle-class youth. *Studies in the literary imagination, 31*(1), 103–126.

Tolkien, J. R. R. (1974). *The lord of the rings.* Boston, MA: Houghton Mifflin. (Original work published 1954)

Tolkien, J. R. R. (1987). *The hobbit, or, there and back again.* Boston, MA: Houghton Mifflin. (Original work published 1937.)

Tönnies, F. (1957). *Community and society (Gemeinschaft und Gesellschaft)* (C. P. Loomis, trans. & ed.). East Lansing, MI: Michigan State University Press. (Original work published 1887.)

Voigt, C. (1983). *A solitary blue.* New York: Atheneum.

Chapter Eight

From Sexist to (sort-of) Feminist *Representations of Gender in the Harry Potter Series*

ELIZABETH E. HEILMAN AND TREVOR DONALDSON

In this chapter, we consider gender representation in the Harry Potter series and examine specific books and characters. Elizabeth is a woman in her forties and Trevor a man in his twenties: we have very different life experiences and ways of approaching the texts, and yet our analyses are similar—the Harry Potter books, like many popular books for children, mostly reinforce gender stereotypes. Many children yearn to be lost in literary worlds where they can experience adventure, heroics and power, and that means that girls read a lot of books with boys as the hero, such as Pony Boy in *The Outsiders*, and Sam Gribley in *My Side of the Mountain*. When boys and girls adventure together, boys usually have more fun. For example, in the *Box Car Children* series, older brother Henry is having the lion share of adventures, while the younger sisters cook and clean, typical of the kind of text that irritates my children. Even *Winnie the Pooh* is dominated by male characters. Pooh, Tigger, Christopher Robin, Owl, Piglet, Eeyore are all male. The only female is Kanga, the mother of the little boy animal, Roo.

Reading the first Harry Potter book with her son, Elizabeth really hated the way Hermione cowered in fear when faced with the troll, and was disappointed that she had to be rescued by the boys. While Ron and Harry successfully and bravely faced a horrible 12-foot tall troll (*Sorcerer's Stone*, pp. 174–176), Hermione couldn't move and had sunk to the floor in fright. Scenes like this, together with the absence of powerful females, were disappointing. As she read through the first four books, it was clear that the Harry Potter books featured females in secondary positions of power and authority and replicated some of the most familiar cultural stereotypes for both males and females. This was the focus of Elizabeth's chapter in the first edition of this book.

But, as it turns out, Harry Potter is a long and complex series with much going on and with multiple, contradictory, and even transgressive representations of gender. Yet, as we will detail, while the last three books showcase richer roles and more powerful females, we find that women are still marginalized, stereotyped, and even mocked. The overall message related to power and gender still conforms to the stereotypical, hackneyed, and sexist patterns of the first four books, which reflect rather than challenge the worst elements of patriarchy.

Why Gender Critique Matters

Is consideration about sexism important, since the books are fun to read and have a lot to recommend them? We think so. Gender representations, like other forms of cultural ideology, both obscure and justify oppressive practices even though interpretations of the meaning of gender can be dynamic and multiple (Connell, 1987, 1991, 1993, 1995; Messner, 1997; Pyke, 1996). Gender representations are personal ways to understand ourselves, others, and society but they are also impersonal reflections of macro-level power relations (Bourdieu, 1977; Chafetz, 1990; Connell, 1996; Foucault, 1980; Lipman-Blumen, 1984). Though both feminist and poststructuralist theories tell us that texts can be read from multiple, contradictory, and even transgressive positions, it is still important for criticism to reveal dominant and hegemonic conventions. Though any one gender stereotype would not be significant, repeated and varied examples of demeaning stereotypes are very significant. In addition, these gender ideologies are especially powerful because the books are pleasurable and popular. Part of the pleasure comes from the "comfort" of the stereotypes and the recognizable character types and situations.

How do these ideologies work? Influence, art, and interpretation lies with the reader rather than the author and text. Sumara (1993/1999) points out that:

> The way in which we come to know ourselves in the literary work is not embedded in the work, but rather emerges from our own interaction with the work. It is in this interactive process, manifested in the feeling of being lost, that the reader of the novel is sometimes able to find feelings, ideas, possible worlds thats/he did not have prior to the reading.
>
> (p. 293)

The most compelling ideology comes in the form of the more subtly suggestive and pleasurable reading. Barthes (1976) describes two types of literary pleasure, *plaisir* and *jouissance*. A reader feels *plaisir* when familiar cultural and ideological situations are mirrored in literature. Readers overwhelmingly describe the Potter books as pleasurable works in which the young reader can readily be lost. In the Potter books, character types and the hierarchies of class, culture, and gender are very much the same as those in other popular books and movies and in real life situations. The type of pleasure called *jouissance*, in contrast, "unsettles the reader, jarring him out of cultural assumptions, bringing her to the brink of the abyss" (Tobin, 1988, p. 213). If this occurs, it seems more likely to be inspired by details of fantasy and by the implicit critique technology described by Sheltrown in this volume. Thus, the Potter books are ideologically conservative, read for *plaisir*, but to some readers could be innovative in plot complexity, language use, or in the visual, technological, and magical detail. Yet, even the more creative and original components do not seem *unsettling*. As Susan Sontag (1990) has asserted, "real art makes us nervous" (p. 8).

All books present ideology and authors do so with different levels of intention.

Sutherland (1985) classifies ideology in children's literature as the politics of assent (which reflects and reinscribes societal norms), the politics of advocacy, and the politics of attack. Ideology is invisible in books focusing on "assent," whereas books featuring the politics of advocacy and attack either promote or denounce particular socio-cultural practices. Yet, this seems too simplistic. In the Harry Potter books, all three occur. The Harry Potter series reflects and reinscribes societal norms; some passages advocate norms and others attack norms. Furthermore, Hollindale's (1988) observations that ideology in children's literature is not "a political policy ... it is a climate of belief" (p. 19) seems more accurate for the Harry Potter books. Below we detail this climate of belief and consider in particular, representation, roles, relationships, masculinity, and mothers.

Gender by the Numbers

In order to reveal dominant conventions, feminist theories of children's literature have pursued multiple levels of analysis, beginning with female representation in literature. How much narrative space is devoted to males? Like *Winnie the Pooh*, the Harry Potter books are dominated by male characters. Among the students named in the first four books, there are 29 girls and 35 boys. By the end of the series, based on the list at Wikipedia and counted by Ellen Ott for this chapter, among characters with some role (as opposed to characters mentioned in passing or historically without developing the plot) there are 115 females to 201 males mentioned in the series as a whole. Further, the more important characters are predominantly male. The main characters are two boys, Harry Potter and Ron Weasley, and a girl, Hermione Granger. The characters, that are frightening, evil, or suspected of evil, are overwhelmingly male in the first four books and primarily male in the later books. These include Voldemort, Draco, Wormtail (Peter Pettigrew), and Severus Snape. In the first four books, those described as Death Eaters, the evil wizards who followed Voldemort, include a married couple, Mr. and

Mrs. Lestrange, and 16 males. Within the first four books, the Ministry of Magic, the seat of power, all of the ministers are male except for Bertha Jorkins, who is described as gossipy and absent minded. Most of the irritating (but not evil) grown-ups are female. These include Mrs. Figg, Professor Trelawney, Rita Skeeter, and Aunt Petunia, who has twice the neck of the usual person, which comes in handy when she is craning her neck over fences for gossip.

The girls on the Quidditch team provide another example of how token inclusion reinforces inequality. Though the girls often score in the earlier books, their scoring rarely wins the game. It is ultimately unimportant. Catching the Snitch wins the game and the Seekers that do this are male. In order to find the Snitch, Cho Chang trails Harry instead of going after it for herself (*Prisoner of Azkaban*, p. 261). The girls are not involved in the most complex moments of play and never play dirty or get badly hurt. Feminist researchers in physical education (Flintoff, 1994; Hasbrook, 1999; Scraton, 1990) have observed that male students and teachers consider competitive sports to be a "naturally male" activity. This concept of naturally competitive males is reinforced by the fact that the captains are male, and their hard, rugged names, Flint and Wood, emphasize their masculinity.

In the *Order of the Phoenix*, however, a startling number of new female characters are introduced and others are newly developed. The expansion is so extreme that it reads as a willful attempt at gender inclusion. Rowling adds numerous female characters into the history of this world and into the present action, and she expands many of the existing girls' and women's roles. This includes the first examples of female villains, such as Bellatrix Lestrange, a Death Eater, who breaks out of Azkaban. Newly introduced is the Order itself as an organized form of power distinctive from the Ministry of Magic and Rowling populates it with women. Harry picks up a photograph of the original Order of the Phoenix in which "those hidden right at the back appeared at the forefront of the picture" (p. 174). This seems like an apt metaphor for the transformation of gender presentation in this book. We find out that prior to Fudge, Millicent Bagnol was Minister of Magic and that Emmeline Vance and Marlene McKinnon were in the Order of the Phoenix. Nymphadora, a.k.a. Tonks, a fighter, and an Auror, is a current member, introduced as a powerful witch amongst the group entrusted with escorting Harry away from the Dursleys. Newly mentioned in the Ministry are Mafalda Hopkirk who works for the *Improper Use of Magic* office, Amelia Susan Bones as Head of the Department of Magical Law Enforcement and interrogator for Harry's trial and many more women in the Ministry who will be detailed later. Amongst the students, Pansy Parkinson, Padma Patil, and Hannah Abbot and are elevated to prefect, and Angelina Johnson expands her role to become captain of the Gryffindor Quidditch team. Ginny is suddenly a sub-stantial person, and George says in reference to her Bat-Bogey Hexes, "size is no guarantor of power" (p. 100). Luna "Loony" Lovegood is introduced as an eccentric but not unimportant collaborator for the good guys. Mrs. Weasley is seen as a political person for the first time since she is a member of the Order of the Phoenix, and we see Mr. Weasley supervising the chopping of meat and vegetables (p. 82) and attending to other domestic tasks while in previous volumes all domestic work was left to Molly.

The Deathly Hallows also introduces a variety of new female characters that play important roles in plot development. Harry and Hermione are nearly killed by Bathilda Bagshot's dead body, which had been inhabited by Voldemort's snake Nagini. They sought her out because of her connection as a friend of the Potters, a mentor to Dumbledore, and author of *A History of Magic.* Professor Burbage is eaten by Nagini in the first scene after being tortured by Voldemort for educating Hogwarts students on Muggle culture, she is something of a revolutionary considering Voldemort's eugenic proposal to eradicate Mudbloods. The introduction of Dumbledore's mother, Kendra, and sister, Ariana, frame his adolescent malevolence to acquire "the Hallows" and rule the Muggle world.

Throughout the series the presence of women develops quantitatively—there are more of them—as well as in terms of their influence—they do more. In the later books, Rowling depicts women in positions of leadership in which they often control the actions or even the thoughts of male characters, as the very many females develop beyond the stereotypical femininity in which they have previously been cast. For example, Mrs. Weasley, initially a narrowly written, exclusively domestically minded, worrying mother, seems transformed in the final battle of *Deathly Hallows*. She sheds the apron and oven mitts for a fierce and aggressive tone as she engages Bellatrix Lestrange in a duel. Harry is surprised but pleased by her change: "Harry watched with terror and elation as Molly Weasley's wand slashed and twirled" (p. 736). Rowling's most matriarchal character finally leaves "The Burrow" and involves herself first-hand in violent conflict with the Death Eaters. Another instance of change in character occurs in the same battle for Hogwarts, where Minerva McGonagall assumes leadership in protecting the school. She questions the Slytherins' loyalty to preserving the school and the wizarding community from Voldemort's control and gives them an ultimatum.

> I shall expect you and the Slytherins in the Great Hall in twenty minutes, also.... If you wish to leave with your students, we shall not stop you. But if any of you attempt to sabotage our resistance or take up arms against us within this castle, then, Horace, we duel to kill.
>
> (p. 602)

In preceding situations McGonagall would have deferred to a male superior or consulted with her colleagues rather than being decisive on the spot.

Throughout the series journalist Rita Skeeter has been solely responsible for reporting all news/gossip to the wizard community by way of the *Daily Prophet*; essentially, besides the Ministry of Magic, she is the voice that the public hears. In *Deathly Hallows*, Skeeter releases a biography, *The Life and Lies of Albus Dumbledore*, in which she reveals Dumbledore's initiative to establish wizard rule over the Muggle world. Rita's persistent ambition and obnoxiousness has finally earned her a big story that changes the way the wizard community views one of their most influential leaders. By exposing Dumbledore, Rita Skeeter secures significant influence in the male-dominated society, which is a first for female characters. Similarly, Dolores Umbridge's position in the Voldemort administration affects the entire wizard community. Umbridge is in charge of filtering all Mudbloods out of the community, her official title reading: "Senior Undersecretary to the Minister, Head of the Muggle-born Registration Commission" (p. 250). Another example is Bellatrix, when in *Deathly Hallows* she asserts her authority as a Death Eater when Lucius Malfoy challenges it, saying "you lost your authority when you lost your wand, Lucius! How dare you! Take your hands off me" (p. 460)! Voldemort trusts Bellatrix with one of the Horcuxes, which she hides in her vault in Gringotts.

Hermione's development in *Deathly Hallows* is showcased when for the first time she gives readers a glimpse of personal ambition. She retorts Scrimgeour's suspicions of her considering a career in "magical law" by saying "No, I'm not, I'm hoping to do some good in the world" (p. 124). With this ambition Hermione separates herself from her partnership with Ron and Harry that has defined her and possibly restricted her for the past six years.

The Final Verdict: Feminist or Sexist?

Female characters become more prevalent as the series continues, their pragmatic femininity develops beyond strictly feminine attributes, and their roles may be more representative of an equally distributed gender hierarchy. But does their presence in authoritative positions satisfy a rich feminist conception of equality? Molly Weasley leaves The Burrow to protect her children and duels to defend her daughter, making her aggressive assertions consistent with her mothering role. Worse, her battle with Bellatrix in which she screams, "YOU BITCH" (cap. *sic*) (p. 736) reads like a catfight added for comic relief. The funniness of the scene relies on mockery of both women. Does McGonagall assume leadership only because Dumbledore is dead? When she is faced with the first opportunity, is it merely her duty by default? Why didn't she initiate the coup before Harry arrived? When McGonagall is portrayed shouting "charge" in battle, it is funny because, like Molly Weasley, she is acting out of character. Rita Skeeter may be the most powerful, independently professional woman in the series, but she is constantly discredited by Harry; her character is manipulative and untrustworthy. Consistent with the series,

Skeeter is another female denigrated because of her less than desirable feminine appearance. Her moving portrait is described as:

> a woman wearing jeweled glasses with elaborately curled blonde hair, her teeth bared in what was clearly supposed to be a winning smile, wiggling her fingers up at him. Doing his best to ignore the nauseating image, Harry read on.
>
> (p. 23)

Rita Skeeter's work is made interesting and, therefore, widely read because of her ability to twist the truth; her lies define her career.

Similarly, deception characterizes Umbridge's and Bellatrix's rise to powerful positions. In the *Order of the Phoenix*, Umbridge was appointed Defense Against the Dark Arts teacher but was working as a spy for Minister Fudge to discredit Harry and Dumbledore. Her work earns her a promotion to "High Inquisitor," a position she abuses to set more tyrannical regulations, until she is appointed Headmistress of Hogwarts. Her resumé of underhandedness eventually earns her the position of Senior Undersecretary to the Minister where she works on a kind of Mudblood genocide of the wizard community. Harry describes her appearance as similar to "a large, pale toad" (*Order of the Phoenix*, p. 146). Bellatrix has an obsequious loyalty that is mocked by Voldemort. Speaking to him, "her voice constricted with emotion, 'it is an honor to have you here, in our family's house. There can be no higher pleasure.'" Voldemort mocks her saying, "that means a great deal Bellatrix, from you" (p. 9). She isn't respected and is only kept because of her faithfulness. She fails Voldemort when her Horcrux is stolen from her Gringotts vault by Harry, Ron, and Hermione. She is ultimately contemptuous to both the good guys and the bad guys.

Hermione's advanced knowledge of magic shows potential beyond the other students, but she has only exercised her gift to aid Harry's quests rather than focusing on her own career. He is the hero; she is but an assistant. In the *Goblet of Fire* Hermione starts S.P.E.W., "Society for the Promotion of Elfish Welfare," an organization to fight for the rights of house-elves. Independently, she pursues the cause but her organization is portrayed invalid or trite in comparison to Harry's endeavors in the school. Hermione is so wrapped up in Harry's goals that hers may be suppressed or unrealized. Ruthann Mayes-Elma (2006) concurs that the pragmatic identity–attitude of female characters is suppressed because they do not actively construct their own identity; only once they figure out they are oppressed can they do something to change their status (p. 80). However, Hermione seems perfectly content with her subordinate partnership with Ron and Harry. Hermione's adolescent preoccupation with Ron an object of romance and her ultimate marriage to Ron solidifies her dependent identity in the trio.

The Helper Females: Hermione and McGonagall

The sexism present at the end is also throughout the series. Males are represented more often, but they are also depicted as wiser, braver, more powerful, and more fun than females. It is not simply who is present, but also how characters are portrayed, and what they do, that matters. Most of the girls are depicted as anti-intellectual and most keenly interested in the low-status magic of the Divination class. At the height of action, females are not typically very involved, and they are always fearful and emotional. The relative powerlessness of females is most evident in the portrayal of the main character, Hermione. In Chapter 16, during the action-filled denouement of the first book (*Sorcerer's Stone*, Chapter 16), Harry, Ron, and Hermione are working together towards the Sorcerer's Stone. Hermione shrieks, screams, and speaks "nervously," reactions the boys do not have. Though Hermione's knowledge helps them along, Harry sends her back. She agrees with this decision, throws her arms around Harry, and says, "Harry—you're a great wizard you know." He says, "I'm not as good as you." And she responds, "Books and cleverness! There are more important things—friendship and bravery and—oh Harry be careful!" (p. 287). Thus, Harry's ability to make friends and be brave establishes him as the true great one, and, he is the great one in every book.

Hermione, and female characters in general, react differently to conflict than male characters do in the series. In *Deathly Hallows*, when Harry and Ron argue about pursuing the remaining Horcruxes, their dialogue is described by shouts, anger, and standing in positions of physical dominance: "his words pierced Harry like scalding knives" (p. 307). Hermione is described as being barely audible over the pouring rain. She transitions from participating in the conversation to becoming the mediator of her infuriated friends, "tears pouring down Hermione's face" (p. 308).

This type of scenario occurs repeatedly. Sometimes females begin an action scene as a token presence, but something usually happens to them. Hermione is primarily an enabler of Harry's and Ron's adventures, rather than an adventurer herself. Though she is much more active and important in *Deathly Hallows* than in the early books, she is asleep in the tent when Ron and Harry get the first Horcrux and oddly, though we are told that she gets the third Horcrux, this is only mentioned in passing, not described in rich detail like the heroics of the boys. Ernelle Fife (2006) defines characters with Hermione's enabling presence as "wise warriors," comparing her to the Greek Goddess Athena, born armed from the head of Zeus, "a mentor and guide to numerous heroes, and is seldom a deity of aggression, but of defensive warfare" (p. 1). Hermione embodies Fife's theory and displays her defensive attitude in their discussion of which of the "Hallows" would be most effective in a confrontation. Hermione chooses the Invisibility Cloak in order to avoid violence and denounces Ron's choice of the unbeatable wand because "the wand would be bound to attract trouble" (*Deathly Hallows*, p. 415).

In the middle of *Harry Potter and the Chamber of Secrets*, Hermione is the one who makes the important Polyjuice Potion, which works fine for Harry and Ron, leading them into further adventures, but goes awry when Hermione uses it on herself. She accidentally turns herself into a cat, which causes her to sob and pull her robes over her head. She is hospitalized for weeks. In another plot twist, she is later immobilized by being turned into a "petrified person" yet, in her immobilized condition, she provides crucial information, which Ron "tugs and twists" out of her hand. Hermione's knowledge is important, but it is primarily used for Harry's adventures, not her own. In the *Goblet of Fire*, she teaches Harry how to summon his broom, which helps him triumph in the Triwizard Tournament and escape Voldemort, but Hermione, of course, does not compete or face Voldemort herself.

Hermione's maternal attributes are reinforced by Harry and Ron. In the *Deathly Hallows*, Hermione assumes an overwhelmingly matriarchal role during her, Harry's, and Ron's time spent alone hiding from Death Eaters in the forest. Throughout the seventh book Hermione is obligated with carrying a magical beaded bag that has no limit to what it can hold, she consistently pulls essentials from the bag that save or make Ron's and Harry's lives comfortable. After sneaking into the Ministry of Magic, they're forced to Disapparate into the wilderness to avoid detection. Hermione's bag wasn't packed in anticipation of a camping trip and they are all hungry. Ron assumes that Hermione is to blame for their lack of food, but it is Hermione that reinforces stereotyping of domestic responsibility in their exchange. Ron complains "my mother can make good food appear out of thin air." Hermione responds arguing "Harry caught the fish and I did my best with it! I notice I'm always the one who ends up sorting out the food, because I'm a girl, I suppose!" (p. 293). Hermione risks going to the supermarket despite the presence of bounty hunters and Death Eaters searching for anyone connected to Harry; she helps Harry regardless of the potential implications of going into public. At Harry's seventeenth birthday party Ron compliments Hermione after she decorates the room with streamers, saying "You've really got an eye for that sort of thing" (*Deathly Hallows*, p. 119). She is rewarded for her feminine characteristics but portrayed as "nerdy" when she tries to compete in the classroom. Harry's masculine tendency to delve head first into conflict drive the action of the stories; accordingly, his style of heroism trumps Hermione's rational and defensive approach. Harry has the final veto for all decisions. Pugh and Wallace explain females in relation to male leaders, saying "women are presented as only taking actions within the purview of men, and their actions are depicted as largely irrelevant or unreasonable when they step outside that authority" (p. 14).

In *Goblet of Fire*, Fleur, a female, is "allowed" to be one of four students competing in the Triwizard Tournament, but she ends up last. During the second task, she gets tangled up in weed and cannot save her own sister.

Harry has to save the sister. Though Fleur is important enough to become one of the "seven Potters" flying as a decoy in the tense opening to *Deathly Hallows*, her inclusion in the mission seems jarring because she is a superficial, love-struck ditz preoccupied with wedding planning in the previous volume, the *Half-Blood Prince*.

In action scenes in each book, these characterizations are repeated. Hermione speaks in a "terrified voice" (*Chamber of Secrets*, p. 336) or a "petrified whisper" (p. 339). Harry and Ron are never described in this way. Furthermore, though Hermione's knowledge is sometimes useful, it is Harry's "stupid" bravery that really saves the day. It is important that both Harry and Ron have knowledge when they need it, but they are not bookish like Hermione. Research on boys' school culture suggests that bookishness and academic achievement are considered feminine (Mac and Ghaill, 1994; Paetcher, 1998). When Harry attacks the troll and rescues Hermione in *Sorcerer's Stone*, it is described as "both very brave and very stupid" (p. 176). In *Harry Potter and the Prisoner of Azkaban*, in a scuffle with a suspected evil doer, Rowling narrates: "Perhaps it was the shock of Harry doing something so stupid, but Black didn't raise the wands in time" (p. 340). In this passage, Hermione is not helpless. She kicks Sirius Black. Yet, when females are given token power, their inequality is reinforced, and their status is not enhanced. The kick is a minor effort and Black turns out to be a good guy, not a serious opponent.

Among the adults, Professor McGonagall seems to mirror Hermione as a smart female of clearly secondary status. Like Hermione, she is book-smart, but not wise, powerful, or brave. Like Hermione, she is a stickler for rules and is often described as having her arms full of books and spilling them (*Sorcerer's Stone*, p. 267; *Goblet of Fire*, p. 205). Her characterization is reinforced by her physical description. Her hair is worn in a bun and she has beady eyes and square glasses. McGonagall's secondary status is also evident in the nature of her interactions with students. Unlike Headmaster Dumbledore, students can trick her. Ron and Harry successfully lie to her, for example, at the end of *Chamber of Secrets*. They told Professor McGonagall that they were on their way to visit Hermione in her sick bed, when, in fact, they were scheming to get into the Chamber of Secrets. It would be hard to imagine Dumbledore being fooled by these two boys. It also would be inconceivable to imagine Dumbledore responding emotionally as McGonagall did, with "a tear glistening in her beady eye" (p. 288). She is sentimental and lacks discernment.

McGonagall is also something of a mother figure, concerned that students get enough sleep and stay well. For example, "The Gryffindor party ended only when Professor McGonagall turned up in her dressing gown and hair net at one in the morning to insist that they all go to bed" (*Prisoner of Azkaban*, p. 265). Professor McGonagall also makes motherly inquiries of Potter: "Are you sure you feel all right Potter?" (*Chamber of Secrets*, p. 90). Even the female students are depicted as motherly and more gentle. Boys are told to back away from unicorns. "They prefer a woman's touch" (*Goblet of Fire*, p. 436). This depiction is consistent with research on the portrayal of women in children's literature. For example, Barnett (1986) found females in children's storybooks to be comforting, consoling, and providers of emotional support, while males were more likely to be represented obtaining a goal or overcoming an obstacle. Tetenbaum and Pearson (1989) also found that female storybook characters were depicted as more caring and concerned about relationships than were males.

McGonagall's secondary status is evident not just in her "soft" relations with students, but also in her relations with peers. She is effectively silenced by men when offering her opinion about what to do next at the dramatic climax of *Harry Potter and the Goblet of Fire*. She is chastised by Dumbledore, who calls her by her first name. "Why are you disturbing these people? Minerva, I am surprised at you" (p. 703). Watch as Professor McGonagall's voice is drowned by Fudge's and see that Dumbledore, in contrast, can assert power. "'Listen to me, Cornelius' said Dumbledore, taking a step toward Fudge, and once again, he seemed to radiate that indefinable sense of power" (pp. 705–706). At the conclusion of this passage, Professor McGonagall's ideas go unheeded and she is dismissed on an errand. She "nodded and left without a word." The relative powerlessness of the two most masterful women in the series only underscores female weakness.

Emotional Females

The females are emotional and cry readily throughout all seven books. In *Sorcerer's Stone*, Hermione overhears Ron saying that she has no friends and soon after, "Harry and Ron overheard Parvati Patil telling her friend Lavender that Hermione was crying in the girls' bathroom and wanted to be left alone" (p. 172). This demonstrates both the portrayal of girls as gossipy and the portrayal of Hermione as emotional and vulnerable. At the end of the first book, Hermione is publicly recognized for "the cool use of logic in the face of fire," and she buries her face in her arms. "Harry strongly suspected she had burst into tears" (*Sorcerer's Stone*, p. 305). Lavender Brown cries when her pet rabbit, Binky, is killed by a fox (*Prisoner of Azkaban*, p. 148). Pansy Parkinson is in tears after Malfoy was "attacked" by a Hippogriff (*Prisoner of Azkaban*, p. 118). In *Deathly Hallows*, after escaping Gringotts on the back of a dragon, "Ron kept swearing at the top of his voice, and Hermione seemed to be sobbing" (p. 544).

Sometimes female crying is described more subtly. McGonagall, regretting her treatment of Pettigrew, "sounded as though she had a sudden head cold" (*Prisoner of Azkaban*, p. 207). In another example, "Mrs Weasley kissed all of her children, then Hermione, and finally Harry. Do take care, won't you

Harry," she said as she straightened up, her eyes oddly bright (*Prisoner of Azkaban*, p. 72). Yet males rarely touch or cry. Acceptable male tears occur when Dumbledore had an aesthetic response to music (*Sorcerer's Stone*, p. 128) or when Wood "sobbed unrestrainedly" after winning the Quidditch game (*Prisoner of Azkaban*, p. 312). Moaning Myrtle reports that Draco was crying in the bathroom and instead of humanizing him, the detail reinforces his weakness of character. Even death is an occasion for female, but not male emotional outburst. At Cedric's death it was only girls who "were screaming, sobbing hysterically" (*Goblet of Fire*, p. 672). As sports team members, the girls exhibited girlish behavior by giggling at the possibility of playing with handsome new captain and seeker, Cedric Diggory. "'He's that tall good looking one, isn't he?' asked Angelina. 'Strong and silent,' said Katie and they started to giggle again." By contrast, the boys concentrate on the implications of new leadership in the opposing team. "'Mustn't relax! Must keep our focus!' shouts Wood, his eyes bulging" (*Prisoner of Azkaban*, p. 169).

Quidditch is not the only context for giggling. The books are littered with references to giggling girls, although there is not a single reference to giggling boys. For example, "Mrs Weasley was telling Hermione and Ginny about a love potion she had made as a young girl. All three of them were rather giggly" (*Prisoner of Azkaban*, p. 70); "Groups of giggling girls often turned up to spy on Krum" (*Goblet of Fire*, p. 317); "Girls giggling around Cho" (p. 396). "Parvati will you go to the ball with me? Parvati went into a fit of giggles" (p. 401).

Though they are portrayed as giggly, emotional, gossipy, and anti-intellectual, many of the girls are hazy characters. Certain traits do not seem to be authoritatively owned by any one female character, but, instead, are presented in groups. In the first four books, Alicia Spinnet, Angelina Johnson, and Katie Bell are typically mentioned en masse and give identical responses to situations. It seems that Rowling was using her "cut and paste" function. When girls are mentioned individually, they are often indistinct. In *Chamber of Secrets* "Fourth year Alicia Spinnet … seemed to be nodding off against the wall behind her. Her fellow chasers, Katie Bell and Angelina Johnson, were yawning side by side opposite" (pp. 107–108). In *Prisoner of Azkaban*, "Wood pointed at Alicia Spinnet, Angelina Johnson, Katie Bell" (p. 144). "Angelina, Alicia and Katie had come over too" (p. 110). Later, "Angelina, Alicia and Katie suddenly giggled" (p. 169) when they found out Cedric Diggory was to be the new Seeker for Hufflepuff.

It is not until *Goblet of Fire* (p. 261) that we find out Angelina is "a tall black girl." This late detail reads as a diversity afterthought. Other grouped female sets are the Parvati Patil, Padma Patil, and Lavendar Brown group and the Pansy Parkinson and Millicent Bulstrode set. At Bill and Fleur's wedding, Fred moves through the crowd dealing with "a gaggle of middle aged witches" and "a pair of pretty French girls who giggled and allowed him to escort them inside" (p. 138). A "group of fourth year girls was whispering and giggling on the other side of the door" (p. 138) to Harry's compartment on the Hogwarts Express in *Half-Blood Prince*. This repeated grouping reinforces a tendency for readers to interpret females as types, rather than as individuals. It also reinforces the idea of the sociological construct of the communal and friendly girl compared to the individual and competitive boy. Chodorow (1978), for example, believes that girls retain pre-oedipal attachments to their mothers and "come to define and experience themselves as continuous with others" (p. 169).

Body and Appearance Obsessed Females

The inferior position of females is further reinforced through characterizations that highlight their insecurities and self-hatred, especially as it relates to their looks, bodies, and specifically feminine attributes. The "Fat Lady" in the portrait at the entrance of Gryffindor Tower is an example of this. She has no personal name and is never called anything but the "Fat Lady" or a very fat woman. Her size and gender define her. She is characterized as lazy, inattentive, gossipy, and more concerned about her appearance than her work. After her portrait (herself) is slashed, a male ghost reports: "'Ashamed your head-ship sir. Doesn't want to be seen. She's a horrible mess. Saw her running through the landscape on the fourth floor, sir, saw her dodging between the trees. Crying something dreadful,' he said happily" (*Prisoner of Azkaban*, p. 161). Strong, negative body image messages are conveyed through the main character, Hermione. It is significant that the two "bright" females are unattractive and unsexy.

Professor McGonagall is a severe-looking, tall woman who has black hair worn in a tight bun, and square spectacles. When Madame Delacour is introduced she is described as "a beautiful blonde woman" who "was most accomplished at household spells and had the oven properly cleaned in a trice" (p. 108). Hermione is introduced in *Sorcerer's Stone* as having "a bossy sort of voice, lots of bushy brown hair, and rather large front teeth" (p. 105). In *Goblet of Fire*, when Rita Skeeter reports that Hermione is "stunningly pretty," Hermione is ridiculed. "Stunningly pretty? Her?" Pansy Parkinson had shrieked the first time she had come face to face with Hermione after Rita's flattering newspaper article had appeared. "What was she judging against—a chipmunk?" (p. 316). Hermione is only presented as the attractive date of Vickor Krum after she has a form of plastic surgery. She lets her teeth remain shorter after a corrective spell (p. 405). She is transformed like Cinderella and, like many tomboys in teen novels, into a "princess." She becomes physically acceptable.

But she didn't look like Hermione at all. She had done something with her hair; it was no longer bushy but sleek and shiny, and twisted up into an elegant knot at the back of her head. She was wearing robes made of a floaty periwinkle blue material, and she was holding herself differently somehow ... the reduction in the size of her front teeth was more noticeable than ever.

(p. 414)

The message to girls is: get a makeover. You are not okay. It is disturbing that the females that are most physically beautiful—the Veelas—are not even human. They are portrayed as male fantasy sex objects able to seduce, beguile, and confuse males. Yet, all females are influenced by super-human standards of beauty. Only some girls who conform to a certain rigid standard of beauty can have a date. Yet, Ron and Harry, not described as good looking themselves, get dance dates with "the two best looking girls in the year" (*Goblet of Fire*, p. 411).

This is a dangerous, and yet a common message. Many females dislike their natural appearance, purchase a variety of products and perform a range of beauty regimens that can be ridiculous, painful, and even life threatening (Fallon, 1990). Women who want aesthetic cosmetic surgery have particularly low self-esteem (Hueston, Dennerstein, & Gotts, 1985). Research also indicates that many adolescent girls value their looks more than their intelligence and schoolwork (Tiggerman and Gardiner, 2000). It is particularly unfortunate that Hermione, a good student, changes her teeth to become more good-looking.

Hermione is not the only female student worried about looks. Eloise Midgen tried to charm away acne and ended up taking off her nose. Moaning Myrtle, a ghost, was an ugly, outcast, pimple-afflicted girl who wouldn't have died had she not been hiding out because, as she explains, "Olive Hornby was teasing me about my glasses" (*Chamber of Secrets*, p. 299). The girls buy WonderWitch love potions and pimple vanishers—not the boys. Research shows that teenagers with acne suffer emotionally and are at higher risk of "psychological disorder" (Papadopoulos, Walker, Aitken, & Bor, 2000). Moaning Myrtle is viciously treated. Looks clearly matter. This portrayal of females, which highlights looks and reinforces low self-esteem, is politically and economically significant. In a capitalistic system, the creation of an insecure female helps to sell clothes, accessories, and various beauty products and processes. As Gilbert and Taylor (1991) explain, gender ideologies are powerful because they "work at an unconscious level through the structuring of desires, as well as at a conscious or rational level" (p. 135).

Mothers and Girlfriends without Boundaries

In spite of their efforts to be beautiful and accepted, the females in the Harry Potter series are often treated with secondary status in familial and romantic relationships, and the women show often inappropriate boundaries in their relationships. Nuclear families, such as the Weasleys and the Dursleys, have stay-at-home mothers and employed, head-of-the-household type fathers. The mothers are bossy, and are so over-involved with their children they are stifling, spoiling, and inappropriate. This includes Molly Weasley, Dudley's mother Petunia, Draco's mother Narcissa and even Lupin's mother. Women are also over-involved and lack self and power in romance. The Auror, Tonks, literally loses her power to metamorphose and begins to "look like moaning Myrtle" because she pines for a man she loves. Lavendar's obsession with Ron is a central satire in *Half-Blood Prince*. Hermione's love-scorned pique with Ron seems out of bounds. Perhaps most dramatically, a poor response to love gone wrong intersects with poor mothering in the figure of Merope, a name that sounds like Morose. She is so mistreated first by her brother and father, and then in her romantic relationship, that she abandons her child through suicide.

If she had been emotionally stronger and been able to maintain better boundaries in her relationships, might she have given Tom Riddle/Voldemort enough love to prevent sociopathy? Harry experienced extreme child abuse like Merope but he is strong enough to feel self-respect after the experience. Some of his confidence comes from the knowledge of his mother's self-sacrificial love. Where is Merope's mother? The central theme of the novels, the battle between good Harry and bad Tom seems to have roots in their mothers—the good, self-sacrificing, pretty, charming mother Lily and the bad, self-destructive, failed, "plain, pale" mother, Merope.

The men have determined Merope's fate and indeed the men are in charge of the relationships. In another family, Albus Dumbledore's little sister, Ariana, was completely at the mercy of the male influences in her life. At six years old, three Muggle boys saw her performing magic and "they got a bit carried away trying to stop the little freak from doing it" (*Deathly Hallows* p. 564). After that she couldn't control her magical abilities and Aberforth, her other brother, describes the damage saying "she was never right again" (p. 564). It became Albus' responsibility to take care of her. She became a burden, and was accidentally killed in a duel between Albus, Aberforth, and Grindelwald, initiated by an argument about Ariana's impediment to Albus and Grindelwald's plans.

Men determine whether the relationships are on or off. Ron decides when to romance Hermione, Lupin decides when to marry Tonks, Harry decides when to romance or break up with Ginny. From the beginning, Harry and Ron are in charge, even as much younger boys, when placed in a dating relationship at the Yule ball and are totally disrespectful to Parvati and Padma Patil, their dates. "Harry felt as if he were a show dog being put through its paces" (*Prisoner of Azkaban*, p. 415). Ron totally "disses" Padma: "'Aren't you going to ask me to dance at all?' Padma asked him. 'No' said Ron, still glaring after Hermione" (p. 423). Early in the series, Ginny is the archetypal girl and is presented as deeply passive, weak, and receptive. She has a crush on Harry, which disables her. She becomes literally mute and still. Later, she is weak enough to be fully possessed and used by the evil Lord Voldemort. In *Deathly Hallows*, she becomes a stereotypical "catch"—the popular girl. Harry's attraction to Ginny is based on her lack of stereotypical female characteristics. "She was not tearful; that was one of the many wonderful things about Ginny, she was rarely weepy. He had sometimes thought that having six brothers must have toughened her up" (p. 116). In his desire for Ginny, Harry defines what attributes are favorable in women, marking all the feminine distinctions that characterize the plurality of female characters as undesirable.

As Luce Irigaray (1985) describes, women become paralyzed or hysterical because they have no means and no metaphors for expressing desire. In *Deathly Hallows* Luna Lovegood is "sucking her finger in a dreamy fashion and looking Harry up and down" (p. 141). Considering her name, her identity is consumed by her sexuality. Cho Chang is the beautiful and exotic Asian love interest of Harry, and serves more as a symbol rather than as a fully developed character. This is disturbingly suggestive of what Kim (1990) describes as race and gender hierarchies that have objectified Asian Americans as permanent outsiders. "Asian men have been coded as having no sexuality, while Asian women have nothing else" (p. 71). In *The Deathly Hallows*, in the midst of planning a coup on the Death Eaters' control of Hogwarts, Harry is distracted by his two love interests.

> Ginny was now climbing through the hole in the wall ... Ginny gave Harry a radiant smile, he had forgotten, or had never fully appreciated how beautiful she was ... Harry's mouth fell open. Right behind Lee Jordan came Harry's old girlfriend, Cho Chang. She smiled at him.
>
> (p. 582)

This scene further excludes women from situations that require leadership. While Harry is concerned about saving the wizarding world, Cho and Ginny are portrayed as aloof to the condition, focused on their attraction to Harry.

In a study of young romance readers, Willinsky and Hunniford (1993) found that because adolescent girls read in a realist manner, texts represent a dangerous seduction. Girls tend to read romance texts as preparation for the romances they foresee as part of their immediate future (pp. 91–93). Willinsky and Hunniford maintain that "[this] reading is like having your fortune read in good faith with the tingle of excitement in watching it unfold in the crystal ball" (p. 94). Yet, both boys and girls potentially suffer from such power imbalances.

Stereotypical Masculinities

In order for a theory of gender identity to be inclusive, gender identity conventions must be understood as *equally though differently alienating* for men and for women. Female archetypes tend to describe types of powerlessness, whereas dominant male archetypes tend to describe types of powerfulness. To the extent that each distort reality and circumscribe choices and free will, each are limiting, hegemonic, and alienating. There are quite narrow and specific identities suggested for both males and females in the Harry Potter series. In the Harry Potter books, boys are stereotypically portrayed, with the strong, adventurous, independent type of male serving as a heroic expression of masculinity, while the weak, unsuccessful male is mocked and sometimes despised.

As R. W. Connell (1996) reminds us, types of gender representations "do not sit side by side like dishes in a smorgasbord; there are definite relations between them." For example, "some masculinities are more dominant than others" (p. 212). The form of masculinity that is culturally dominant in a given setting is called hegemonic masculinity. Hegemonic cultural practices are those in which most people give "spontaneous consent" to the "general direction imposed on social life by the dominant fundamental group" (Gramsci, 1978, p. 12). A certain type of boy "naturally" seems better. Often people do not realize the extent to which their ideas of gender are culturally created. As Connell explains, "hegemonic" signifies a position of cultural authority and leadership, not total dominance; other forms of masculinity persist alongside. The hegemonic form need not be the most common form of masculinity; it is simply the most valued (Connell, 1996, p. 211). Hegemonic masculinity is straight, strong, domineering, and oppresses not only women, but also the many men excluded from it. Even "subscribers" may find its norms unattainable (Messner, 1997, pp. 7–8). David Wallace and Tison Pugh (2006) conclude that the protagonist's masculinity, Harry's, must be stronger than that of all other surrounding male characters, "especially in relation to gender and sexual orientation difference" (p. 2). Therefore, Harry can act independently, while male characters around him may not be capable. Although Ron is a very important male character, he doesn't have the capacity to act independently; an adolescent with a very protective mother often shows this in his personality. Lupin, Sirius, Dumbledore, and Mad-Eye Moody all die, allowing Harry to overcome the adversity of losing his strong male influences, and develop is own dominant masculinity.

Nearly all of the males seem to be engaged in power struggles. Yet, the reader has a very clear idea of which males are in top positions. The coolest males seem to be Harry, Dumbledore, and Bill Weasley, who works for Gringotts (the bank) in Egypt and has a ponytail. The traits of powerful males include bravery, confidence, class status, and personal charisma. Although the

Weasleys are poor, Bill's status is different. He displays both cultural and financial power. Dumbledore is a leader and is interested in chamber music, which is suggestive of upper class status. We know that even Harry has money.

Harry's status is interesting. At first he appears to be an outsider and thus neither dominant nor powerful. He is a skinny boy with tousled hair who is trying to find his place. And yet, as the stories progress, he obtains significant status. He becomes rich and famous. He has some of the best stuff, such as a top quality broom and an Invisibility Cloak. He is also a school sports star able to get a date with one of the prettiest girls in the school. Part of Harry's appeal comes from the fact that he is introduced to us as a skinny, orphaned outsider and yet he goes on to have success in every important venue of masculinity. He seems anointed. Research suggests that maintaining peer status and moving from "nerd to normal" are chief preoccupations of the young adolescent (Kinney, 1993). Harry's success is satisfying to any reader who wants power or vindication. Yet, if Harry simply achieved status and remained unproblematically popular, there would be little narrative tension. Thus, Rowling often places Harry in situations in which other students or the wizarding world are mistrustful of Harry. He is repeatedly vindicated.

Harry's triumphs are reinforced by the fact that in the series, most males are not powerful or in positions of cultural authority and leadership. Just as token inclusion reinforces the inequality of the females, the multitude of males who are insecure, low status, and less than fully masculine reinforce the dominance of hegemonic masculinity. Percy Weasley lacks power because his Hermione-like rule following undermines his masculinity. Cedric Diggory is not a dominant male because of what appears to be his social class status. Hufflepuffs are loyal and good workers, but not intelligent leaders.

Being a pretty boy "thickheaded" Hufflepuff is unmanly. "'He's that tall good looking one isn't he?' said Angelina. 'Strong and silent,' said Katie. 'He's only silent because he's too thick to string two words together,' said Fred impatiently" (*Prisoner of Azkaban*, p. 169.)

> Cedric displays a form of working class masculinity. When male self-esteem is undermined by being an insubordinate and taking orders from others, men who are working class reconstruct their position as embodying true masculinity by focusing on their strength, endurance, and capacity to tolerate pain.
>
> (Donaldson, 1991; Pyke, 1996)

This is the sort of tough, dumb masculinity Cedric possesses.

There are numerous non-dominant adult males in these books who are deeply undesirable. These include Argus Filch, Professor Flitwick, Gilderoy Lockhart, Professor Slughorn, Professor Quirrell, and Peter Pettigrew or

"Wormtail." Their negative portrayal serves as a textual warning. They demonstrate the consequences of failed masculinity. No boy readers would want to be like any of them. Argus Filch is the failed wizard owner of Mrs. Norris, the cat. Owning and doting on the cat makes him seem effeminate. Filch is a Squib, which means that he was born of a wizarding family but cannot do magic. The frustration this failure causes contributes to his anti-social behavior and his nasty bullying of students. "Tiny little Professor Flitwick" drinks cherry syrup and soda with ice and an umbrella, decorates with live fairies, speaks in a squeaky voice, and is emotionally sensitive. For example, when he was afraid, "he let out a squeal" and then "burst into tears." He faints after telling everyone that there is a troll in the castle in *Harry Potter and the Sorcerer's Stone*. This portrayal is in the same book: "Now don't forget that nice wrist movement we've been practicing!" squeaked Professor Flitwick, perched on top of his pile of books as usual. "Swish and flick, remember, swish and flick" (p. 171). Professor Flitwick is characterized with words and images that are connotative of crude cultural stereotypes of gay men.

Such negative portrayals reinforce the vilification of non-dominant masculinity and femininity common in many school settings. There are no gay people nor gay couples in these books and they end with a virtual parade of heterosexual married pairing. Gay young people and young people who do not conform to dominant gender identities are at particular risk, and this series reinforces heteronormativity. We find Rowling's claim, after the series was completed, that Dumbledore was gay as offensive since a recognizably gay Dumbledore could have helped reduce stigma. There is no evidence of this. Gay teens are much more likely than their peers to be the victims of violence and harassment, to drop out of school and to think about and attempt suicide (O'Conor, 1995; Stoelb & Chiriboga, 1998). In the Harry Potter books, numerous expressions of non-dominant masculinity are instead mocked.

Gilderoy Lockhart is characterized as a deeply conceited man whose bravado and mannerisms serve to hide his utter incompetence and fearfulness. He carries stacks of autographed pictures with him most of the time and is jealous of attention given to Harry. He has coiffed golden, wavy hair and wears curlers at night. He wears robes in a wide array of colors, including forget-me-not blue, lavender, turquoise, mauve, lurid pink, deep plum, jade green, and midnight blue. Certainly this vain, fearful, pink-robed, curler-wearing man is less than masculine, even though many young female students like him.

Both Quirrell and Wormtail are weak males. Their physical possession by Lord Voldemort emphasizes their lack of masculinity. Professor Quirrell is nervous, prone to fainting, pale, and often trembling. Who would suspect p-p-poor, st-stuttering Professor Quirrell of being connected with Voldemort? Quirrell became a host and a slave to the disembodied Voldemort.

Peter Pettigrew, known as "Wormtail" since he can take the form of a rat, is described in his student days as that "fat, little boy" by Madame Rosmerta (*Prisoner of Azkaban*, p. 207). McGonagall recalls him with the description, "Stupid boy ... foolish boy ... he was always hopeless at dueling" (p. 208). McGonagall says Pettigrew "hero worshiped Black and Potter" but was "never quite in their league, talent wise" (p. 207). His failure to compete with the dominant males leads him to be vulnerable to possession and use by the evil Voldemort.

The boys who do not measure up to the masculine ideal are consistently derided and are actively excluded from participation in school social life. This is quite similar to what occurs in many schools in Great Britain, Australia, and the U.S.A. (Epstein, 1997, 1999; Martino, 1995, 1999; Kehily & Nayak, 1997). In Rowling's books, boys establish their masculinity by avoiding behaviors common to the girls and the less masculine males. Hegemonic males do not express fear, cry, giggle, or gossip, and they are not concerned about their appearance. Hegemonic males are good at sports and have access to things, money, and prestige. Socialization into this type of competitive, unflinching masculinity helps to create consumers, soldiers, and corporate strivers. It also reinforces contempt rather than sympathy and public support for the downtrodden.

Among the students, Neville and the brothers, Colin and Dennis Creevey, are portrayed, in varying degrees, as "wimps." Language used to describe them reinforces their lowliness. Creevey sounds like creepy. Neville sounds like snivel. Although other boys are often hurt in Quidditch, Neville leaves in disgrace after he fell off a broom during a Quidditch lesson. "Neville, his face tear-streaked, clutching his wrist, hobbled off with Madam Hooch." (*Sorcerer's Stone*, p. 147). He is viciously mocked. His unattractiveness to girls is emphasized by Pansy. "'Ooh, sticking up for Longbottom?' said Pansy Parkinson, a hard-faced Slytherin girl. 'Never thought *you'd* like fat little cry-babies, Parvati'" (p. 147). Neville is also victimized by teachers, such as Snape. During Potions lessons, "Neville regularly went to pieces" (*Prisoner of Azkaban*, p. 125). Snape says "tell me boy, does anything penetrate that thick skull of yours?" Neville is described as "pink and trembling. He looked like he was on the verge of tears" (p. 126). Neville is a poor student and a poor athlete. The misery this boy experiences is a testament to the consequences of failed masculinity. Slowly, he fights back, starting with standing up to bullies and eventually transforms. Neville's reinvention as an important friend of Harry's, as a member of Dumbledore's Army, and ultimately as a boy capable of surviving a face off with both Bellatrix and Voldemort serves as an echo case to Harry's, and enhanced the trope of emerging masculinity. Both begin as weak, skinny, outsiders and yet become men.

Implications: Disrupting Gender Stories

As Walkerdine (1990) explains, there is a need for gender-neutral stories that are equally appealing to gender-confining, stereotypical, and prejudicial material. Can this be? Such books would create a different kind of reading pleasure. We believe that part of the popularity of the Harry Potter books stems from their highly familiar depictions of gender and power. Novels that confronted readers' stereotypes would elicit either rejection or the unsettling pleasure of *jouissance*. Yet, all texts can be resisted, read against the grain, and deconstructed. We urge Harry Potter readers to think about these portrayals. Even though we are experienced critical and feminist readers of texts, our formal examination of these books revealed more than initial casual reading. Children talking with each other, with parents, or with teachers should question how to achieve "common sense" ideas about femininity and masculinity and consider who is served and who is harmed through gender ideologies. Certainly books such as these help to normalize a world in which most child-care workers and secretaries are female and most world explorers, engineers, and firefighters are male. In educational settings, critical discussions about literature, culture, and gender ideology can be very productive (Davies, 1989, 1993, 1997; Lee & Beach, 2001; Peyton, 2000; Yeoman, 1999). Children can learn what Bronwyn Davies (1989) describes as the discursive practices of society. When this happens, children "are able to position themselves within those practices in multiple ways, and to develop subjectivities both in concert with and in opposition to the ways in which others choose to position them" (p. xi).

Given the enormous readership of the Harry Potter texts, scholarship on these works and thoughtful consideration of ways to introduce critical themes into curriculum is very important. Such critiques help readers, parents, and classroom teachers to consider the ways that literary portrayals potentially reproduce and legitimize inequality, and even help create identity. Even if young readers are not actively seeking lessons in gender identity, they can be learned. For this reason, feminist critical pedagogy encourages educators to examine the ways in which popular texts, such as these books, mirror dominant relations and function to legitimize such relations of power and gender experiences (Lewis, 1997; Luke, 1997). In this way, the critical gaze, rather than the books themselves, become the focus of reading and of curriculum. These texts are particularly useful starting points for discussions because they embody both engaging and constricting themes and images.

References

Barnett, M. A. (1986). Sex bias in the helping behavior presented in children's picture books. *Journal of Generic Psychology, 147*, 343–351.

Barthes, R. (1976). *The pleasure of the text* (R. Miller, Trans.). New York: Hill & Wang.

Bourdieu, P. (1977). *Outline of a theory of practice*. New York: Cambridge University Press.

Chafetz, J. (1990). *Gender equity*. Newbury Park, CA: Sage.

Chodorow, N. (1978). *The reproduction of mothering*. Berkeley, CA: University of California Press.

Connell, R. W. (1987). *Gender and power*. Stanford, CA: Stanford University Press.

Connell, R. W. (1991). Live fast and die young: The construction of masculinity among young working-class men on the margin of the labour market. *Australian and New Zealand Journal of Sociology, 27*(2), 141–171.

Connell, R. W. (1993). The big picture: Masculinities in recent world history. *Theory and Society, 22*(5) 597–623.

Connell, R. W. (1995). *Masculinities.* Los Angeles, CA: University of California Press.

Connell R. W. (1996). Teaching the boys: New research on masculinity, and gender strategies for schools. *Teachers College Record, 98*(2), 2086–2238.

Davies, B. (1989). *Frogs and snails and feminist tales: Preschool children and gender.* Sydney: Allen & Unwin.

Davies, B. (1993). *Shards of glass: Children reading and writing beyond gendered identities.* Cresskill, NJ: Hampton Press, Inc.

Davies, B. (1997). Constructing and deconstructing masculinities through critical literacy, *Gender and Education, 9*(1), pp. 9–30.

Donaldson, M. (1991). *Time of our lives: Labor and love in the working class.* Sydney: Allen & Unwin.

Epstein, D. (1997). Boyz' own stories: Masculinities and sexualities in schools. *Gender and Education, 9*(1), 105–115.

Epstein, D. (1999). Real boys don't work: "underachievement," masculinity and the harassment of "sissies." In D. Epstein, J. Elwood, V. Hey, & J. Maws (eds.), *Failing boys: Issues in gender and achievement* (pp. 96–108). London: Open University Press.

Fallon, A. (1990). Culture in the mirror: Sociocultural determinants of body image. In T. E. Cash & T. Pruzinsky (eds.), *Images: Development, deviance, and body change* (pp. 80–109). New York: Guildford.

Fife, E. (2006). Wise warriors in Tolkien, Lewis, and Rowling. *Mythlore, 25*(1–2), 147.

Flintoff, A. (1994). Sexism and homophobia in physical education: The challenge for teacher educators. *Physical Education Review, 17*(2), 97–105.

Foucault, M. (1980). *Power/knowledge: Selected interviews & other writings, 1972–77.* C. Gordon (ed.). New York: Pantheon.

Gilbert, P., & Taylor, S. (1991). *Fashioning the feminine.* Sydney: Allen & Unwin.

Gramsci, A. (1978). *Selections from the prison notebooks of Antonio Gramsci* (Q. Hoare & G. Nowell-Smith, Trans. & eds.). New York: International Publishers.

Hasbrook, C. A. (1999). Young children's social constructions of physicality and gender. In J. Coakely, & P. Donnelly (eds.), *Inside sports* (pp. 7–16). London: Routledge.

Hollindale, P. (1988). Ideology and the children's book. *Signal 55*(1), 3–22.

Hueston, J., Dennerstein, L., & Gotts, G. (1985). Psychological aspects of cosmetic surgery. *Journal of Psychosomatic Obstetrics and Gynecology, 4,* 335–346.

Irigaray, L. (1985). *This sex which is not one* (Catherine Porter with Carolyn Burke, Trans.). Ithaca, NY: Cornell University Press.

Kehily, M., & Nayak, A. (1997). Lads and laughter: humour and the production of heterosexual hierarchics. *Gender and Education, 9*(1), 69–87.

Kim, E. H. (1990). Such opposite creatures: Men and women in Asian American literature. *Michigan Quarterly Review 29* (Winter 1990).

Kinney, D. A. (1993). From nerds to normals: The recovery of identity among adolescents from middle school to high school. *Sociology of Education, 66*(1), 21–40.

Lee, G., & Beach, R. (2001). Response to literature as a cultural activity. *Reading Research Quarterly 36*(1), 64–74.

Lewis, C. (1997). The social drama of literature discussions in a fifth/sixth grade classroom. *Research in the Teaching of English, 31*(2), 163–204.

Lipman-Blumen, J. (1984). *Gender roles and power.* Englewood Cliffs, NJ: Prentice Hall.

Luke, A. (1997). Texts and discourse in education: An introduction to critical discourse analysis. In M. Apple (ed.). *Review of research in education* (Vol. 21, pp. 3–48). Washington, DC: American Educational Research Association.

Mac an Ghaill, M. (1994). *The making of men: Masculinities, sexualities and schooling.* London: Open University Press.

Martino, W. (1995). Deconstructing masculinity in the English classroom: a site for reconstituting gendered subjectivity. *Gender and Education, 7*(2), 205–220.

Martino, W. (1999) "Cool boys," "party animals," "squids" and poofters: Interrogating the dynamics and politics of adolescent masculinities in school. *British Journal of Sociology of Education, 20*(2), 239–263.

Mayes-Elma, R. (2006). *Females in Harry Potter: not all that empowering.* Lanham, Maryland: Rowman and Littlefield Publishers, Inc.

Messner, M. (1997). *Politics of masculinities: Men in movements.* Thousand Oaks, CA: Sage.

O'Conor, A. (1995). Breaking the silence: Writing about gay, lesbian, and bisexual teenagers. In G. Unks (ed.), *The gay teen: Educational practice and theory for lesbian, gay, and bisexual adolescents* (pp. 13–15). New York: Routledge.

Paetcher, C. (1998). *Educating the other: Gender, power and schooling.* London: Falmer Press.

Papadopoulos, L., Walker, C., Aitken, D., & Bor, R. (2000). The relationship between body location and psychological morbidity in individuals with acne vulgaris. *Psychology, Health & Medicine, 5*(4), 431–439.

Peyton, J. (2000). Boy talk: Critical literacy and masculinities. *Reading Research Quarterly, 35*(3), 312–338.

Pugh, T., & Wallace, D. (2006). Heteronormative heroism and queering the school story in J. K. Rowling's Harry Potter series. *Children's Literature Quarterly, 31*(3), 260–281.

Pyke, K. (1996). Class-based masculinities: The interdependence of gender, class, and interpersonal power. *Gender & Society, 10*(5), 527–550.

Rowling, J. K. (1997). *Harry Potter and the sorcerer's stone.* New York: Scholastic.

Rowling, J. K. (1998). *Harry Potter and the chamber of secrets.* New York: Scholastic.

Rowling, J. K. (1999). *Harry Potter and the prisoner of Azkaban.* New York: Scholastic.

Rowling, J. K. (2000). *Harry Potter and the goblet of fire.* New York: Scholastic.

Rowling, J. K. (2007). *Harry Potter the deathly hallows.* New York: Scholastic.

Scraton, S. (1990) *Gender and physical education.* Geelong, Australia: Deakin University Press.

Sontag, S. (1990). *Against interpretation.* New York: Anchor Books.

Stoelb, M., & Chiriboga, J. (1998). A process model for assessing adolescent risk for suicide. *Journal of Adolescence, 21*(44), 359–370.

Sumara, D. (1993/1999). Of seagulls and glass roses. In W. Pinar (ed.), *Contemporary curriculum discourses: Twenty years of JCT* (pp. 289–311). New York: Guildford.

Sutherland, R. (1985). Hidden persuaders: Political ideologies in literature for children. *Children's Literature in Education, 16*(3), 143–157.

Tetenbaum, T. J., & Pearson, J. (1989). The voices in children's literature: The impact of gender on the moral decisions of storybook characters. *Sex Roles, 20*(7–8), 381–395.

Tiggerman, M., & Gardiner, M. (2000). I would rather be size 10 than have straight A's. *Journal of Adolescence, 23*(6), 645–660.

Tobin, M. (1988). Bridging the cultural gap: Eighteenth-century narrative and post-modernism. *CLIO: A Journal of Literature, History, and the Philosophy of History, 17*(3), 211–223.

Walkerdine, V. (1990). *Schoolgirl fictions.* London: Verso.

Willinsky, J., & Hunniford, R. M. (1993). Reading the romance younger: The mirrors and fears of a preparatory literature. In L. Christian-Smith (ed.), *Texts of desire: Essays on fiction, femininity and schooling* (pp. 87–105). London: Falmer.

Yeoman, E. (1999). How does it get into my imagination? Elementary school children's intertextual knowledge and gendered storylines. *Gender & Education, 11*(4), 427–441.

Chapter Nine

Monsters, Creatures, and Pets at Hogwarts
Animal Stewardship in the World of Harry Potter

PETER DENDLE

Though Harry Potter's England is a tangible and familiar one in many outward respects, superimposed on it and suffused imperceptibly throughout it is a shadow world of wizards and witches, of curious creatures and fantastic beasts. Many aspects of this hidden world of wizardry, of course, prove upon closer inspection to be parallels or parodies of features characterizing our own society. Bureaucratic politicians, unscrupulous tabloid journalists, inter-racial tension (cast as inter-species tension), and institutional injustice provide an endless stream of moral challenges for a young man already struggling with friendships, schoolwork, and hormones. Among numerous other real-world social and moral issues reinterpreted in fantasy terms, J. K. Rowling devotes significant attention to animals and animal sentience, the nature of monstrosity, and the relationship between humans (or "wizards") and the natural world. The responsibilities of stewardship over the realm of "magical creatures" is a continuous anxiety in the Harry Potter series, and one that maps interestingly—in capturing many of the same successes and hypocrisies alike—onto the actual human relationship with animals at the turn of the third millennium.

The line between human and animal, or indeed between animate and inanimate, is fluid throughout the series.[1] Werewolves abound, and even Harry's godfather Sirius Black is an Animagus who regularly becomes a dog. Ron's pet rat turns out to be a Hogwarts alumnus, hiding from justice in rat form. In class, Hogwarts students are constantly turning objects into animals, and back again, and the novice student often winds up with an animal–object hybrid by mistake. A silver snuffbox at Number Twelve Grimmauld Place bites Sirius, and a silver instrument like a pair of tweezers with many legs scuttles up Harry's arm; a Fanged Frisbee tries to take bites out of tapestries in passing.[2] *The Monster Book of Monsters*, a text assigned for Hagrid's Care of Magical Creatures class, is itself a monster, savage and dangerous.[3] Harry himself seems part animal at times: he can converse with snakes through the innate Parseltongue ability, and in *Harry Potter and the Order of the Phoenix*, because of their linked essence, he adopts the first-person point of view of Nagini the serpent.[4] Through their Expecto Patronum spells, wizards and witches can create a protective magical force that takes the shape of an animal. Each individual seems to create a different guardian species, sometimes matched to his or her character, as though each person has a unique animal totem.[5] Animals and plants blend into one another, also: among Hermione's texts is *Flesh-Eating Trees of the World*, and Neville's *Mimbulus mimbletonia* plant evolves into something that croons affectionately when petted.[6]

This fluid ambiguity between living and non-living creatures—this implicit animism potentially suffusing human, animal, plant, and object—raises interesting moral problems. Margaret Oakes writes,

> The unsuccessful attempts of Harry's friend Dean Thomas to turn a pincushion into a hedgehog in their Transfiguration class leave Dean with a pincushion that curls up defensively if someone tries to stick a pin in it. These examples tell us that both the animate creatures and inanimate objects that magical beings encounter can have a heightened sense of consciousness: almost any living thing or object can be considered something which must almost be treated as an equal, a partner, or an adversary in some way.[7]

The moral relationship of humans with lesser creatures is a recurring theme in the Harry Potter series, but by this very fact, it also winds up presenting an uncomfortable obstacle Rowling must navigate as she crafts humorous scenes that often involve the exploitation and sometimes pain of lesser creatures. Many memorable scenes of the series involve comical attempts to wrangle willful lesser species, such as de-gnoming the garden, de-infesting the drapes of doxys, or dealing with the uncontrolled chaos of "freshly caught" Cornish pixies let loose in Gilderoy Lockhart's useless Defence Against the Dark Arts class.[8] The potential sentience of these and other species is usually skirted in the narrative, though the continuous attention to rights in non-human species in the series as a whole creates an ambivalent moral space in which uncomfortable questions are raised.

Empathy for animals is one of the moral signposts Rowling employs in the Harry Potter series to direct the reader's sympathy for various characters. Among the many reasons we don't like Aunt Petunia, it is surely not to her credit that she "hated animals."[9] Conversely, one of the principal reasons we like Hagrid, aside from his loyalty to Harry, is his limitless empathy for animals and creatures of all sorts—especially the ugly, repulsive, or dangerous ones least likely to garner sympathy from most casual animal enthusiasts. Firenze the centaur—not an easy species to impress, even under the best of circumstances—states that Hagrid "earned my respect for the care he shows for all living creatures."[10] We see Hagrid caring not only for majestic Hippogriffs and terrifying dragons but also for tiny, disagreeable Bowtruckles: when his cabin is burned from an Incendio spell, he mourns for the Bowtruckles caught therein, whose fragile legs he had bound to help them convalesce.[11] In fact, Hagrid serves as one of the main ambassadors to the world of magical creatures.[12] He is their steward and advocate, and (on some unfortunate occasions) their cheerfully resilient chew-toy. In this respect he represents the conscience of the wizarding world at its simplest, purest, and perhaps finest. He loves creatures from an immediate and unapologetic appreciation for what they are. When Draco Malfoy asks maliciously of Blast-Ended Skrewts, "what do they *do*? ... What is the *point* of them?" Hagrid is stumped, and he is all the more endearing for that: he just doesn't understand the question.[13] Hagrid values animals intrinsically, for the sake of their uniqueness and peculiarity, rather than for their utility. Next to his primal empathy for all creatures, Hermione's elf rights campaign comes across as over-cerebral and dogmatic.

The elf rights subplot of the series is not among Rowling's greatest successes. Some have seen Hermione's campaign as at least raising challenging moral problems and providing a variety of approaches for children readers,[14] but the overall sense is that by the end of the series, the author has simply lost interest in the concerted political sympathy she was at such pains to rally for elves in the fourth book.[15] The lot of house-elves is unquestionably one of abject servitude throughout the wizarding world. Dobby the house-elf, in his racially charged pidgin, laments that elves "are the lowly, the enslaved, us dregs of the magical world."[16] Even kindly and nurturing Mrs. Weasley states that she wishes she had a house-elf to do the ironing. This casual remark is cruelly recalled later in the same book, when Dobby irons his own fingers as penance for having tried to prevent Harry from going to Hogwarts.[17] Rowling plays Dobby's self-abuse as a darkly comic element, which would not be so disturbing if Harry's own typically unreflective use of house-elves and laissez-faire apathy for Hermione's S.P.E.W. crusade or for the related issues raised did not predominate by the end of the series.[18]

There are a number of intelligent, language-using species in the wizarding world, all of whom have had uneasy relations with wizards historically: merpeople, centaurs, etc. It is goblins and especially elves, though, that present the two most conspicuous contrast species, embodying issues of both race and class. It has been commented that goblins embody many caricatured traits of stereotypical Jews, and that the history of slavery and African American race relations are overtly projected onto the elves.[19] Brycchan Carey is right to point out that Rowling is fairly safe in choosing to craft her rhetoric of domination by drawing from such a politically neutral issue as slavery, a historical phenomenon that—even though structures of racism of course persist, deeply rooted in institutions as well as in attitudes—has no contemporary defenders anywhere across the political spectrum.[20] Rowling is nuanced and detailed in her depictions of how racism and imbalanced power relations can form and persist for centuries: among the various species relations in her *oeuvre*, we witness such historically complicated processes as the internalization of inferiority, the institutionalization of unequal access to power and participation in the political discourse, and the rewriting of history. In this climate of political and historical awareness (even if thinly recast in non-human species in a fantasy setting), the discourse of animal sentience comes quite close to the surface a number of times.

In *Order of the Phoenix*, the extent of a being's capacity to feel is offered as a benchmark regarding whether or not the creature is to be treated morally. Dumbledore explains to Harry that Sirius should have treated the elf servant Kreacher with kindness and respect, but that he didn't because apparently Sirius never "saw Kreacher as a being with feelings as acute as a human's."[21] In the final book, *Harry Potter and the Deathly Hallows*, we are clearly meant to view the goblin Griphook as cruel because he "laughed at the idea of pain in lesser creatures,"[22] but, in fact, the wizarding community has itself been guilty of this sort of thing repeatedly. Lesser creatures are systematically exploited by wizards for utility, recreation, and ornament, and Rowling regularly introduces these elements casually for comic effect.[23]

The wizard world's attitude toward animals and animal welfare, much like our own Muggle world attitude, is riddled with ambiguity and hypocrisy. The house-elf heads mounted on the wall at Number Twelve Grimmauld Place are meant to be macabre, reflecting generations of barbarous abuses against the loyal elf servants. In the very same corridor, however, it is comical when Tonks knocks over the troll-leg umbrella stand (a parody of Victorian-era elephant-leg stands, prizes of the Big Hunt): that dismembered relic is morally acceptable, presumably, because trolls are inherently brutish and violent.

There are no vegetarians that we know of in the wizard world, and indeed wizards' use of animals for food, clothing, companionship, and entertainment very much mirrors our own. Leather and dragon hide appear side by side as clothing materials in the world of wizards, though dragonskin seems to be more prestigious. Lavish feasts at Hogwarts feature "a hundred fat, roast turkeys" and "mountains of roast," alongside other traditional fare.[24] Sausages and meat pies are regular grub at the Weasleys' house, and turkey and gravy are on offering there at the holidays, just as at Hogwarts.[25] We know that the Weasleys keep chickens and eat eggs, but in general the wizarding world's source of food—if not their source of scullery labor in the basement of Hog-warts—remains entirely mysterious. Early in the series Mrs. Weasley is said to conjure an entire meal, but this is somewhat at odds with statements made in the final book that food cannot be created out of nothing:

> "Your mother can't produce food out of thin air," said Hermione. "No one can. Food is the first of the Five Principal Exceptions to Gamp's Law of Elemental Transfigur[ation] … It's impossible to make good food out of nothing! You can Summon it if you know where it is, you can transform it, you can increase the quantity if you've already got some."[26]

This raises interesting questions concerning the economic underpinnings of the wizard world food supply. Are livestock raised in low numbers some-where, sold to wizards in small portions, and then increased in quantity for serving at the table? Or does the industrial scale of food served daily at Hog-warts imply that there are also larger supply farms somewhere? Rowling does not address these issues directly, though the way the questions are framed suggests something of a paradox—similar to why elf labor is needed at all in the basement, when we know that (for instance) dishes can wash themselves and put themselves away with a flick of the wand.

As in our world, the wizard community has centrally organized species management, and seems to mount deliberate conservation campaigns to protect species. Dragon populations must be carefully monitored, allowing them to propagate but not letting their numbers become dangerous to Muggles or wizards.[27] These structures point to a society interested in animal welfare and ecological balance. On the other hand, there are wizard versions of pet stores, such as Magical Menagerie on Diagon Alley—retail pet stores and the keeping of caged animals are sites of more obvious controversy in the human world, and begin to raise more problematic questions.[28] Animals are regularly used in Hogwarts classes for Vanishing, in a parallel manner to our own use of animals in biology classes for dissection. At Hogwarts, however, all the animals are living. In Transfiguration class, they start out Vanishing small mice, and work up to cats: "Hermione had actually progressed to Vanishing kittens" (the more complex the creature, we are told, the more difficult it is to Vanish).[29] This is in their fourth year; it is not stated what sorts of animals are Vanished in the final years of the Hogwarts curriculum. Beyond these ethical issues, creatures are also commodified and banalized in the magic world, just as in ours. A Hippogriff calendar is sent to a convalescing patient at St. Mungo's hospital: the Healer tells Broderick Bode, "And look, Broderick, you've been sent a pot plant and a lovely calendar with a different fancy Hip-pogriff for each month; they'll brighten things up, won't they?"[30]

Some of the uses to which wizards put lesser creatures in the wizard world would be considered exploitative and even abusive in the contemporary Muggle world. Leprechauns serve as cheerleaders at the Quidditch World Cup in *Harry Potter and the Goblet of Fire*, but they could well be willing participants in that national event.[31] Dwarves, absurdly dressed up as cupids with golden wings and harps, distribute valentine cards throughout Hogwarts on Valentine's Day in *Harry Potter and the Chamber of Secrets*. Their willingness is somewhat less obvious, since it is said they look "surly."[32] In *Harry Potter and the Philosopher's Stone*, Halloween is celebrated at Hogwarts with a display of 2000 live bats, used purely for effect.[33] For Christmas, Professor Flitwick in *Harry Potter and the Prisoner of Azkaban* decorates his classroom with real, fluttering, shimmering fairies; hundreds of live fairies are again used as decorations in *Goblet of Fire* for Christmas decorations.[34] Mandrake plants, whom we come to view as intelligent as we witness their coming-of-age adventures in *Chamber of Secrets*, are simply lobbed as weapons against the dark forces in the final book.[35] Finally, a dragon—a noble creature, as we have learned from Hagrid and from Charlie Weasley—is kept chained in the dungeons of Gringotts, as a security feature. He is a miserable, unhealthy specimen, who has not seen daylight in a long, long time: "The beast's scales had turned pale and flaky during its long incarceration under the ground; its eyes were milkily pink; both rear legs bore heavy cuffs from which chains led to enormous pegs driven deep into the rocky floor."[36] It does not have room in the cramped chamber even to spread its wings. The creature has also been subject to abuse, as part of its training: "Harry could see it trembling, and as they drew nearer he saw the scars made by vicious slashes across its face, and guessed that it had been taught to fear hot swords when it heard the sound of Clankers."[37] This harsh training was presumably inflicted by goblins, but wizards have apparently shown no moral outrage about the means used to keep their treasure safe.[38]

Part of the intended effect of introducing this sickly, abused dragon, of course, is to present an opportunity for Harry to liberate it. Indeed, Harry is a perennial liberator of all manner of creatures: a boa constrictor from the zoo, Buckbeak the Hippogriff, and Dobby, to name a few. Most often he seems to free such creatures as an expedience or even by accident, rather than from any great personal yearning for the freedom of all caged or oppressed creatures.[39] He uses the dragon, for instance, simply as his own means of escaping the deep vaults of Gringotts. If his means of exit were not cut off, there is no indication he would pay the dragon any attention. He has a personal connection with Dobby, but seems utterly uninterested in universalizing this principle of freedom to any other elves. Our last major scene involving elves is their siding with the wizards against the Dark Lord at the Battle of Hogwarts, but here our closing visualization of them is hardly flattering: "hacking and stabbing at the ankles and shins of Death Eaters, their tiny faces alive with malice."[40] Why malice? Neville, Harry, McGonagall, and many others all fight in the same battle: are they too beings of malice?

It seems we are meant to applaud Harry's kindly and respectful treatment of Dobby, and to view Kreacher's conversion away from the dark side as a step forward. Yet Kreacher has merely learned, over the course of the series, to be a good servant to Harry. By Chapter 12 of *Deathly Hallows*, he has become polite and respectful:

> "Shoes off, if you please, Master Harry, and hands washed before dinner," croaked Kreacher, seizing the Invisibility Cloak and slouching off to hang it on a hook on the wall, beside a number of old-fashioned robes that had been freshly laundered.[41]

The closing sentence of the entire seven-book series (save for the Epilogue) shows Harry himself—who had once been surprised to learn of the existence of a servant class in the wizard world—as having internalized the treatment of Kreacher as a menial servant:

> "That wand's more trouble than it's worth," said Harry. "And quite honestly," he turned away from the painted portraits, thinking now only of the four-poster bed lying waiting for him in Gryffindor Tower, and wondering whether Kreacher might bring him a sandwich there, "I've had enough trouble for a lifetime."

The casual thought of Kreacher as caterer of convenience hardly does the elf justice as a hero from the Battle for Hogwarts, which Kreacher proved himself to be. If Kreacher is a homophone for "creature," then this bodes ill for the future of animal dignity and welfare in the wizarding world.

While we are meant to commend Harry's liberating of Buckbeak the Hippogriff from his scheduled execution, there is no indication that the general use of them in the curriculum will be subject to any change. We know of the Hippogriffs in Hagrid's Care of Magical Creatures class that they "didn't seem to like being tethered like this."[42] Presumably, this is a necessary exigency in training a new generation of wizards how to interact with Hippogriffs and manage their well-being. Owls, on the other hand, have a worse situation in the wizard world. Hedwig, though she enjoys Harry's attention, is hardly allowed to live a life of freedom and dignity. Harry is locked up one summer at Privet Drive, and so Hedwig must apparently share his misery: though the lawns and fields outside abound in mice and other natural prey, Hedwig is kept in her cage, starving also. When Aunt Petunia slides Harry in a bowl of cold, canned soup, he downs half of it in one gulp, and pours the rest of the soggy vegetables into Hedwig's cage: "She ruffled her feathers and gave him a look of deep disgust."[43] Harry has a dream that night: "He dreamed that he was on show at the zoo, with a card reading 'Underage Wizard' attached to his cage."[44] Apparently Harry is incapable of extending this intuition to

Hedwig, who sometimes returns to her cage only resentfully, peering out at the world of freedom and potential prey longingly. In fact, Hedwig dies violently for Harry, though it is never addressed why a flying creature that has an innate ability to find people wherever they are is transported in a cage and subjected to such a high-risk sortie in the first place.

Sometimes when Rowling is dismissive of a species or includes the animal's pain in a humorous or sympathetic episode, she employs a specific narrative strategy to absolve the reader of bad feelings: she paints that species as violent or aggressive. We have seen trolls as hateful, foul creatures in *Philosopher's Stone*, and know furthermore that they are incapable of being civilized: a tapestry of trolls in Hogwarts portrays them clubbing Barnabas the Barmy for attempting to teach them ballet.[45] We also know that wizards enjoy (or in the past have enjoyed) troll hunting. During Harry's exams, we learn that the first Supreme Mugwump of the International Confederation of Wizards, Pierre Bonaccord, lobbied to put an end to troll hunting: "but Liechtenstein was having problems with a tribe of particularly vicious mountain trolls."[46] Bonaccord is misguided in his idealistic attempt to grant protection to a species undeserving of it for their brutish ferocity.

We see a similar strategy with regard to garden gnomes. First introduced to Harry in the lawn at The Burrow, gnomes in the Harry Potter series are capricious imps with heads like potatoes. They are a far cry from the conceptualization in the popular 1977 illustrated book *Gnomes* (with sequels and a host of ancillary materials), which painted the rich culture of gnomes in realistic detail.[47] Now, gnomes are a traditional British staple, a cutesy accoutrement of the tidy English middle-class lawn: Rowling's recasting of them as pests that need to be periodically lobbed over into adjacent fields is inspired. As rationalization, Ron explains, "It doesn't hurt them—you've just got to make them dizzy so they can't find their way back to the gnomeholes."[48] As further justification for the practice of de-gnoming, Rowling includes the detail that one gnome sinks its "razor-sharp teeth" into Harry's finger. As a result of that, "Harry learned quickly not to feel too sorry for the gnomes."[49] The violence of a natural species defending its home territory somehow morally justifies the Weasleys in evicting them. The scene is more or less replayed in *Deathly Hallows*, when Luna Lovegood lingers to say hello to the gnomes, while her father idealistically muses, "Such a glorious infestation! How few wizards realize just how much we can learn from the wise little gnomes."[50] Moments later Luna shows up having been bitten: obviously she and her father are meant to be seen as romantic flakes. The fact that gnomes lash out at those who bother them renders them less worthy of respect, though this is actually behavior that one would presume of any normal species acting in fear and defense. Not unlike Muggles, wizards disrupt natural patterns of fauna and flora for arbitrary ideals of garden and landscape aesthetics, and blame whatever species wind up serving as obstacles.[51]

The gnomes are somewhat bestialized in a scene when one comically tugs at a worm, and then once it is extracted, sits up against a rhododendron sucking it happily.[52] We know that gnomes are sufficiently intelligent to use language, however: they squeal "Gerroff me! Gerroff me!" during the gnome-tossing episode, and we later learn that the gnomes in the Weasley lawn who have spent too much time around Fred and Bill have picked up "a lot of excellent swear words."[53] Surely this problematizes the treatment of these creatures who are accorded no more regard than moles or groundhogs. Ron arbitrarily takes a kick at a gnome who is poking out from a bush, and Hermione's cat Crookshanks is free to chase them around the lawn.[54] Finally, Fred mischievously treats a gnome to humiliating repayment for a minor injury: the angel atop the Weasleys' Christmas tree is actually a gnome "that had bitten Fred on the ankle as he pulled up carrots for dinner. Stupefied, painted gold, stuffed into a miniature tutu and with small wings glued to its back, it glowered down at them all."[55] Only Fred, George, Harry, and Ron are in on the secret—and the reader, of course, who is meant to wink at them over everyone else's head and have a good laugh. It's hard to see how this would be funny were it a squirrel or chipmunk, and if the species in question is more intelligent than those, then it's even worse. In short, Rowling tries to have her cake and eat it too, drawing from the common lore of sentient, language-using Little People inhabiting our lawns and forests, while simultaneously exploiting them to create moments of prankish comedy that must then be rendered morally "safe."

There is moral ambivalence surrounding a number of larger, more complex magical creatures, such as giants and werewolves. These sided with Voldemort during his first rise to power, and stand in danger of doing so again. One of the things Voldemort has to offer the (mostly) neutral creatures such as giants is freedom—the freedom, according to Lupin, "we've been denying them for centuries."[56] In that light, their willingness to side with Voldemort is hardly incomprehensible, and the very notion of Dark Creatures is undermined. Lupin himself—a good werewolf—further reinforces that it is more difficult to divide species into good and evil camps than one might think. Parvati Patil's division of the animal kingdom into "proper creatures" and "monsters" is untenable ("That's more what I thought Care of Magical Creatures would be like ... proper creatures like unicorns, not monsters").[57] One is reminded of the Muggle propensity to value species in accordance with our own needs, whims, and ideals of cuteness, and to make conservation decisions accordingly.[58] Searching for a consistent moral ethic of wizards' treatment of various creatures is probably as futile as searching for one in the Muggle world. Certain species, for historical, emotional, and cultural reasons, are dear to us, while others are expendable.

The emotional need to express domination symbolically runs deep in both worlds also. When Buckbeak is wrongly thought to have attacked Draco out of uncontrolled savagery, the Committee for the Disposal of Dangerous Creatures is called in to investigate, and they recommend putting the Hippogriff to death. This is not a measure for public safety, but vengeance: Tom Riddle tells Hagrid, "The least Hogwarts can do is make sure the thing that killed their daughter is slaughtered."[59] This recalls the real world practice of calling for the destruction of animals that have killed or maimed humans, even if the human was clearly intruding on the animal's natural inhabit or provoking the creature needlessly.

In fact, ours is a society with a great many contradictions with regard to animal welfare and suffering. The Animal Welfare Act of 2006 (United Kingdom) allows for all activities that occur in the normal course of fishing, though ornamental fish and farmed fish are protected by cruelty and duty-to-ensure-welfare statutes. Free range game birds are not protected, but birds sold as pets are. Circuses, performing animals, and animal trainers are carefully provided for, as are animals used in testing. Specific provisions exist for farm animals, including laying chickens kept in non-cage systems, laying chickens kept in conventional cages, laying chickens kept in "enriched" cages, and calves confined for rearing and fattening.[60] The United Kingdom is generally considered in advance of many other nations regarding the humane treatment of animals. In the United States, the Animal Welfare Act of 1966 (amended several times since) does not cover reptiles, fish, amphibians, insects, or other invertebrates. Also excluded from the Animal Welfare Act definition of "animal" are birds, rats of the genus *Rattus* and mice of the genus *Mus*, farm animals, and animals used in research. Finally, "Animals sold in retail facilities are also exempt from the regulations, except wild or exotic animals."[61] This hodge-podge of *ad hoc* exceptions reveals not the consistent application of philosophically or morally articulated principles, but the catering of definitions and practices to our own wants and needs. At the time of this writing, the last horse slaughterhouse in the U.S. has just been ordered by the courts to close, while some 35 to 40 million cattle are slaughtered per year. In 2006, $38.5 billion were spent on pet products and services in the U.S. (including the growing industry of pet psychiatry and even pet psychics),[62] while some 1300 species remain on the U.S. endangered species list. My point here is not to suggest any particular resolution for these highly complex issues that have evolved over time, but to draw attention to several among the many contradictions Muggles hold with regard to their relationship with, and stewardship over, animal species. Because of the medieval exoticism that informs much of the atmospheric backdrop of Rowling's wizarding world, the wizards' reliance on animals is manifestly greater than our own. They still use animals for courier service and even as the principal writing medium (parchment is stretched and scraped animal skin). This casual antiquarianism forms an especially pronounced contrast with the highly modern political and ideological questions raised in the series.

Carey calls the Harry Potter series "among the most politically engaged novels to have been written for children in recent years," and writes, "Harry's personal struggle with the dark lord Voldemort ... provides a site for discussion of a democratic society's response to elitism, totalitarianism, and racism."[63] Though the narrative centers on a melodramatic battle between good and evil, the moral problem of animal suffering and animal stewardship seems to me equally present, though not taken up as an active political cause in the way that Hermione takes up the elf cause. Animal cruelty is specifically raised as an issue in the series,[64] but Rowling is hardly likely to be mistaken for an animal rights activist. Indeed, she seems to take a swipe at the radical Animal Liberation Front in Ron's suggestion that Hermione call her S.P.E.W. campaign the "House-Elf Liberation Front" instead.[65] Nonetheless, readers are drawn into contemplating some uncomfortable power dynamics of the natural realm: it is apparently acceptable to toss gnomes for fun and for lawn aesthetics, while noble creatures such as the Hippogriff should be admired and protected. The moral contours of the uneasy relationship between "wizards" and subordinate creatures are neither simple nor consistent, and in this way—whether Rowling intended it or not—they can serve readers as abstract thought experiments whose intuitions can then, perhaps, be applied variously to the very real problems and challenges of real world monsters, creatures, and pets.

Notes

1. See Elaine Ostry, "Accepting Mudbloods: The Ambivalent Social Vision of J.K. Rowling's Fairy Tales," in Giselle Liza Anatol, ed. *Reading Harry Potter: Critical Essays* (Westport, CT and London: Praeger, 2003): 89–101, 90–91.
2. Snuffbox and instrument: *Order of the Phoenix* 108; Fanged Frisbee: *Half-Blood Prince* 210. The Harry Potter editions consulted herein are abbreviated as such: *Philosopher's Stone*: *Harry Potter and the Philosopher's Stone* (London: Bloomsbury, 1997); *Chamber of Secrets*: *Harry Potter and the Chamber of Secrets* (London: Bloomsbury, 1998); *Prisoner of Azkaban*: *Harry Potter and the Prisoner of Azkaban* (London: Bloomsbury, 1999); *Goblet of Fire*: *Harry Potter and the Goblet of Fire* (London: Bloomsbury, 2001); *Order of the Phoenix*: *Harry Potter and the Order of the Phoenix* (London: Bloomsbury, 2003); *Half-Blood Prince*: *Harry Potter and the Half-Blood Prince* (London: Bloomsbury, 2006); *Deathly Hallows*: *Harry Potter and the Deathly Hallows* (New York: Arthur A. Levine/Scholastic, 2007).
3. *Prisoner of Azkaban* 15, 44
4. *Order of the Phoenix* 419, 425.
5. On the mythical significance of animals in Harry Potter, see M. Katherine Grimes, "Harry Potter: Fairy Tale Prince, Real Boy, and Archetypal Hero," in Lana A. Whited, ed. *The Ivory Tower and Harry Potter: Perspectives on a Literary Phenomenon* (Columbia and London: University of Missouri Press, 2002): 89–122, esp. 107, 118–119.
6. *Half-Blood Prince* 334; *Order of the Phoenix* 762.
7. Margaret J. Oakes, "Flying Cars, Floo Powder, and Flaming Torches: The Hi-Tech, Low-Tech World of Wizardry," in Giselle Liza Anatol, ed. *Reading Harry Potter: Critical Essays* (Westport, CT and London: Praeger, 2003): 117–128, 126.
8. Gnomes: *Chamber of Secrets* 33; doxys: *Order of the Phoenix* 95–98; "Freshly caught" pixies: *Chamber of Secrets* 79–80.
9. *Prisoner of Azkaban* 23.
10. *Order of the Phoenix* 533.

11. *Half-Blood Prince* 715.
12. See Iver B. Neumann: "Hagrid is a being of the boundary, a messenger, a mediator between species and realms, even between culture and nature" ("Naturalizing Geography: Harry Potter and the Realms of Muggles, Magic Folks, and Giants," in Daniel H. Nexon and Iver B. Neumann, ed. *Harry Potter and International Relations* (Lanham, MA, *et al.*: Rowman & Littlefield, 2006): 157–175, 165).
13. *Goblet of Fire* 174.
14. Brycchan Carey observes, "a significant aspect of Rowling's project is the promotion of political participation for young people and, rather than be narrowly prescriptive, she instead offers a range of political models for young people to explore and emulate" ("Hermione and the House-Elves: The Literary and Historical Contexts of J.K. Rowling's Antislavery Campaign," in Giselle Liza Anatol, ed. *Reading Harry Potter: Critical Essays* (Westport, CT and London: Praeger, 2003): 103–115, 106).
15. Writing after the release of the fourth book, Carey predicted of elves in the context of Hermione's elf freedom campaign, "it is plain that their story will be expanded in future installments of the series, and this narrative expansion may well include a resolution" (113). This did not turn out to be the case. Writing after the release of the fifth book, Steven W. Patterson argued not only in favor of the moral justness of Hermione's campaign, but moreover the immorality of apathy toward it, in "Kreacher's Lament: S.P.E.W. as a Parable on Discrimination, Indifference, and Social Justice," in David Baggett and Shawn E. Klein, eds. *Harry Potter and Philosophy: If Aristotle Ran Hogwarts* (Chicago and La Salle, IL: Open Court, 2004): 105–117. Rowling herself has apparently tried to correct the deficiency somewhat, explaining to her fans in a live chat hosted by Bloomsbury.com (July 30, 2007) after publication of the seventh book that Hermione continues to fight for elf rights after her graduation from Hogwarts:

> Hermione began her post-Hogwarts career at the Department for the Regulation and Control of Magical Creatures where she was instrumental in greatly improving life for house-elves and their ilk. She then moved ... to the Dept. of Magical Law Enforcement where she was a progressive voice who ensured the eradication of oppressive, pro-pureblood laws.
> (Retrieved March 30, 2008 from www.accio-quote.org/articles/2007/0730-bloomsbury-chat.html)

There is something depressing about this facile sort of *post hoc* narrative afterthought in a chat room.
16. *Chamber of Secrets* 133. On his comical dialect, reminiscent of the stock African American dialect in early cinema, see Carey 103–104. Shortly after the publication of *Chamber of Secrets*, Jar Jar Binks in George Lucas' *Star Wars Episode I: The Phantom Menace* would famously incur charges of racism for a dialect with similar features.
17. *Chamber of Secrets* 27, 132.
18. Elves do contribute to Harry's success in the final book, both indirectly (the goblin Griphook agrees to help Harry retrieve a Horcrux—Helga Hufflepuff's golden cup—from Gringotts after seeing Harry bury Dobby with his own hands (*Deathly Hallows* 486)) and directly (they side with the wizards in the final battle against Voldemort (*Deathly Hallows* 734–735)). The house-elf Kreacher urges his fellow elves into battle with the cry, "Fight for my Master, defender of house-elves!" (*Deathly Hallows* 734). In fact, Harry has only defended a single elf, and shows little sign of broader social consciousness. When elves fight against Voldemort, it is either out of servitude for their wizarding masters (reminiscent in some respects of African Americans who fought for the Confederacy during the Civil War) or else—as with many other sentient species—because they vaguely recognize the better of two evils.
19. A casual google search of "goblins" and "Jews" launches one into the midst of an active online discussion of the topic, conducted mostly in personal blogs, such as Matt Zeitlin, "Harry Potter and the Jewish Goblins" (whippersnapper.wordpress.com). For elves and African Americans, see Carey 107–113.
20. Carey 107.

21. *Order of the Phoenix* 733. This quotation is explicitly recalled once more, in the final book of the series (*Deathly Hallows* 199).
22. *Deathly Hallows* 509.
23. Ostry has drawn attention to the ambivalence of Rowling's ideological vision: she understands the slave mentality and depicts it accurately, but then downplays its evils or else plays it for laughs (96; see also Julia Park, "Class and Socioeconomic Identity in Harry Potter's England," in Giselle Liza Anatol, ed. *Reading Harry Potter: Critical Essays* (Westport, CT and London: Praeger, 2003): 179–189, 185).
24. *Philosopher's Stone* 149.
25. *Chamber of Secrets* 31, *Half-Blood Prince* 404.
26. Conjures meal: *Chamber of Secrets* 53; Hermione's recital: *Deathly Hallows* 292–293.
27. *Half-Blood Prince* 12.
28. *Prisoner of Azkaban* 48.
29. *Order of the Phoenix* 295. The detail that it is kittens Hermione is Vanishing, rather than cats, reinforces Rowling's dark humor and her assault on the banality of our societal obsession with cuteness.
30. *Order of the Phoenix* 453. The American version of *Harry Potter and the Order of the Phoenix* changes "pot plant" to "potted plant."
31. *Goblet of Fire* 95–101.
32. *Chamber of Secrets* 176.
33. *Philosopher's Stone* 127.
34. *Prisoner of Azkaban* 141, *Goblet of Fire* 359. In the brief companion piece *Fantastic Beasts and Where to Find Them* (London: Bloomsbury, 2001), which Rowling penned for the Comic Relief charity, Rowling provides details that might justify such practices: "The fairy is a small and decorative beast of little intelligence ... being excessively vain, it will become docile on any occasion when it is called to act as an ornament" (16–17). In the absence of such ancillary materials, the more obvious and prevalent conceptualization of fairies as a sentient, intelligent species with their own culture naturally prevails. Much of the information in the introduction and individual entries of *Fantastic Beasts and Where to Find Them* seems similarly motivated to help justify the ethical questions raised with regards to lesser creatures in the series. Puffskeins represent "a docile creature that has no objection to being cuddled or thrown about" (34), and of leprechauns it is said, "alone of the 'little people,' leprechauns can speak" (25)—which is entirely at odds with what we know of gnomes from the series (more below), and arguably of pixies from this companion book itself (they produce a "high-pitched jabbering intelligible only to other pixies," 32).
35. The Mandrakes are said to become "moody and secretive" as they enter adolescence, for instance, and in their teens they throw a loud party in a tree-house (*Chamber of Secrets* 175, 186); *Deathly Hallows* 620.
36. *Deathly Hallows* 535–536.
37. *Deathly Hallows* 536.
38. The dragon's employment in this capacity is widely known to wizards. As early as Chapter 5 of the first book, during Harry's first trip to the bank, Hagrid nonchalantly mentions, "They say there's dragons guardin' the high-security vaults" (*Philosopher's Stone* 51).
39. Thus Ostry: "Harry gives Dobby, the house-elf who defies his master to help the boy, his freedom, but only incidentally" (96).
40. *Deathly Hallows* 735.
41. *Deathly Hallows* 225.
42. *Prisoner of Azkaban* 88.
43. *Chamber of Secrets* 22.
44. *Chamber of Secrets* 22.
45. *Order of the Phoenix* 345.
46. *Order of the Phoenix* 640.
47. Wil Huygen and Rien Poortvliet (illustrator), *Gnomes* (New York: H.N. Abrams, 1977).
48. *Chamber of Secrets* 33. The claim that it doesn't hurt them is somewhat reminiscent of the long-standing Muggle chestnut, as unprovable as it is improbable, that lobsters feel nothing when dropped into a pot of boiling water.

49. *Chamber of Secrets* 33.
50. *Deathly Hallows* 140.
51. Harry enjoys a more rustic look to a garden: watching the lawn spruced up for Bill and Fleur's wedding, Rowling tells us that he "liked it in its overgrown state" and "thought that it looked rather forlorn without its usual contingent of capering gnomes" (*Deathly Hallows* 107).
52. *Half-Blood Prince* 409. Scrimgeour says conversationally, "Funny little chaps, aren't they?"
53. *Chamber of Secrets* 33, *Deathly Hallows* 140.
54. *Deathly Hallows* 107, *Goblet of Fire* 56 and 60.
55. *Half-Blood Prince* 391.
56. *Order of the Phoenix* 81, and see *Half-Blood Prince* 397.
57. *Goblet of Fire* 383.
58. David L. Stokes, "Things We Like: Human Preferences among Similar Organisms and Implications for Conservation," *Human Ecology* 35 (2007): 361–369.
59. *Chamber of Secrets* 184.
60. Retrieved March 30, 2008 from http://www.defra.gov.uk/animalh/welfare/farmed/on-farm.htm. For historical context and development, see Hilda Kean, *Animal Rights: Political and Social Change in Britain since 1800* (London: Reaktion Books, 1998). "Enriched" cages provide at least 750 cm² (as opposed to around 450 cm² in traditional chicken batteries), and must contain a nest and litter.
61. Retrieved March 30, 2008 from http://www.aphis.usda.gov/lpa/pubs/fsheet_faq_notice/faq_awusda.html.
62. Retrieved March 30, 2008 from http://www.appma.org/press_industrytrends.asp.
63. Carey 105.
64. For instance, the brusque fiasco in which Harry crashes his trolley into the wall at King's Cross, and spills Hedwig's cage onto the floor, causes "a lot of muttering about cruelty to animals from the surrounding crowd" (*Chamber of Secrets* 55). Of course, this muttering comes from ignorant Muggles who don't properly understand the situation.
65. Carey 106.

Chapter Ten

Harry Potter, the War against Evil, and the Melodramatization of Public Culture

Marc Bousquet

Voilà! In view, a humble vaudevillian veteran, cast vicariously as both victim and villain by the vicissitudes of Fate. This visage, no mere veneer of vanity, is a vestige of the vox populi, now vacant, vanished. However, this valorous visitation of a by-gone vexation, stands vivified, and has vowed to vanquish these venal and virulent vermin vanguarding vice and vouchsafing the violently vicious and voracious violation of volition. The only verdict is vengeance; a vendetta, held as a votive, not in vain, for the value and veracity of such shall one day vindicate the vigilant and the virtuous.

(V for Vendetta)

Detective Martin Prendergast: "Let's go meet some nice policemen. They're good guys. Let's go."
    Bill Foster. "I'm the bad guy? How did that happen? I did everything they told me to. Did you know I build missiles? I help to protect America. You should be rewarded for that."

(Falling Down)

This chapter explores the Harry Potter series in the context of the Reagan–Bush–Thatcher–Blair "war against evil" and an intensifying reliance on melodrama in political culture. The core observation that I make is twofold. First, melodrama can be an extraordinarily effective organizer of public opinion in service of imperial, dominative ambition, whether employed by the black shirts of the Third Reich or by recent occupants of the White House. The powerful appeal of simple, binary melodramatic ethics (pure good versus unmitigated evil) and its core subjectivity—the victimized, misunderstood hero, who often appears paranoid or delusional to others—is a significant component of the success of the Harry Potter series. That same powerful appeal, when employed by state power and corporate media, helps to organize feelings of national victimization (by the Jews! by radical Islam! by the "haters of freedom" and "our way of life"!) in support of domination. The totalizing ethics of melodrama lean toward justification of violence—i.e., torture can be "good" when employed against "evil" people. In this way, by organizing nationalist—even imperial—feelings in support of the violent exercise of state power against persons, people, cultures, and other states, melodrama justifiably raises enormous concerns for critical observers of the United States as a political and cultural agent on the world stage.

One way of reading the Harry Potter series, therefore, is in the mode of cultural pathology: i.e., as a potentially harmful cultural artifact that disseminates a melodramatic worldview and therefore prepares the way for the abuse of state power. There is of course substantial support for such a reading. Over the course of the series, there is also substantial support for a complementary reading that would show Rowling—like many others working in a melodramatic mode—employing the melodramatic grammar of white hats versus black hats to introduce many fine shades of gray. This second reading would be compatible with numerous associated lines of thought, especially those springing from prevailing tendencies in Birmingham-school cultural studies. For these readers, the question is not how Rowling intended the series, or whether there was some firm allegorical meaning "in" the text that was itself dangerous to young readers' moral, ethical, or political sensibility. Rather, these critics would explore the complex, ambiguous—and often liberatory— ways that readers employ texts, even the politically distasteful elements of very regressive texts, often against the author's intentions.

The second core observation that I make is more difficult than the first, and leads to much edgier, but perhaps more subtle and fruitful, readings of Harry Potter as a cultural artifact than those suggested above.

The key thought is that melodrama's broad appeal has much to do with its origins in the revolutionary working-class insurrections that saw the establishment of democratic states between 1798 and 1848. With that in mind, I point out that both historically and at present melodrama has never been only a rhetoric of state power, of false victimhood assumed by imperial storm troopers in service of domination. It has been and remains also a rhetoric of liberation. The appeal of melodrama as a liberatory rhetoric may in part explain its success when hijacked by the state. Of particular interest is the striking example of the film *V for Vendetta*, which—astonishingly in the current climate of repression—represents the political violence of its victim hero in extraordinarily sympathetic terms in his campaign against state repression. It is a powerful, disturbing, exhilarating film that (re)captures the revolutionary, democratic sensibility of the melodrama. It explicitly calls up the language, iconography, and subjectivity of victimization established in the democratic revolutionary theater in an explicit attempt to once again build popular insurrectionary feeling and name democracy's common enemy—in those who have hijacked the democratic state and the public sphere.

Since there are numerous parallels in the ways the later installments of the Potter series handle the abuse of state power, we must ask the difficult question: how, then, shall we respond to the melodramatic sensibility in Harry Potter, especially as it unfolds over the course of the series, with Rowling visibly struggling with the established melodramatic grammar of the novels in the aftermath of the intensified adoption of melodramatic rhetoric to justify broad extensions of state power in both Britain and the United States after September 11, 2001?

Taking the series as a whole, can we dismiss its deployment of melodrama simplistically as social-psychological bad medicine for young minds? Or are there ways in which the series is like *V for Vendetta*? While noxious as a rhetoric of domination, is melodrama perhaps still a viable and necessary rhetoric from below? We may not wish, in other words, to throw out the revolutionary baby with the right-wing bathwater.

Finally: are we so sure that that we know what the "correct" alternatives to melodrama might be?

Melodrama, History and Form

Melodrama (black hats vs. white hats, pure good vs. pure evil, as in Sergio Leone westerns, Rocky and Bulwinkle, etc.) originates in the eighteenth century working-class theater and its emerging iconography of the French revolution. The villains wore black, the dark evening clothes, and top hats of the aristocracy. The heroes wore the homespun, often undyed clothing of the working class and peasantry. Melodrama placed villains in black top hats with specific rhetorical consequences. It functioned to "name the enemy" for working-class audiences, fostering a sense of class solidarity against the aristocratic oppressor. As a victim, the hero's character generally doesn't develop, but is always, simply, "good." Consequently, much of the dramatic action has to do with being misunderstood or victimized. The character doesn't change, but his circumstances change or his true identity is revealed.

Peter Brooks analyzes the core feature of melodrama as this moment of enlightenment or clarification, the climactic revelation of truth. It is therefore a drama of knowledge. The action ends when the mystery is dispelled and/or the misunderstood hero's always-extant goodness is at last recognized. Brooks' analysis in this regard is particularly helpful because the "good versus evil" iconography of melodrama has, of course, a much longer history.[1]

The special contribution of the melodrama is the creation of a victim hero, misunderstood and misrecognized, in a plot that drives relentlessly toward clarification and recognition. The story is over when the victim hero's virtue is known. This means that one of the genre's most common plot engines is misrecognition by a figure in authority—a parent, employer, spouse, police officer, politician, cleric, headmaster, or teacher. Sometimes the mistaken authority in melodrama is "the public" itself, or a figure for the public sphere, such as a journalist or sports audience. Typically the ultimate recognition of the hero's goodness is accompanied by other revelations: the identity or true character of the villain, clarification of plot lines, and so forth. As Brooks points out, the melodramatic aesthetic introduces ambiguity and complexity only to drive it from the scene, emphasizing that "the *reward* of virtue is only a secondary manifestation of the *recognition* of virtue" (27).

Overwhelmingly, the dominant form of the nineteenth-century stage and the twentieth-century film industry, melodrama incorporates Enlightenment/ Encyclopedic ideology about the relationship between knowledge, education, and social change. In melodrama, when the problem is fully understood, the problem is resolved. This faith that the exposure of wrongs leads inevitably to their redress is widespread among educators and cultural actors throughout the West. Sustained by melodramatic cultural forms, including journalism, political speech, and educator practice, the belief in the transformative power of knowledge, speech, and publicity emerged in the eighteenth century, rose to dominance in the nineteenth century, and remains dominant today.

Accordingly, melodrama did not long remain revolutionary working-class propaganda. It was incorporated into the project of political modernism more broadly. Promptly appropriated by the elites, professionals, and managers who controlled the theaters, it was adapted to literary purposes and influenced political discourse, political iconography, and political thought from the early nineteenth century through the present. Little studied nor discussed in academic circles today, melodrama has far from waned. If it has become more difficult to grasp critically, it is only because it saturates the political and cultural atmosphere. It is the single most influential mass-media form today. It is nearly omnipresent in big-budget Hollywood films—many of whose video-store "genres" of western, thriller, action, horror, etc, are best understood as subgenres of classic melodrama. (Many of them have two centuries of antecedents in working-class theater.) Ditto for almost all video games, especially the "first person shooter" variety. Melodrama structures bestselling fiction and television narrative. It shapes tabloid and television journalism. It provides a powerful set of tropes to political speech, especially in wartime, or in struggles analogized to war (as in the "war on drugs"). In political discourse, including partisan speech and television news reporting, melodrama's capacity to "name the enemy" and consolidate a collective antagonist to the "evil" Other is most effectively deployed by those whose interests are shared by corporate media interests.

Ever present in modern political discourse, melodrama is not, however, always dominant. For instance, the wartime melodramatic register established in the struggle against fascism continued unabated in the subsequent McCarthyism. Subsequently, however, the melodramatic policy complex of anticommunist geopolitics through the 1960s and 1970s steadily gave ground. Even in the midst of the Reagan–Bush–Thatcher reaction, Reagan's "evil empire" remark was therefore received as startling and regressive, one which caused bitter divisions even within the ranks of his strongest supporters and closest advisors.

Today, however, melodramatic conventions are once again policy and the manufactured consensus of political culture, including the conviction that evildoers are less than human. George W. Bush's rhetoric of a "war against evil" frames and sustains a broader public commitment regarding "evildoers." This rhetoric casts the United States in the role of blameless victim, a virgin tied to the tracks while top-hatted dictators of oil wealth gleefully twirl their mustaches.

The fact that Saddam Hussein had no connection to the events of September 11th only intensifies the melodramatic register, because the United States is now not only blameless, but misunderstood on the world stage. The Bush administration experiences its crisis of legitimacy in relation to the Iraq war in the manner of the heroes of most Schwarzenegger, Stallone, or Willis star vehicles. From Rambo and the Terminator to Willis's John McLane, these violent avengers are all compulsively and repetitively misunderstood by employers, politicians, spouses, and the public. The action of the plot moves in installments toward clarification—a clarification powered by authority's long-awaited recognition of the hero's essential, unvarying, misunderstood goodness. As the misunderstood hero of J. S. Jones' 1838 classic, *The People's Lawyer*, has it: "You shall one day know who I am and be sorry for this injustice!" (398). Invoking the language, iconography, and psychology of melodrama, the Bush administration appears to have the same desire—to be recognized by last-minute intervention (the confession of an evildoer, the discovery of a missing document or witness, etc.). The Bush administration compulsively repeats its need to be acknowledged as having been wholly good and blameless from the beginning. At the end of the mayhem, the hero's reward is an acknowledgement that he was right all along, however paranoid, irrational, and antisocial he seemed throughout the plot.

Educators, Critics and Literary "Realism"

By contrast, many commentators and critics cast the Bush administration within the narrative of bildungsroman or bourgeois realism. These narratives go a bit like this: facing a test of character and growth, the Bush administration fails to change, reflect, or develop. This conserves the traditional reference point of literary realism: the "realistic" representation of the psychological development of bourgeois subjects.

Those of us working in the academic wing of the culture industries typically value these "realist" and classically liberal-bourgeois narratives of character growth—of overcoming internal obstacles and changes of attitude by the hero—more highly than we value melodramatic narratives of overcoming external obstacles and consequent changes of attitude by persons other than the hero. We tend to view bourgeois realism and melodrama as very different from each other. We further believe bourgeois realism to have tremendous merits—literary, ethical, psychological, educational—that melodrama all but completely lacks. To a strong extent, our academic rejection of melodramatic cultural forms reflects our strong commitment to classically liberal values, including those of liberal education. Bourgeois-realist forms of narrative ascribe enormous merit to all activities associated with character development (including, broadly, education). Bourgeois, or psychological, realism resolves plots happily with personal growth, and unhappily with failure to grow.

The discomfort of liberal educators with melodrama is understandable. Liberal educators commonly conceive of liberal education as in part encouraging students to "develop" in relation to melodramatic forms. The presumption is one of a trajectory: away from melodramatic forms associated with the unschooled juvenile (first-person shooter video games, cartoons, comics) toward the bourgeois-realist forms generally prized in close proportion to schooling. These preferred texts include, for instance, novels dealing with contemporary social themes such as race, gender, and cultural difference. Significantly, however, these preferred texts rarely address the theme of social class (except through highly ideological mediations such as race).

In addition to positive and prosocial messages regarding the importance of character-building against racism and gender bias, these novels typically require a grasp of such new-critical values as ambiguity, complexity, and irony. With more of these things, more internal navigation of ambiguity and complexity, and less melodramatic binarizing and simplification, we believe, perhaps the Bush administration would have urged us to saddle up to Saddam's hanging party in vain.

In short, liberal educators view melodrama through a melodramatic lens. We view melodrama, purely, and simply, as "bad." In the academic imagination, melodrama is bad literature, bad culture, bad politics, bad education. It stands in opposition to "good" literature, politics, and education.

This leads those of us with educator's tin stars pinned to our vests to a clear, simple, straightforward conclusion: We need more schooling to stamp out the juvenile attachment to melodrama. Melodrama is the enemy.

But is it?

The Unexpected Ambiguities of Melodrama

Thinking about melodrama requires us to go a little further, to explore some unexpected ambiguities of the melodramatic structure of feeling. One complexity to consider is that bourgeois realism and melodrama have a lot in common—especially the shared tradition of romantic, heroic, individualism. Pursuing the growth of bourgeois character in bildungsroman, literary realism developed in close relationship to the social psychology of a professional, managerial fraction of the working class: persons for whom an extended apprenticeship of schooling and prosocial character development ends with the reward of a good income and status recognition, a rough analogue of the character-building adventures of the bourgeois son in bildungsroman, not yet ready to direct his father's wealth-building enterprise. From the latter half of the nineteenth century through the present, professionals and managers have consumed a literature valorizing the overcoming of internal obstacles, of psychological growth associated with external rewards. In a way, literary realism is simply the flexible form of the melodrama, with the obstacles to recognition moved inward. Melodramatic heroes are misunderstood by authority; realist heroes misunderstand themselves or others. Realism also depends on a series of recognitions; it, too, is an epistemological drama. But in realism the liberal subjectivity—Rorty's liberal ironist, Anderson's imperial self—becomes both the object and subject of recognition. Both as a matter of cultural history and emotional content, the liberal conviction of the educator and administrator that the virtues of schooling will be rewarded is not so very far from the convictions of the melodramatic hero. Both progress toward the ultimate recognition of virtue.

Another consideration is that melodrama functions more like grammar than a prescription or formula. It shapes what can be said, but is not fully determining. Even in its most industrialized and commodified form, Hollywood film, artists working with the grammar of melodrama have found a way to navigate complexity, ambiguity, and irony. This is the intention of Joel Schumacher's Falling Down, based on an Edgar-award winning original screenplay by Ebbe Roe Smith. In many ways a classically modernist film with the auteurist ambition of featuring Everyman on the edge, the film thematizes the inadequacy of the melodramatic register of contemporary subjectivity—"I'm the bad guy? But I build missiles to protect America!"—while relying entirely on dominant, melodramatic film grammar to make the point. This is the core observation of Birmingham-school cultural studies approaches to commodified mass culture: ideology critique of mass culture in the Frankfurt school tradition, while valuable, is not enough. Even the most ideologically narrow cultural artifacts bear contradictory meanings and can be put to use against the grain of the intended significance. Pursuing Bourdieu's dictum regarding mass culture—"There is another production called consumption"—the Birmingham school traces the ways that ordinary citizens constantly pry ideologemes from their intended meanings and creatively re-deploy them to liberatory purpose.

In short, both producers and consumers of melodrama are in the habit of making the language of black and white signify in every shade of gray.

This contradictory deployment of melodrama as both the object of critique and the grammar of the critique itself, is also true of mainstream responses to the Bush administration's "war against evil" rhetoric. On *The Daily Show*, Jon Stewart, and on *The Colbert Report*, Stephen Colbert, for instance, constantly skewer the Bush administration's melodramatic worldview. But Stewart's own trope for the vice-president and president are iconically melodramatic villains. For him, Cheney is Darth Vader, the aristocrat-villain caped in black. He correspondingly casts Bush in the role of pure evil's comic sidekick with an imitation ("heh-heh-heh") redolent of such familiar second villains as Muttley, Dick Dastardly's dog in the Hanna–Barbera series. Colbert's performance is even more interesting: as a liberal ironist, he nightly performs the role of someone who, as he says, "sees the world in black and white," with the apparent intention of inviting his audience to consider the distance between the worldview of the egotistical simpleton he portrays and their own. Yet it's never clear that the gap is as large as he would like.

The best critique of the melodramatic worldview is that it simplifies reality and can be used to overwhelm dissenting speech and critical thought. The Bush administration's assignation of white hats and black hats makes it much harder, for instance, to speak or even imagine parallels between the historical tactics of American rebel-patriots (roadside sniping by nonuniformed combatants) and those of contemporary Iraqi resistance to American occupying forces. There is little to defend in the worldview of an imperial nuclear superpower that grasps international relations in the cartoonish and paranoiac mode of an "axis of evil." Deploying melodramatic epistemology well in advance of its brigades, the Bush administration seeks—just as Elisabeth Anker contends—to place state power beyond the realm of democratic politics and the possibility of debate: "Thoughtfulness was replaced by the imperative toward retributive action" (33). The administration's binarization into camps of "for" and "against" is, of course, a form of totalization, an intellectual reign of terror. Anker is right to name melodrama as the mode through which Bush and the corporate media "took power away from citizens by encouraging them to assume that state power was an unquestionable moral imperative in fighting the eternal battle between good and evil" (36). By way of melodrama, the Bush administration and corporate media framed a national consensus that a) all those dubbed evildoers by the administration can and should be tortured to clarify the plot; b) that there can be no relief to good until the evil other is destroyed; and c) because "you're either with us [good] or against us [evil]," anyone disturbing these clarities is potentially an enemy of the state.

On the other hand, Anker probably misses out on something by describing melodrama as having primarily "dangerous ramifications" for democratic citizenship (22). As we've seen with Colbert and Stewart, even liberal ironists are drawn to melodrama's power to name the enemy, creating a solidarity of antagonism. Any full consideration of melodramatic utterance has to acknowledge, for instance, the breathtaking challenge to liberal orthodoxy posed by a courageous film like the Wachowski brothers' *V for Vendetta*, which attempts to recapture the revolutionary melodramatic worldview, wresting the language, iconography, and yearning for justice of melodrama away from state propaganda and back to its roots in popular insurrectionary feeling.

Is it only a question of the Bush administration using the wrong cultural mode? Or is it a question of the cultural mode being deployed to name the wrong enemy? *V for Vendetta* makes a compelling case for the latter. One has to wonder whether it can be accidental that a major film so fully capturing the democratic revolutionary feeling emerges after three decades of a reactionary class war from above, producing globally unprecedented extremes of inequality and a security state far closer to the totalitarian imaginings of Orwell's 1984 than most U.S. observers ever thought possible.

Furthermore: clarification remains a liberartory aim in many circumstances. As I was finishing up this piece, journalist John Cloud published his piece on Dumbledore's sexuality in Time magazine, igniting a variety of reactions, many akin to this letter to the editor, anxiously trying to contain its meaning: "The Harry Potter story is about Harry and his best friends working together to fight evil. It is not a p.c. statement about sexuality. It is not Harry and the Angry Inch. J. K. Rowling's story started as a children's book and evolved into teenage reading material. That is it." (Van den Herik) As liberal educators, our typical reaction to this anxious demand for clarity is a rueful smile. Of course, we say, the story is really about Dumbledore's sexuality. That good and evil stuff is for children and the unsophisticated.

Notwithstanding our sense of superiority for mastering the arts of subtextuality, if we push even a bit at the liberal valorization of ambiguity, complexity, and irony, we can't be so sure that these modes are automatically preferable in all circumstances. Anyone remotely familiar with U.S. labor law understands that the Reagan–Bush reaction has not proceeded with cartoonish references to "evil empires" alone. It has also proceeded with the canny work of battalions of lawyers and bureaucrats dedicated to producing regulatory complexity and ambiguity around such terms as "work" and "worker." These masters of subtext all trained in classes like ours. They too chuckled at the letter-writer who insisted that the story was really about a bunch of kids "working together to fight evil." We taught them to do that.

The consequence of these regulatory ambiguities—crafted by our best students—has been profound for tens of millions of workers. Persons working as "independent contractors" aren't workers. Undocumented immigrants can work, but cannot claim the rights of labor. Persons employed "part-time" don't enjoy many worker protections, and now work more than full-time— just at multiple part-time jobs. At the height of the faculty unionization movement, faculty in private colleges were dubbed "supervisory" personnel, and can be legally retaliated against for attempting to unionize. Following the same legal ambiguity, even nurses who have no subordinates have been legally construed as supervisory personnel, and denied labor protections.

If there is a mode that characterizes the class war from above, it turns out not to be melodrama after all. Instead, class war from above relies on new-critical textual manipulation: regulatory ambiguity, the million-dollar-a-year lawyer's production of interpretive complexity, and the ironic mode, which allows our liberally-educated "best students" to live with themselves while they service capital.

The same points about nuance, complexity, and ambiguity might be made with respect to the law and discourse surrounding torture, or the Supreme Court's endorsement of Bush's electoral "victory" over Gore in a state governed by his brother.

Harry Potter, Victim Hero

Over the course of the series, Rowling's ambitions for her central character change and grow. He begins a classically melodramatic victim hero, and becomes, with the longer novels (four to seven), more of a bourgeois-realist hero, with *bildungsroman*-style challenges that establish the growth and evolution of his character. Perhaps the most dramatic challenge Harry faces is the evolution in his feelings toward the situation of the house-elves, a growth that takes place so slowly that for several installments of the series it is hard to credit Rowling with what appears to have been her ultimate intention, for Harry to move toward the greater sympathy with their situation evidenced by Hermione and, eventually, Dumbledore. The melodramatic grammar established in the first novels remains firmly in place throughout the saga, and the more ambitious novels have as one of their core challenges the expression of moral ambiguities—albeit with a vocabulary designed to eliminate them.

As we first meet him, Potter is described in the classic melodramatic posture of the victim hero, whose true identity is obscured even from himself: "he slept on, not knowing he was special, not knowing he was famous" (*Sorcerer's Stone* 18). Throughout the subsequent decade, Harry yearns to be known, and we are presented with a montage foreshadowing the satisfaction of this desire, showing a parade of strangers over the years inexplicably waving at him, bowing to him, shaking his hand, and so forth (*Sorcerer's Stone* 27). During this period, and really throughout this novel, Harry's character doesn't struggle to develop, so much as it struggles simply to emerge—to pass into the limelight, pressing past obstacles into vision and recognition. The Dursleys function to cloak his virtue, actively concealing evidence of his good qualities, his past, his identity—his very existence. Relegated to a closet under the stairs, he is absent from the family photographic record, and misinformed about his parents and culture. Above all, the Dursleys are repeatedly underscored as persons who couldn't appreciate Potter's virtues even if they were inclined to do so. This sets up the drama of unveiling that the first novel, and the entire series, compulsively repeats: Harry's essential virtues are misunderstood by figures in power and authority, then recognized, then misunderstood once more.

The world of school initiates the first definitive revelation of Potter's character with the traditional melodramatic device of the waylaid document. The protracted struggle over the admissions letter is the first direct confrontation that the boy initiates: for the first time, he makes demands and outright refuses the authority of the Dursleys: "Harry didn't move. 'I WANT MY LETTER!' he shouted" (31). This is entirely a struggle over knowing: the Dursleys seek at all costs to prevent revelation while Harry and his eventual sidekick Hagrid struggle to bring it about.

That moment of enlightenment is partly the revealed memory of trauma (the moment of his parents' murder), troped on limelight: "As Hagrid's story came to a close, he saw again the blinding green light, more clearly than he had ever remembered it before" (46).

On the melodramatic stage, this revelation scene would have been accompanied by a flash of light revealing the characters frozen in place in a carefully composed picture, or tableau, as well as by a sharp sound effect, such as thunder, an organ chord (ta-da!) or, as when Sweeney Todd lifts his razor high and pauses, a steam whistle. Frequently the tableau is accompanied by the echoing laugh of the villain, which is what accompanies Harry's revelation: "and he remembered something else, for the first time in his life, a high, cold, cruel, laugh" (46).

This first achievement by our hero is an achievement of self-assertion, of insisting on being known in his proper character—in this case, as a potential master of the arts of traditional, liberal, college-preparatory schooling, here troped as magic. One of the great weaknesses of the melodrama as a vehicle for working-class solidarity was its early, pronounced tendency to reveal the identity of the hero as someone who doesn't belong to the working class at all, typically an aristocrat in disguise or blocked from his inheritance and title by accident or conspiracy. In some cases of Jacksonian-era melodrama, the hero's working-class roots and rough manners are celebrated in the form of a "nature's aristocrat," a version that survives today in, for instance, Bruce Willis vehicles or television police/legal procedurals, in which sexist or rough-talking police officers nonetheless reveal themselves as having "hearts of gold." More commonly, however, as in the 1839 J. S. Jones classic, *The People's Lawyer*, the hero proves to have been not nature's nobleman but, more simply, an actual aristocrat in disguise. In these cases, the recognition of the hero's identity is accompanied by a pot of money, status, and, typically, the power to resolve any remaining conflicts in the plot.

This tendency captures the desire of the working-class audience to escape its condition, albeit in a way unlikely to advance working-class revolution. This device has particular social-psychological appeal for the emergent professional-managerial fraction of the working class, for whom schooling and liberal bourgeois ideology represented the possibility of a concrete, personal satisfaction of their individual desire to escape the working-class condition—without incurring the personal risks and cost of transforming underlying social relations.

The experience of schooling is surprisingly consistent with melodramatic ideology for the professional-managerial class: sentenced, like other members of the working class, to a lifetime of labor, of working in order to live, schooling is the experience that reveals their meritoriousness, validates their claim to an income some fraction or multiple of the income of others who work in order to live. Through schooling, the professional-managerial class supplants the "nature's nobleman" artisan hero of some Jacksonian melodrama with the lords of the grade-point average, the seigneurs of standardized testing, and so on. Potter, Hermione Granger, and Dumbledore are all variants of this version of heroism, which includes a fairly conventional dismissal of the (rest of) the working class (the dullard Hufflepuffs), accompanied by an equally typical lionization ("griffin"-dor) of the hard-working, but modestly leisured, bourgeois "good" members of the ruling class comprising entrepreneurs, professionals, managers, and venture capitalists by distinction from the leisured, aristocratic "bad" members of the ruling class in Slytherin. One of the reasons the scholarly Ravenclaw house is largely absent from the plot through the series is because the heroism of Griffyndor is functionally reliant on schooling. The text fails to distinguish Gryffindor from Ravenclaw to the extent it distinguishes it from the other two houses because Gryffindor is schooling plus bourgeois virtue (and sometimes schooling *as* bourgeois virtue), together with the habits of rule. Gryffindor represents the professional-managerial contradiction—of striving to prove merit "democratically" through schooling, but which turns out to be an opportunity to display a plausibly bourgeois meritoriousness that associates social power with belonging to the ruling class, or at least conformity with its interests. Which may explain in part why the biggest-selling of the books about Potter may well turn out to be the one that offers "leadership wisdom from the world of wizards," Tom Morris' *If Harry Potter Ran General Electric*, a compendium of platitudes purporting to explain how to be a "great man" in the world of capitalist exploitation.

The revelation of Potter's identity follows this pattern of schooling-as-revealed-bourgeois-merit closely. The recognition of his virtue is accompanied in short order by the revelation that he is, in fact, an aristocrat in the world of schooling, and a splendidly rich celebrity to boot: "It's an outrage! ... not knowin' his own story when every kid in our world knows his name!"(*Sorcerer's Stone* 44). With considerable dramatic economy, Rowling makes Potter's first working-class sidekick the agent of this revelation

("Hagrid looked at Harry with warmth and respect blazing in his eyes" (47)), so that the hero's new aristocratic status is properly set off by the freely given deference of the working class, as well as by the (harder-won) new deference of the professional-managerial suburbanite Dursleys. As an aristocrat in the world of schooling, he is summoned away from the destiny arranged for him by these false parents ("He's going to Stonewall High and he'll be grateful for it.") into the boarding-school destiny arranged by his true parents and their surrogates, such as Dumbledore—"His name's been down ever since he was born" (47).

The nature of Potter's belonging to a ruling class is the source of considerable plot consideration over the course of the series. The continuous recycling of the revelation plot over the course of the series—Potter misunderstood, Potter recognized—retains some vitality by using these repeated scenes of misrecognition to parse more and more finely the hero's relationship to other heroes and villains, often on the basis of socioeconomic class and class fractions. What one observer has convincingly described as "Rowling's close detail of a late capitalist, global consumer culture" therefore at least to an extent navigates some of the "social inequities and injustices that masquerade behind the draperies of democracy" (Westman 306–307). In this way, Potter's aristocracy of the boarding school is quickly distinguished from the aristocracy of the Malfoys (who retain their ancient association, like all of the series' villains, with the iconic clothing, manner, grammar, and plot function of the landed class enemy of the revolutionary melodrama). Potter's qualifications for the ruling class are also quickly distinguished from the professional-managerial scholasticism of Hermione, and the lower-middle-class institutional loyalties of the civil-servant Weasleys, as well as the commercial interests of the Dursleys (though Potter himself later dabbles in venture capitalism, supporting the Weasley twins' desire to rise from their background by enterprise). Later episodes deal with the more difficult parsings represented by Tom Riddle/Voldemort, Snape, and Dumbledore, as different dimensions of Potter's character are revealed.

The series derives tremendous energy from continuously recycling the revelation plot. The series reveals over and over again that Harry is, indeed, good, right, and virtuous after being mistaken by family, friends, the wizarding public, the Muggle public, and even parental surrogate Dumbledore: at a few points Potter is even mistaken about himself, and the plot functions to reveal Harry's goodness to himself. The revelation plot works for Harry's various doppelgangers as well, both those who are eventually revealed as standing with good, and those who are eventually revealed as standing with evil. Indeed, nearly every significant character in the book takes a turn in the revelation plot.

The corollary to the revelation of the hero's identity is the revelation of the villain, as in the climactic Chapter 17 of the *Sorcerer's Stone*, "The Man With

Two Faces." As in the melodrama and nineteenth-century serial fiction emulating it, Rowling has brought down the curtain in Chapter 16 with the villain revealed in a tableau of shadows: "There was already someone there—but it wasn't Snape. It wasn't even Voldemort" (208). After the cinematic beat of the chapter break, Chapter 17 begins on the next page as if with the snap of a floodlight:

> It was Quirrell.
>
> "*You!*" gasped Harry.
>
> Quirrell smiled. His face wasn't twitching at all.
>
> "Me," he said calmly. "I wondered whether I'd be meeting you here, Potter."
>
> "But I thought—Snape—"
>
> "Severus?" Quirrell laughed and it wasn't his usual quivering treble either, but cold and sharp. "Yes, Severus does seem the type, doesn't he? So useful to have him swooping around like an overgrown bat. Next to him, who would suspect p-p-poor st-stuttering P-Professor Quirrell?"
>
> Harry couldn't take it in. This couldn't be true, it couldn't.
>
> "But Snape tried to kill me!"
>
> "No, no, no. *I* tried to kill you."
>
> (*Sorcerer's Stone* 209)

The first three volumes, the shortest in the series, turn almost entirely around revelation plots: Quirrell and Snape in the first, Tom Riddle in the second, and Sirius Black in the third ("YOU'VE GOT THE WRONG MAN!" Harry shouts into the face of the befuddled minister Fudge (*Prisoner of Azkaban* 285)).

Whenever the dramatic tension is not about Harry's mistaken identity, the tension remains epistemological—will the character be revealed as good or revealed as evil? Sometimes this truth is concealed from the reader, and known to characters in the fiction; in other cases, the reader knows, and the plot action is effectively an epistemological car chase, a frenetic struggle to rectify the mistaken identity. In some cases, the revelation plot is used to rehabilitate characters—the Malfoys—previously revealed as evil. Even minor characters are continuously subjected to revelation scenes, as when the *Chamber of Secrets*' Gilderoy Lockhart, a version of the classic melodramatic hero, à la Dudley Do-Right, is revealed as a coward. Lockhart functions to position Harry within the melodramatic tradition—as a Clark Kent professional-managerial hero, modestly seeking to escape his celebrity.

The longer novels, fourth through seventh in the series, increasingly incorporate plots featuring the development of Harry's character. But this doesn't reduce their reliance on the melodramatic economy of revelation, of tension regarding the misunderstanding of character, rather than its development. The *Goblet of Fire* derives significant tension from the traditional device of establishing the allegiance of Lupin, for instance. More interestingly, the *Order of the Phoenix*—the first published after the assault on the World Trade Center—broadens the field on which Harry and his allies, doubles, and mentors are misunderstood. In *Harry Potter and the Order of the Phoenix*, Harry, Dumbledore, and Arthur Weasley—as well as their entire cadre—become the object of state terror and misinformation, with Harry subjected to relentless public scorn and "a full criminal trial" signifying the willingness of the state to abuse its power.

The fifth and sixth volumes display the most complex engagement with the melodramatic structure of feeling. The *Order of the Phoenix* highlights what happens when agents of state power appropriate melodramatic rhetoric with the eager collaboration of the corporate media. This inaugurates both an intensification of melodramatic plot drivers and a distinct effort to distance or bracket the series' reliance on melodramatic logic. As the object of state terror in the *Order of the Phoenix*, Harry's sense of being misunderstood reaches its peak. His interior monologue captures the reader's own fatigue with the much-repeated misrecognition plot, "How many more people were going to suspect that he was lying or unhinged?" (198). Cast in the government-scripted melodrama as public enemy number one, Harry experiences kinship with the falsely accused and eventual fugitive Dumbledore and, especially, the wrongly imprisoned Sirius Black: "Harry thought Sirius was probably the only person who could really understand how he felt at the moment, because Sirius was in the same situation" (269). This drives Harry into the prototypical defiance of the melodramatic hero: "They'll know we're right in the end," but, he wonders, how many more assaults would "he have to endure before that time came" (199).

Simultaneously, however, this theme of the misunderstood victim hero is for the first time in the series—after literally dozens of repetitions—rendered problematic by Rowling. In the context of Hermione Granger's sustained campaign to raise awareness regarding structural exploitation in the wizarding world, and the complicity of wizards and their institutions, including schools, in that exploitation, Harry's sense of perpetual victimization at last grows thin. "Oh, stop feeling all misunderstood," Granger finally snaps (*Order of the Phoenix* 441). Together with Dumbledore, Hermione in the final three novels becomes increasingly visible as a tutelary agent moving Potter from self-absorption to an actual interest in others. In this novel, the privileged Harry's perennial "feeling of ill-usage" (152) is handled as a character problem that he must struggle to overcome—i.e., an element in a *bildungsroman* or literary-realist plot—and no longer functions uncomplicatedly as a melodramatic plot driver. This is accompanied by a formal rejection of melodramatic logic by father-surrogate Sirius Black, "'Yes, but the world isn't split into good people and Death Eaters,' said Sirius with a wry smile." (271). Now a "wry" liberal ironist, Rowling attempts to wrench Black from the misrecognition plot—innocence mistaken for evil—that gives him his name ("serious black"). Similarly, at the conclusion of the *Half-Blood Prince*, while Harry is still dubbing Snape a villain, Hermione backs him off: "'Evil's a strong word,' Hermione said quietly" (595).

This more psychological handling of Harry—the effort to treat him with the devices of literary realism—doesn't imply a repudiation of the melodramatic, but rather an effort to make the melodramatic signify in psychologically complex ways, as in Harry's intensifying self-reflection throughout the final three novels. Utilizing almost exclusively the Romantic trope of the doppelganger, this self-reflection constructs moral ambiguity in the language of good and evil: Harry struggles to understand how he can be both "good" and intimately, profoundly, inescapably tied to "evil," as he increasingly involuntarily experiences manifestations of his own consciousness as a "kind of aerial that was tuned in to tiny fluctuations in Voldemort's mood" (*Order of the Phoenix* 489). This psychological handling is accompanied by the classic psychological plot—the overcoming of the father. Whereas melodramatic psychology yearns for recognition by the father or patriarchal authority (the gaze of the magistrate, teacher, detective, etc.), literary-realist psychology commonly problematizes the father: after yearning to be like his father, Potter in the fifth novel discovers that his father was a bully, and at last wonders, "But did he want to be like his father any more?" (588). To a substantial extent, this literary-realist ambition shares space with melodrama in the final three volumes. The series' climax is therefore dual. In the last pages of the final volume, we have both a melodramatic climax—in Chapter 34, which opens "Finally, the truth." (*Deathly Hallows* 554) and closes with the traditional "flash of green light"—as well as a literary-realist climax, in Chapter 35. Like "Incident at Owl Creek Bridge," the story by Ambrose Bierce most often described as the prototypical literary-realist text, Chapter 35 is essentially a dream sequence that takes place in psychological reality. Bierce's story takes place during the execution by hanging of a Confederate prisoner, recording his imagined escape and reunion with his family during the instant in time it takes to plummet to the end of his rope: at the conclusion of Harry's similar psychological adventure, Dumbledore plays English professor: "Of course it is happening inside your head, Harry, but why on earth should that mean it is not real?" (579).

These literary-realist ambitions in the final three volumes are accompanied by what might be called a profound "melodrama fatigue." On the one hand, the effort to draw plot energy from the established economy of the series leads to increasingly tired efforts to breathe life into the struggle between good and evil. As even the first film based on the series makes clear, it is already a dramatic and semiotic challenge for Alan Rickman to perform Snape's evil in the mode of a black-clad lisping aristocrat when there are at least three other black-clad villains with sibilant speech patterns in the same episode alone!

Unsurprisingly, by the sixth volume, for Voldemort even to be legible as a villain in the melodramatic register, he has to be described in magnificently amplified terms, in a very long exposition by Dumbledore as having traveled "beyond the realm of what we might call usual evil" (*Half-Blood Prince* 464). In the same exposition, Harry is once more recast as the hero "pure of heart" originating with melodrama—drawing strength from "the incomparable power of a soul that is untarnished and whole" (478).

On the other hand, at the same height of fatigue with melodrama, the series in this sequence revives the Hegelianism current at the rise of revolutionary melodramatic popular logic—the claim that ruling-class evil gives rise to its own gravediggers, best formulated by Marx in the Communist manifesto, and here paraphrased by Rowling in Dumbledore's explanation to Potter: "Don't you see? Voldemort himself created his worst enemy, just as tyrants everywhere do! Have you any idea how much tyrants fear the people they oppress?" (477). While this is hardly the stuff of the children's literature produced by the actual, vital culture of Western Marxism (see Mickenberg, especially "The Commies Go After the Kids," 136ff), it does represent at least the possibility of pushing back at a tyrannical ruling class.

In assessing the meaning of the melodramatic logic animating this series of more than 3000 pages, we have to acknowledge that Rowling's work engages the strengths of melodramatic mode as well as its weaknesses. Even to the extent that it participates in the hidden melodrama of professional-managerial heroism—merit at last revealed by education institutions—the series finds time to raise questions about that complicity, giving us Dumbledore's flirtation with fascism. And just where it confirms our educators' bias in favor of safe fictions with "positive messages" of character development, it moves onto the terrain of *V for Vendetta* and asks us whether we professionals and managers do need to join with the house-elves and goblins and start naming the enemy who turns out to be Tom Riddle, a double of our own successes through schooling. And finally, it asks us whether our heroism through schooling, however essential, can ever be enough.

It isn't easy for educators to "name the enemy." They're often quite literally forbidden to do so, with intensifying ruling-class control of curriculum and teacher speech. It is, in any event, an act generally outside of normative pedagogy. By contrast, Anker's call for "more complex and nuanced ways of understanding contemporary national life," is perfectly conventional and sensible within the frame of liberal orthodoxy in contemporary electoral politics. Her call for nuance exactly captures such authoritative positions as that advanced by the authors of the recent Carnegie text, *Educating for Democracy*, which associates educating for "responsible political engagement" with fostering the disposition toward critical thinking defined in classic new-critical terms as the disposition to "appreciate complexity and ambiguity" (55). In that book, the 60-year-old orthodoxies of the post-war literary "new criticism," emerging in part as a mode of delegitimizing the militant and class-conscious fiction of American proletarian writers, now functions not just as a literary but as a political orthodoxy within the education establishment. Even knowing the specific political content framing this neutral orthodoxy doesn't make it easy to challenge.

But perhaps the difficulty of arguing with these conventional beliefs and normative pedagogy is the point. Is "responsible political engagement" always best served by nuance? Was the political sophistication of the American population improved by banishing texts addressing class, class struggle, and the class war from above from curricula and even postsecondary literary history (albeit by the soft banishment of being judged insufficiently tinged with ambiguity, complexity, and irony)? Are there not moments when incivility, finger-pointing, and naming the enemy ("demonization") is the most responsible political act? It is easy to lionize civility when one is not being tortured, exploited, unfairly terminated from employment, evicted, educated in a rat-infested schoolhouse, or discriminated against. It is easy to appreciate ambiguity and complexity when it is the economic well-being, nutrition, and health care of others at stake.

Full, fair, informed consideration of any utterance in the melodramatic mode—including Rowling's—cannot come from the narrow, cold-war standpoint of a long-outmoded branch of literary criticism. Ultimately, thoughtful consideration of the continuing appeal of melodramatic utterance in political democracy has to at least consider the extent to which the revolutionary social promise of political democracy remains incompletely fulfilled.

Notes

1. As many commentators on Harry Potter have noted, including some that focus on the political culture and international relations, e.g., Neumann 160.
2. This is a fairly contested point, with the traditional readers of melodrama, such as Dan Gerould, associating it primarily with revolutionary feeling, and more recent readers, such as Bruce McConachie, emphasizing the evolution of the genre's audience and ideological import. See their tart exchange in TDR, sparked by Gerould's review of McConachie's influential Melodramatic Formations. Similarly, Elaine Hadley reads melodrama as a "contestatory mode" while Jeffrey Mason reads it in relation to "the myth of America."
3. For more on the "violent avenger" and the emergence of heroic individualism and its relationship to liberal hegemony, see McConachie, Mason, and Bousquet.
4. This is precisely the standpoint of the most interesting analysis of melodrama as a "pervasive cultural mode" after 9/11, Elisabeth Anker's UC Berkeley dissertation and forthcoming book, which convincingly reads Bush administration rhetoric and media coverage to describe how the U.S. "became signified as a morally powerful victim ensnared in a position that required it to transform victimization into heroic retributive action" (22). I think this is a very important line of analysis, but that it is limited by demonizing the melodramatic mode (as I did in my own dissertation, which also positioned melodrama as the undesirable other of democratic culture).
5. This is a point made eloquently with reference to the melodramatic "technoculture" surrounding the Potter phenomenon by Peter Appelbaum in the first edition of this volume:

   > One thing I have learned from cultural studies is that textual analysis is not enough.... It is especially important to learn from people how they "use"

popular culture resources to make sense of their lives, their culture, and their fears and fantasies, and through such mediation, to construct new modes of meaning.

(26)

References

Anderson, Quentin. *The Imperial Self.* New York: Knopf, 1971.

Anker, Elisabeth. "Villains, Victims, and Heroes: Melodrama, Media, and September 11." *Journal of Communication* 55, 1 (March 2005): 22–37.

Appelbaum, Peter. "Harry Potter's World: Magic, Technoculture, and Becoming Human." In *Critical Perspectives on Harry Potter* (1st edition). Ed. Elizabeth E. Heilman. New York: Routledge, 2003.

Bousquet, Marc. "The Emergence of the Melodramatic as a Social Instrument." Chapter 3 of "The Practice of Association." Ph.D. Dissertation, CUNY Graduate School, 1997.

Brooks, Peter. *The Melodramatic Imagination: Balzac, Henry James, Melodrama and the Mode of Excess.* New Haven, CT: Yale University Press, 1995.

Cloud, John. "Put Dumbledore Back in the Closet." *Time,* October 22, 2007. Retrieved March 25, 2008, from http://www.time.com/time/arts/article/0.8599,1674550,00.html.

Colby, Anne, Elizabeth Beaumont, Thomas Ehrlich, and Josh Corngold. *Educating for Democracy: Preparing Undergraduates for Responsible Political Engagement.* San Francisco: Jossey-Bass, 2007.

Falling Down. Director Joel Schumacher, screenplay Ebbe Roe Smith. Warner Bros., 1993.

Gerould, Daniel. Review of *Melodramatic Formations* by Bruce A. McConachie. *TDR* 37, 2 (Summer 1993): 181–184.

Gerould, Daniel and Bruce A. McConachie. "Marxism, Melodrama and Theatre Historiography." *TDR* 38, 1 (Spring 1994): 31–34.

Hadley, Elaine. *Melodramatic Tactics: Theatricalized Dissent in the English Marketplace, 1800–1885.* Stanford, CA: Stanford University Press, 1995.

Jones, John Stevens. *Solon Shingle, or The People's Lawyer.* National Theatre, Boston, 1839.

McConachie, Bruce. *Melodramatic Formations: American Theater and Society, 1820–1870.* Iowa City, IA: Iowa University Press, 1992.

Mason, Jeffrey D. *Melodrama and the Myth of America.* Bloomington, IN: Indiana University Press, 1993.

Mickenberg, Julia L. *Learning from the Left: Children's Literature, the Cold War, and Radical Politics in the United States.* New York: Oxford University Press, 2006.

Morris, Tom. *If Harry Potter Ran General Electric: Leadership Wisdom From the World of Wizards.* New York: Doubleday, 2006.

Neumann, Iver B. "Naturalizing Geography: Harry Potter and the Realms of Muggles, Magic Folks, and Giants." In *Harry Potter and International Relations.* Eds. Daniel H. Nexon and Iver. B. Neumann. Lanham, MD: Rowman and Littlefield, 2006.

Rorty, Richard. *Contingency, Irony, and Solidarity.* Cambridge: Cambridge University Press, 1989.

Rowling, J. K. *Harry Potter and the Sorcerer's Stone.* New York: Scholastic, 1997.

Rowling, J. K. *Harry Potter and the Prisoner of Azkaban.* New York: Scholastic, 1999.

Rowling, J. K. *Harry Potter and the Order of the Phoenix.* New York: Scholastic, 2003.

Rowling, J. K. *Harry Potter and the Half-Blood Prince.* New York: Scholastic, 2005.

Rowling, J. K. *Harry Potter and the Deathly Hallows.* New York: Scholastic, 2007.

V for Vendetta. Director James McTeigue, screenplay Andy and Larry Wachowski, based on the graphic novel series by David Lloyd. Warner Bros., 2006.

Van den Hesik, Kristy. Letter to the Editor, *Time,* November 8, 2007. Retrieved March 25, 2008, from http://www.timie.com/time/magazine/article/0,9171,1682285-2,00.html.

Westman, Karin E. "Specters of Thatcherism: Contemporary British Culture in J.K. Rowling's Harry Potter Series." In *The Ivory Tower and Harry Potter.* Ed. Lana A. Whited. Columbia, MD: University Missouri Press, 2002.

Literacy Elements and Interpretations

Part III

Literacy
Elements
and
Interpretations

Chapter Eleven

Playing the Genre Game
Generic Fusions of the Harry Potter Series

ANNE HIEBERT ALTON

We shall not cease from exploration
And the end of all our exploring
Will be to arrive where we started
And know the place for the first time.

(**T. S. Eliot,** *Four Quartets*)

Since its first appearance in 1997, J. K. Rowling's Harry Potter series has become one of the most popular series, not to mention one of the most intriguing phenomena, of our time. It has been credited for a renaissance in reading for children all over the world, despite competition from the supposedly more accessible forms of entertainment available on videos, television, or the internet, and has already become an integral part of our popular culture and academic discourses. Given the tremendous degree and variety of attention paid to the series over the last decade, it is impossible not to wonder about the underlying causes of its popularity and notoriety: what specifically makes Harry Potter so special that people read and reread the books and continue to discuss them, particularly now that Rowling has finished and published the final book in the series? While clearly the series works on a number of different levels, all of which contribute to its tremendous popularity, I argue that one of the major reasons for its appeal lies in Rowling's treatment of genre, particularly in relation to her incorporation of a vast number of genres in the books.[1] Genres traditionally dismissed as "despised genres" (Ursula Le Guin's term, not mine)—including pulp fiction, mystery, gothic and horror stories, detective fiction, the school story and the closely related sports story, and series books—appear throughout the Harry Potter books, along with more mainstream genres (at least in children's literature) such as fantasy, adventure, and quest romance. Rather than creating a hodgepodge with no recognizable or specific pattern, Rowling has fused these genres into a larger mosaic, which enhances readers' generic expectations and the ways in which the series conveys literary meaning.

One of the primary functions of genre, at least in terms of generating readership, is as a marketing device: how books are generically categorized tends to influence how readers think about them even before picking them up.[2] This tradition, which can be seen particularly clearly in works of pulp fiction and children's magazines in the late nineteenth and early twentieth centuries, is a feature of the Harry Potter series. Though not pulp fiction in the strict sense, since it lacks such defining features as sentimentality, eroticism, sensationalism, and (in a physical sense) the poor paper quality of tabloid fiction, the series does contain certain pulp elements, particularly in titles and dust jackets. The titles—all beginning with the phrase "Harry Potter and"— suggest series books, while the rest of the phrases encourage readers to formulate more specific generic expectations. *Harry Potter and the Sorcerer's Stone*[3] suggests fantasy, magic, and myth, while elements of mystery or even horror are evoked by *Harry Potter and the Chamber of Secrets*. *Harry Potter and the Prisoner of Azkaban* sounds like a racy crime thriller, and *Harry Potter and the Goblet of Fire* invokes images of adventure and mysticism. *Harry Potter and the Order of the Phoenix* carries the medieval connotations of chivalry and knighthood (associated with "order") along with the promise of hope and rebirth (associated with "phoenix"), while the mystery implicit in *Harry Potter and the Half-Blood Prince* not only raises questions of identity but also picks up on one of the troubling sub-texts of the series by invoking the contrasts between the Muggle and wizard worlds. Finally, *Harry Potter and the Deathly Hallows* has connotations of not only a Gothic tale but also the sense of deadly mystery.

The dust jackets demonstrate an even stronger link with pulp fiction. Like late nineteenth century pulp novels' covers, which were designed to capture purchasers' attention by seeming to represent the "contents of the magazine in an appealing, vivid, alluring light" (Scott 42), the covers of the Harry Potter books tend to be connected to certain generic assumptions. For example, the American edition of *Sorcerer's Stone* shows Harry—a clumsy-looking, skinny boy with messy hair and glasses—flying on a broomstick and trying to catch the Golden Snitch, while the cover of the British edition portrays him as a skinny, puzzled schoolboy standing on Platform 9¾ before a red train engine labeled Hogwarts Express. While this cover appears to be somewhat less fantastic than its American counterpart, the colors—predominately pinks and purples, with orange and blue in the background—traditionally indicate fantasy, while the figure on the back cover could be nothing but a wizard. The rest of the covers have similarly powerful generic implications, though there are differences. The cover of the American edition of *Chamber of Secrets* shows Harry grasping the tail-feathers of a red and gold phoenix as the two float past the entrance to the Chamber of Secrets, while the cover of the British edition portrays Harry, Ron, and Hedwig the owl in a flying blue car against the background of a calm blue sky. Here, the cover for the American version seems to indicate a substantially more adventurous and perhaps threatening story, in contrast to the reassurance of the happy faces and calm colors of the British edition. While both the British and American editions of *Prisoner of Azkaban* portray Harry and Hermione riding a Hippogriff, the British edition portrays the characters looking more serious than does the American version, which shows Harry, Hermione, and the Hippogriff smiling and looking excited.

As the series progresses, the differences between the British and American covers become more dramatic, yet both continue the pulp fiction tradition of catching attention as well as encouraging certain generic expectations. For example, with *Goblet of Fire*, the red, gold, and black tones of the British cover hint at some of the book's serious content—the life-and-death struggle of the Triwizard Tournament tasks, for example—and indicate to readers that this will be a tale of fantasy, adventure, and conflict. In contrast, the shades of green, copper, and black on the American cover seem far less threatening, while the expression on Harry's face suggests a sparkling and exciting tale along with a tamer and potentially less dangerous fantastic world. With *Harry Potter and the Order of the Phoenix*, the contrasts indicated by the covers have intriguing implications: the golden majesty of the phoenix on the British cover, along with the colorful statues in the foyer of the Ministry of Magic, project a far more optimistic and upbeat tone than the book contains; conversely, the American cover, with its deep blue hues, conveys a dark and threatening impression far more in keeping with the darker narrative of *Order of the Phoenix*, and the image of Harry looking over his shoulder produces a strong sense of uneasiness not indicated by the British cover. The trend continues with the covers of *Half-Blood Prince*, where the British one highlights Harry's immediate and active participation in strong magic, as indicated by the ring of fire around Harry and Dumbledore; the American cover portrays a more contemplative magic, with Harry and Dumbledore peering into what looks like the Pensieve. Moreover, the back cover for the American edition is particularly interesting, since it portrays a very dark image—the Dark Mark—along with other characters from the tale, but does not suggest the sort of panic that they should be displaying when faced with such a portent.

The covers for the American and British editions shift dramatically throughout the series in terms of the mood they portray. The American covers for the first three books in the series are far darker and more serious than their British counterparts, perhaps indicating different expectations these two societies seem to hold for fantasy. While this tendency seems reversed with *Goblet of Fire*, with the British cover portraying a far more dangerous scene than the American one, it reappears with *Order of the Phoenix* and *Half-Blood Prince*. Not until *Deathly Hallows* do the two covers seem to indicate similar generic messages in terms of their degree of optimism: the British one, which portrays Harry, Ron, and Hermione in the vault at Gringotts bank along with what turns out to be Griphook's arm brandishing a sword behind them, indicates some of the swashbuckling action of this part of the story, while the American cover shows Harry and Voldemort during their final confrontation: a part of the story which should be tremendously action-packed and yet which seems, at least from the cover, to be a quieter moment than one might expect. The color schemes for both, however—gold and red for the British cover and yellow, orange, and red for the American—suggest the ultimate triumph of Harry and the forces of good over Voldemort's forces of evil.

In terms of content, the series shares other elements of pulp fiction, including the ease of identification with the protagonist, something that hooks the reader of such fiction. Indeed, all three of the main protagonists appeal to readers; everyone can either identify with or knows someone like brainy Hermione, faithful and funny Ron, and orphaned yet courageous Harry. Moreover, the books contain the wish-fulfillment of the need to be special—and how much more special can one be than to be admitted into a magical world filled with like-minded people who have talents above and beyond the real world? Pulp fiction also tends to contain elements of luxury like those that appear in thriller movies (Palmer 113), like Hogwarts' magical meals or the comfort of Harry's tower room complete with velvet-curtained beds for all five inhabitants. Conspiracy, which is an underlying thread throughout the series and is also a marker of pulp fiction, appears in the Death Eaters' conspiracy to assist Voldemort in gaining control of the world and Draco's ineffective attempts to kill Dumbledore in *Half-Blood Prince*. More significantly, conspiracy is an element not only in Snape's actions throughout the series to protect Harry for Lily's sake, but ultimately in Dumbledore's grand plan to vanquish Voldemort, revealed in full to no one except for Harry during their conversation at King's Cross station. Moreover, as Lee Siegel points out, the books have

> mastered the conventions of the James Bond movies. So far, every book ends with the standard Bond wrap-up, in which the captured British agent—in this case, Harry Potter—waits patiently to be killed while the villain helpfully explains the fine points of the plot, reviews the highlights of his villainy, and discusses his plans for the future.
>
> (Siegel 6)

We see this during Harry's and Voldemort's confrontation in *Goblet of Fire*, and again during their final conflict in *Deathly Hallows*.

Pulp fiction is also characterized by elements of lawlessness, violence, and cruelty (Hilton 13), all of which become more pronounced as the series progresses. Cruelty exists not only in the Dursleys' treatment of Harry but also in more graphic scenes, such as when Dolores Umbridge not only forces Harry to magically cut the words "*I must not tell lies*" into his own hand and write the lines on parchment with his blood (*Order of the Phoenix* 267), but also authorizes whippings for Fred and George as well as the use of the Cruciatus curse on students who cross her. Violence appears with the murder of Cedric Diggory, while lawless behavior permeates the series from the beginning: Harry gets away with breaking school rules regularly, while Hermione is permitted to use time-travel to pursue her studies and later—in an action sanctioned by Dumbledore—uses the Time-Turner to help Sirius. More seriously, Voldemort flouts natural laws in his quest to regain a human body and to split his soul into Horcruxes to avoid death.

These elements of violence, while characteristic of pulp fiction, also evoke both ghost and horror stories. The traditional ghost story portrays something that should be dead invading the world of the living, which happens in Harry Potter with Peeves the poltergeist or the Houses' Ghosts. The use of Gothic elements leads to an atmosphere that tends to be frightening, yet is realistic enough for the terrors to be quite believable. While the ghosts are not scary, Gothic elements appear throughout Hogwarts, specifically in its dungeons (where Snape's Potions classes take place), subterranean passages, hidden entrances, and secret rooms. Other sorts of supernatural elements typical to the Gothic story appear with such creatures as vampires like Sanguini (*Half-Blood Prince*), zombies or inferi (*Half-Blood Prince* and *Deathly Hallows*), and even spirits of the dead, which appear most poignantly (and somewhat anti-Gothically) with the reappearance of James, Lily, Sirius, and Lupin to Harry as he walks through the Forbidden Forest to give himself up to Voldemort near the climax of *Deathly Hallows*. Unexpected and mysterious disappearances also abound: in addition to Hermione's mysterious vanishing in *Prisoner of Azkaban*, we have Bertha Jorkins' more sinister disappearance in *Goblet of Fire* and Dumbledore's disappearances in both *Order of the Phoenix* and *Half-Blood Prince*. While the Gothic convention of the beautiful heroine suffering at the hands of the cruel villain appears in *Chamber of Secrets* with Ginny's possession by Tom Riddle's diary-persona, overall Rowling has shifted this convention onto Harry, as he is repeatedly attacked by Voldemort in various guises. Elements of horror also appear throughout the series, with such moments as the vision of the apparition drinking the blood of a slain unicorn in *Sorcerer's Stone*, the threatened attack of the giant spiders and the whispered "…*rip … tear … kill*…" Harry hears in *Chamber of Secrets* (137), Wormtail cutting off his own hand to resurrect Voldemort and the entire "Flesh, Blood, and Bone" chapter in *Goblet of Fire*, the repeated Jekyll and Hyde parameter of the use of the Polyjuice potion throughout the series, and the torturing of Hermione in *Deathly Hallows*.

Two other genres commonly associated with pulp literature and that appear throughout the Harry Potter series include mystery and detective elements, especially solving a problem, usually in relation to a violent crime such as murder, a disappearance of some sort, or a hidden identity. The pattern in both genres is similar: a secret about the crime is first hidden and then revealed, usually through the discovery of the villain's identity by a detective figure who reveals the secret and reconstructs what happened. The main mystery throughout the series pertains to Harry and Voldemort, raising such questions as who is Harry Potter? Who is Voldemort, why does he want to kill Harry, and why does he keep failing? What form will their ultimate confrontation take, and what will be the end result? Specific mysteries also appear in each book as well as through the series: *Sorcerer's Stone* creates a mystery around the stone and its significance, as well as about Voldemort's reasons for trying to kill baby Harry; *Chamber of Secrets* constructs a traditional detective story with the petrification incidents as well as discovering the source of the horrific whispers Harry hears; *Prisoner of Azkaban* deals with the mysterious identity of Sirius Black as well as the antagonism between Scabbers and Crookshanks; *Goblet of Fire* entails mysteries including the Riddle family's cause of death, how and why Harry's name appeared in the Goblet of Fire, and the odd behavior of Ludo Bagman and Mr. Crouch, the Minister of Magic. The mysteries in *Order of the Phoenix* involve the remote behavior of Dumbledore towards Harry as well as the actions of the Order. In *Half-Blood Prince*, readers wonder about the identity of the half-blood prince, Slughorn's modified memory, and the identity and location of the Horcruxes, while *Deathly Hallows* not only continues Harry's search for and destruction of the Horcruxes but also adds the mystery of the Hallows. Another generic aspect of mystery appearing throughout the series is the exoneration (and sometimes physical rescue) of the innocent, which is particularly strong in *Chamber of Secrets* and *Half-Blood Prince*. Snape's heroics and the motivations and machinations of Dumbledore are also exonerations.

A sub-genre of mystery is detective fiction, which usually features a detective figure who is an outsider of some sort—someone who is not a member of so-called regular society—and who thus not only holds different values than the norm, but also can see the problem differently and more clearly than other people. Here Harry clearly fits the bill: being from a Muggle background but of stellar heritage in relation to the wizard world, he does see the problem of Voldemort differently, which in the end helps Harry overcome many of his threats. In the traditional detective story, the detective discovers the solution to the problem and solves the mystery by interpreting a variety of physical and psychological signs and, at times (like the prototypical detective, Sherlock Holmes), by thinking like the villain. This sort of behavior appears with not only Harry but also Dumbledore, for example, in *Half-Blood Prince*, where the two attempt to trace Tom Riddle's past as well as analyze his psyche in order to identify and locate the objects he used as Horcruxes, and Harry continues the pattern through *Deathly Hallows* in his quest both for the Horcruxes and the Hallows. In several of the earlier other books, too, the protagonists act as detectives in various ways. In *Sorcerer's Stone* they research the provenance of the Stone and prevent Voldemort from obtaining it. In *Chamber of Secrets* they discover the identity and motive of Tom Riddle, who is petrifying a number of people in the castle. In *Prisoner of Azkaban* Ron and Hermione help Harry elude, capture, and free Sirius Black; and in *Goblet of Fire* Harry acts as "sleuth" in completing the three tasks of the Triwizard Tournament, thwarts Voldemort's attempts to kill him again, and discovers that Voldemort has not only regained human form but is amassing support to control the world (Zipes 179).

Of all the novels, however, *Chamber of Secrets* is the one that best conforms to the traditional elements of detective fiction. Detective stories begin with the discovery of the crime, which is followed by other events that impede progress towards resolution. Here, this appears in the first and subsequent discoveries of the petrified victims. Various false and true clues appear throughout the narrative, such as Hagrid's mistaken belief that the spiders led by Aragog will be helpful, or the mirror that Hermione drops just before being petrified. Delaying tactics slow down the action in order to build suspense, as with Ron, Hermione, and Harry's attempts to reveal Malfoy's part in the crime (he is not directly involved), while blocking figures and suspects also interfere: Filch, Mrs. Norris, Peeves, and even Snape (albeit inadvertently) all act as blocking figures, and Hagrid is arrested as a false suspect. Finally, the taciturn "Great Detective" is assisted in his detective work by a garrulous assistant and a cast of "grotesques" or odd characters (Porter 330). While Harry is not especially taciturn, nor are Ron and Hermione particularly garrulous, the grotesque character appears with the ghost of Moaning Myrtle. Moreover, Harry is willing to risk everything to catch the petrifier and thus not only clear his name but prevent further danger to his fellow Hogwarts residents—thus further establishing his heroic role in the series.

Another connection to popular or pulp fiction appears in the Harry Potter books' generic identity as series books,[4] particularly in terms of shelf appeal, where series readers will read the cover design or logo for reassurance that the book belongs to a particular series. This fulfills a certain desire for the predictability series books provide with similar plot structures and style. Here Rowling delivers. Her writing style does not vary with each installment, and the structure of the plot remains generally the same: each book takes place over the duration of one school year, and most begin with Harry unhappy at home with the Dursleys; he is then rescued or escapes to the magical world of Hogwarts, where he and his friends Ron and Hermione solve a mystery involving Voldemort or one of his followers; after surviving an encounter with Voldemort or his representative, which adds another clue to the ongoing mystery of Voldemort and develops the escalating conflict between good and evil, Harry returns home for another summer with the Dursleys. This repeated structure reassures readers of a happy ending while allowing them to experience the vicarious enjoyment of adventure, drama, and danger.

Series books also tend to include the same groups of characters, and as the Harry Potter series progresses readers re-encounter old friends as well as old enemies. In addition to the central characters of Harry, Ron, and Hermione, each installment features fellow Gryffindors Neville Longbottom, Dean Thomas, Seamus Finnigan, and the twins Fred and George Weasley, along with foes Draco Malfoy and his gargantuan sidekicks, Crabbe and Goyle. Headmaster Dumbledore appears in all seven books, despite his demise at the end of *Half-Blood Prince*, along with fierce Professor McGonagall, squeaky Professor Flitwick, and menacing yet enigmatic Professor Snape, while the arch-villain, Voldemort, fails to appear only in *Prisoner of Azkaban*. Rowling also adds or develops new and significant characters throughout the series, including a different Defense Against the Dark Arts teacher each year, along with Tom Riddle (*Chamber of Secrets*), Sirius Black, Remus Lupin, and Peter Pettigrew (*Prisoner of Azkaban*), Viktor Krum and Mad-Eye Moody (*Goblet of Fire*), Nymphadora Tonks, Dolores Umbridge, and Bellatrix Lestrange (*Order of the Phoenix*), and Horace Slughorn and a more developed Narcissa Malfoy (*Half-Blood Prince*). While *Deathly Hallows* is the only installment that does not introduce significant new characters, Rowling compensates by not only developing apparently minor characters from earlier books, including Griphook (first introduced in *Sorcerer's Stone*) and Kreacher (*Order of the Phoenix*), but also delving far more deeply into Dumbledore's and Snape's characters as she reveals details from their childhoods and young adulthoods that reveal key elements of their characters as well as the narrative as a whole.

Rowling's characterization is one of her strongest points: her characters are, almost without exception, realistic and convincing, due to her economic yet effective description. Perhaps the best example appears in her introduction of Hagrid, Hogwarts' caretaker and eventual Care of Magical Creatures professor:

> He was almost twice as tall as a normal man and at least five times as wide. He looked simply too big to be allowed, and so *wild*—long tangles of bushy black hair and beard hid most of his face, he had hands the size of trash can lids, and his feet in their leather boots were like baby dolphins. In his vast, muscular arms he was holding a bundle of blankets.
>
> (*Sorcerer's Stone* 14)

Hagrid's tender nature is revealed when he bids baby Harry farewell: after giving him "what must have been a very scratchy, whiskery kiss" he howls and sobs with grief (*Sorcerer's Stone* 15). His emotional connection with Harry appears throughout the series, right unto the last, when he cradles the unconscious (and apparently dead) Harry in his arms and, weeping, carries him back to Hogwarts. Such strength of characterization provides verisimilitude, another of the pleasures of reading series fiction, with its sense of providing answers to the question of what really happened to characters who have become like close friends or mortal enemies to readers.

The strongest appeal of series fiction lies in this sense of resolution, or at least in "a series of profoundly satisfying narrative or thematic closures" (Watson 7). This is absolutely true for the Harry Potter series, for each book—or installment, since Rowling maintained she was really writing a seven-part novel (Stahl)—achieves a certain closure, either thematically or in terms of plot or both. By the end of *Sorcerer's Stone*, the stone has been destroyed and Harry has been able to see his parents, or at least their photographs. At the end of *Chamber of Secrets*, Tom Riddle and his diary have been vanquished and Harry's confirmation as a Gryffindor rather than Slytherin has been assured. *Prisoner of Azkaban* concludes with no less than the saving of Sirius Black's and Buckbeak's lives, along with Harry's discovery of a sympathetic guardian. The ending of *Goblet of Fire* is a significant turning point in the series: while it concludes with Harry once again surviving an attack from Voldemort, it also begins a new order of alliance within the wizard world, with much stronger lines being drawn between the sides of good and evil than have appeared before. This pattern is confirmed with the ending of *Order of the Phoenix*, where not only Harry and his D.A. followers battle with Death Eaters, but where Voldemort and Dumbledore come face-to-face. Similarly, the ending of *Half-Blood Prince*, the penultimate book in the series, ends with the death of Dumbledore and the fleeing of Snape, but places Harry back into the original strong triangle of friendship with Ron and Hermione. Each of these endings, while thematically satisfying, creates curiosity about what is going to happen next and feeds the reader's expectations to a frenzy that can be satisfied only with the conclusion to the series. With *Deathly Hallows*, Rowling not only brings the major conflicts of the series to a satisfying conclusion, but also resolves many of her dangling plot lines: Dumbledore's ultimate plan is finally revealed, we discover more (though not everything) about Harry's lineage, and Snape's motivations throughout the series finally become clear, and connect resoundingly with the thematic implications of love raised first in *Sorcerer's Stone* and followed throughout the series. Rowling's Epilogue provides even more closure, with Harry's forgiveness for Snape, along with the thematic resonance of synthesis, apparent in the name of his third child, "Albus Severus," while the book's final lines—"All was well" (*Deathly Hallows* 759)—provide a perfect example of Watson's notion of profound satisfaction.

One of the potential problems of a literary series in which the characters grow and mature as the books progress is that, at least in a successful series, they must do so without losing any of their initial appeal. Since the middle of the twentieth century, following the tradition of glorifying innocent childhood begun by such poets as Wordsworth and Blake, the growth from childhood to adulthood has been regarded as a loss rather than a happy progression. As Watson suggests, "it is a bold series-writer who proceeds beyond this point, for to do so must challenge the great western cultural assumption that the *potential* adulthood of the young is more charismatic than *achieved* adulthood" (206). This is particularly true for the Harry Potter books, whose protagonists start out at age 11 and mature to the age of 17. However, Rowling has avoided the potential problems by making the series a typical *bildungsroman* (novel of formation) or *erziehungsroman* (novel of education). This genre focuses on the physical, intellectual, moral, and spiritual development of the protagonist from childhood to adulthood, charting various situations and crises that lead to the protagonist's maturity and recognition of his/her identity and place in the world. At the opening of *Sorcerer's Stone*, Harry is quite literally a child—a baby, in fact—with no knowledge of the world or his special powers; as the first few chapters progress, he starts to become aware not only of his orphan status and resulting poor lot in life (who in their right mind would want to be stuck with the Dursleys?) but also that odd things seem to happen around him. As the series develops, Harry experiences a number of events that lead to his growth, change, and maturation: he learns that he is a wizard, and that he is already famous for having vanquished Voldemort (though he has no idea how he managed to do so); he leaves the world of Muggles for Hogwarts to begin his formal education and he adapts to the many challenges of this new environment; he makes friends as well as enemies; he encounters evil in a variety of forms and each time manages to triumph over it; and he starts to contemplate his future and consider what career path he might pursue after he graduates from Hogwarts and becomes a fully fledged adult wizard. This is followed by his acceptance of his role as the "Chosen One" who is prophesized either to vanquish Voldemort or die in his attempts, his tracking down of the Horcruxes, and his wrestling with the temptation of finding and using the Hallows. Having faced his mortality and accepted the belief that only his own death will bring about the downfall of Voldemort, he achieves true adulthood by not only realizing his identity and his true place in the world but also by offering one final chance of mercy to Voldemort: "Think, and try for some remorse, Riddle" (*Deathly Hallows* 741). In the end, we see Harry 19 years later, a happy husband and father, sending off his two eldest children to Hogwarts.

The Harry Potter series also can be considered *bildungsroman* in the way it embodies three motifs common to the genre: the loss of the father and the search for a surrogate parent, the realization of conflict between the gentlemanly ideals of the past and the struggle in the present for survival and identity, and the search for and discovery of love (Gohlman 249). *Sorcerer's Stone* opens with the death of Harry's parents, and as the series progresses the effects of this loss appear not only in his occasional pang of wondering what his parents were like—to the extent where he is willing to risk being caught by Filch just to catch a glimpse of them in the Mirror of Erised—but also in his fierce defense of his father when he is criticized by the Dursleys, Aunt Marge (whom he inflates like a balloon), Draco Malfoy, and Snape. His delight when he realizes that Sirius Black is innocent of his crimes and thus can be a true godfather to him, and his love for and protection of Sirius in *Goblet of Fire* and *Order of the Phoenix*, signifies at least partial closure for this first stage.

The second motif, Harry's realization of the conflict between the ideals of the past and the reality of the present, appears not only in the discord between Harry's life with the Dursleys and his life at Hogwarts, but also in the tensions that develop between the old and new orders within the wizard world. Even more significantly, it appears throughout *Deathly Hallows*, as Harry struggles between his loyalty to Dumbledore and his plan to locate and destroy the remaining Horcruxes and his discovery of the Hallows and the temptation to find them to use against Voldemort. The last motif, the search for and discovery of love, is worthy of a paper in its own right, so here I will go into only one line of argument, which focuses on the love for family, the love for a romantic partner, and the love for humanity as a whole. The first initially appears with the emphasis on Lily Potter's love for her son as one of the factors that saved Harry from the worst of Lord Voldemort's wrath, and this ties into the romantic love—revealed at last in *Deathly Hallows*—that Snape felt for Lily and which accounts for many of his actions throughout the series. The third, the love for humanity as a whole, appears not only with the character of Dumbledore, whose devotion to protecting all of the world—Muggle and wizard—from Voldemort suggests such a love, but also with Harry, whose willingness to sacrifice himself for the greater good invokes a similar love for humanity. As he says to Voldemort,

> I was ready to die to stop you from hurting these people … I've done what my mother did. They're protected from you. Haven't you noticed how none of the spells you put on them are binding? You can't torture them. You can't touch them.
>
> (*Deathly Hallows* 738)

Such a show of maturity nicely addresses and overturns the potential problem of characters in series fiction losing their charismatic appeal as they grow older, suggesting that this is not a necessary outcome: Harry is arguably at his most appealing when he reaches this point of development.

Genres such as series books and *bildungsroman* overlap very closely with school stories, another of the formative genres in the Harry Potter books. Given their subject matter of a seven-year period of education at the premier (and apparently only) school for wizards in Britain, what better place to chart those formative adolescent years than something akin to a British public school? While some critics have suggested that the traditional school story has been dead—or at the very least passé—for the last several decades,[5] Harry Potter signifies a return to the traditional Victorian boarding school or public school story, but with the element of fantasy added. Hogwarts follows the general organization of a British public school in that students are assigned houses—Gryffindor, Ravenclaw, Hufflepuff, and Slytherin—and take all of their meals and classes with their fellow house-mates, as well as sleep in dormitories belonging to these houses and spend free time in their house common rooms. The school system of rewards and punishments is built around the houses, which compete each year for the greatest number of points in order to win the School Cup. These house divisions have the effect of promoting both house and school spirit, as can be seen very clearly in the scene when Gryffindor wins the Quidditch match in *Prisoner of Azkaban*, as well as encouraging excellence both in and out of the classroom: house points are awarded for winning at Quidditch, for good or insightful answers to professors' questions during class, or for other behavior that demonstrates the traditional values of chivalry, fair play, or courage, as when Neville is awarded the winning ten points for having had the courage to stand up to his friends (*Sorcerer's Stone*). Points are deducted from houses for breaking school rules (Fred and George Weasley are regular offenders here), disorderly conduct, incorrect answers in class, or showing disrespect to a teacher. Like British public schools during the Victorian age, either in fact or fiction, Hogwarts also has a selection criteria, but rather than accepting students from particular social or economic spheres, the criteria to be accepted at Hogwarts is simply that students must be wizards; whether they are from Muggle or non-Muggle backgrounds is irrelevant.

In terms of structure, the series contains a few of the basic elements of the generic school story pattern, though in a way that revises rather than conforms to the genre norm, where a boy enters school feeling somewhat nervous but also ambitious, suffers from loneliness and the discipline of both his schoolmasters and the school's games, gradually makes a few friends and starts to flourish and even rebel, eventually "learns duty, self-reliance, responsibility and loyalty as a prefect," and finally leaves school for the real world with regret, but permanently formed through his school's code of conduct and seal (Richards 6). Certainly Harry starts out at Hogwarts feeling nervous, but his reasons are not the usual ones: instead of being the typically invisible new boy, he is known throughout the wizard world for his encounter with Voldemort, and is instantly recognizable because of the scar on his forehead. His ambition is to become less—rather than more—visible, and yet concurrently to live up to his reputation, as well as to remain in Hogwarts so that he no longer has to deal with the Dursleys. Nor does he initially suffer from loneliness: he and Ron become friends on the Hogwarts Express before they arrive at the school, and Harry is greeted by Hagrid the moment he gets off the train. Like Hermione, he welcomes the discipline of his classes (except for Potions, taught by Snape), and he revels in his natural talent for Quidditch. The seeds for his rebellion have been sown in him, courtesy of the Dursleys, long before he arrived at school, and in many ways his self-reliance results from their poor treatment of him rather than from any lessons he learns at Hogwarts. However, his experiences at school do teach him about the concepts of duty, responsibility, and loyalty, though much of this results from his learning about the history of the wizard world and his place in it in relation to Voldemort. While Ron and Hermione, rather than Harry, become Prefects, the pattern remains intact when even that choice is explained satisfactorily, at the end of *Order of the Phoenix*, to Harry by Dumbledore. His decision not to return to Hogwarts, made at the end of *Half-Blood Prince* and followed through *Deathly Hallows*, certainly is tinged with regret, and his eventual choice to continue his search for the Horcruxes despite the temptation of the Hallows further cements the code of conduct exemplified by Dumbledore.

The Harry Potter books do conform to the generic conventions of school stories in that they depict "schooldays as they should be" complete with practical jokes, sports, mischief, studying, "and Dickensian Christmas hols" (Richards 12), but again with the added ingredient of fantasy. Fred and George Weasley provide much fodder for humor with their continued eye for mischief, plenty of attention is given to regular Quidditch practices and matches, and studying takes on a completely new dimension when students must do homework for such classes as Potions, Transfiguration, Herbology, Charms, Care of Magical Creatures, Divination, and Defense Against the Dark Arts. The depth of description devoted to the classes is a minor departure from the tendency that traditional school stories have of ignoring the academic part of schooling, but here the details add to the enjoyment of the books because of the intriguing areas of study. Christmas holidays, however, are very much in keeping with the genre's traditions: when Harry, Ron, and (in *Prisoner of Azkaban*) Hermione remain at Hogwarts over Christmas, they enjoy sumptuous meals, snowball fights, no studying, greater freedom than usual to wander around the school, and the sight of their professors and teachers becoming more relaxed and therefore more human—at least for the duration of the break.

The teachers at Hogwarts also share a number of characteristics with teachers in traditional school stories, and many of them serve as role models for proper behavior, with Professor McGonagall as the ultimate example of propriety as well as discipline: "It's one o'clock in the morning. *Explain yourselves*" (*Sorcerer's Stone* 243). In contrast, Professor Snape acts as an anti-role model, with his favoritism of Draco Malfoy and the Slytherins and his grudge against Harry. Most importantly, Dumbledore embodies the typical attributes of the school story headmaster by representing "all that is real—virtue, merriment, and humanity" (Quigly 36). With Thomas Arnold (1795–1842), the prototypical public school headmaster immortalized in *Tom Brown's Schooldays*, Dumbledore shares elements of charismatic leadership and kindness, along with the power of influence in making Hogwarts (like Arnold's English public school) "a place to train character" (Richards 3). In contrast, teachers such as Madame Hooch, the Quidditch teacher, zany Professor Trelawney, or self-centered Professor Slughorn add not only comic relief but also the message that even apparently insignificant teachers can play very real roles in character development.

The schools in school stories often represent microcosms of the larger world. In this isolated environment children act in different ways than they would if they were living under the constraints of their parents' rules and regulations, and they also construct their own social order and culture. Certainly this is true for the world at Hogwarts, particularly in terms of its society. While the students must answer to Dumbledore, their professors, and their house masters, they have far more freedom than they would enjoy in the outside world: for example, Hogwarts has no apparent curfew, and students can remain in their house common rooms studying or socializing as late as they please. In addition, since the children at Hogwarts seem, almost without exception, to be happy to have been selected as students, they tend to attend most of their classes without complaint and usually pay attention in class—though the incentive to do so may be helped along by the knowledge that they could be turned into toads if they fail to pay attention.

As in all societies, they also deal with the usual issues of friendships and social hierarchies. Harry spurns Malfoy's advice to help him avoid choosing "the wrong sort" of associations (*Sorcerer's Stone* 108) and befriends Ron Weasley; later, he, Ron, and Hermione sort out their initial differences and become fast friends after their encounter with the mountain troll. The initial tension between Harry and Draco Malfoy builds throughout the series, with their rivalry appearing not only in their classes but also in the dining hall, on the Quidditch field, and anywhere else the two are forced to meet. While Harry finds Malfoy a constant irritation, he is but a symptom of the larger evil that Harry faces in his continuing battle with Voldemort, and his role is played out very nicely with his inability in the end to kill Dumbledore as well as his crucial loss of his wand to Harry in *Deathly Hallows*. Neville Longbottom, too, becomes an integral part of their group, and by the end of *Order of the Phoenix* he has become an accomplished as well as valued member of the D.A.; his role becomes pivotal in *Deathly Hallows*, when he—like Harry in *Chamber of Secrets*—calls Gryffindor's sword out of the Sorting Hat and uses it to behead Nagini, Voldemort's last remaining Horcrux. Rowling keeps the school story patterning consistent throughout the series, with the final battle between the Death Eaters and Dumbledore's Army taking the form of an enormous, unruly mêlée (a sports match with an edge) throughout the school grounds and hallways. Fittingly, the final confrontation between Harry and Voldemort takes place in the Great Hall, which functions as Hogwarts' central meeting ground.

The emphasis placed on Quidditch, the ultimate sport for wizards, that appears in the Harry Potter series illustrates its generic identity as a sports story. Indeed, as Nicholas Tucker suggests, "Hogwarts pays almost as much attention to success at Quidditch as *Tom Brown's Schooldays* does to winning on the rugger field" (225). As the youngest house Quidditch player in a century, Harry quickly earns a name for himself as a Seeker and, like many a child, he fantasizes about being good enough someday to play for England and represent his country internationally. In addition to teaching such team values as loyalty, courage, and leadership, sports activities were also traditionally considered a means of redirecting aggression and energy that students might feel towards each other into something less unsettling or dangerous; certainly their participation in Quidditch matches allows Harry and Malfoy to battle out some, though by no means all, of their aggressions. In addition, sports were supposed to teach the ability to be a good loser, a lesson that Harry seems to have learned well, as suggested by the way he accepts his impending death in *Deathly Hallows*. For other students, however, winning becomes more important than the values that Quidditch ideally should teach. The Slytherin team is portrayed throughout as being sore losers who are willing to go to any lengths to win a game, including personal fouls on Harry and disguising themselves as Dementors to break his concentration (*Prisoner of Azkaban*). Even Oliver Wood, the Gryffindor team's captain, cannot stop obsessing over game strategy before a significant match against Slytherin, and he is so devastated when the team loses a match to Hufflepuff that he cannot bear to visit Harry in the hospital wing after he falls off his broom (*Prisoner of Azkaban*). Both reactions serve to highlight Harry's healthier philosophy: while he certainly would prefer to win, he is not nearly as angry as the Slytherins or as devastated as Wood when his team loses. Instead, he takes pleasure in being recognized as a good Quidditch player, which takes some of the focus away from his connection with Voldemort.

More significantly, however, the game functions as a major part of Harry's education and one that eventually contributes to his routing of Voldemort. As team Seeker, his role is to chase after the Golden Snitch and catch it to win the game; he must be quick, both in terms of his wits and in terms of coordination, level-headed, and not be shaken when he doesn't immediately succeed. The game helps Harry keep his mind off his fellow students' hostility when they shun him for being able to speak Parseltongue (*Chamber of*

Secrets), and he enjoys playing Quidditch to escape from his tumultuous emotions when awaiting his trial in *Order of the Phoenix*. Moreover, the physical skills he learns from the game pay off when he uses his proficiency at precision flying to avoid the Hungarian Horntail dragon and retrieve the golden egg during the Tournament, again when he confronts Voldemort in the graveyard in *Goblet of Fire*, and at the end of *Deathly Hallows* when he, "with the unerring skill of the Seeker, caught the [Elder] wand in his free hand as Voldemort fell backward" (744).

The significance of the sports story genre also appears in the detailed description of the game and its rules. Terminology such as Beaters, Chasers, and Keepers, along with Bludgers and Quaffles, and the vivid descriptions of flying and minute details pertaining to Harry's original Nimbus Two Thousand broom and his new Firebolt keep readers interested and intrigued. Finally, good sports stories of the modern era bring readers right into the game, which Quidditch does, despite the fact that readers can play it only in their imaginations. Rowling does this not only through her detailed descriptions of Harry's experiences while training and playing, but also through the commentaries of Lee Jordan and, later, Luna Lovegood. By placing readers in the position of being spectators, Rowling makes the fantastic elements of a game played by players flying on broomsticks and chasing a magically enchanted object with wings seem more convincing and believable.

The ability to combine fantasy and reality is one of Rowling's greatest strengths, and she makes it effortless for readers to invoke their willing suspension of disbelief. It helps that the Harry Potter books take place in the real world, some of which is quite aware of the wizard world. Hogwarts appears to exist in the England of today, but is protected from the Muggle world by spells or enchantments (Hermione's theories about just how this might be done appear in *Goblet of Fire*), and is reached from that most prosaic of locations, King's Cross station in London, but from the magical portal of Platform $9\frac{3}{4}$ on the Hogwarts Express. In numerous other ways, the series is steeped in reality: students attend classes, do homework, and experience the same sorts of rivalries and tensions that they might experience at any British public school. Indeed, as Pico Iyer suggests, what

> makes the Harry Potter books fly ... [is] their fidelity to the way things really are (or were, at least, when quills and parchment were still more common than computers): wizards, Harry Potter's world suggests, are only regular Muggles who've been to the right school.

The right school here, of course, involves magic as a part of the students' everyday lives, and that becomes the focus of their studies. They take classes focusing on the history of the wizard world, along with specific skills such as flying and wand use, while they learn charms and spells to create light

("Lumos"), levitate objects ("Wingardium Leviosa"), deflate Boggarts ("Riddikulus"), and charms for defense like the Patronus charm Harry learns against dementors ("Expecto Patronum") or, most crucially, "Expelliarmus" to disarm an enemy.

Fantasy elements include other specific details, with owl post utilized for mail delivery, live photographs appearing on the collectible trading cards that come in packages of chocolate frogs, and encounters with Blast-ended Skrewts, Flobberworms, and Thestrals during Care of Magical Creatures classes (*Order of the Phoenix* 444–445). This exactness of detail appears in all elements of the wizard world, which has its own financial system, with 17 silver sickles to a galleon and 29 knuts to a sickle; its own transportation system, with not only the Hogwarts Express but also Floo Powder, Portkeys, and the Knight Bus for stranded wizards; its own political system, complete with departments such as the Misuse of Muggle Artifacts Office, where Ron's father works; and its own hospital system, with St. Mungo's Hospital for Magical Maladies and Injuries.

Two other generic fantasy elements appear as well: a strong sense of place and originality.[6] The series is populated with intriguing and believable settings such as Diagon Alley and its shops like Eeylops Owl Emporium, Florean Fortescue's Ice Cream Parlor, or Flourish and Blotts bookshop; Hogwarts School with its turrets, long and drafty corridors, cozy common rooms, and 142 staircases; Hagrid's cottage filled with a cheerful muddle of animals and assorted possessions; the wizard settlement of Hogsmeade, complete with the Shrieking Shack where Professor Lupin used to take refuge during his worst throes of werewolfhood; and The Burrow, the Weasleys' home, where Harry learns to deal with garden gnomes by tossing them over the fence, and where Fred and George enjoy a spirited match of dining table jousting in *Goblet of Fire*. Along with the original details already mentioned, Rowling demonstrates other sorts of inspiration: indeed, the scene in which Harry gets his wand from Mr. Ollivander (*Sorcerer's Stone* 83–85) and the initial Sorting Hat episode (*Sorcerer's Stone* 116–122) are some of the most resonant and original in modern fantasy. Similarly, inventions including the Pensieve, Nifflers and Kneazles (such as Hermione's cat Crookshanks), and the Marauder's Map have contributed to the series' near-mythic status, while Bertie Bott's Every Flavor Beans, the pocket Sneakoscope, howlers, and Fred and George's many inventions—including Extendable Ears, spectacular magical fireworks and portable swamps—add to its immense popularity. In the end, the series exemplifies the characteristic of good fantasy questioning the prevailing worldview by asking just how fantastic our notions of reality are, and creating alternatives to what we think of as the real world. While clearly Rowling's inventions are fantastic, they nevertheless suggest a way of defining ourselves through our own wishes and desires.

Elements of fairy and folk tales also appear throughout the series, particularly in relation to the use of certain motifs. For example, the tale of the Elves and the Shoemaker appears in relation to the liberation of Dobby from Lucius Malfoy's employ via the gift (however inadvertently presented) of clothes. Similarly, the Cinderella motif is invoked by Harry's home life before he becomes informed of his wizardry. Harry's situation can also be connected to the folk tale of King Arthur, particularly in terms of the hero's initially unclear origins: popular folk belief suggests that Arthur was of unknown parentage and raised as a foster son by Sir Ector; his lineage, of which he can be proud (as the legitimate son of the King), is revealed later. Similarly, while Harry knows the name of his father, he knows very little else about him until the final volume in the series, at which point his connections to the original owner of the Invisibility Cloak—and by extension the three brothers who were challenged and eventually defeated by the Deathly Hallows in the children's tale—are revealed. In addition, both tales invoke the significance of a sword: for Arthur, his ability to pull the sword from the stone, on which is engraved: "Whoso pulleth out this sword of this stone and anvil is rightwise king born of all England" (Malory I:5), while for Harry, it is his ability to summon help from Dumbledore and thus receive Godric Gryffindor's sword that proves his rightful place in Gryffindor. As Dumbledore comments, "Only a true Gryffindor could have pulled *that* out of the hat, Harry" (*Chamber of Secrets* 334). The significance of certain numbers also invokes folk and fairy tale motifs, where both three and seven tend to be significant. We see this here not only with the three tasks the champions must complete during the Triwizard Tournament, but also in the appearance of the three Deathly Hallows. Similarly, the significance of the number seven appears in the seven years students spend at Hogwarts, the seven books that comprise the series, and Voldemort's attempt to split his soul into seven parts to create Horcruxes and outwit death.

Traditional fairy and folk tale settings and magical creatures also appear throughout, with both the towers of Hogwarts and Hagrid's cottage on the grounds. The Forbidden Forest also appears numerous times: Harry is punished there near the end of *Sorcerer's Stone*, he and Ron encounter Aragog and the giant spiders there in *Chamber of Secrets*, and the children trek through the woods to meet Grawp and then later lead Umbridge into the woods to be ambushed by the centaurs in *Order of the Phoenix*. Numerous forests populate *Deathly Hallows*, but the most significant of these is the Forest of Dean, where Snape plants the sword of Gryffindor for Harry to find. Moreover, the series is populated with magical or otherworldly creatures typical to fairy or folk tales. Dragons appear in *Sorcerer's Stone* with Norbert, again in *Goblet of Fire* as Harry battles the dragons in the Triwizard Tournament, and finally with the guard-dragon that Harry, Ron, and Hermione ride to break out of Gringotts in *Deathly Hallows*, while giants appear not only with Hagrid and Madame Maxime but also with Hagrid's brother Grawp. Goblins serve as guards as well as bank-tellers at Gringotts, and the goblin Griphook plays a small but significant role in *Deathly Hallows*. Werewolves appear too, most traditionally with the figure of Fenrir Greyback in *Half-Blood Prince* and *Deathly Hallows*, but also with the more benevolent figure of Remus Lupin.

Numerous other figures throughout the series draw upon a rich variety of folkloric beliefs. For instance, in English folklore Bowtruckles are tree-guardians of wand trees, Hinkypunks appear in West country folklore, and Grindylows are water demons of Yorkshire folklore; Kappas, in contrast, allegedly have a source in Japanese folklore that suggests that they appear as water spirits that drag their victims into the water to drown and mutilate them. Both Veela and Mandrakes appear in European folklore: Veela are female shape-shifting spirits dwelling in forests, lakes, mountains, and clouds, whose effects on young men are exactly as those that appear in *Goblet of Fire*, although folkloric belief suggested that men who encountered them while dancing were fated to dance until they died of exhaustion. Similarly, the baby Mandrakes that grow to adolescence in *Chamber of Secrets* were European plants with forked roots that, with some imagination, might appear human-like; they were believed to utter a deadly shriek if pulled from the ground, and were thought to be endowed with magical properties due to their medicinal uses as painkillers, sleeping aids, and anaesthetics.

Creatures common to Greek mythology also appear, such as Fluffy (from *Sorcerer's Stone*), who resembles Cereberus, the three-headed giant dog guarding the entrance to the Underworld, and the sphinx who poses an Oedipus-like challenge to Harry in *Goblet of Fire*. Similarly, the phoenix has connections with both ancient Greek and Egyptian mythology, where it was associated with the cycle of the sun; during the Middle Ages it became part of Christian symbolism, representing death, resurrection, and eternal life, while in Chinese mythology, the phoenix is a symbol of power, integrity, loyalty, honesty, and justice—an appropriate choice for Dumbledore's Patronus. Finally, Aragog, the giant spider, can be traced back to the African folk tale of Anansi the spider, a trickster as well as a story keeper and wise figure who was believed to provide a link between humans and the gods.

Fantasy usually involves a quest of some sort, which ties it to traditional forms of both adventure and quest romance. Certainly the series contains all of the typical elements of the adventure tale. In addition to blending the familiar with the unexpected, thus offering readers comfort and excitement concurrently, adventure tales focus on a noble-natured hero who is removed from the comforts of home and the controls of normal society and forced to face innumerable dangers. Due to his intelligence, courageous spirit, resourcefulness, and self-reliance, the typical adventure hero overcomes the odds and wins the battle against his adversaries. Harry is quite happy to be removed from his extremely uncomfortable domicile with the Dursleys, and Hogwarts quickly becomes his second—and beloved—home, and from there he faces and conquers such fantastic dangers as three-headed dogs, fire-breathing dragons, deadly serpents, and Dementors who suck out souls along with happy memories. The adventure hero is usually accompanied on his adventures by a faithful companion, and receives aid from a helper figure who possesses more information than he does. Here, both Ron and Hermione fill the role of faithful companions, while helper figures such as Dobby and, later, Griphook appear. Adventure plots tend to be fast-paced, heavy on dialogue and description, and maintain a buoyant and optimistic tone throughout, even though the hero at times may be tempted to give in to despair, and the books fit this description exactly as well. The climax of the adventure story usually occurs during the final battle against the most powerful opponent, and generally arises "from the theme of honor preserved against the dangers of intrigue, betrayal and the clash of loyalties" (Fisher 109). This can be seen initially with Harry's repeated encounters with Voldemort and how Harry's reliance on the memory of his parents and their love for him gives him the strength or protection necessary to survive those encounters. Later, this paradigm is developed as Harry's loyalties clash with his instincts, and as he suffers feelings of betrayal in relation to both Ron and Dumbledore in *Deathly Hallows*. Adventure tales conclude with the triumphant return of the hero to his true home, where he is rewarded by discovering his proper worth and/or identity, and the ending of the series follows through with Harry's realization of his identity as well as a resounding sense of his own worth.

Finally, the series adheres to many of the generic elements of quest romance, both in terms of character and pattern. Harry clearly appears as the hero, who in quest romance is analogous to the deliverer or mythical Messiah, and certainly at the beginning of the story he is recognized in the wizard world as the person who vanquished Voldemort. The hero is often of a mysterious origin, whose true father is concealed, and Harry's origins on his father's side remain a mystery to him for most of the series and are not ever fully explained, though he finds out a little more about his heritage in *Deathly Hallows*. Traditionally the hero represents spring, vigor, and youth, and we see this in Harry's initial identity as a child, as well as in his continued growth throughout the series. Similarly, Voldemort appears as the foe or villain of quest romance, corresponding to "the demonic powers of a lower world" (Frye 196). Traditionally the foe represents winter, darkness, confusion, sterility, and old age, and certainly Voldemort and his representatives cause darkness as well as chaos, while notions of winter and sterility appear in the meaning of his name, with *volde* being the Old English word for earth or land and *mort* the French word for death. Other character types from quest romance also appear throughout the series, with faithful companions such as Ron, who provides practical knowledge through experience of the wizard world, and Hermione, who provides wisdom through book learning. The heroine, too, a female complement to the hero playing a supporting role, appears in Ginny Weasley, while Dumbledore appears as the "old wise man …

often a magician who affects the action he watches over" (Frye 195). The "true father," while sometimes conflated with the figure of the old wise man, here appears not only in Sirius Black but also in the eerie appearance of James Potter, represented by his ghostly voice in *Goblet of Fire*, through Snape's memory in the Pensieve in *Order of the Phoenix*, and in his ethereal appearance near the end of *Deathly Hallows*. Privileged and aloof characters occur with Draco Malfoy as well as Severus Snape, while comic and colorful characters, who provide depth as well as comic relief, appear with Hagrid and Luna Lovegood. Finally, both Firenze and Kreacher function as spirits of nature, figures that traditionally elude the moral antithesis of villainy or heroism and who function as servants or friends of the hero.

The pattern of quest romance consists of three defined stages, with which the series corresponds almost perfectly: *agon* or conflict, *pathos* or death-struggle, and *anagnorisis* or discovery. The first stage, *agon*, begins with the hero's perilous journey, during which he moves into a new landscape, distinct from his normal world, full of secrets and enchantments. This describes the series' opening, with Harry's perilous journey into the wizard world and Hogwarts, both of which are not only distinct from his normal, Muggle world, but also are filled both with secrets and, quite literally, enchantments. During this first stage, the hero receives his training, and Harry is trained in the basic precepts of wizardry as well as in other more significant ways to become the hero. True to the pattern, he also engages in a number of preliminary minor conflicts, which include his encounters with Sirius Black in *Prisoner of Azkaban*, his participation in the Triwizard Tournament—particularly in relation to the dragon and the merpeople—in *Goblet of Fire*, his clashes with Umbridge in *Order of the Phoenix*, and his repeated conflicts with Snape throughout the series. More important, however, are Harry's preliminary conflicts with Voldemort: in *Sorcerer's Stone*, with Voldemort possessing Quirrell's body, in *Chamber of Secrets*, with Tom Riddle's diary persona, in *Goblet of Fire*, after Voldemort's re-embodiment, and in *Order of the Phoenix*, at the Ministry of Magic.

The second stage of quest romance, *pathos* or death-struggle, entails the crucial battle in which either the hero or his foe, or both, must die, which occurs in *Deathly Hallows*. During this stage, the hero leaves his resting-place and goes forth into his great contest, and for Harry this begins in *Half-Blood Prince* as Harry leaves the resting-place of his childhood behind and shoulders the burden of the prophecy. Also during this second stage, the hero must travel through a wilderness or dark forest and face challenges of despair and threats of death; Harry has been facing threats of death throughout the series, and the wilderness is something we see after Harry and his friends leave the relative security of Grimmauld Place and begin to search for the Horcruxes. The notion of despair has already been set up by the death of Dumbledore at the end of *Half-Blood Prince*, but Rowling extends this significantly with the deaths of Mad-Eye Moody and Hedwig near the beginning of *Deathly Hallows* and with the dubious behavior of Lupin after his marriage to Tonks. The feeling is further developed by Ron's defection from Harry's quest, and then by the heart-wrenching death of Dobby. Harry's despair reaches its height with the first battle at Hogwarts when Fred is killed in battle, Snape dies at the hands of Voldemort, and Harry returns to see Lupin's and Tonks' bodies added to those of the dead. In his despair, he experiences Snape's memories and gives himself up to Voldemort. What follows marks the climax of quest romance, where the hero's fears fall away and release him from guilt, fear, and weariness; this stage encompasses Tolkien's notion of "Eucatastrophe," or the sudden joyous turn. Here, Harry discovers that he hasn't actually died and that he at last possesses a real chance of defeating Voldemort; upon his return he does just this, with significant help from his friends, though Rowling removes the responsibility of Voldemort's murder from her hero's shoulders by allowing Voldemort's own "Avada Kedavra" curse to rebound and kill him instead of Harry.

The third stage of quest romance, *anagnorisis* or discovery, focuses on the recognition of the hero: having proved his heroism the hero is acclaimed, but upon returning home he finds he is no longer like those he left behind. Interestingly, Rowling changes the pattern here, and allows Harry to have the "normal" life he's always desired, rather than showing him to be so damaged by his experiences that he can no longer live fully in the world (as is Frodo at the end of *The Lord of the Rings*). Had Rowling ended the story with the final chapter, rather than adding her "Epilogue," it would be possible to argue the series as typical quest romance in every way. However, the "Nineteen Years Later" chapter suggests two other possibilities: either Rowling is inviting readers to rethink their notions of quest romance and allow a different ending, thus changing the nature of this particular genre, or instead to rethink just how closely the story follows the pattern of quest romance.

Northrop Frye suggests that the nearer the quest romance approaches to myth, "the more attributes of divinity will cling to the hero and the more the enemy will take on demonic mythical qualities" (187), and this is true to a certain extent of both Harry and Voldemort. In some senses, Harry has already taken on divine attributes, starting off as "the boy who lived" and then surviving increasingly serious attempts on his life. It is even truer of Voldemort, who by the end of *Goblet of Fire* has quite literally risen from the dead to become a malevolent figure who seems larger than life. From there, the story continues to move in the direction of myth, in terms of both allusions and Rowling's creation of her own mythic elements such as the Mirror of Erised and the Devil's Snare (*Sorcerer's Stone*), the significance of Parseltongue (*Chamber of Secrets*), the Whomping Willow (*Prisoner of Azkaban*), the Pensieve (*Goblet of Fire*), Thestrals and the Room of Requirements (*Order of the Phoenix*), the concept of Horcruxes (*Half-Blood Prince*), and the notion of the Deathly Hallows (*Deathly Hallows*). Her treatment of such themes as the true nature of good and evil, the concept of immortality, and the significance of love suggests her movement towards the genre of epic, whose narrative chronicles the heroic character's achievements through an important part of history. Moreover, her invocation of the significance of story in *Deathly Hallows* suggests the series' very significance: that a good story not only allows us to enter into it fully and go somewhere completely unknown and perhaps even unimagined, but also to return with a different view of our own life and the world. Ideally, stories give us the gift, at least in our imaginations, of walking in someone else's life for a moment, an experience that when surrendered to provides a kind of imaginative understanding that we cannot gain from leading our own solitary life. Moreover, good stories not only have a life that outlasts our own—as Philip Pullman suggests, "Once upon a time lasts forever"[7]—but, more broadly, a significance that can change the world, as "The Tale of the Three Brothers" in *The Tales of Beedle the Bard* proves to hold for Harry.

Reading Harry Potter through the various lenses inherent within a multi-genre approach leads to the realization that genre, rather than being a mere classification tool, has taken on significance as a communication system. Because of their conscious or unconscious awareness of the various genres fused in the books, readers gain the delight of recognition as they read something that feels familiar in form: they know the conventions of the game, or the story, before they begin, and thus are looking for the tags, or signs, of fantasy, or pulp fiction, or the school story, or detective fiction. As they read the story, or progress through the game, they not only find these tags but also start to anticipate how Rowling will include others specific to the genre they are reading. However, Rowling takes the game one step further: as new tags of each genre appear, they reflect links to other genres as well and change the meaning of the tags that have preceded them, thus modifying the initial genre to which they belonged, and the cycle starts all over again. By fusing the genres in this way, Rowling has created something new: a generic mosaic made up of numerous individual pieces combined in a way that allows them to keep their original shape while constantly changing their significance. The ways in which these pieces operate vary and change depending on the generic tags being interpreted at any given time by any particular reader.

When speaking of genre, questions of hierarchy almost inevitably seem to come into play: what's on top? However, reading the Harry Potter series as a generic game makes this question irrelevant, at least in terms of genre. In a game that is constantly changing and rearranging its pieces, no single genre can claim top place in the hierarchy; instead, it is the continual interplay among the tags and thus the genres that becomes most significant, as this interplay is what creates the multiple meanings of the whole. The perpetual shifting of the mosaic's pieces encourages readers to reread the text as they succumb to the very human temptation of trying to find the "real" meaning of the series. In the end, the delight that millions of readers have discovered and will continue to experience in Harry Potter is the sense of wonder that results from their repeated experience of Eliot's notion of "knowing the place for the first time."

Notes

1. The term genre is usually invoked when referring to works sharing a similar form or style. Until the eighteenth century, the major generic classifications were lyric, epic or narrative, and dramatic, and critics tended to insist on each genre remaining "pure" and not mixed with other genres; moreover, genres were assumed to be hierarchically arranged, with epic and tragedy at the top and other (or "minor") genres at the bottom. Over the last 50 years it has become more critically acceptable to consider works in relation to a variety of generic traditions and conventions. Generic distinctions based on content are no longer exclusive, nor are they set in stone: indeed, Alastair Fowler notes that "every literary work changes the genres it relates to" (23). This is particularly appropriate when considering the ways in which Rowling combines genres, which is starting to change the way we perceive the study of genre as a whole.
2. The appearance of different editions for child and adult readers—books with exactly the same textual content but different covers, prices (the "adult" editions were more expensive), and placement in bookstores—also suggests the ways in which marketing affects generic expectations in relation to children's literature versus adult literature.
3. In Britain and other English-speaking countries, the title of the first book in the series is *Harry Potter and the Philosopher's Stone*.
4. For the purposes of this discussion, I will focus on the conventions of literary series written by the same author, rather than what Watson refers to as publishers' format-series written by authors given publishers' house names, such as *The Bobbsey Twins*, *Tom Swift*, *Nancy Drew*, and *The Hardy Boys* series.
5. Critics including Richards, Quigly, and Townsend have commented on the death of the genre since the 1960s.
6. Eleanor Cameron's article on High Fantasy has influenced much of my thinking about fantasy and its components.
7. Pullman concludes his Carnegie Medal acceptance speech for *Northern Lights* (1995)—better known in North America as *The Golden Compass*—with the suggestion that "We don't need lists of rights and wrongs, tables of do's and don'ts: we need books, time, and silence. Thou shalt not is soon forgotten, but Once upon a time lasts forever."

References

Cameron, Eleanor. "High Fantasy: *A Wizard of Earthsea*." *Crosscurrents of Criticism: Horn Book Essays 1968–1977*. Ed. Paul Heins. Boston, MA: The Horn Book, 1977. 333–341.

Eliot, T. S. *Four Quartets*. London: Faber and Faber, 1944.

Fisher, Margery. *The Bright Face of Danger: An Exploration of the Adventure Story*. Boston, MA: The Horn Book, 1986.

Fowler, Alastair. *Kinds of Literature: An Introduction to the Theory of Genres and Modes*. Cambridge, MA: Harvard University Press, 1982.

Frye, Northrop. *Anatomy of Criticism: Four Essays*. Princeton, NJ: Princeton University Press, 1957.

Gohlman, Susan Ashley. *Starting Over: The Task of the Protagonist in the Contemporary Bildungsroman*. New York: Garland, 1990.

Hilton, Mary. "'The Blowing Dust': Popular Culture and Popular Books for Children." *The Prose and the Passion: Children and Their Reading*. Ed. Morag Styles, Eve Bearne, and Victor Watson. London: Cassell, 1994. 9–19.

Iyer, Pico. "The Playing Fields of Hogwarts." *New York Times on the Web*. October 10, 1999.

Retrieved March 7, 2007, from http://www.nytimes.com/books/99/10/10/bookend/bookend.html.

Le Guin, Ursula K. "The Despised Genres: Women Writers and the Canon." Lecture. University of Calgary (September 24, 1996).

Malory, Thomas. *Le Morte d'Arthur*. 1485. *Works*. Ed. Eugène Vinaver. 2nd edn. Oxford: Oxford University Press, 1971.

Palmer, Jerry. *Thrillers: Genesis and Structure of a Popular Genre*. New York: St. Martin's Press, 1979.

Porter, Dennis. "Backward Construction and the Art of Suspense." *The Poetics of Murder: Detective Fiction and Literary Theory*. Ed. Glenn W. Most and William W. Stowe. New York: Harcourt Brace Jovanovich, 1983. 327–340.

Pullman, Philip. "Carnegie Medal Acceptance Speech." Retrieved November 19, 2007, from http://www.randomhouse.com/features/pullman/author/carnegie.html.

Quigly, Isabel. *The Heirs of Tom Brown: The English School Story*. Oxford: Oxford University Press., 1984.

Richards, Jeffrey. "The School Story." *Stories and Society: Children's Literature in its Social Context*. Ed. Dennis Butts. London: Macmillan, 1992. 1–21.

Rowling, J. K. *Harry Potter and the Philosopher's Stone*. London: Bloomsbury, 1997.

——. *Harry Potter and the Sorcerer's Stone*. 1997. Illus. Mary Grandpré. New York: Scholastic, 1998.

——. *Harry Potter and the Chamber of Secrets*. London: Bloomsbury, 1998.

——. *Harry Potter and the Chamber of Secrets*. Illus. Mary Grandpré. New York: Scholastic, 1998.

——. *Harry Potter and the Prisoner of Azkaban*. London: Bloomsbury, 1999.

——. *Harry Potter and the Prisoner of Azkaban*. Illus. Mary Grandpré. New York: Scholastic, 1999.

——. *Harry Potter and the Goblet of Fire*. London: Bloomsbury, 2000.

——. *Harry Potter and the Goblet of Fire*. Illus. Mary Grandpré. New York: Scholastic, 2000.

——. *Harry Potter and the Order of the Phoenix*. London: Bloomsbury, 2003.

——. *Harry Potter and the Order of the Phoenix*. Illus. Mary Grandpré. New York: Scholastic, 2003.

——. *Harry Potter and the Half-Blood Prince*. London: Bloomsbury, 2005.

——. *Harry Potter and the Half-Blood Prince*. Illus. Mary Grandpré. New York: Scholastic, 2005.

——. *Harry Potter and the Deathly Hallows*. London: Bloomsbury, 2007.

——. *Harry Potter and the Deathly Hallows*. Illus. Mary Grandpré. New York: Scholastic, 2007.

Scott, Alison M. "They Came from the Newsstand: Pulp Magazines and Vintage Paperbacks in the Popular Culture Library." *Pioneers, Passionate Ladies, and Private Eyes: Dime Novels, Series Books, and Paperbacks*. Eds. Larry E. Sullivan and Lydia Cushman Schurman. New York: Haworth Press, 1996. 39–46.

Siegel, Lee. "Harry Potter and the Spirit of the Age: Fear of Not Flying." *New Republic*. November 22, 1999. Retrieved March 7, 2007, from http://web.archive.org/web/20000304132127/http://www.thenewrepublic. com/magazines/tnr/112299/siegel112299.html.

Stahl, Lesley. "60 Minutes: *Harry Potter*." Interview with J. K. Rowling. CBS. September 12, 1999.

Tolkien, J. R. R. *The Lord of the Rings*. 1954–1955. Boston, MA: Houghton Mifflin, 1994.

——. "On Fairy Stories." *Tree and Leaf*. London: Unwin, 1964. 11–72.

Townsend, John Rowe. *Written for Children: An Outline of English-Language Children's Literature*. 1965. 6th edn. London: Bodley Head, 1990.

Tucker, Nicholas. "The Rise and Rise of Harry Potter." *Children's Literature in Education* 30:4 (December 1999): 221–234.

Watson, Victor. *Reading Series Fiction: From Arthur Ransome to Gene Kemp*. London and New York: Routledge, 2000.

Zipes, Jack. "The Phenomenon of Harry Potter, or Why All the Talk?" *The Troublesome Success of Children's Literature from Slovenly Peter to Harry Potter*. New York and London: Routledge, 2001. 170–190.

Chapter Twelve

Harry Potter and the Secrets of Children's Literature

MARIA NIKOLAJEVA

There will be books written about Harry—every child in our world will know his name!

(Minerva McGonagall in *Harry Potter and the Philosopher's Stone*)

It is tempting today, with ten years in the rear-view mirror, to claim that the resolution of the Harry Potter saga was predictable. We can but speculate whether the ending of the final volume, *Harry Potter and the Deathly Hallows*, has been part of the original design or influenced by the unprecedented success of the first volumes. It is intriguing to explore the novels in terms of their compliance with or deviation from the conventions of children's literature; both can, paradoxically, account for their popularity.

Harry Potter is a child of serendipity, appearing just when the international children's book market was in acute need of a new type of character. The flat, one-dimensional, mind-numbing characters of formulaic fiction, though satisfying the basic desires of less sophisticated readers, had for decades vexed conscious critics, librarians, and teachers. The ambivalent characters, praised by critics, have often been rejected by young readers as too demanding. The fortunate blend of the straightforward and the reasonably intricate, the heroic and the everyday in Harry Potter became a response to these contradictory needs, and, sarcastic voices notwithstanding, seems to have reconciled the incompatible desires.

In the first edition of my chapter "Harry Potter—a Return to the Romantic hero" I explored the Harry Potter novels in terms of displacement of myth, in Northrop Frye's sense (*Anatomy of Criticism*), and of genre eclecticism. My argument point was that in contemporary Western children's fiction, most of the child characters seem to appear on low mimetic and ironic levels. The universal appeal of Harry Potter can be ascribed to the fortunate attempt to reintroduce the romantic character into children's fiction. The Harry Potter figure has all the necessary components of the romantic hero. There are mystical circumstances around his birth, he is dislocated and oppressed and suddenly given unlimited power. His innocence and intrinsic benevolence make him superior to the evil—adult—forces. He bears the mark of the chosen on his forehead, and he is worshiped in the wizard community as the future savior. The pattern is easily recognizable from world mythologies, even though Harry is not claimed to be a god or a son of god, which, in Frye's typology, disqualifies him as a genuine mythic hero, displacing him to the level of romance. Yet Harry Potter is a product of the twenty-first century, demonstrating ambiguity in the concepts of good and evil, gender transgression, and other tokens of the postmodern aesthetics, satisfactory for critics. The adult appeal originates from other layers of the books: adult issues, the richness of allusions, elaborate linguistic games, or social satire. Yet for most readers, the lure of Harry Potter is his total conformity with the idea of a romantic hero.

Harry Potter provides the sense of security that characters such as another young magician in Diana Wynne Jones' *The Lives of Christopher Chant* or the sign reader Lyra in Philip Pullman's *His Dark Materials* have subverted. In following Harry's (mis)adventures, the issue is not whether he wins, but how he gets there. The *Goblet of Fire* offers a masterly balance of suspense and confidence in the final scenes. We know that the hero will be miraculously saved in the last moment, and we keep on reading to learn exactly how this happens. The extratextual knowledge about the existence of the three remaining volumes adds to our belief in the positive outcome. The sequels cannot possibly go on without Harry. Neither can he be killed and resurrected in the next volume, since mortality is included as a part of the universe. Harry is not a mythic "returning god."

To assess Harry as a modern—or rather postmodern—hero, two closely related critical theories are highly significant: carnival and queer, both dealing with power and both subcategories of a more encompassing theoretical field of heterology, discourse on the Other (Certeau). Carnival theory, developed by Mikhail Bakhtin (Bakhtin) and successfully applied to children's novels, focuses on the literary depiction of a temporary reversal of the established order when power structures change places. If queer theory has primarily been utilized to investigate gender relationships, carnival theory has primarily been applied to texts that clearly show carnivalesque features: hyperbole, upside-down-world, grotesque, scatological humor, theater, circus, market place, jester trickery, and so on. Far too seldom do scholars embrace Bakhtin's overall view of literature as carnival, a symbolic representation of a socially liberating process, a disguised interrogation of authorities. Bakhtin presents the essence of the medieval carnival (a short period of grotesque festivities and excesses preceding Lent), as a temporary reversal of the established order when all societal power structures changed places. Carnival was sanctioned by the authorities who therefore had control over it. Moreover, the temporary nature of carnival presupposed the restoration of the initial order. Yet carnival had a subversive effect, since it showed that social hierarchies were not unquestionable. Bakhtin views literature as a narrative device used to describe reality in a distorting mirror, in a state of temporary deviation from the existing order, as well as total freedom from societal restrictions.

Carnival theory is highly relevant for children's literature. Children in our society are oppressed and powerless, having no economic resources of their own, no voice in political and social decisions, and subject to laws and rules that the adults expect them to obey without interrogation. Yet, paradoxically enough, children are allowed, in fiction written for their enlightenment and enjoyment *by adults*, to become strong, brave, rich, powerful, independent—on certain conditions and for a limited time. Even though the fictional child is usually brought back to the security of home and parental supervision, the narratives have subversive effect, showing that the rules imposed on the child by the adults are in fact arbitrary. Carnival elevates the child to the superior position of the romantic hero. Yet, the inevitable re-establishment of order in the end of a carnivalesque children's story brings the characters down to the high mimetic, low mimetic or ironic levels, at which they are only slightly more powerful than their environment, equal to it or inferior to it.

Queer theory, with its emphasis on (hetero)normativity, explores other dimensions of societal inequalities. Labeling the Harry Potter books as queer, Michael Bronski points out that the original queer-theoretical meaning of this concept, homosexual, has acquired a broader significance, referring to general deviation and nonconformism (Bronski, "Queering Harry Potter"). Going a step further, queer theory demonstrates, first, that norms are arbitrary, and second, and more important, that the whole argument about "norms" and "deviations" gives the norm priority, and thus more authority and power. Queer theory does replace one norm with another, but claims that all conditions are equally normal. Queer studies test how we can exchange an established pattern, in the case of children's literature, adult normativity, for another one, and examine what happens with the child in power as norm and the powerless child a deviation. The essence of queer theory, in this interpretation, is the interrogation of any single condition as a norm. It is in this broader sense I am using the term queer in this chapter, and as deviating, interrogative, unconventional, queer is if not synonymous with carnivalesque then at least very close, which Bronski also suggests in drawing parallel between queer and Misrule, a variant of carnival. I do not, however, view the Harry Potter books as inherently queer (in the sense of them being a disguised depiction of a coming-out), but rather apply heterological tools to expose some additional aspects of the much-researched series. The queer, or gender-related, features of Harry Potter, such as blurring the gender-segregated school system (Pugh and Wallace, "Heteronomative Heroism"), is merely one aspect of a more comprehensive power structure.

Power hierarchies in the series are unequivocal. Wizards are superior to non-wizards. Other writers, such as Diana Wynne Jones, have created worlds where magic is opposed to non-magic, but she never presents non-magical worlds or people without magical powers as inferior. Jones frequently portrays a higher authority that unscrupulously governs ordinary people, much like the Ministry of Magic imposes its rules on Muggles. Yet in Jones' worlds, the authority is repeatedly interrogated, both explicitly and through the subject position offered by the text.

In the Harry Potter universe, full-blood wizards are superior to Muggle-born, and the persecution of the Muggle-born in the final volume is reminiscent of the worst genocides in human history. British wizards are superior to foreign wizards, some of which are bestowed by ridiculous Eastern European names. Within the wizard community, foreign-born are never given prominent roles (the Patil twins loom in the periphery, tokens of Hogwarts' equal opportunity policy). Squibs—wizard-born without magic powers—are the lowest of the wizard world. Translated into reality it may correspond to contempt toward mentally impaired people. Human beings are superior to goblins, elves, centaurs, and giants—grotesque bodies, or physically impaired. Men are superior to women. It suffices to compare Professor McGonagall's status with the male teachers; to consider the Divination professor Trelawney's constant humiliation, or the open mockery made of Professor Umbridge. The ambiguous role of Hermione and particularly her restricted agency is unobstructed. Gryffindor's Quidditch team features a couple of girls kept in the background; Luna is looney, and Tonks gender-neutral, which is accentuated by her self-imposed androgynous name.

The rich are not unexpectedly superior to the poor, and here Ron's position becomes blurred, or queered: as a male and full-blood he is superior to Hermione, but since his family's financial circumstances are constrained, Hermione appears a cut above. Harry himself is well-provided for and can be generous toward others, and even though he never abuses his power, it is understood that he is better than students with less pecuniary assets. The authorities, represented by the Ministry of Magic, are naturally superior to the rank-and-file, and even the mighty Dumbledore must comply. In the Hogwarts' student hierarchy, ageism is tangible. First- and second-year students are not allowed to go to the village, and older students openly bully younger ones. Most of the racist, sexist, imperialistic, and other ideologically dubious aspects of the novels have been thoroughly investigated before. Yet all these power structures are employed to support the central one: adults are superior to children.

The protagonist fulfills all the power criteria except one, and thus is presented as the bearer of normativity. Concerning the adult/child tension,

Harry is allowed a temporary, carnivalesque superiority, under absolute adult control, on adult conditions, and as long as the adults please to let the child play on his own. The adult world takes over in various ways when it is time to restore order. For Bakhtin, the issue would be whether the hero, and thus the reader, can make inferences from the carnivalesque experience and view the existing power positions as arbitrary, hence something that can be changed. Translating the favorite concept of queer theory, heteronormativity, to the conditions of children's literature, we can speak about adult normativity, or aetonormativity (of Latin *aetas*, age; ageism). The adults have by right of age unlimited power in our society. But what happens if the adults are no longer the smartest, the richest, and the most powerful in the child/adult relationship? What happens if we substitute child normativity for adult normativity? It seems that the Harry Potter books instead endorse the adults as norm.

The books have also been discussed as novels of adolescence (Trites, "The Harry Potter Novels"). Paradoxically enough, the adolescent novel denies the protagonists the power that books for younger children allow through carnivalization. In a young adult novel, society catches up with the protagonist, depicted in transition from being oppressed to becoming an oppressor—unless he perishes on the way. In the Harry Potter books, power clearly reproduces itself. Harry and his friends are initially scornful about Ron's older brother Percy, who is appointed prefect and uses every occasion to point out his supremacy. Throughout the books, we watch Percy's progression until he finally leaves childhood and gets an important job at the Ministry of Magic. In the *Order of the Phoenix*, Ron and Hermione become prefects, and Percy congratulates his brother on the first step in his bureaucratic career. Harry never makes it to prefect, thus his special position is amplified, his freedom to break school rules is not put to trial, but in the first place the prefect appointment is connected with loyalty toward the adults. Naturally, being prefects does not prevent Ron and Hermione from following Harry on his increasingly dangerous adventures, but both take their responsibility according to adult prescriptions. With Ron's and Hermione's foretaste of power, their final incorporation into adult hierarchy is anticipated.

Carnival Commences: the Premises of Children's Literature

Harry is a perfect illustration of the archetypal figure in children's literature. Born into the world of humans, he is dislocated from his rightful environment. A child deprived of his or her birthright is one of the most common mythical and folktale motifs, occurring in stories as diverse as Cinderella and the Bible. The romantic convention prompts to the reader that the weak and the oppressed will be empowered and returned to their proper positions in the social hierarchy. Harry is reintroduced to the community from which he has been temporarily expelled and given seemingly unlimited power, even though, with a marvelous ironic twist, he is yet to learn how to use it.

Moreover, although restored in his rightful position, Harry is yet to prove himself worthy of it, and is therefore subjected to a number of trials. Each volume of the Harry Potter saga is a duplication of this trial pattern (cf. Zipes 176f.). The conventions of the romantic mode dictate that the hero pass the trial and win the combat with the evil forces. In this, Harry is equipped with an army of gurus and supporters and an infinitely evil and powerful opponent. However, his innocence and his intrinsic benevolence make him superior to the evil—adult—powers.

The removal of parents is the premise of children's literature. The absence of parental authority allows the space that the fictive child needs for development and maturity, in order to test (and taste) his independence and to discover the world without adult protection. At the same time, the child cannot be left completely without adult supervision; therefore there are substitutes, who provide security, but also maintain the rules that the adult world has set up. It is less offensive to get rid of *in loco parentis* figures than the biological parents, but such surrogates are essential in many senses. Not least as the protagonist approaches adolescence, parental figures are needed so that he can rebel against them. As the novels progress, new father substitutes pop up, positive as well as negative: in addition to Uncle Vernon, Voldemort, Dumbledore, Hagrid, and Snape, also Sirius, Lupin, Arthur Weasley, Mad-Eye Moody, Lucius Malfoy, Cornelius Fudge, and so on.

With an orphan hero, the identity search theme is amplified while he is also exposed to more serious trials than would be possible with adult protection. He is, however, never totally on his own, since it is children's books written by an adult, and the adult world must have control over the child. Compared to real parents, substitutes decrease adult power over the child without abolishing it. Thus Harry Potter books are based on the imperative convention of children's literature. From a psychological point of view it may seem unreasonable for Dumbledore to leave infant Harry with his wicked relatives (even though there is a half-rational explanation). Similarly, it feels irresponsible of the Hogwarts teachers to let Harry and his friends run about at night rather than locking them in the dorm with a magic spell and protecting them from danger. However, this negligence is not only indispensable for the plot (what could possibly happen if Harry slept obediently in his bed?) but also for character constellations. It is quite significant that more and more parent substitutes are gotten rid of, finally even Dumbledore. In the last book, friends and supporters are sacrificed in gross detail.

The overwhelming majority of fantasy novels feature ordinary children temporarily empowered through a magic agent. Those who believe Harry Potter to be the first child protagonist endowed with magic powers have forgotten Ged from Ursula Le Guin's *Earthsea*, Will from Susan Cooper's *The Dark Is Rising*, or Christopher from Diana Wynne Jones' *The Lives of Christopher Chant*, just to name a few. However, in all these books, including Harry

Potter, the young wizard's power is initially limited. Like Ged, Will, and Christopher, Harry must learn to use magic; it is not a matter of merely waving a wand. As a wizard, Harry is omnipotent only compared to Muggles, notably his foster family. He is in many ways superior to his peers at Hogwarts: famous since birth, unbeatable in Quidditch, and indisputably more energetic and mischievous—virtue in his classmates' eyes, if not the teachers'. He is braver, but in a typically heroic manner: he acts as a hero because he is a hero. In some respects, Harry is inferior to his schoolmates; for instance, not particularly good in academic achievements. Harry and the other wizards are not omnipotent gods, immune to laws of nature: they can be injured, get sick, and die. Some wizards are more powerful than others: Dumbledore is among the most powerful, and as we eventually learn, he is not beneath abusing his power. Harry is born with enormous power as compared to many other characters in fantasy, yet his power is subjected to a set of regulations. For instance, he is not supposed to use magic in the Muggle world, and he can at any time be locked in his cupboard. When in the *Order of the Phoenix* Harry summons a Patronus to save Dudley, the wizard community tries to punish him severely. The child may have an illusion of unlimited power during carnival, while it is actually restricted by the adults. Although empowered, the child is not given full control; and even though it is understood that Harry is the only one to match the evil force of Voldemort, until the ultimate battle Harry has to comply with the rules imposed by adults. In the end, Dumbledore, the father substitute, has the final say.

The choice of a male protagonist is naturally not a coincidence. The romantic narrative is by definition masculine (Hourihan), and contemporary attempts to place a female character in a masculine plot merely results in a simple gender permutation, creating a quasi-female, "a hero in drag" (Paul). Our gender awareness notwithstanding, males are still superior to females, and being male puts Harry in a privileged position by definition. In Harry's defense, if he needs defense, or rather in his creator's defense, Harry, his machismo notwithstanding, is not a gender stereotype. Applying one of the many standard schemata for masculinity/femininity (e.g., Stephens, "Gender"), reveals that Harry displays quite a few traits normally associated with feminine stereotypes. He is non-violent, non-aggressive, emotional, caring, and vulnerable, which definitely makes him different from the conventional romantic heroes. Yet, he never reaches the complexity of some contemporary fantasy protagonists.

Carnival Continues: the Hero on Top

Fantasy mode is the foremost strategy of empowering a child. It is in no way a coincidence that fantasy is so dominant in children's fiction as compared to general literature where it is considered a low genre. Oppressed and humiliated in the ordinary world, Harry is displaced into a magical world where anything can happen. Harry is transported by means of the magical train (not in any way a new invention; a similar device was employed by Edith Nesbit almost a century before, and by many other fantasy writers). He comes into possession of a large variety of magical agents: his fantastic flying broom, his magic wand—a phallus symbol, as a psychoanalytically oriented critic would not fail to notice—an invisibility mantel, a magical interactive map, and so on. These attributes make him better equipped than his classmates and most of his teachers. Ron and Hermione become his helpers, and their specific talents, as well as later Luna's and Neville's, fill in when his own magical powers prove insufficient. Harry's triumphant ascent from his oppressed position with the Dursleys to fame, perpetual riches, and his privileged existence at Hogwarts is an easily recognizable fairy-tale pattern.

As in most fantasy novels, Harry is the Chosen One, the coming messiah. There is a prophecy about his mission, exactly as in other fantasy novels, from *The Lion, the Witch and the Wardrobe* to *His Dark Materials*. Fantasy heroes, or romantic heroes in Frye's sense, lack complexity, as appropriate for young readers from a didactic viewpoint. They know no nuances, being 100 percent heroic, they never doubt, fear, or despair. If described at all, they possess a standard set of traits: strong, brave, clever, kind, or beautiful. Their moral qualities are impeccable: they are just, loyal, and devoted to the cause they pursue. The premise for the romantic child hero is the idealization of childhood during the Romantic era, based on the belief in the child as innocent and therefore capable of conquering evil. Although this ideal child is now interrogated (see essays in McGavran, *Literature and the Child*), it affects the ways in which child heroes are still constructed in certain text types. Harry is no exception. His chief strength is the very fact that he is a child, and it is stressed that as an infant, he already had the power to protect himself against Voldemort. His intrinsic goodness is his most momentous weapon.

John Stephens limits his discussion of carnival in children's fiction to fantasy (Stephens, *Language* 120–157). There are, however, other ways of empowering the child without magic, and many of these are present in the Harry Potter novels, due to the remarkable genre eclecticism. High mimetic characters, in Frye's model, are humans superior to other humans, for instance, in terms of bravery, wisdom, or patriotism. Superior to other young people, high mimetic characters serve as models not only for the other characters in the story, but for the readers as well. In children's fiction, such characters are used for educational purposes. Adult readers may find Harry quite satisfactory as a model for children: he is humble, well-mannered, respectful toward his seniors, a perfect English gentleman. Young readers may appreciate other traits in Harry. As pointed out before, Harry is superior to his peers in terms of fame, bravery, and sports achievements. He is favored by his teachers, for instance, selected against the rules for the Quidditch team; in the *Goblet of Fire* he is allowed to participate in the Triwizard Tournament, which is likewise against the rules (and as we learn later, the result of an evil conspiracy).

Another genre that allows Harry to be superior in a typically carnivalesque manner is mystery. Mystery novels for children, such as *Nancy Drew* or the *Hardy Boys* series, empower the protagonists by letting them be smarter than the adults, to succeed where real detectives fail, and to happen to be in the right place at the right moment. Although devoid of supernatural features, mystery novels are no more realistic than the most incredible fairy tales, and the young heroes are far from ordinary. Indeed, they excel in everything: they can drive cars and fly airplanes, have quick brains, intuition, and observation aptitude; they can perform chemical analyses, operate obscure machinery, and find their way around without maps or compass; they come safe out of the most dangerous situations. Incidentally, Nancy Drew is also exceedingly good at sports and wins golf tournaments just in passing, while busy solving another mystery. Harry Potter is very much like these popular heroes. In each novel, he must solve a mystery, using his wits, courage, defiance, curiosity, deduction ability, and not least physical dexterity.

The boarding-school story provides excellent opportunities for empowerment. In boarding-school novels, with *Tom Brown's Schooldays* as an early model, the plot revolves around ordinary adventures: lessons, homework, sports, celebration of the first and last day of school, competition between dormitories, mischief, nightly orgies, forbidden outings to off-bound places, spying for enemies, the arrival of new students and teachers, bullying, revenge, and so on. Apart from the ongoing progressive plot featuring the struggle of good and evil, the bulk of the Harry Potter volumes contain a chain of everyday episodes, albeit generously seasoned with magic. In all of these, Harry is allowed to be brilliant, even though the triviality of adventures somewhat dilute the heroic nature of our hero. The ordinariness of Harry is magnificently emphasized by his name, which clearly stands out as plain and unpretentious beside Dumbledore, McGonagall, or Draco Malfoy. While these associative names are used to contribute to their bearers' individualities, Harry's name underscores his Everyman nature. Contemporary characters are not meant as examples for young readers to admire, but as equal subjectivities. While Harry is undoubtedly more lucky than most of us, his exceptionality is balanced by his more down-to-earth qualities, including his poor sight. Yet, with his old-fashioned, broken glasses Harry sees better than any other Hogwarts student, a quality especially appreciated by the members of his Quidditch team. Through Quidditch the novels adhere to the sports novels, another excellent genre to empower the child who is initially inept but eventually wins the competition.

The naughty-boy story is also prominent. The protagonist's strength is his intrinsic goodness, which allows him to perform pranks without being punished. Harry repeatedly breaks school rules, but since he does so with the best intentions, he is always forgiven. A comic effect is created when the teachers draw points from Gryffindor because Harry and his friends have been out after hours, while they award the house tenfold for Harry saving Hogwarts from mortal peril. Similarly the adventure story places the child in an extraordinary situation, an exotic and dangerous setting in which he can show his courage better than in everyday life: reveal villains, solve mysteries, and find treasures. The premise of adventure is chance: the hero happens to overhear a conspiracy or get important intelligence, a carnivalesque, empowering device. The conventions of adventure genre dictate that the hero accomplishes his mission. There is a touch of W. E. Johns' Biggles novels when Harry and Ron take the magical flying car to get to school when they miss the train.

All these genres are interwoven, and the attraction of the novels lies exactly in the fact that they do not clearly adhere to a particular genre. Yet all the various generic features, and all the levels of the narrative, from mythic down to ironic, in Frye's terms, cooperate to elevate the hero offering him a wide scope of opportunities to show himself superior to others—as long as the adults in the background have control over the situation.

Carnival Terminates: the Adults' Triumph

It would seem that, being a wizard, Harry is empowered permanently. However, the prerequisite of romantic fiction is the return to the initial order, the disempowerment of the hero, and the re-establishment of adult authority. The classic mythic hero kills his father and usurps the father's place, which would be highly improper in a children's book. Instead, Harry's father is, in accordance with children's literature tradition, conveniently killed off while Harry is still a baby, and in the end, Harry does not even have to kill Voldemort. Within the romantic mode, the child hero is brought back from magical journeys to alternative worlds or histories to the ordinary, sometimes being explicitly stripped of the attributes of previous power, most tangibly seen in the transformation of the Kings and Queens of Narnia back to children at the end of *The Lion, the Witch and the Wardrobe*. The magical object is irretrievably lost or loses its magical power (*The Story of the Amulet* by Edith Nesbit), the magical helper is removed (*Mary Poppins* by Pamela Travers), and the character stands alone without assistance, no longer a hero.

After each year at Hogwarts, Harry returns to the Dursleys. Apart from being a suitable narrative element, providing a natural frame for each school year, the return reminds of Harry's temporary departure from the ordinary and his temporary empowerment through the magical setup. The author follows the tradition from the Grand Old Lady of contemporary fantasy, Edith Nesbit, who, according to interviews, was one of Rowling's childhood favorites. In Nesbit's novels, magic is never omnipotent and often tricky. We may feel sorry for Harry, but for the sake of the plot his staying with the Dursleys is indispensable. When the family are no longer instrumental for the narrative, they are quietly got rid of, and we never hear about them again.

More important, Harry is not omnipotent in the wizard world either. The only one equal with Voldemort in magic force, he must still obey the adult wizards' commands. School setting emphasizes this power structure, spelled out, for instance, through Mrs. Weasley's utterance: "You are still at school and adults responsible for you should not forget it!" (*Order of the Phoenix* 83). Harry tentatively questions this by exclaiming bitterly to himself: "Just stay out while the grown-ups sort it out, Harry!" (495). Yet his silent rebellion has no effect. Dumbledore pops up like *deus ex machina* and concludes Harry's victory with an appreciative pat on the shoulder. It is especially noticeable in the *Order of the Phoenix*: as Harry and his friends fight Voldemort's supporters in the secret rooms of the Ministry of Magic, and as all hope is lost, Dumbledore, who has been waiting backstage, steps forward, and the narrator lets the reader in a most didactic manner share Harry's thoughts: "*they were saved*" (805; emphasis in the original). Here is the essence of adult normativity in a nutshell: the child hero can be as brave, clever, and strong as he pleases, but in the end, an adult will take over. Here is perhaps the secret behind those children's books that we sometimes call the masterpieces of children's literature. In some incredible way, such books manage to solve the dilemma: both to empower the child and to protect him from the dangers of adulthood, to try, against common sense, to hold the child within the innocence of childhood, since it is part of the adults' power strategy.

Carnival Reiterated: the Purpose of Sequels

The carnival structure is faithfully repeated in the first six volumes, following the master pattern of myth and folktale: home—away—home. Harry starts with his abominable foster family, goes to school where a new adventure awaits, allowing him to confirm his position as a hero, whereupon he is exiled to his humiliating existence with the Dursleys. Just as we may rejoice that Harry at long last will have a proper family with Sirius, the latter is appropriately removed. There are inventive variations within the volumes, and Harry's tasks become increasingly more dangerous and complicated, but the general plot structure is the same. This repetitiveness, or sameness, which some critics associate with the essence of children's literature (Nodelman, "Interpretation"), is prominent in series fiction, such as *Nancy Drew*, the *Famous Five*, or *Just William*, in which the order of reading is irrelevant since each of the books is a complete and independent narrative. The protagonist does not change nor grow older. It is claimed that the monotony of series fiction offers readers a sense of security, both concerning the invincibility of the hero, the stability of the plot, and their own reading skills. The Harry Potter novels presuppose a chronological order. Even though the summary of the previous events are provided in the beginning of each volume, details and characters reappear in later books, and the reader is expected to recognize them. While it is possible to read the books at random, as each plot is neatly rounded up, much of the suspense is lost when, for instance, the true nature of certain characters is already revealed or if circumstances behind key events have already been explained. Plotwise then, the novels are not serial fiction (cf. Watson, *Reading Series Fiction*).

The other essential trait of series is the static character. Harry undeniably becomes a year older in each book; he is neither Nancy Drew who is forever 16 (or perhaps 18, to enable her to drive in all states) nor William, deep-frozen at 11. However, character development can be of two kinds, chrono-logical and ethical. No matter what some critics say about the increasing scope of Harry's emotions, we are not given Harry's thoughts or feelings, if he is at all bestowed with the ability to think and feel. He is not a character encumbered by complex inner life. We are told that he is scared or lonely, but these are narrator's statements, not representations of mental states that demand more sophisticated narrative devices. This mediated narrative tech-nique does not allow penetration into the character's mind; in fact, from the later volumes we know more about Voldemort's state of mind through the glimpses Harry gets due to the supernatural connection between the two. Harry does not develop much as a character, but we cannot demand psycho-logical credibility from a character deliberately constructed as a romantic hero. Heroes are by definition static and flat. Even though Harry acquires a touch of ambiguity through his ties with Voldemort, even if he is allowed some slight imperfection, such as temper outbursts, his development is chronological, not ethical. In the last volume, the 17-year-old Harry is not radically different from his 11-year-old self. He does not encounter any adolescence-related problems, as he is too busy saving the world. Even his ubiquitous Parseltongue ability is not a minor inherent flaw in an otherwise perfect hero, but part of the injury inflicted by Voldemort. Like fairy-tale heroes, Harry hardly ever has any ethical dilemmas or moral choices. He may misjudge people or follow false clues, but this is indispensable in a mystery novel. Contemporary modes of conveying psychological states are demand-ing, since they are ambivalent in allowing the reader to determine the source of utterance. The Harry Potter novels are unequivocal and straightforward in this respect. Harry does contemplate his identity and his mysterious connec-tion with Voldemort, but mostly his thoughts revolve around what is to be done and how to do it; in other words, they propel the plot, but do not con-tribute to characterization. The novels are clearly action-oriented rather than character-oriented, which, to some critics, is the intrinsic feature of children's fiction (e.g., Nodelman, *Pleasures* 192).

According to the myth scholar Mircea Eliade, three aspects are essential for the rite of passage: the sacred, death, and sexuality (Eliade, *The Sacred and the Profane*). While Harry is excessively exposed to the sacred in the magic world he inhabits, his initiation into the two other components is more problematic. True, Harry's parents died under most horrible circumstances, yet as mentioned before, parents' foremost obligation in children's fiction is to be absent, preferably dead. Death is not a character's existential experience, but a necessary narrative device. When Cedric is killed before Harry's eyes in *The Goblet of Fire* it may seem tragic, but who is Cedric to Harry other than rival? In romantic fiction, rivals are to be disposed of. In the *Order of the Phoenix*, Sirius is sacrificed, which could signal a step towards Harry's maturation. However, Harry has hardly developed any serious affection toward his new foster father: Sirius is a promise of family that Harry lacks, so this is what Harry really mourns. Furthermore, Sirius dies in a merciful off-stage manner, rather symbolically than physically, which is another convention of children's literature. The author is considerably more cautious in the depiction of death as compared to her many contemporary fellow writers who have portrayed a child's confrontation with death in realistic as well as fantastic modes. The fantasy genre makes is especially easy to dispose of characters since it is not perceived as disastrous as in "real" life. When friends and enemies are killed in the final battle in *Deathly Hallows*, we take it for granted.

Sexually, Harry is eternally pre-pubertal. Hermione is a helper, a squire, a mind trust, a fellow combatant. Harry's infatuation with Cho is just another attribute of the romantic hero: the chivalrous worship of a pretty—and exotic—lady. When Cho does show some interest he hurriedly retires to the safety of Hermione's side. A few innocent kisses is the farthest our hero ever gets. In a psychological interpretation, Harry is amazingly infantile and immature for his age, both emotionally and physiologically. However, as a literary character he can only be what his creator makes him, and she is extremely prudent in depicting Harry's sexual awakening. As compared to some sexually advanced teenagers in contemporary young adult fiction, Harry is ridiculously uninformed. Yet this is also a children's literature convention. Critics who have traced character development in the Harry Potter novels have fallen into the pit of wishful thinking. As adults we want the child to grow up and become one of us, the powerful. At the same time, we want to keep the child innocent and ignorant, since we then have power over him.

In the final volume, all loose ends are tied together. In fact, it is astounding how many tiny details from the previous volumes turn up and prove highly significant. Yet it is still only on the plot level this conclusiveness is visible. As a character, Harry emerges from his carnival without the wisdom that carnivalesque subversivity usually presupposes.

Carnival Interrogated: the Permanence of Adult Normativity

What has then changed in the power hierarchy of the Harry Potter universe as the saga has been concluded? What has been interrogated and what has been confirmed?

Wizards are obviously still superior to Muggles, and no questions about possible cooperation are ever raised. Although Muggles have been just as much threatened by dark forces as the wizards, they have not been invited to join the battle. Unlike *The Lord of the Rings* or Lloyd Alexander's *Prydain Chronicles*, wizards have no intention of leaving the ordinary world; on the contrary, their control is as strong as ever. Wizard children are still attending the elite school, closed to Muggles. Muggle-born are not persecuted as severely as under Voldemort's rule, but the distinction remains. Harry is still wealthy and thus respected. Gryffindor is still considered better than Slytherin. Prefects are still enjoying their privileges riding in a separate carriage on Hogwarts Express and having a separate bathroom at school. Bill Weasley has married a girl from an inferior nation, but she has never learned proper English (a true token of the author's condescension), and the neighbors, we can assume, refer to her as "that French wife of his." The only free house-elf, Dobby, has died for the good cause, while the other elves have presumably returned to Hogwarts kitchen, happy as ever to serve their masters. Kreacher, whom Harry has inherited as a bonus to the house from Sirius, apparently cooks, cleans, and washes clothes in the large Potter household. Grawp the giant, Hagrid's half-brother, has shown his loyalty to Harry, but the other giants are bad and have presumably been slaughtered or exiled together with other supporters of You-Know-Who. The goblins have once again demonstrated their unreliable nature. There is, in other words, no indication of equal rights.

Hermione, Ginny, and other female characters have demonstrated valor in battle, but Neville is given the honor of killing Voldemort's snake, which almost places him on par with Harry in heroism (it has indeed been speculated before whether Neville rather than Harry is "the Chosen One"). The girls find happiness in marriage, and if they are at all like the model wife and mother, Mrs. Weasley, they wait for their husbands with hot dinner as these come home for work, and they see to it that the children pack their trunks properly before leaving for Hogwarts. Apparently neither Hermione nor Ginny has made any academic career in their old school. Instead, Neville has replaced the female Professor Sprout in Herbology. And while Ron and Hermione have a boy and a girl, Harry and Ginny are blessed with two sons already acting superior toward their little sister. Whatever happens with the Muggles, in the wizard world there is no room for diversity, for single or same-sex parents: traditional family values are permanent.

Generally, all the values of the Harry Potter books are traditional. Christian fundamentalists have accused Harry Potter of Satanism, while other critics have argued more seriously about their Christian undertones (e.g., Dickerson and O'Hara, 227–251). On reading the books carefully, the Christian ideas are transparent, alongside its many other levels, and are especially amplified in the last volume. This is not only, and not primarily the fact that wizards celebrate Christmas and Easter, and that at some point the house ghosts burst out in "Come all ye faithful." The Christian holidays are poor match with the otherwise pagan world of magic; perhaps some official at the Ministry of Magic considered the festivities worth importing from the Muggle world, alongside radio and steam engines. In any case, celebrations are depicted exclusively from a child's point of view, focusing on presents and food. Further, snakes are associated with evil in Christianity, and this idea is fully developed in the series. The Christian allusions, however, lie deeper beyond the surface and can, for those who so wish, be read as a much stronger Christian allegory than the Narnia chronicles. Although Harry is not born of a virgin (the notion which, incidentally, in contemporary exegetics has proven to be a mistranslation of a passage in the Old Testament; Isaiah 7:14), there are miraculous circumstances around his early infancy. There is a prophecy about him, and he is chosen to bear his people's pain and sorrow on his shoulders. He is repeatedly tempted by evil and withstands the temptation; he acquires a group of disciples and is pursued by the infidels. During the hour of respite that Voldemort gives him in one of the final chapters, Harry is, like Christ in Gethsemane, torn between the desire for the cup to pass from him and the sense of duty. He dies a voluntary sacrificial death, and Voldemort presents his limp body with a triumphant "Ecce Potter" to a crowd of mourners. He is resurrected and thus delivers the world from evil (the wizard world only, but that is another matter). He is also spared having murder on his conscience. The force that wins over evil is love. If this is not a Christian message, what is? Moreover, Christianity prescribes forgiving those who trespass on us, and consequently Harry's arch-enemy, Draco Malfoy, is forgiven. Even Percy, the prodigal son of the Weasleys, returns to the family. Dumbledore promises Harry eternal life in wizard heaven, where the faithful will meet again. In *His Dark Materials*, Pullman interrogates not only the church as institution, but any celestial authority. The Harry Potter books confirm the social order based on conventional Western values, on solid beliefs in indisputable dogmas, and on unquestionable authorities.

Most important, however, in terms of power hierarchies is the adult/child axis. When Dumbledore dies at the end of the *Half-Blood Prince*, it appears that Harry is finally left on his own, with only his many substitute fathers' legacies to fulfill his quest. As it turns out, all his success, not only in the final volume but throughout the series, has depended wholly on Snape's protection, which in its turn is the sign of Snape's eternal love for Harry's mother, an issue somewhat beyond the scope of a child's priorities. In fact, from what Snape's memories reveal for Harry in the Pensieve (in case we can trust these), the focus of the whole story may easily shift onto Snape. His devotion to the son of his dead beloved is so immense that he is prepared to bear a mark of the Dark Arts on his body, to live a life as a double spy, a life of lies and pretence, of contempt and hate from fellow teachers as well as students, including the object of his concerns. While Harry's life is full of risk and danger, yet with high stakes to win, Snape's is utter misery and no reward. Thus the seven-volume epic can be viewed as a distressing story of a pathetic man who longs for the son he has never had. Going along these lines, we are definitely not dealing with a children's book; this perhaps explains why it has held adult readers spellbound, even though they may have been unaware of this particular aspect. Ironically, the safeguard Harry has always been told was provided by his mother's love turns out to be the safeguard of her rejected devotee. The keyword "love" once more becomes a pivotal point in the series.

Dumbledore's irresponsible use of Harry "for the greater good" (a Jesuit motto), revealed in the last volume, corroborates that the child is secondary and instrumental to the wishes and purposes of adults. Precisely as in the previous volumes, Dumbledore summons Harry—from beyond the grave, so powerful is his clutch on the poor boy—to explain to him everything Harry has not understood, everything the adults have concealed from him "for his own good," everything he has not been considered mature enough to grasp, everything they have lied about, everything they have abused him to perform for their benefit. The didacticism of this final dialogue with Harry's primary guru echoes and amplifies the ideological charge of the whole series.

Finally, the epilogue shows Harry living happily ever after, married and a father of three children, to whom he now can preach and whose fates he has decided once and for all. The wheel of power has gone full circle. Adult normativity is irreversibly cemented.

Yet conventional does not mean mediocre. The Harry Potter novels are certainly well over the mediocre level in every respect. On the contrary, they are an excellent example of what children's literature is and what it does.

References

Alexander, Lloyd. *The Book of Three*. New York: Holt, 1964.
Alexander, Lloyd. *The Black Cauldron*. New York: Holt, 1965.
Alexander, Lloyd. *The Castle of Llyr*. New York: Holt, 1966.
Alexander, Lloyd. *Taran Wanderer*. New York: Holt, 1967.
Alexander, Lloyd. *The High King*. New York: Holt, 1968.
Bakhtin, Michail. *Rabelais and His World*. Cambridge, Ma: MIT Press, 1968.
Bronski, Michael. "Queering Harry Potter." *Z Magazine Online* 16 (2003) 9. Retrieved December 20, 2007 from http://zmagsite.zmag.org/Sept2003/bronski0903.html.
Certeau, Michel de. *Heterologies. Discourse on the Other*. Minneapolis, MN: University of Minnesota Press, 1986.
Cooper, Susan. *The Dark Is Rising*. London: Chatto & Windus, 1973.
Dickerson, Matthew, and David O'Hara. *From Homer to Harry Potter. A Handbook on Myth and Fantasy*. Grand Rapids, MI: Brazos Press, 2006.
Eliade, Mircea. *The Sacred and the Profane*. New York: Harper & Row, 1961.
Frye, Northrop. *Anatomy of Criticism. Four Essays*. Princeton, NJ: Princeton University Press, 1957.
Hourihan, Margery. *Deconstructing the Hero. Literary Theory and Children's Literature*. London: Routledge, 1997.

Jones, Diana Wynne. *The Lives of Christopher Chant.* New York: Greenwillow, 1988.

Le Guin, Ursula. *A Wizard of Earthsea.* New York: Parnassus, 1968.

Lewis, C. S. *The Lion, the Witch and the Wardrobe.* New York: Macmillan, 1950.

McGavran, James Holt, ed. *Literature and the Child. Romantic Continuations, Postmodern Contestations.* Iowa City, IA: University of Iowa Press, 1999.

Nesbit, Edith. *The Story of the Amulet.* London: Benn, 1906.

Nesbit, Edith. "The Aunt and Amabel." *The Magic World.* New York: Macmillan, 1912.

Nikolajeva, Maria, "Harry Potter – a Return to the Romantic Hero", *Critical Perspectives on Harry Potter*, 1st edn., ed. Elizabeth Heilman, New York, Routledge, 2002. 125–140.

Nodelman, Perry. *The Pleasures of Children's Literature.* New York: Longman, 1992.

Nodelman, Perry. "Interpretation and the Apparent Sameness of Children's Literature." In *Children's Literature: Critical Concepts in Literary and Cultural Studies.* Ed. Peter Hunt, vol. 1, London: Routledge, 2006, pp. 88–113.

Paul, Lissa. "Enigma Variations. What Feminist Criticism Knows About Children's Literature." In *Children's Literature: Critical Concepts in Literary and Cultural Studies.* Ed. Peter Hunt, vol. 3, London: Routledge, 2006, pp. 208–223.

Pugh, Tison, and David L. Wallace. "Heteronomative Heroism and Queering the School Story in J. K. Rowling's Harry Potter Series. *Children's Literature* 34 (2006): 260–281.

Pullman, Philip. *Northern Lights.* London: Scholastic, 1995.

Pullman, Philip. *The Subtle Knife.* London: Scholastic, 1997.

Pullman, Philip. *The Amber Spyglass.* London: Scholastic. 2000.

Rowling, J. K. *Harry Potter and the Philosopher's Stone.* London: Bloomsbury, 1997.

Rowling, J. K. *Harry Potter and the Chamber of Secrets.* London: Bloomsbury, 1998.

Rowling, J. K. *Harry Potter and the Prisoner of Azkaban.* London: Bloomsbury, 1999.

Rowling, J. K. *Harry Potter and the Goblet of Fire.* London: Bloomsbury, 2000.

Rowling, J. K. *Harry Potter and the Order of the Phoenix.* London: Bloomsbury, 2003.

Rowling, J. K. *Harry Potter and the Half-Blood Prince.* London: Bloomsbury, 2005.

Rowling, J. K. *Harry Potter and the Deathly Hallows.* London: Bloomsbury, 2007.

Stephens, John. *Language and Ideology in Children's Fiction.* London: Longman, 1992.

Stephens, John. "Gender, Genre and Children's Literature." *Signal* 79 (1996): 17–30.

Tolkien, J. R. R. *The Fellowship of the Ring.* London: Allen & Unwin, 1954.

Tolkien, J. R. R. *The Two Towers.* London: Allen & Unwin, 1954.

Tolkien, J. R. R. *The Return of the King.* London: Allen & Unwin, 1955.

Travers, Pamela. *Mary Poppins.* London: Collins, 1934.

Trites, Roberta Seelinger. "The Harry Potter Novels as Test Case for Adolescent Literature." *Style* 35 (2001) 3: 472–485;

Watson, Victor, *Reading Series Fiction: From Arthur Ransome to Gene Kemp.* New York: Routledge, 2000.

Zipes, Jack. *Sticks and Stones. The Troublesome Success of Children's Literature from Slovenly Peter to Harry Potter.* New York: Routledge, 2001.

Chapter Thirteen

Harry Potter and the Horrors of the *Oresteia*

ALICE MILLS

A classical Greek and Roman context for the story of Harry Potter is first hinted at in the opening pages of the first volume, *Harry Potter and the Philosopher's Stone* (*Philosopher's Stone*) with the introduction of Albus (Latin for "white") Dumbledore, then in chapter 3 with the mention of Hagrid's Christian name, Rubeus (Latin for "reddish"). On Harry's first train journey to school he learns the name of an unpleasant fellow student, Draco (Latin for snake or dragon, from the Greek δράκων). Readers encounter centaurs derived from Greek mythology who live in the Forbidden Forest alongside unicorns derived from mediaeval bestiaries. Harry's quest in *Philosopher's Stone* leads him to meet the menacing Fluffy, a half-comic version of the three-headed dog, Cerberus, who guards the entrance to the classical underworld. Fluffy's classical provenance is fleetingly confirmed when Hagrid admits that the dog was sold to him by a "Greek chappie I met in the pub las' year" (141). With the exception of Fluffy, it is mediaeval and Renaissance mythic material that Rowling most fully utilizes in *Philosopher's Stone*, such as the lore of the unicorn and the art of alchemy.

As the series continues, further classical allusions are to be found in the Latin spells and the Greek and Roman names given to many of Rowling's characters. The list of classically named characters includes Draco's nasty parents Lucius (a Latin word whose connection to lux, meaning "light" is ironic, considering Lucius' inclinations towards evil) and Narcissa. This reference to classical myth is perplexing, as it is Narcissa's love for her son that enables her to abandon her allegiance to evil; she is not given to the self-absorption that caused the death of Ovid's Narcissus although her life is narrowly devoted to family. Rowling's good werewolf is surnamed Lupin (from the Latin, *lupinus*, "of a wolf") and his friend who can transform himself into a dog is called Sirius (the Latin name of the dog-star). The most powerfully evil of Sirius' disagreeable female cousins is called Bellatrix (Latin for "female warrior"), while the indomitable Professor McGonagall's Christian name is Minerva (Roman equivalent to the Greek goddess Athene). Harry's arch-enemy, Voldemort, (whose name derives from Latin via French, *vol* signifying "wish" and *mort*, "death") has among his supporters Amycus (a name taken from an obscure figure in classical myth, with an ironic allusion to the Latin word *amicus* meaning "friend") and his sister Alecto's name is taken from one of the Greek Erinyes,[1] and is derived from the Greek ἄλληκτος, meaning implacable.

Until the start of volume 7, *Harry Potter and the Deathly Hallows* (*Deathly Hallows*), such classical allusions could be dismissed as playful flourishes of erudition, incidental to a story predicated on the Judaeo-Christian division of sentient beings into those who adhere to good and those who support evil. This kind of division does not exist in the classical Graeco-Roman mythology from which such names as Minerva and Alecto are taken. Professor Dumbledore's Christian name, Albus ("white"), aligns him with Tolkien's Gandalf the White, also leader of an order dedicated to fighting against the Dark Lord of evil, and hints at the albedo stage of the alchemical process, as the name Rubeus hints at the rubedo stage; Lucius Malfoy eventually sees the light and while not precisely joining the forces of good, stops actively persecuting them: but these are exceptional among those of Rowling's characters given classically derived names. In Graeco-Roman myth, human characters such as Andromeda (after whom Tonks' mother is named) and gods such as Minerva/Athene were represented as neither good nor evil. The gods intervened in human affairs as it pleased them: Minerva/Athene cherishes Odysseus not because his cause is exceptionally worthy but because he is exceptionally clever and crafty. The Greek Erinyes are no monsters from hell inflicting torments upon the damned but implacable ministers of justice in the world of the living. In the end, there is no doubt that Dumbledore and Harry are in fact acting for the good of all humankind and that Harry and Hermione in particular are working for the good of all sentient beings. Opposed to them are Voldemort and his supporters, whose evil is a given for the story; the reader is afforded no room for doubt on this matter. While a handful of characters who have supported Voldemort eventually achieve some form of redemption via impulses towards mercy, love for their child, or gratitude for having been saved by Harry from death, in general evil is presented in these volumes as an absolute and final choice. Rowling's fantasy world is built on the Augustinian concept of our own world as a venue for the spiritual war between the forces of evil and those of good. In such a drama, allusions to Greek and Roman language and mythology can carry no moral or spiritual weight as alluding to a competing worldview.

The moral schema of a war between the forces of good and those of evil has been so strongly and systematically established in the course of the first six volumes that for those readers familiar with Greek drama, the first epigraph to *Deathly Hallows*, taken from Aeschylus' tragedy *The Libation Bearers*, may well seem extraordinarily inapplicable:

> Oh, the torment bred in the race,
> the grinding scream of death
> and the stroke that hits the vein,
> the hemorrhage that none can staunch, the grief,
> the curse no man can bear.
>
> But there is a cure in the house,
> and not outside it, no,
> not from others but from *them*,
> their bloody strife. We sing to you,
> dark gods beneath the earth.
>
> Now hear, you blissful powers underground—
> answer the call, send help.
> Bless the children, give them triumph now.

A brief account of the history of this house (that is, the family of Atreus, Agamemnon, and Orestes) may be helpful here. *The Libation Bearers* is the second play in Aeschylus' trilogy, and it sets up more than one seemingly intractable moral dilemma. Should a son follow a god's command and kill his mother in order to avenge her killing of his father? Having done so, does he deserve punishment? The trilogy's theme of kin-slaying looks back long before the start of the first play. Three generations previously, Pelops was cut up, cooked, and served to the gods by his father Tantalus. The child was resurrected by the gods. Pelops' favorite son was killed by his two rivals, Pelops' other sons, Atreus and Thyestes. Later Thyestes killed Atreus' son whereupon Atreus killed Thyestes' sons and served them to him as a meal. Aeschyus' first play in the *Oresteian Trilogy*, the *Agamemnon*, begins when King Agamemnon is returning from Troy to a kingdom ruled by his wife Clytemnaestra and her paramour Aegisthus, another of Thyestes' children. Agamemnon has murdered his daughter ten years previously, arguing that this deed was a ritual sacrifice enjoined by the gods in exchange for fair winds to Troy. Clytemnaestra justifies her murder of Agamemnon on the grounds that he murdered their daughter, but it is to her great benefit to rid herself of an unwanted, unloved husband, and Aegisthus can simultaneously be avenged for his siblings' murder by Atreus. *The Libation Bearers* tells how Orestes, the son of Agamemnon and Clytemnaestra, now come to manhood, kills his mother with the encouragement of his sister Electra. Despite the justification of his act as retribution for the murder of his father, the Erinyes are roused to assail his mind and drive him to madness. These Erinyes, deities of retribution, take a particular vengeful interest in children who kill their mothers. Agamemnon is not tormented by them for killing his daughter, nor Clytemnaestra for killing her husband. Aeschylus' third play in the *Oresteian Trilogy*, the *Eumenides*, is concerned with a closely argued resolution achieved by divine intervention. Orestes' torments are relieved when Athenian law is shifted away from the *lex talionis*, and Athene finds a new function and new honors for the Erinyes, now bereft of their ancient task of tormenting kin-slaughterers.

Both Orestes' plight in *The Libation Bearers* and the eventual cure found for his house's (that is, his family's) cascade of vengeful murders are morally complex and as such, quite unlike Harry Potter's difficulties in working out what he should do in the course of *Deathly Hallows* or the self-evident right-ness of killing Voldemort. Aeschylus' words, in the epigraph to *Deathly Hallows*, could perhaps be stretched to apply to some of the characters and events in Rowling's novels. The children who ask for help could be associated with Harry, Hermione, and Ron (although they are only of the same house in the sense of a school house, which does not carry a curse), while Voldemort's cult of pure blood could be loosely linked to the "torment bred in the race," but the Harry Potter novels' curse is not restricted to the house (that is, in the Aeschylean sense of family) of Voldemort. Rather than narrowing its focus to the appalling consequences of retributive murder within a single family, Rowling's final volume expands to epic scope in its account of a host of characters assembling for the decisive battle whose consequences affect a nation if not the whole world.

Neither the epigraph nor the pattern of murders in and before the *Oresteia* can be mapped convincingly onto the overall narrative of the Harry Potter books or onto *Deathly Hallows* in particular. The question then arises whether any of the individual stories of kin-slaughter within these novels can provide a more apt pairing with these Greek myths. Kin-slaughter occurs repeatedly within the present action of the Harry Potter books as well as in the back stories of various families, perhaps most poignantly in the case of Sirius Black. The "Black" family name indicates their propensity for evil and antagonism to the cause of the good Albus ("white") Dumbledore. They have long espoused the hateful doctrine of pure blood promulgated by Voldemort. When Sirius Black dares to champion Harry, he is (probably) killed by his cousin Bellatrix. Unlike Aeschylus' Orestes, Bellatrix appears to have no qualms about the righteousness of her act and she suffers no mental anguish on account of murdering her kin either during the murder or in the months that follow. No equivalent of the Aeschylean Erinyes arrives to torment her. Instead she triumphs. When Bellatrix eventually dies, it is not at the hands of an avenging family member, continuing the pattern of bloody retribution. For Bellatrix, the killing of Sirius becomes just one among her attacks on Dumbledore's and

Harry's supporters. Sirius' death is thus a matter of pathos rather than tragedy in high Aeschylean style.

While kin-slaughter is not given any tragic privilege in this instance, the death of Sirius does raise some other issues that prove far from straightforward to resolve. Sirius dies because he fights Bellatrix and her spell strikes him in the chest, but he is not without responsibility for his own death in that he chooses, against strong advice, to leave his safe house and fight alongside Harry. It is his longing to be both at liberty and of use, what might be termed his "dogged" determination against all sensible advice, that draws him to the dueling ground. That determination is fueled by his years of enduring the horrors of imprisonment in Azkaban and his months of hiding after his escape, believed to be a traitor by the forces of good. Who, then, is responsible for Sirius' death? As in Aeschylus' play, reasons for his death go back and back into the blood-soaked past.

Even my cautious statement that Bellatrix kills Sirius is open to question. Towards the end of *Harry Potter and the Order of the Phoenix* (*Order of the Phoenix*) Rowling gives this account of what happens:

> The second jet of light hit him squarely on the chest.
>
> The laughter had not quite died from his face, but his eyes widened in shock...
>
> It seemed to take Sirius an age to fall: his body curved in a graceful arc as he sank backwards through the ragged veil hanging from the arch.
>
> Harry saw the look of mingled fear and surprise on his god-father's wasted, once-handsome face as he fell through the ancient doorway and disappeared behind the veil, which fluttered for a moment as though in a high wind, then fell back into place.
>
> Harry heard Bellatrix's triumphant scream, but knew it meant nothing—Sirius had only just fallen through the archway, he would reappear from the other side any second.
>
> (*Order of the Phoenix*, 700–701)

This episode can be understood in two conflicting ways. In one, Sirius is struck to the heart by Bellatrix's spell and dies from the wound, toppling through the veil as he does so. The text's strong suggestion that this is the veil between our mortal world and the world of the dead has no relevance to the cause of Sirius' death: he would have toppled to the floor and died there if the veil had not been in his way. This reading is supported by Rowling's account of Bellatrix's death in volume 7:

> Bellatrix laughed the same exhilarated laugh her cousin Sirius had given as he toppled backwards through the veil...

Molly's curse soared beneath Bellatrix's outstretched arm and hit her
squarely in the chest, directly over her heart.

Bellatrix's gloating smile, froze, her eyes seemed to bulge: for the
tiniest space of time she knew what had happened, and then she
toppled.

(*Deathly Hallows*, 590)

Here, a parallel is explicitly drawn with Sirius' death, preceded by his exhila-
rated laughter and look of fear and surprise. The alternative reading of Sirius'
fall is that Bellatrix's spell was not the immediate cause of his death; it struck
him in the chest, knocking him off-balance, but what actually killed him was
the act of toppling through the veil. As in classical mythology, crossing the
boundary between life and death can only be done in one direction for all but
the most exceptional of heroes. The chapter heading, "Beyond the Veil," supports this reading of Sirius' death as due to his crossing of a boundary that he
cannot recross, as does Lupin's determination not to let Harry pass through
the veil after the lost Sirius: "if Sirius was not reappearing out of that archway
when Harry was yelling for him as though his life depended on it, the only
possible explanation was that he could not come back" (*Order of the Phoenix*,
712). In this version of events, both Bellatrix and Harry are deceiving themselves in crediting her with his murder. From Rowling's words, there is no
way of knowing the exact cause of Sirius' death.

While this matter remains ambiguous, Rowling leaves no doubt that Sirius
is aligned with good (despite his habitual mistreatment of his house-elf). Nor
is there any doubt that Bellatrix is dedicated to the cause of evil. The complexity of the episode in which Sirius dies resides within the question of responsibility for that death and not with the issue of retribution, whereas Aeschylus
makes it extremely clear just who kills whom and his plays focus on issues of
familial retribution and justice. Bellatrix deserves and eventually receives punishment, but not for the death of her cousin in particular, and not at the
hands of another family member, nor as part of a familial sequence of
revenges.

Sirius himself can be accused of symbolic if not literal mother-slaying. The
portrait of his dead mother is to a limited extent his actual mother, and is so
named by him; it exhibits the same bigotry and the same contemptuous
hatred for her son that she is said to have displayed when alive. (The relationship between such a sentient, speaking portrait and the dead person in the
afterlife remains obscure in these volumes.) Animated by any loud noise, Mrs.
Black hurls at Sirius and his friends the only weapons she can still effectively
wield, insulting words. His response is to force shut the curtains over her face:

"*Yooou!*" she howled, her eyes popping at the sight of the man. "*Blood
traitor, abomination, shame of my flesh!*"

"I said—shut—UP!" roared the man, and with a stupendous effort he and Lupin managed to force the curtains closed again.

(*Order of the Phoenix*, 74)

Since the portrait is in some sense the woman, she can be said to die again each time the curtains silence her. The black comedy of the monstrous mother who can never be finally silenced behind her veiling curtains, the repressed returning yet again from the dead, is the obverse of Sirius' pathos-laden death, lost behind curtains from which he can never return. In this reading of Mrs. Black as a Clytemnaestra figure, it must be noted that Sirius did not in fact kill his mother when she was still a living woman. Nor is he now her only killer; that task devolves onto Harry, his would-be adopted son, and more generally onto any of the Order who happen to be present. With these provisos, both Sirius and Harry can be compared to Bellatrix as kin-slayer: she both is, and is not, Sirius' killer while Sirius and Harry both are and are not mother-killer and adoptive grandmother-killer, respectively. Neither Harry nor Sirius suffers any remorse or guilt for their treatment of Mrs. Black, who is no more than a nuisance to them, and her continuing efforts to make their lives a misery are the only form of retribution that they must endure. In Aeschylean terms, Mrs. Black has become her own Erinyes, screeching and screaming in judgment on her son who defends himself by killing her yet again. Sirius and Harry are no Orestes, to lose command of their wits because of her insults. Rather, like Bellatrix, they live on unscathed.

Within the Crouch family, kin-slaying also takes place. Barty Crouch Senior judges his son guilty of atrocious crimes on doubtful evidence and sentences him to the living death of imprisonment in Azkaban: this could be viewed as symbolic son-killing and late in *Harry Potter and the Goblet of Fire* (*Goblet of Fire*) the father renounces his son as any kin of his: "I'm your son!" he screamed up at Crouch. "I'm your son!"

"You are no son of mine!" bellowed Mr. Crouch, his eyes bulging suddenly. "I have no son!" (*Goblet of Fire*, 517–518). In this case the kin-slayer changes his mind, persuaded by his dying wife to rescue their son. Mrs. Crouch voluntarily sacrifices her life for that of her son, and she is already mortally ill, so that her death is not an instance of mother-slaying; there is, however, no doubt, once all the facts have been revealed, that Barty Junior goes on to murder his father. As with the death of Sirius, the question of who is responsible for Barty Senior's death can be given more than one answer. Barty Junior is no Aeschylean Orestes, to be caught up in an inexorable flow of retribution. He is described as smiling insanely while confessing to his father's murder (*Goblet of Fire*, 600) and is possibly so psychotic that he can be assigned no criminal responsibility for the killing. He resembles the gloating Bellatrix, who can be judged pathologically lacking in conscience. No anguish besets him as he gleefully recounts the story of his father's death, and the reader is given no indication that he has grieved for his mother. As with Bellatrix, his own death is brought about by someone outside his family and incurs no retribution; by this stage the entire Crouch family may well have died out.

While the Aeschylean epigraph to *Deathly Hallows* does not sit well with the kin-slayings within the Black and Crouch families, it seems at first to sit much better with Dumbledore's scandal-ridden past. When the story of the Dumbledore family is first bruited, it is suggested that he killed his sister Ariana after conniving at her imprisonment and concealment for most of her short life. Perhaps Albus' brother Aberforth attacked him at their sister's funeral and broke his nose in an attempt to avenge this act of kin-slaughter. It is eventually revealed that not Albus, but Ariana, was the killer of their mother, in a fit of madness, and that she was not maddened in Aeschylean fashion by retributive Erinyes but as a result of being attacked while a young child by Muggles afraid of her magical talents. Thus her killing of her mother has nothing in common with Orestes' carefully planned murder of Clytemnaestra in *The Libation Bearers*. Ariana's brothers do not contemplate taking vengeance upon her, for she is not mentally competent to be assigned criminal responsibility for what she has done. As in the cases of the Black and Crouch families, responsibility arguably goes back in part to events that took place years previously, in Ariana's case to the Muggle attack that brought about her madness. Where Ariana's own actions are concerned, Aberforth's summing up of events seems a fair one: "it was an accident. Ariana could not control it" (*Deathly Hallows*, 456).

The killing of Ariana's mother is thus fully accounted for but the killing of Ariana poses more unsolved problems than any of the novels' other episodes of kin-slaughter. The identity of her killer is never definitively revealed. Aberforth remains uncertain which of the three young men lashing out at one another with their wands, himself, his brother Albus, and Gellert Grindelwald, actually brought about her death. Speaking to Harry in the afterlife, Albus implies that Gellert was the killer:

> The argument became a fight. Grindelwald lost control. That which I had always sensed in him, though I pretended not to, now sprang into terrible being. And Ariana ... after all my mother's care and caution ... lay dead upon the floor.
>
> (*Deathly Hallows*, 574)

The question of the killer's identity is left open, however, when Harry decides not to ask his beloved headmaster directly: "Harry did not ask whether Dumbledore had ever found out who struck Ariana dead. He did not want to know, and even less did he want Dumbledore to have to tell him" (576). Is Harry merely anxious to spare Albus any fresh grief in revisiting the event, or is he not at all certain that Gellert was the killer, and afraid that Albus might incriminate either himself or his brother? It thus remains unclear whether

Ariana's death was another tragic accident or a deliberate act of murder by the enraged Gellert. Albus is blamed by his brother, and also blames himself, for not caring adequately for his sister; whether or not it was his spell that killed her, he is responsible in that it was his intoxicating and ill-judged friendship with Gellert that brought the stranger into the household where the fatal quarrel took place.

Albus Dumbledore not only blames himself for Ariana's death but, according to Harry, has been tormented by guilt ever since it happened. Arguing with Aberforth, Harry puts forward a perplexing interpretation of what Albus meant by his strange words when driven mad by Voldemort's potion:

> [Aberforth] "And Albus was free, wasn't he? Free of the burden of his sister, free to become the greatest wizard of the—"
>
> "He was never free," said Harry.
>
> "I beg your pardon?" said Aberforth.
>
> "Never," said Harry. "The night that your brother died he drank a potion that drove him out of his mind. He started screaming, pleading with someone who wasn't there. *Don't hurt them, please ... hurt me instead* [...] He thought he was back there with you and Grindelwald, I know he did," said Harry, remembering Dumbledore whimpering, pleading. "He thought he was watching Grindelwald hurting you and Ariana ... it was torture to him, if you'd seen him then, you wouldn't say he was free."
>
> (*Deathly Hallows*, 457–458)

Harry's assertion here, "I know it was," is as odd as his later deliberate choice not to ask Dumbledore who had killed Ariana. All of Harry's other interpretations of what Dumbledore did or intended are eventually either confirmed or refuted by independent evidence, and Harry's patchy record in *Deathly Hallows* as a decoder of secrets may not inspire the reader with complete confidence here. Moreover, the episode to which Harry is referring, their trip to the hidden lake, was narrated in a previous volume, long before any of the painful details of Albus' early life were revealed, so that this outcry of his could not have been given such an interpretation at the time. The headmaster's words of anguish, when first narrated in *Harry Potter and the Half-Blood Prince* (*Half-Blood Prince*), invite the reader's speculation:

> "I don't want ... don't make me..."
>
> [...] "Make it stop, make it stop," moaned Dumbledore.
>
> [...] "It's all my fault, all my fault," he sobbed, "please make it stop, I know I did wrong, oh, please make it stop and I'll never, never again..."
>
> [...] "Please, please, please, no ... not that, not that, I'll do anything..."
>
> (534–535)

Could Albus be channelling the phrases of some victim of Voldemort when he sobs these broken phrases out? His words, "make it stop," might be taken by the puzzled reader of *Half-Blood Prince* as referring to the liquid that Harry is pouring down his throat. Even when the episode is reviewed from the basis of fuller information given in *Deathly Hallows*, doubt may persist as to Harry's version of what Dumbledore means here. Could the headmaster, maddened by the potion, be so untrue to his convictions as to promise the hallucinated Gellert that he would "do anything" to save his siblings pain? And even if the reader accepts Harry's act of mind-reading and makes allowances for Albus' induced madness, it remains significant that Harry does not mention to Aberforth this phrase, "I'll do anything," guaranteed as it is to enrage Aberforth and redouble his scorn for his brother.

Albus' entire career tends to confirm this reading of his words of madness as yielding to Gellert, promising him anything he wants, for he has held back from advancement to the Ministry of Magic in fear of becoming corrupt once more if he were to enjoy so much power. Mentally, then, Dumbledore has not moved on from a frightened concept of himself as Gellert's ready co-conspirator, just as emotionally he cannot let go of his anguish over his sister's fate, even after his own death. Among Rowling's characters he is the one who most closely resembles Aeschylus' Orestes, but a more wretched Orestes uncertain whether he may have struck the fatal blow, assailed by inner Erinyes of guilt and remorse who can never, it seems, be placated.

Tom Riddle, Lord Voldemort, is another kin-slayer. His mother dies shortly after his birth and though he is not her literal killer, the pregnancy is likely to have contributed to her state of extreme poverty and debilitation. In an effort to conceal his Mudblood origins, Tom kills his Muggle father and grandparents once he has attained enough magical power, and probably implants false memories of the killing in his Muggle uncle, who confesses to the killings and dies in Azkaban as Voldemort's fourth, indirect family victim. As usual in Rowling's work, these instances of kin-slaying are far from Aeschylean in their motivation and outcome. No curse of retribution hangs over the house of Voldemort; he murders with no inner qualms; his family appears to have no other surviving member who might attempt vengeance. Far from becoming the target of the Erinyes' retributive wrath, Voldemort eventually numbers among his followers a woman named after a Roman Fury, Alecto Carrow. She is no minister of just retribution against kin-slayer, as the Erinyes are, but a hellish tormentor of children who have done nothing criminal.

Voldemort does not halt his kin-slaying activities with the deaths of all his male relatives. He cannot allow his father's body to rest in its grave. In a grue-some ceremony, he causes part of his father's skeleton to be raised from the grave and plunged into a cauldron of boiling liquid: *"Bone of the father, unknowingly given, you will renew your son!"* (*Goblet of Fire*, 556). This rite of renewal has overtones of Medea's sorcery, when she boils her enemy alive in a cauldron under the pretence of renewing his youth. It can also be understood as the obverse of the cannibalistic feasts that inaugurate and continue the sequence of murders in the house of Tantalus and Atreus. Tantalus' cannibalistic feast is made up of his own son, Atreus' of his brother's sons; neither feast is consumed by the man who devises it, but both are designed to appall and pollute the eater. It is only by divine intervention that Tantalus' son is resurrected, and Thyestes' sons do not rise again from the dead. In contrast, Voldemort is the only consumer of his feast. He ingests his father's bone, as well as Wormtail's hand and Harry's blood, in order to rise again in an adult, more or less human body.[2]

In an Aeschylean context, Apollo's defense of Orestes in *The Eumenides* has a bearing on this ritual of renewal. The god argues:

> The mother is not the true parent of the child
> Which is called hers. She is a nurse who tends the growth
> Of young seed, planted by its true parent, the male.
>
> (*Eumenides*, lines 657–659)

Voldemort is reborn by means of an all-male trio of donors who with some reluctance provide their blood, flesh, and bone, while the only feminine element in this rebirth is the cauldron as womb. This rebirth can be read as a parodic enactment of Apollo's argument, after the psychopathic Voldemort has parodied Orestes' parent-slaying in *The Libation Bearers* with the multiple guilt-free murders of his family.

The extraordinarily intimate relationship between Harry and Voldemort adds to the implications of the ritual and its consequences. Harry has carried part of Voldemort's soul within himself since babyhood and Voldemort now carries some of Harry's blood as part of himself; to this extent they can be viewed as the same person. Because of this sharing of parts, Voldemort's bursts of fear and rage possess Harry's consciousness: Harry functions as an Orestes suffering hallucinatory torments for crimes that he does not commit. It is only when Voldemort "kills" Harry that this possession completely ends. In its stead, Voldemort appears doomed to suffer agony without end, reduced after his own death to the suffering baby whom Harry has already encountered in the afterlife (even though Voldemort is still alive). (The relationship between this baby and the yet-living man is as obscure as that already mentioned, between sentient portrait and dead human being.) Rowling does not identify the flayed, shuddering infant as Voldemort but Harry says to the living Voldemort, urging remorse: "It's your one last chance," said Harry, "it's all you've got left ... I've seen what you'll be otherwise" (*Deathly Hallows*, 594). Apart from the lack of external confirmation, there is no reason to doubt Harry's assessment here. In the afterlife, Voldemort will presumably never grow up, never become capable of experiencing anything except abandonment and pain. Such a fate harks back to his ritual of rebirth, when he is lowered into the boiling water in the form of a grotesque creature the size of a baby:

> The thing Wormtail had been carrying had the shape of a crouched human child, except that Harry had never seen anything less like a child. It was hairless and scaly-looking, a dark, raw, reddish black. Its arms and legs were thin and feeble, and its face—no child alive had a face like that—was flat and snake-like, with gleaming red eyes.
>
> (*Goblet of Fire*, 555–556)

In the ritual of rebirth, Voldemort succeeds in being parented to instant adulthood, while in the other world his other self is being assigned to eternal babyhood (and once his original human eyes have been destroyed in *Hallows*, perhaps this afterlife baby is now blinded too). In *The Libation Bearers*, Agamemnon's murderers live in fear that his son Orestes will grow up to take revenge: for Voldemort (vol-de-mort), the pursuit of death shapes him into a child that can never grow up. In this, as in so many other senses, Voldemort's story is an anti-*Oresteia*.

The final chapter of *Deathly Hallows* qualifies as an anti-*Oresteia* in a different sense. Here the reader is informed of the enduringly happy, fertile marriages between Harry and Ginny Weasley, Ron Weasley and Hermione, Bill Weasley and Fleur (with her French name, Victoire is most likely to be their daughter). Victoire is reported to be snogging the son of the dead Lupin and Tonks, and Harry's daughter Lily promptly speculates on the likelihood of their marriage. Thus the story of Harry Potter ends in celebration of the happy Weasley family as it multiplies and prospers. At the start of this chapter I noted that while Harry, Hermione, and Ron belonged to the same school house, they were not members of the same house in the Aeschylean meaning of family; now, a generation after Voldemort's death, all three of them belong to the Weasley family by birth or marriage into it. In the course of the novels, members of the Weasley family have acted heroically and with great folly, fallen out with their parents, been wounded, and died, but the family has not been locked into an Aeschylean cascade of retributive murder, generation after generation. There is no curse on this house, nor has there ever been one; rather, it functions as an ideal against which all others in the novels are measured. In the *Agamemnon* Cassandra laments:

> Alas for human destiny! Man's happiest hours
> Are pictures drawn in shadow. Then ill fortune comes,
> And with two strokes the wet sponge wipes the drawing out,
> And grief itself's hardly more pitiable than joy.
>
> (*Agamemnon*, 1325–1328)

To this grim and tragic vision of human destiny, Rowling's final chapter stands opposed. Here happiness, based on goodness, not only endures but flourishes, untainted by any imperatives of vengeance: this is a profoundly anti-Oresteian view of human life.

Notes

1. In this article I use the Greek name for these beings rather than the more familiar Latin "Furies," as in classical Greek drama the Erinyes were ministers of justice in the upper world as well as denizens of the underworld while the Roman Furies were more closely associated with the underworld only.
2. The use of these ingredients obscenely hints at Genesis 2.23: "And Adam said, This is now bone of my bones, and flesh of my flesh: she shall be called Woman, because she was taken out of Man." The sexual connotations of Voldemort's act and its connection with the elements of rape and incest in the Oresteian mythic material would make a fascinating study in their own right but lie beyond the scope of the present chapter.

References

Aeschylus. *The Oresteian trilogy*. Trans. Philip Vellacott. Harmondsworth: Penguin, 1956.

Rowling, J. K. *Harry Potter and the philosopher's stone*. London: Bloomsbury, 1997.

——. *Harry Potter and the goblet of fire*. London: Bloomsbury, 2000.

——. *Harry Potter and the order of the phoenix*. London: Bloomsbury, 2003.

——. *Harry Potter and the half-blood prince*. London: Bloomsbury, 2005.

——. *Harry Potter and the deathly hallows*. London: Bloomsbury, 2007.

Tolkein, J. R. R. *The lord of the rings: The fellowship of the ring*. London: George Allen and Unwin, 1954.

——. *The lord of the rings: the two towers*. London: George Allen and Unwin, 1954.

——. *The lord of the rings: the return of the king*. London: George Allen and Unwin, 1954.

Chapter Fourteen

Philosopher's Stone to Resurrection Stone
Narrative Transformations and Intersecting Cultures across the Harry Potter Series

KATE BEHR

Many people (myself included) were more anxious about the final installment in the Harry Potter series than any of its predecessors. Could Rowling pull it off? How could she not only write the last book in the series, but also achieve a satisfactory ending, one that would answer questions and fulfill expectations raised by the previous six books? In the end, *Harry Potter and the Deathly Hallows* does cap the series, answer questions, and offer satisfying closure to the reader. Rowling works this magic through transformation—a significant element in the narrative structure across the novel series and a repeated theme at the heart of the story. Narrative transforms familiar elements of our culture like language, class, authority, genre, so that the ordinary becomes extraordinary (Natov, Lacoss). Transformation occurs not just at the level of plot and character, but also in Rowling's presentation of overlapping cultures that are similar yet different. We find transformation in the details of the wizarding world, its language, and customs; we find transformation at a deeper level through the narrator's focus on Harry Potter's character as he moves through adolescence to adulthood, making more and more difficult choices; and we find transformation at the heart of the series itself as Rowling recapitulates the first book in the last, emphasizing some motifs but changing or transforming the myths.[1]

At its simplest, narrative *is* transformation. Elements transform when joined by narrative. Further narrative transformations occur when the story changes, whether we use the phrase as part of a linguistic or psychoanalytic analysis. Psychoanalytically, narrative transformations do not so much change the desires or the facts as the participants' perceptions of relationships and their dynamics. Thus the plot (to borrow the Formalist distinction) remains the same but the narrative, the connecting flow, and thus the story presented to the reader/auditor is changed (usually for therapeutic effect). Todorov reaches similar conclusions in his essay on narrative transformations, though his work focuses on syntax rather than interpretation. For Todorov, a narrative transformation occurs when a predicate—a single action—is expanded, either simply, by adding an operator, or as a complex transformation, by grafting two predicates together (Todorov 225).[2] Just like the psychoanalytic understanding, the facts remain unchanged, but narrative transforms the relationship between them.

Rowling highlights this relationship between narrative and transformation within her text from the first moment we see Ron trying to cast a spell: "Sunshine, daisies, butter mellow/Turn this stupid, fat rat yellow" (*Harry Potter and the Sorcerer's Stone* (hereinafter *Sorcerer's Stone*) 105). Words change (or should change, in Ron's case) what is spoken about. All spells, therefore, show the relationship between narrative and transformation: the best example is the Riddikulus charm to neutralize a Boggart, which demonstrates in *Harry Potter and the Prisoner of Azkaban* (hereinafter *Prisoner of Azkaban*) that a magical narrative transformation can defeat fear. When faced with a shape-shifting Boggart, each person faces his or her own worst fears; to repel that Boggart each person has to dominate his or her fear and "force it to assume a shape that you find amusing" (134). In other words, the "Riddikulus" charm enables the individual concerned to change the context, to add details that change the relationship between the facts and the way that the onlooker perceives them. Professor Lupin's students have transformed their fears by creating complex predicates for them—illustrating Todorov's narrative transformations. Laughter enables the students to achieve emotional distance, to free themselves from paralysis, and to stop being victims.

Language can also make people into victims—another form of transformation. Rowling shows the transformative power of language and narrative most clearly in her depiction of the press, which first changes (transforms) the subject matter as it changes the discourse and then completes the narrative transformation by altering the readers' perception. Rita Skeeter, irritating muckraker and reporter for the *Daily Prophet*, is a perfect example:

> Frowning, he avoided her gaze and looked down at words the quill had just written: *Tears fill those startling green eyes as our conversation turns to the parents he can barely remember.*
>
> "I have NOT got tears in my eyes!" said Harry loudly.
>
> (*Harry Potter and the Goblet of Fire* (hereinafter *Goblet of Fire*) 306)

As well as narrative transformation, Rowling here demonstrates her capacity for mirroring Muggle journalese. "He can hardly remember his parents" is effortlessly transformed by Rita's "Quick-Quotes Quill" into something far more marketable. Rita's interviews with Harry for the *Daily Prophet* and *Witch Weekly* almost destroy Harry's credibility, making him seem an attention-seeking, violently disturbed young man. Hermione, recognizing the power of the press and the spoken word—no coincidence that she is the one who points how important the correct word invariably is: "Europa's covered in ice, not mice" (*Goblet of Fire* 300)—reverses the trend homeopathically. If a dose of fantasy masquerading as reality is enough to destroy Harry's reputation, then, she reasons, a dose of reality masquerading as fantasy (Rita's *Quibbler* interview) should restore it. However, Harry is not the only subject and victim of Rita's poisonously green quill. Dumbledore, with whom she sparred when interviewing Harry initially (Dumbledore said she had called him "an obsolete dingbat," (307)), is transformed by her unauthorized biography of him in *Harry Potter and the Deathly Hallows* (hereinafter *Deathly Hallows*). That biography, a narrative within the narrative, is itself a transformation of the narratives told to her. Rita's dark hints about Dumbledore's family, about the death of his sister, and about his fascination with handsome but dangerous Gellert Grindelwald change Harry's, and through Harry the reader's, perception of Dumbledore, hitherto an icon of unfailing wisdom, benevolence, and gentle humor, into yet another untrustworthy adult and unreliable narrator.[3]

As we have seen, transformation is a function of narrative, evident in the way that plot and characters evolve across the series, but transformation is also apparent in Rowling's conception of her magical world. Transformation is integral to the magical world; indeed "Transfiguration" is a difficult academic subject that the students must study to pass an exam at Ordinary Wizarding Level. Several characters literally transform themselves from human to animal and back again at different points in the story, and the context for their change (and whether or not they can control it) is significant to the narrative. In a sense, this is narrative transformation: the teller shapes and controls the story by joining, selecting, and choosing the elements that create the tale and the ending desired. Therefore, young wizards (like Harry in *Sorcerer's Stone* and, more disturbingly, Ariana Dumbledore in *Deathly Hallows*) who cannot control their magic, which bursts out, changing the world around them as well as themselves—think of Harry's hair—are dangerous. The education system for witches and wizards exists to help them learn to control and use the magic they have (Dickinson). Similarly, consider the difference between Animagi, who can control their transformations, bear some physical mark corresponding to the creature into which they transform, and have to register their identifying characteristics with the Ministry of Magic, and the werewolves. Harry and the readers perceive werewolf Remus Lupin as kind, sensitive, and attuned to his students while in his human phase, but he is dangerous and untrustworthy during his change—unless it is *controlled* by magic, a potion that domesticates a hungry werewolf and transforms him into something relatively harmless.

Magic transforms the ordinary or the extraordinary into something else, which is just what Rowling does through narrative, by paralleling our "Muggle world" with the magical one. She presents our culture afresh to us, her readers, twice over: once as a version of "our" reality, which appears strange and rather limited when seen through the eyes of the wizarding Weasley family—"Mum's got a second cousin who's an accountant, but we don't talk about him" (*Sorcerer's Stone* 99)—and once more as the wizarding world itself, which is our culture defamiliarized, transformed, and enchanted.

What is the fascination of this kind of narrative transformation? Why should readers experience such pleasure in the magical re-presentation of elements of their own culture? Peter Brooks' classic work on the power of narrative provides one answer. Like Brooks, who follows Lacan, I would argue that the power of the narrative exists in the interplay between signifier and signified; unlike Brooks, I would apply Lacan's interpretation of Saussure's algorithm to the Muggle and wizard cultures rather than to language (Brooks 54). Lacan's interpretation concerns language: the bar dividing signifier (or word or language) and signified (or concept) indicates repression, the inaccessibility of the true signified (Lacan).[4] Therefore language, the chain of signifiers, is constantly underpinned by a meaning that it can never quite articulate, but which is always pressing close to the surface.

When applied to the two cultures presented in the Harry books, this algorithm elegantly describes the relationship between Muggle and wizard worlds—M/W.[5] Our mundane, Muggle world is the signifier—recognizable as everything apparent on the surface and also the controlling, defining language, but below (and sometimes alongside) it is the signified wizard world, which exists largely in the gaps in Muggle perceptions. Though there are witches, wizards, and other magical creatures living all over the British Isles, they do so imperceptibly. Large magical sites like Diagon Alley, Platform 9¾, Hogwarts and Hogsmeade don't appear on Muggle radar. "The people hurrying by didn't glance at it. Their eyes slid from the big book shop on one side to the record shop on the other as if they couldn't see the Leaky Cauldron at all" (*Sorcerer's Stone* 68). Rowling's wizard world is a shadow world, an underground, almost a conspiracy (given that some Muggles are aware of it) that exists in the gaps of the "real."[6]

If we extend the analogy between signifier and signified, Muggle and wizard worlds, we find that the dynamic force powering the narrative is not the gap between words and meanings as Brooks would have it—though that is nicely demonstrated in the playfulness of Dumbledore's opening address to the students in *Sorcerer's Stone*: "Before we begin our banquet, I would like to say a few words. And here they are: Nitwit! Blubber! Oddment! Tweak!" (*Sorcerer's Stone* 123). Instead, the meaningful gap is the one across which the two worlds co-exist and interact, which Harry describes in Book Five as "the great invisible wall that divided the relentlessly non-magical world of Privet Drive and the world beyond" (*Harry Potter and the Order of the Phoenix* (hereinafter *Order of the Phoenix*) 37). The wizard world exists only in relation to the "real" world, echoing/mirroring all its customs and discourse, and thus reflects our Muggle world—transformed by narrative.

Wizard institutions are absurd, transformed versions of our own. The Ministry of Magic, with its many Departments (Magical Sports and Games, Magical Law Enforcement, Control of Magical Creatures), headed by the Minister of Magic, Cornelius Fudge dressed in—what else?—a pinstriped cloak, satirizes the workings of bureaucracy, especially the British Civil Service. Percy Weasley's fussy obsession with his first report on standardizing the thickness of cauldron bottoms recalls the many dicta handed down by the EU. Even the rites of passage are familiar: like many young Muggles trying to pass the driving test, young wizards like Charlie Weasley often fail their first attempt at the Apparition license: "Charlie had to take the test twice.... He failed the first time. Apparated five miles south of where he meant to, right on top of some poor old dear doing her shopping" (*Goblet of Fire* 57). Thus, mundane elements of life—bureaucracy, tradition, becoming independently mobile—are renewed when re-presented and transformed via the wizard world.

Although the wizarding world seems to be the shadowside of the Muggle, mimicking its concerns, bureaucratic structure, and weaknesses, narrative transformation makes it *more* concrete than the culture whose discourse, traditions, and customs it mirrors. Superficially, it appears otherwise, as wizards typically use spells where Muggles use technology or machinery (for light, heat, cooking, heavy lifting, transportation, etc.). Magic does not create an egalitarian society, however; the social and financial differences between the Weasleys and the Malfoys mirror class divides in the Muggle world. Interestingly, though, intangibles in the Muggle world are frequently made real in a wizarding context. This too demonstrates the signifier/signified relationship. Where the signifier, Muggle money, has virtual rather than intrinsic value—only the word exists; wizard money, the signified, is made of precious metal and has real value. Similarly where Muggle photographs capture one moment and are static thereafter, wizard photographs capture a moment and give it pseudo-life so that figures move, wander off, get bored, wave, interact with each other, and so on. Muggle memories are evanescent, transitory signifiers; wizard memories, the signified, can be physically captured and stored in a Pensieve for later sifting and retrieval. Also wizard memories captured in books can have a life of their own like Tom Riddle's 50-year-old diary. Even your dreams can become real: the magical Mirror of Erised can show you your innermost heart's desire even if you can't articulate it yourself. Punishments, too, can take on an awful life: Dolores Umbridge's version of writing lines literally engraves her message into the body of the culprit. In each case, the Muggle signifier is nothing but a word, while the wizarding world, the shadow world, acts as the signified, supplying the full concept, a fullness that Muggle language can only hint at.

Invariably, this sort of transformation has a comic effect at first. Harry and the reader together marvel at the wizarding world, which seems absurd in its ability to render the fantastic as real. However, once that world becomes familiar to the reader, Rowling promptly defamiliarizes it by shifting the tone and effects from comic to menacing. As the series develops, spells or situations that initially seemed amusing or harmless become threatening. Polyjuice potion, for example, is comical in *Harry Potter and the Chamber of Secrets* (hereinafter *Chamber of Secrets*) when the students use it—Harry and Ron become the hulking bullies Crabb and Goyle, and Hermione accidentally gets a cat face—but an instrument of torture and potential agent of destruction for the fake Mad-Eye Moody in *Goblet of Fire*, and then a desperate measure, the only means for Harry, Ron, and Hermione to get into the Ministry of Magic, in *Deathly Hallows*. Similarly, fussy Fudge, the Minister of Magic, is initially a comic figure, but is transformed and corrupted by power as the series continues (Barton). Initially, Hagrid describes Cornelius Fudge as a "bungler" who "pelts Dumbledore with owls every morning asking for advice" (*Sorcerer's Stone* 65). He is a figure of fun in his pinstriped cloak, fussy but surprisingly kind when he reassures Harry about the consequences of inflating his aunt in *Prisoner of Azkaban*, and decently horrified that the Dementors would even consider administering the Kiss to an innocent boy at the end of that book. By the end of *Goblet of Fire*, however, Fudge has changed:

> He had always thought of Fudge as a kindly figure, a little blustering, a little pompous, but essentially good natured. But now a short, angry wizard stood before him, refusing, point-blank to accept the prospect of disruption in his comfortable and ordered world.
>
> (*Goblet of Fire*, 707)

The man who trusted Dumbledore implicitly in the early books is now furiously rejecting an unpalatable truth, and has become an enemy by *Order of the Phoenix* because it is easier for him, he thinks, to protect his position/status by fighting Harry and Dumbledore than it is to accept Voldemort's return and fight him. Dumbledore tells Fudge in *Goblet of Fire* that he is blinded by his admiration for power and for his own office, and Fudge demonstrates this claim in *Order of the Phoenix*, not only by trying to arrest Dumbledore (and failing), but also by his reluctance to accept the truth at the end, even while standing in the wrecked foyer of the Ministry of Magic after a battle in which other wizards saw Voldemort. The narrative transformation is not a volte face in character—as one might see in a soap opera, for instance, where writers adapt characters to a constantly changing plot. Instead, Harry perceives elements of Fudge's personality, apparent but understated in the early books, become stronger and dominate him. Power and status have eroded the kindly Fudge, leaving naked ambition and fear behind to control his reactions to a crisis.

The change in Harry's (and, therefore, the reader's) perceptions indicate how the narrative transforms as the series progresses. Core facts remain the same from first to last, but the reader's perceptions change as the stories and characters grow in complexity and acquire a history. Our understanding moves in a hermeneutic circle, as clues or references planted by Rowling in earlier books are only appreciated in the light of later events, usually moving from a mood of comic relief to one of tragic intensity. However, Rowling does not just create comical effects by using spells. She also shifts the effects of environments by changing the context for the action from comic entertainment to life and death battles—more narrative transformations. Bathrooms, for instance, are ludicrous but unnerving in Rowling's magical world, places where children battle trolls, brew potions, and prepare to fight evil (Mills). One of the most important locations in Hogwarts begins as a comical anecdote about a bathroom. Remember the unnamed mystery room full of chamber pots that magically appeared one morning when Dumbledore had a full bladder? Harry did, and that memory eventually gave him the location for his unauthorized Defense Against the Dark Arts classes. The Room of Requirement appears again and again throughout the series, often in the same guise but used for increasingly sinister or desperate purposes. For example, as Hogwarts's magical lumber-room, the place where objects are abandoned or hidden, it features in several novels: Harry uses it to hide his Potions book in *Half-Blood Prince*; Draco Malfoy works there on the Vanishing Cabinet to plan his attack against Dumbledore; Voldemort hid one of his precious Horcruxes in it many years ago; and finally, it is the site for life and death as Crabbe is killed there and Harry saves Malfoy's life. The Room of Requirement is also a haven: Fred and George use it as a place to hide from Filch; Dobby uses it as place where Winky (a drunken house-elf) can sleep off her binges; and it functions as a sanctuary for the rebellious students in *Deathly Hallows*, who would be tortured and killed without it. In each case, the room undergoes multiple narrative transformations as the purpose of that room changes from light relief to serious intent.

Clearly, the narrative arc for Harry and the reader moves from wonder, innocence, and comedy to fear, experience, and tragedy as the series progresses. This trajectory is not whimsy but a function of narrative. A reader's innocence cannot be maintained because narrative works within time and space, and every story starts, develops, and finishes. As a story develops, readers (and often characters) acquire experience and lose their innocence;

indeed, a reader, caught by the "passion for reading," is actively trying to lose his/her innocence (Brooks 19). One example that demonstrates how seemingly innocent events or decisions accrue significance as the series progresses is the choice of Harry's House. The Sorting Hat initially hesitates over whether to place him in heroic Gryffindor or ambitious Slytherin because Harry is potentially both brave and powerful. We don't begin to realize the significance of that choice until Harry agonizes over it in *Chamber of Secrets*, marking the awakening of Harry's moral consciousness.

The Sorting Hat's decision is not an isolated incident but illustrates a pattern; something innocent or incidental in an early book becomes complex, significant, and central to the developing character or plot of a later one. Another good example of this is the question, posed at the end of *Sorcerer's Stone*, which transforms into the hidden mainspring for the action of *Order of the Phoenix* and causes Voldemort's destruction in *Deathly Hallows*. Harry asked Dumbledore why Voldemort targeted him as a baby, and the long delayed answer to that question at the end of *Order of the Phoenix* results in Dumbledore's revising and transforming his own narrative as he explains his faulty reasoning, his attempt to preserve Harry's innocence, which caused him to keep Harry dangerously in ignorance from year to year. Dumbledore begins his explanation/confession with a reference to a sign or mark that exemplifies the hermeneutic drive of narrative: Harry's scar. Initially, the scar is simply a lightening bolt mark on his forehead that identifies the "Boy Who Lived"; as the books progress, however, the scar becomes more and more important, more and more painful, recognized by Dumbledore and Harry as a barometer that registers Voldemort's anger, and as a visible sign of the connection between Harry and the Dark Lord. By the end of *Order of the Phoenix*, knowing the answer to the question he posed in *Sorcerer's Stone*, Harry is burdened: "An invisible barrier separated him from the rest of the world. He was—and he had always been—a marked man. It was just that he had never really understood what that meant" (*Order of the Phoenix* 856–857). Dumbledore's explanation, given as a narrative summarizing each year that Harry has spent at Hogwarts and decoding what seemed inexplicable or a lack of trust, simplifies the story while it removes Harry's innocence. The narrative moves onto a well worn track for fantasy literature; throughout the series, the fairy-tale pairing of Harry and Voldemort becomes more evident as M. Katherine Grimes observes. Initially, Harry was presented (and saw himself) as almost a random victim of Voldemort's evil, but as the narrative progresses and the connections/similarities increase, Harry's relationship with Voldemort is retold. In fairy-tale or fantasy, readers expect a close family connection between good and evil (Bettleheim), so the revelations at the end of Book 5 satisfy readers' expectations with a retold, simplified narrative, while horribly confirming and complicating Harry's relationship to Voldemort. Now he knows he and Voldemort are locked in a predestined life-and-death struggle for "*NEITHER CAN LIVE*

WHILE THE OTHER SURVIVES" (*Order of the Phoenix* 841). However, although this knowledge is the basis for Harry's actions in the following book, the narrative transforms still further at the conclusion of the series when, at last, access to Snape's memories tells Harry that he has been preserved and protected not to fight Voldemort to the death but to accept death himself, "raising him like a pig for slaughter" as Snape bitterly comments (*Deathly Hallows* 687).

Harry's growth is another narrative transformation affecting the reader's perception of present and past events. Identified with Harry, the reader initially found every wizard technique astounding, and his/her attention, like Harry's, was drawn to the details of the marvelous wizarding world. Bertie Bott's Every Flavor Beans, Owl Post, Howlers, and photographs that move captivated 11-year-old Harry and his readers. As the series progresses, however, the details are neither as frequent nor as absorbing (few new spells are introduced, for instance), and the reader's attention has been shifted from Harry's environment to Harry himself as he transforms from a wide-eyed, innocent schoolboy to a suspicious, angry adolescent and then to a knowledgeable adult. M. Katherine Grimes indicates how this aspect of character development makes a direct appeal to an adolescent and young adult audience, who see Harry as a "real boy" who no longer thinks solely in black-and-white terms—good parents do not have to be dead, and bad ones are not necessarily step—or surrogate parents as is the case in fairy tales (Whited and Grimes 100).[7] We see these changes in Harry who is forced to re-evaluate his heroes as the series progresses. Things are no longer black and white: in the earlier books, his father and his father's friends are heroes of whom Harry is rightfully proud and whom he is quick to defend: "For nearly five years, the thought of his father had been a source of comfort, of inspiration" (*Order of the Phoenix* 653). But, when Harry peeks at Snape's painful memories in *Order of the Phoenix*, Rowling suggests another, uncomfortable, interpretation of Harry's personal narrative—one that casts Harry's father as a conceited bully and the hated Snape as a victim (644–650). Even Sirius' judgment, unquestioned since Harry accepted his innocence in *Prisoner of Azkaban*, is clearly flawed, and Harry, just as impulsive, shares the same flaws. Snape's memories prompt Harry's further development in *Deathly Hallows*. Privy to Snape's most intimate memories, Harry has to re-evaluate his personal narrative—his heroes, his family, and his choices—once more.

Harry has been losing his heroes since *Order of the Phoenix*. Though the prophecy is the factual secret that powers the action of that book, Harry's relationships with his fathers are the emotional dynamo. His relationships with all his fathers shift: he entertains doubts about James, the idealized father whom he has never known but whom he strongly resembles; he loses his godfather and has to hear some (to Harry) unpalatable truths about his character; and, for most of *Order of the Phoenix* he thinks he has lost Dumbledore's affection and regard. From the first, Dumbledore was presented to the reader and to Harry as immensely wise, ("great man, Dumbledore,") the one wizard whose powers rivaled Voldemort's, and consequently the only one who could stand against him—the last line of defense. Dumbledore is an archetype of the Wise Wizard, not just to Harry but to the wizarding world as a whole. Although not present for the successive confrontations with Voldemort from book to book, Dumbledore was nonetheless consistently present symbolically, protecting Harry providentially. In *Sorcerer's Stone*, Harry reflects: "I think he [Dumbledore] knows more or less everything that goes on here, you know. I reckon he had a pretty good idea we were going to try, and instead of stopping us, he just taught us enough to help" (302). Dumbledore, of course, was there at the end to save Harry from Quirrell. In *Chamber of Secrets*, Dumbledore supplied Harry with Fawkes the phoenix and Godric Gryffindor's sword even though he himself had been removed from office; in *Prisoner of Azkaban*, he provided the hint that allowed Hermione and Harry to use the Time-Turner to save Buckbeak and Sirius; and in *Goblet of Fire*, he saved Harry from the fake Mad-Eye Moody at the end.

The pattern changes in *Order of the Phoenix, Half-Blood Prince*, and *Deathly Hallows*. Dumbledore certainly saves Harry at the beginning, outsmarting Fudge and his minions in the kangaroo court, but the wizarding world no longer regards him as a sage and has taken away his Order of Merlin, his Chairmanship of the International Confederation of Wizards, and his position as Chief Warlock on the Wizengamot. In *Half-Blood Prince*, though vindicated, Dumbledore is once again on the fringes of wizarding society as the Ministry continues to suspect him even though the Minister has changed. He does not even spend much time at Hogwarts, but is constantly absent. Finally, of course, Dumbledore is defeated—his weakness seems both physical and spiritual as he slumps against the tower parapet before Snape, the person he trusted, kills him. From *Order of the Phoenix* onwards, therefore, he is steadily removed from the narrative, first emotionally distant, then physically absent, then dead. Harry has to deal with unpleasantness without his most powerful father figure. Even though Dumbledore is still Headmaster when Umbridge is terrorizing the Defense Against the Dark Arts class, Harry won't go to him. "He was not going to go to Dumbledore for help when Dumbledore had not spoken to him since last June" (*Order of the Phoenix* 273). Dumbledore has reasons for maintaining his distance, just as he had reasons for leaving Harry to ten years of misery at the Dursleys, but all Harry—and therefore his readers—can perceive is abandonment and betrayal.

The most painful confrontations from *Order of the Phoenix* onwards are not, unlike earlier books, between Harry and Voldemort, but between Harry and Dumbledore, or Harry and his friends. In *Order of the Phoenix*, Harry is bereft and angry and Dumbledore "hatefully calm" as he talks about Harry's suffering, suffering that Harry does not want to acknowledge because he cannot face the source—Sirius' death. Rowling emphasizes that Harry sees

Dumbledore's age, his tiredness, and his frailty in this moment: "he felt even angrier that Dumbledore was showing signs of weakness. He had no business being weak when Harry wanted to rage and storm at him" (834). Wanting to escape the human burden of emotional pain, Harry does not want Dumbledore to be human either. He wants a tower of strength that he can batter himself against and be sheltered by. Rowling dismantles that final childish protection, when Dumbledore retells the Harry/Voldemort conflicts from his point of view, completing the transformation of Harry's narrative as he reveals his own motives and answers questions. She continues the theme of Dumbledore's weakness into *Half-Blood Prince*, where Dumbledore's physical weakness is made clear in his cursed, blackened hand and his breakdown at the lake, and explains and transforms those incidents in *Deathly Hallows* in the context of Dumbledore's personal narrative, which reveals him as both fallible and guilty.

The example of Dumbledore shows clearly that, as the narrative continues, it becomes harder for Harry (and consequently for the reader) to distinguish good wizards from evil ones—the more we know, the more the narrative transforms. Harry's battles against Voldemort, repeated and intensified in each book further demonstrate these narrative transformations. Voldemort himself experiences more than one kind of transformation: he literally transforms from book to book: beginning as something with a half-life, merged with the back of Quirrell's head, he is a potent memory of young Tom Riddle in *Chamber of Secrets*, is hideously reborn in *Goblet of Fire*, is a snake-faced demon in *Order of the Phoenix* and *Half-Blood Prince*, and reverts back to something spiritually deformed at the close of *Deathly Hallows*. As the series progresses, we become increasingly aware that Voldemort has acted as an agent in his own narrative (by changing his name and persona from Tom Malvolo Riddle to Lord Voldemort to "He-Who-Must-Not-Be-Named") and in Harry's. Voldemort literally creates Harry's narrative through his reaction to the prophecy, which indicated that a wizard boy, born at the end of July, whose parents were both in the Order of the Phoenix and had barely escaped Voldemort three times, would have the power to vanquish the Dark Lord. Dumbledore reveals that these criteria applied to Harry Potter and also to Neville Longbottom. *Either* boy could have been Voldemort's opponent but Voldemort chose Harry—and marked him with the scar:

He saw himself in you before he had ever seen you, and in marking you with that scar, he did not kill you, as he intended, but gave you powers and a future, which have fitted you to escape him not once, but four times so far.

(*Order of the Phoenix* 842)

Voldemort chose the boy most like himself. Voldemort's choices, like Harry's, transform the narrative. Their clashes become more complicated as Harry's resemblances to Voldemort multiply and his moral awareness becomes more sophisticated. The reader increasingly feels that characters operating on the "good" side are neither necessarily attractive nor kind. According to Veronica L. Schanoes, Rowling deliberately subverts the reader's expectations like this in order to force her readers to think beyond Harry's conventional character assessment. Snape's allegiance was hotly debated before *Deathly Hallows* was released,[8] and the saga of Dolores Umbridge demonstrates that not all sadistic, intolerant villains are Death Eaters. Part of Harry's growing up, aided by his two forays into Snape's memories, has been to understand how complicated all human motives are. No surprise, therefore, that Harry's halfway house between life and death in *Deathly Hallows* is not black and white and hard edged, but gray and vaporous.

Harry has changed a great deal by the last book of the series and, fittingly, here the greatest transformations occur. Rowling's seventh book, the conclusion to the Harry Potter *bildungsroman*, not only brings the hero and villain face to face for the final confrontation, but also recapitulates and transforms the themes laid down in the first volume. Now we can see that themes and motifs, already replayed and subtly changed throughout the series as Harry's (and the readers') awareness and understanding grow, are transformed from cartoon-like myth to the basis for belief and adult decisions.

Correspondences between all the novels are legion but are particularly evident between first and last as Rowling replays and transforms similar plot devices. In each novel, there is a quest for a stone; the Invisibility Cloak is essential; something is stolen from Gringotts; Harry bands together with Ron and Hermione, but has to face Voldemort alone; mothers fight for their children; Snape seems sinister but is revealed to be a reluctant protector; Neville saves the day; Voldemort is defeated by his own killing curse and lack of love; Dumbledore offers some explanation; and Harry has to make a choice. The plot may be similar, but, after seven books, the *story* is completely different.

Harry's attitude to death is what primarily changes the story, marking the most significant of all Rowling's narrative transformations, and that change is revealed through the two stones. Each stone offers a different type of transformation, putting transformation at the center of the series: as the alchemical myth, the Sorcerer's Stone (or Philosopher's Stone) is itself an agent of transformation, turning base metals into precious ones; the Resurrection Stone also transforms, bringing the dead to life. Throughout the series, Rowling, through Dumbledore, consistently reinforces two things about Voldemort's character: that he is terrified of death, and that he cannot understand love: "If there is one thing Voldemort cannot understand, it is love. He didn't realize that love as powerful as your mother's for you leaves its own mark" (*Sorcerer's Stone* 299). The blood-red Sorcerer's Stone (or Philosopher's Stone) postpones death, and thus offers Voldemort a chance of prolonged life (which is how he understands immortality). The black, damaged Resurrection Stone reaches through death to bring life and consequently is of no importance to Voldemort who neither wants to die himself nor to confer a second life on others. As Dumbledore observes, "as for the stone, whom would he want to bring back from the dead? He fears the dead. He does not love" (*Deathly Hallows* 721).

When Harry realizes that he can only win his battle against Voldemort by losing his life, Rowling recapitulates his mother's sacrifice and reinforces all Dumbledore's comments about love. In the first book, the quest for the stone, a quest to avoid death, led to the novel's climax, as Harry and Voldemort fought and struggled to stay alive. Harry's survival was the focus from the beginning of the novel—the Boy Who Lived—to the end. However, in the last book, Harry cannot survive with his integrity intact by avoiding death: he must embrace it. Choosing death is the only way he can win. Harry's love, Harry's relationships, and Harry's self-sacrifice without hope of gain are the climax to *Deathly Hallows* where they were only the background to the action of *Sorcerer's Stone.*

Rowling, therefore, closes her series by referring not to a classical under-standing of life without death but to the Christian one of death overcoming death. She introduced the theme in *Sorcerer's Stone* as part of Harry's history: his mother died to save him, something that has protected Harry throughout his childhood. However, Lily's self-sacrifice, though significant, is not exactly the same as the choice her son makes in the final volume. Lily Potter acted through love and her willing death protected her son, but she acted out of maternal instinct and her sacrifice simply substituted one death for another. Harry's sacrifice is different: he has to think, to go willingly and deliberately to his death with no thought of gain. "He envied even his parents' deaths now. This cold-blooded walk to his own destruction would require a different kind of bravery" (*Deathly Hallows* 692). Harry does not know that his inevitable death will protect his friends; indeed, he expects simply to die. He relin-quishes his part in the action, and only then does he realize how he can access and use the Resurrection Stone—not to ensure his own resurrection, not for gain, not for greed, not to hang on to his loved ones, but to bring them back to accompany him while he walks to join them.

Once Voldemort has struck him down, Rowling puts Harry into an other-worldly waiting area—nicely recapitulating another part of the first book, because the place reminds Harry of Platform 9¾—where he has to choose again between death and life: go on or go back. The original Platform 9¾ exists in a gap between the Muggle world and the wizarding one, a romantic, slightly old-fashioned place that was the starting point for Harry's journey into a new life as a wizard. Harry's metaphysical Platform exists in a gap between life and afterlife, a static place outside time that is also the starting point for a journey into a new life. Rowling has completed a double narrative transformation, from station to magical station, to magical station as metaphor for the afterlife made real. Once again, something in the wizarding world is more solid than Muggle metaphysics.

Harry is not the only person to sacrifice himself willingly in *Deathly Hallows*. Neville Longbottom does too. Neville saved the day for his House in *Sorcerer's Stone* when Dumbledore awarded him, Neville, the crucial ten points that ensured Gryffindor won the House Cup from Slytherin rather than tying for it. Neville's bravery was recognized then, "It takes a great deal of bravery to stand up to our enemies, but just as much to stand up to our friends" (*Sorcerer's Stone* 306). He was a joke in *Goblet of Fire*, improved out of all recognition as part of the D.A. in *Order of the Phoenix*, and in *Deathly Hallows* he has become a hero of the Resistance. Harry might have been a rallying cry at Hogwarts but Neville was the present student leader. It's fitting that Neville should be the one to kill Nagini, the last Horcrux, and that he should take the sword from the Sorting Hat to do it just as Harry had done in *Chamber of Secrets*. Here, Neville gets the hero's role and Harry has had to recognize and play an adult role—Dumbledore's—sending someone he knows and likes to almost certain death because it must be done: "This was crucial, he must be like Dumbledore, keep a cool head, make sure there were backups, others to carry on" (*Deathly Hallows* 696).

J. K. Rowling has pulled it off. Over seven books, she has told, retold, enlarged her story and told it again. Eleven-year-old Harry grows throughout the series, continually making choices, re-evaluating what he thinks he knows and growing in wisdom. Rowling's narrative concludes as the now-adult Harry defeats the much older but still spiritually childish Voldemort. Like Harry encountering the black-haired, orphaned Tom Riddle, or the snake-faced tyrant, or the stunted, flayed near-child, we continually meet the stranger face to face and find that he is us, transformed by narrative.

Notes

1. For other critical approaches to transformation in the Potter series, see chapters three and eight.
2. E.g., "X commits a crime" might transform into "X intends to commit a crime" or "X must commit a crime." The important thing for the single transformation is that only one predicate is involved—when two are used, the transformation is complex. Todorov gives the example. "X kills his mother" and transforms it into a complex predicate: "X thinks he has killed his mother." Note that the transformation ceases when the two predicates are separate and not dependent.
3. Even though the series is finished, Rowling is still transforming the narrative (and our perceptions of it and its characters)—most recently on October 19, 2007 when she revealed that Dumbledore is/was gay (Weingarten and Tyre).
4. Lacan never actually says that the bar equals repression; however he does comment on the relationship between the two, the sliding of the signified beneath the signifier and finds that language works as metaphor.
5. Note that M and W mirror each other.
6. More Muggles than the Dursleys and other relatives of witches and wizards know about the wizarding world: in *Prisoner of Azkaban*, Cornelius Fudge officially informed the British Prime Minister of Sirius Black's real identity (*Prisoner of Azkaban* 38), and *Harry*

Potter and the Half-Blood Prince (hereinafter *Half-Blood Prince*) begins by describing the interview between an incredulous, Muggle Prime Minister and the departing, discredited Fudge (*Half-Blood Prince* 3–18).

7. Grimes also points out that some readers began reading the Harry Potter saga at age ten or thereabouts and have been growing up at approximately the same rate as Harry himself; thus, Harry's development parallels theirs.

8. Speculation appeared in print between the publications of *Half-Blood Prince* and *Deathly Hallows* (Odell and Harte, Berner and Card).

References

Barton, Benjamin H. "Harry Potter and the Half-Crazed Bureaucracy." 104.6 *Michigan Law Review*. May 2006: 1523–1538.

Berner, Amy and Orson Scott Card. *The Great Snape Debate: The Case for Snapes Guilt/Innocence.* Borders, 2007.

Bettleheim, Bruno. *The Uses of Enchantment: The Meaning and Importance of Fairy Tales.* New York: Alfred A Knopf, 1976.

Brooks, Peter. *Reading for the Plot: Design and Intention in Narrative.* 1984; repr. Cambridge, MA and London, England: Harvard University Press, 1992.

Dickinson, Renée. "Harry Potter Pedagogy: What we Learn about Teaching and Learning from J.K. Rowling." 79.6 *Clearing House.* July/Aug. 2006: 240–244.

Grimes, M. Katherine. "Harry Potter: Fairy Tale Prince, Real Boy and Archetypal Hero" in Lana Whited (ed.). *The Ivory Tower and Harry Potter: Perspectives in a Literary Phenomenon.* Columbia and London: University of Missouri Press, 2002: 89–122.

Lacan, Jacques. "The Agency of the Letter in the Unconscious or Reason since Freud" in *Ecrits.* trans. Alan Sheridan. 1977; repr. London: Routledge, 1989.

Lacoss, Jann. "Of Magicals and Muggles: Reversals and Revulsions at Hogwarts" in Lana Whited (ed.). *The Ivory Tower and Harry Potter: Perspectives in a Literary Phenomenon.* Columbia and London: University of Missouri Press, 2002: 67–88.

Mills, Alice. "Harry Potter and the Terrors of the Toilet." 37.1 *Children's Literature in Education.* March 2006: 1–13.

Natov, Roni. "Harry Potter and the Extraordinariness of the Ordinary" in Lana Whited (ed.). *The Ivory Tower and Harry Potter: Perspectives in a Literary Phenomenon.* Columbia and London: University of Missouri Press, 2002: 125–139.

Odell, Joyce and Wendy B. Harte. *Who Killed Albus Dumbledore? What Really Happened in Harry Potter and the Half-Blood Prince? Six Expert Harry Potter Detectives Examine the Evidence.* Port Hadlock: Zossima Press, 2006.

Rowling, J. K. *Harry Potter and the Sorcerer's Stone.* New York: Scholastic Press, 1997.

——. *Harry Potter and the Chamber of Secrets.* New York: Scholastic Press, 1998.

——. *Harry Potter and the Prisoner of Azkaban.* New York: Scholastic Press, 1999.

——. *Harry Potter and the Goblet of Fire.* New York: Scholastic Press, 2000.

——. *Harry Potter and the Order of the Phoenix.* New York: Scholastic Press, 2003.

——. *Harry Potter and the Half-Blood Prince.* New York: Scholastic Press, 2005.

——. *Harry Potter and the Deathly Hallows.* New York: Scholastic Press, 2007.

Schanoes, Veronica L. "Cruel Heroes and Treacherous Texts: Educating the Reader in Moral Complexity and Critical Reading in J.K. Rowling's Harry Potter Books" in Giselle Liza Anatol (ed.). *Reading Harry Potter: Critical Essays.* Westport, CT, London: Praeger, 2003: 131–146.

Todorov, Tzvetan. *The Poetics of Prose.* New York: Cornell University Press, 1977; repr. 1984.

Weingarten, Tara and Peg Tyre. "Rowling Says Dumbledore is Gay." *Newsweek.* Online. October 19, 2007. Retrieved October 20, 2007 from http://www.newsweek.com/id/50787

Whited, Lana, and M. Katherine Grimes. "What Would Harry Do? J. K. Rowling and Lawrence Kohlberg's Theories of Moral Development" in Lana Whited (ed.). *The Ivory Tower and Harry Potter: Perspectives in a Literary Phenomenon.* Columbia and London: University of Missouri Press, 2002: 182–208.

Cultural Studies and Media Perspectives

Part IV

Cultural Studies and Media Perspectives

Chapter Fifteen

Lost in Translation?
Harry Potter, from Page to Screen

PHILIP NEL

I know all about you, of course—

> Hermione Granger, to Harry Potter, *Harry Potter and the Philosopher's Stone*[1]

Harry Potter. Our new—*celebrity*.

> Severus Snape, *Harry Potter and the Philosopher's Stone*[2]

Know who you are, of course, the famous Harry Potter.

> Justin Finch-Fletchley, *Harry Potter and the Chamber of Secrets*[3]

In J. K. Rowling's Harry Potter novels, the title character needs no introduction. Upon meeting him, Hermione says, "I know all about you, of course— ... you're in *Modern Magical History* and *The Rise and Fall of the Dark Arts* and *Great Wizarding Events of the Twentieth Century*." "Am I?" Harry asks, "feeling dazed."[4] Knowing that their films will face legions of knowledgeable Potter fans, filmmakers may have felt dazed, too. In the first film, some of screenwriter Steve Kloves' dialogue suggests the anxiety of adapting a series so well known and loved. After Hermione reveals that Harry's father played Quidditch, Ron exclaims, "She knows more about you than you do!" Harry replies, "Who doesn't?"[5] Fans' devotion to and expertise on Potter make these novels especially challenging to adapt. As Linda Hutcheon writes in *A Theory of Adaptation*, it is "easier for an adapter to forge a relationship with an audience that is not overly burdened with affection or nostalgia for the adapted text": "The more popular and beloved the novel, the more likely the discontent."[6] Citing Harry Potter as an example of this problem, Hutcheon points to a remark made by Christopher Columbus, director of the first two films: "People would have crucified me if I hadn't been faithful to the books."[7]

However, the attempt to be completely faithful hampers those first two films; recognition of the impossibility of being completely faithful liberates the third, fourth, and fifth films. One can understand (and sympathize with) Columbus for seeking fidelity. Certainly, he, Steve Kloves, and the films' producers all deserve praise for insisting on British actors and a British setting. Steve Norris, head of the British Film Commission, puts it this way: "Harry Potter is something that is weirdly about us.... It's culturally British and the thought of it being made anywhere but here sent shudders down everyone's spines. It's like taking *Catcher in the Rye* and setting it in Liverpool."[8] If the threat of an Americanized Potter makes a strong argument for fidelity, a film nevertheless cannot be perfectly faithful to its source text: books and movies each have different strengths and constraints. Neither medium can do exactly what the other does. Though Columbus must grasp this fact, the first two Harry Potter movies betray little awareness of it. In contrast, Alfonso Cuarón, Mike Newell, and David Yates—the directors, respectively, of the third, fourth and fifth films—each seem keenly aware of the impossibility of fidelity. Each director's willingness to bring his own creative vision to the project makes *Harry Potter and the Prisoner of Azkaban*, *Harry Potter and the Goblet of Fire*, and *Harry Potter and the Order of the Phoenix* more successful adaptations than the first two films. Where Columbus' movies are like historical re-enactments, the films of Cuarón, Newell, and Yates are dynamic and make us see the original novels anew. The Harry Potter films offer a case study in the perils and possibilities of adaptation—from Columbus' literalism, to Cuarón's symbolically laden realism, Newell's psychologically astute Young Adult movie, and Yates' dark dystopian mystery.

In many ways, small but meaningful details make the novels work. In the first book, Harry buys a variety of sweets from the Hogwarts trolley, inviting Ron to help himself, and providing occasion for their nascent friendship to develop. That Harry "had never had anything to share before, or, indeed, anyone to share it with" highlights Harry's generosity, but also reminds us of the privation he has endured in ten years with the Dursleys.[9] Or, to take a comparably small example from the fourth book, Dumbledore's comment about his brother Aberforth being "prosecuted for practicing inappropriate charms on a goat" conveys the headmaster's mischievous sense of humor, but also his compassion, since he is using the anecdote to cheer up Hagrid.[10] Neither of these moments appear in the movie versions (though Aberforth's goat has a cameo in the fifth film), but, of course, no film could possibly include each interesting detail from the books.

A film can, however, aspire to translate what the adapters—foremost, the director, but also the screenwriter—perceive as the novel's core experience.

Central to Dumbledore's character is a balance between seriousness and humor. As Steve Kloves puts it, "Dumbledore bears such a tremendous dark burden … and the only way that he can keep that at bay, the darkness, is to be whimsical and humorous."[11] Newell can omit Dumbledore's wry remark about Aberforth because, as Cuarón's film does, Newell's provides many examples of the headmaster's sense of humor, restoring this aspect of his personality after its near-absence from the first two movies. In one moment not in the novel, the fourth film has Dumbledore telling Harry that "the licorice snaps are a wee bit sharp" (as Harry discovers, they snap at your fingers if you don't eat them promptly). When visiting Harry in his dormitory near the movie's end, Dumbledore observes, "I never liked these curtains. Set them on fire in my fourth year—by accident, of course." In contrast, the Columbus films and Yates' make Dumbledore a more stern, Gandalf-like figure, less because of any difference in actors' interpretations, and more because the third and fourth films grant more comic lines to Michael Gambon than the fifth does or than the first two offered to the late Richard Harris.

If the absent Aberforth joke in *Goblet of Fire* shows how a small change can have a little impact on an adaptation, the alterations to the "sweets" scene in *Philosopher's Stone* exemplify how small changes can create larger ripples. Instead of using the moment on the Hogwarts Express to focus on the developing friendship between Harry (portrayed by Daniel Radcliffe) and Ron (Rupert Grint), Columbus uses it to display special effects, providing chocolate frogs that actually jump. In her novel, Rowling provides not jumping frogs but conversation, giving us insight into the characters—Ron's embarrassment about his family's lack of money, and Harry's anxiety about attending wizarding school. Columbus and Kloves do find ways to underscore the importance of friendship, as when, during the quest for the Philosopher's Stone, Hermione (Emma Watson) dismisses Harry's claim that she is a better wizard: "Me—books and cleverness. There are more important things— friendship and bravery."[12] However, had the adaptation focused more on the characters' relationships, it would have less cause to insert this somewhat sentimental, moralizing line.

Where Columbus favors special effects over character development, Cuarón and Newell give the characters space to interact; Yates falls somewhere in between, providing more space than Columbus but less than Cuarón or Newell. With the possible exception of the relatively one-dimensional Dursleys, Rowling provides complex characters who feel "realistic" to readers. Her ability to create characters whom readers care about is key to the novels' success, but Columbus' films retain few reasons for the audience to connect with Harry and his friends. As Rosemary Johnston has noted, Rowling's narrator imagines an audience who is "clever, perceptive, imaginative,… and on side with the narrator," but Columbus' first film "position[s] viewers in a position of dominant and aesthetic spectacularity."[13] Indeed, both films convey the impression that viewers need a steady diet of gags and tricks in order to be entertained. The first film aspires to amuse by having Seamus Finnigan blow himself up repeatedly. When Seamus attempts a spell that should turn water into rum, he causes an explosion, singeing his hair; when he tries the "Wingardium Leviosa" spell, boom! and his hair is singed again. Neither scene occurs in the book, and Rowling's spells have very specific effects when poorly executed—they don't all create smoke. Beyond needlessly bending the logic of Rowling's universe, exploding Seamus furthers neither plot nor character, and so might have been cut in favor of the conversations that do.

Though his storytelling is darkly efficient and his special effects usually serve a clear narrative purpose, Yates does not always manage to create an emotional bond between viewer and character. His short scenes swiftly advance the plot, but provide little time to get acquainted with the characters. In Rowling's "Snape's Worst Memory" chapter, through the Pensieve, Harry visits the scene of his father and Sirius bullying Snape. Experiencing the memories of his father's schoolboy arrogance through the Pensieve allows Harry time to reflect on their behavior and to feel a deep sense of shame. Afterwards, Harry feels "horrified and unhappy," because he knows "how it felt to be humiliated in the middle of a circle of onlookers" and concludes that James Potter "had been every bit as arrogant as Snape had always told him."[14] The film allows no occasion for such self-examination. Instead of watching the memory unfold in the Pensieve, Harry just glimpses it after launching a "Protego" spell against Snape, who was attempting Legilimency on Harry. Borrowing from the novel's "Seen and Unforseen" chapter, the movie has the spell allow Harry to observe fragments of Snape's unhappy childhood, and then immediately moves on. Harry's capacity to feel sympathy for others— even those whom he does not like, such as Snape—is central to his character, making this omission a significant one. That said, condensing ten pages from the "Snape's Worst Memory" chapter into just a few seconds may have been necessary: as the longest book in the series, *Harry Potter and the Order of the Phoenix* must have been especially difficult to adapt. However, an unfortunate side effect is that the film offers few glances into the thoughts and feelings of the characters.

Yates does make the attempt, certainly. At number twelve Grimmauld Place, Harry confesses to Sirius that he *was* the snake who attacked Mr. Weasley, and asks, "What if the reason is that I'm becoming more like him [Voldemort]? [...] What if I'm becoming bad?" Screenwriter Michael Goldenberg has Sirius respond with a sentence from earlier in Rowling's novel— "The world isn't split into good people and Death Eaters"[15]—and adds two new sentences. Sirius (portrayed by Gary Oldman) continues, "We've got both dark and light inside of us. What matters is the part we choose to act on.

That's who we really are." This conversation dramatizes Harry's inner struggle, and highlights two central themes of Rowling's series—that good and evil
have a close and complex relationship, and that choices (not birth) convey a
character's moral worth. It also shows Sirius as a paternal figure to Harry,
underscoring the depth of loss he will feel: as Dumbledore tells Harry in the
novel's penultimate chapter, losing Sirius is losing "the closest thing to a
parent you have ever known."[16] In Yates' film, moments like these are too few.
As a result, the film never drags, but nor does it offer much opportunity for
emotional engagement.

Newell and Cuarón are the most successful in making the characters' interior lives visible. Even when Harry is invisible, Cuarón shows us what he is
feeling. After covertly hearing McGonagall and Fudge telling Madame Rosmerta that Sirius Black betrayed Lily and James Potter, Harry is upset. Since
his protagonist is still beneath the Invisibility Cloak, Cuarón conveys Harry's
anger by keeping the camera focused on the unseen figure creating footprints
in the snow, knocking over a group of carolers. The swift pace of the camera
coupled with Hermione and Ron's reactions to this violent action register
Harry's agitated mood. Hermione and Ron chase after Harry, stopping suddenly to see a trail of footprints leading up to a rock. Accompanied by the just
audible sound of Harry's sobs, the camera watches Hermione carefully
approach the rock. It cuts to the perspective of the (still invisible) Harry,
showing us Hermione's sympathetic expression. As she kneels beside the rock
and reaches for Harry's cloak, a close-range shot of her look of worried interest combines with Harry's slightly louder sobs to amplify the serious mood. In
a reverse shot, the camera focuses on where Harry should be, and Hermione
removes his cloak, revealing Harry with head bowed. Focus back on
Hermione: regarding Harry with a concerned expression, she asks, "Harry,
what happened?" Reverse shot to Harry, still looking down, as he says, "He
was their friend. And he betrayed them." His tears turn to tears of rage, as he
looks up and shouts, "He was their friend!" The camera cuts back to a long
shot, suggesting the range of Harry's voice. As it returns to focus on
Hermione's concerned face, we hear Harry say, "I hope he finds me." Then,
showing Harry's face: "Because when he does, I'm going to be ready." As the
camera gradually zooms in, Harry shouts, "When he does, I'm going to kill
him!" Cuarón and Kloves have significantly altered the scene from the novel,
compressing it to bring out its emotional intensity.

Displaying Harry's shift from anguish to anger not only lays the ground-
work for the emotionally volatile Harry of book five but also suggests that—at
times—Harry's temper brings him psychologically close to Draco Malfoy.
Rowling's novel highlights the unexpected affinity between these two characters when, back at Hogwarts after hearing of Black's betrayal, Harry remem-
bers Malfoy's words: "If it was me, I'd hunt him down myself … I'd want
revenge." Ron's reply—"You're going to take Malfoy's advice instead of

ours?"[17]—reminds us that, as the Sorting Hat said, Harry "*would* have done well in Slytherin."[18] Cuarón's film does not make the Harry–Draco connection as explicit, but the scene in which Harry announces his intent to kill Sirius (discussed in the previous paragraph) does show that Harry, like Draco, has a capacity for rash and vindictive behavior. As Cuarón has said of the third Potter novel, "The strength of the book is not the magic itself, though the magic is great, but the strength of human emotions."[19]

In addition to emotions, a strength of each book is Rowling's narrative drive—that is, her novels are both character-driven *and* plot-driven. Columbus' emphasis on sets and effects slows the pace. For example, when the students approach Hogwarts for the first time, the camera shows the castle as boats approach, then shows the first-years looking awed, then lingers on the castle once more, then moves to a close-up of awed students' faces again, and finally moves back to linger on the castle … again. After nearly a minute of switching back and forth between the castle and the children's faces, what began as an impressive sight grows tedious. Apparently unconscious of his cumbersome style, Columbus has explained, "In the first film, we spent 45 minutes just soaking up atmosphere, exploring Hogwarts Academy. That's behind us now. Now, we can let the adventure begin."[20] Though the more tightly structured second novel does aid Columbus in producing a faster-paced film, the director nonetheless excises suspense in favor of more "atmosphere." During the scene in which they discover the entrance to the Chamber of Secrets, the film devotes two minutes to Lockhart, Harry, Ron standing around while Harry talks with Moaning Myrtle. The three stand beside the sink, as fixed as the column supporting it. Next, Columbus devotes 30 seconds to the machinery of sinks moving around, while Harry, Ron, and Lockhart slowly step back in unison, as if in a chorus line. The loud, slow machinery begs the question of how the Basilisk could possibly have slipped out unnoticed—surely half a minute's clanking would have given it away? Wisely, the novel dispatches this scene more efficiently: "The sink, in fact, sank, right out of sight, leaving a large pipe exposed, a pipe wide enough for a man to slide into."[21] Rather than insist that we admire the machinery, the novel allows the machinery of the plot to propel the action forward.

In contrast, Cuarón's dynamic direction creates suspense from the moment *Harry Potter and the Prisoner of Azkaban* begins. As the camera approaches a distant light, the glow at first appears to emanate from behind the Warner Brothers logo, and then, drawing nearer, from a second-floor bedroom window. Looking through the window, the camera reveals the light's source: a figure sitting up beneath bedsheets. Finally, the camera moves into the room, and the figure—now revealed as Harry Potter—sticks his head out from the sheets, and lies down, feigning sleep. After Uncle Vernon has opened the door to check on him and then closed it again, Harry sits up and ducks under his sheets once more. The camera travels under the sheets where a glowing wand tip illuminates a book open to "Extreme Incantations," as Harry practices saying "Lumos Maxima." Cut to Harry's face as he says it a third time, causing the wand to glow brightly. Suddenly, the camera zooms backwards out of the window to the title of the movie. Critics might fairly point out that having Harry practice spellwork at home should have brought a warning from the Ministry of Magic, but the lit wand makes the scene more dramatically effective on screen. In the opening minute and ten seconds, Cuarón establishes the air of mystery that makes the novels such page-turners.

Although Mike Newell's direction also generates suspense and mystery, it leaves several mysteries unsolved, creating narrative gaps that the fifth film needs to reckon with. Those who either speak Latin or have read the book will understand how Dumbledore's "Priori Incantatem" remark explains what happened when Voldemort's wand short-circuited. Other viewers may be baffled because, apart from these two words, the film is silent on this point. For this and other significant omissions, Newell's *Goblet of Fire* is a fun dramatization for a knowing audience, but a slightly confusing one for an unknowing audience. As Linda Hutcheon points out, "For an adaptation to be successful in its own right it must be so for both knowing and unknowing audiences."[22] To be fair, however, *Goblet of Fire* is much longer than any of the previous three and, since this is a movie and not a mini-series, the film-makers had either to make more cuts or to make two films—as Columbus originally wanted to do.[23] Perhaps the need to condense justifies both the omission of the S.P.E.W. subplot and the decision not to reveal Karkarov as a Death Eater. Yet, even if we concede the necessity of greater cuts (such as these), the film omits several more plot elements important to the next novel: Harry giving his Triwizard earnings to Fred and George for their joke shop, and Snape going off to spy on the Death Eaters.

David Yates and Michael Goldenberg—the fifth film's director and screen-writer—certainly had their work cut out for them. They had not only to adapt the longest of the seven novels, but also to account for gaps left by the fourth movie. To their credit, Yates and Goldenberg pick up some of the plot elements dropped from the fourth film. Newell's *Harry Potter and the Goblet of Fire* excises Dumbledore's attempt to persuade Fudge of Voldemort's return (from near the end of the fourth novel), but the fifth film brings it back, establishing Fudge's unthinking denial and highlighting Dumbledore's emphasis on diplomatic persuasion. At Harry's trial before the Wizengamot, Dumbledore tries to reason with Fudge, using some of the language from Rowling's *Goblet of Fire*: "I implore you to see reason. The evidence that the Dark Lord has returned is incontrovertible."[24] Fudge replies, "He has not." He has, along with the composite character "Nigel," an apparent amalgam of Rowling's Creevey brothers. Yates and Goldenberg may have decided to include him to be consistent with the fourth film, in which Nigel first appears—after all, their choices need be sufficiently congruent with the decisions of the previous screenwriter and directors.

Other gaps in the narrative make significant shifts in Rowling's meaning and, in some cases, may puzzle the unknowing audience. Perhaps taking its cue from Newell's film, Yates' film omits Snape's role as the Order of the Phoenix's spy in the Death Eaters' organization, lessening some of his appealing ambiguity: more often than not, the film's Snape appears to be trying to help Harry. As is true of Newell's film, Yates' also might be preceded with the announcement that, in tonight's performance, the role of Dobby will be played by Neville Longbottom. In the fourth film, *Neville* delivers the Gilly-weed to Harry; in the fifth, *Neville* finds the Room of Requirement in which Dumbledore's Army practices their defensive spells. True, in taking on the absent Dobby's tasks, Neville gains a more central role, perhaps compensating for his omission from other areas—most significantly, from the prophecy. Yet removing Neville from the prophecy makes the morality of choice less central to Rowling's epic. In pointing out that Voldemort chose Harry over Neville, Rowling's novel emphasizes that the Dark Lord's choices make him immoral, just as Harry's choices make him moral. Focusing more on Harry's choices and less on Voldemort's, Yates' film decreases the parallels Rowling has drawn between the characters. Modified meanings are adaptation's inevitable by-product, but alterations that confuse the uninitiated are avoidable. For the most part, Yates minimizes the confusing ones. For example, showing us that Tonks can change her appearance but not explaining how she does it (she's a Metamorphmagus) may make viewers of the film curious, but it need not throw them off the narrative track.

If the fifth and especially the fourth films work best for knowing audiences (who can fill in the gaps), then the first two films should work best for unknowing audiences (who, unfamiliar with the plot, may tolerate the slow pace), and the third should please both knowing and unknowing audiences. However, such an assessment assumes a great deal about audiences. Many devout Potter fans—definitely a *knowing* audience—very much enjoyed the first two films for their attempted fidelity to Rowling's novels. For these fans, Columbus' versions offered the pleasures of the familiar. A fan who writes under the pseudonym Witherwings admits that Columbus' films had "no flashes of genuine creative brilliance, but they faithfully and fondly brought Rowling's stories to life. Columbus constructed a mythical Hogwarts using warm honey hues."[25] For this fan, "faithfully and fondly" trump "creative brilliance." In contrast, Witherwings reports feeling "bitter tears of humiliation" in watching Cuarón's "immense, imposing Hogwarts drained of its warmth," but felt that Rowling's tale had "emerged altered but ultimately unshattered by the film adaptation."[26] The fourth film goes too far for this fan's taste. She or he lamented the "precious few seconds of those silken Lucius locks" and that Hermione wore "a pale pink dress instead of the lovely periwinkle blue robes described in the book." Witherwings asked, "Why did this movie hate me and all that I regard as holy?"[27] The emotionally charged language—"bitter tears of humiliation" and "Why did this movie hate me"—underscores the personal nature of Witherwings' relationship with a Harry Potter text. For Witherwings, at least, a Harry Potter novel is a "holy" text that can only be adapted by and for the faithful.

Those who have read the Potter novels will inevitably compare the films with the books. A knowing audience experiences what Hutcheon calls "an interpretive doubling, a conceptual flipping back and forth between the work we know and the work we are experiencing."[28] However, a careful analysis should move beyond simple comparison to consider how an adaptation interprets Rowling's source text. To evaluate what is lost and what is gained in the translation from novel to movie, one might understand adaptation as a kind of translation. As Walter Benjamin notes in "The Task of the Translator," "no translation would be possible if in its ultimate essence it strove for likeness to the original. For in its afterlife ... the original undergoes a change."[29] Resisting that change, Columbus' ambition to duplicate the originals hamper the filmic translations of the first two Potter novels. In that same essay, Benjamin suggests that "[t]he task of the translator consists in finding that intended effect [intention] upon the language into which he is translating which produces in it the echo of the original."[30] What the director perceives as the intended effect is key to evaluating adaptations of Rowling's series. Our enjoyment of the adaptation may depend upon the degree to which what the *director* sees as the intended effects matches what *we* see as the intended effects. That said, even if we and the director agree on the intended effects, if the director expresses those effects in a way that is unintelligible to us, then we may yet find ourselves at odds with the film. Or not. After all, much enjoyment may come from a film that highlights facets of a novel we had not considered, or that makes us see the work anew.

Yates, Newell, and Cuarón see representing adolescence's emotional landscape as vital parts of the third and fourth Harry Potter novels' intended effects. Teen-age longings are less prominent in *Harry Potter and the Prisoner of Azkaban* (in which Harry turns 13) than they are in *Harry Potter and the Goblet of Fire* (in which he turns 14). Appropriately, Cuarón's film places less emphasis on this dynamic than Newell's—though Cuarón does add moments of awkwardly understood desire that do not occur in Rowling's book. Rowling has Harry, upon seeing Cho Chang on the Quidditch pitch, feel "a slight jolt in the region of his stomach that he didn't think had anything to do with nerves."[31] Cuarón skips Harry's attraction to Cho (her small role in the novel disappears from the film) in favor of making manifest some of the latent attraction between Ron and Hermione. At Hagrid's Hippogriff lesson, as Harry approaches Buckbeak, Hermione grabs Ron's hand in fright. Ron looks down at her hand, the two exchange a glance, Hermione releases his hand, and they swiftly move apart from one another. Later, in Hogsmeade, Hermione and Ron stand staring at the Shrieking Shack. She says conversationally, "It's meant to be the most haunted building in Britain," and adds "Did I mention that?"—punctuating this last statement with a breath that resembles a nervous half-laugh. Ron awkwardly replies, "Twice." Hermione asks, "Do you want to move a bit closer?" Ron looks at her in surprise, and says, "Huh?" She replies, "To the Shrieking Shack." Relief in his voice, he says, "Ohh" and adds, "Actually, I'm fine here." Both added scenes give depth to the relationship between Ron and Hermione, displaying the romantic feelings neither is yet ready to admit.

Newell's film—like Rowling's fourth novel—is the first obviously "Young Adult" work in the series, and with the characters well into their teens, the fifth and sixth novels continue to focus on the psychological and emotional experience of adolescents. Wisely, then, Newell and Kloves retain a version of Hermione and Ron's argument following the Yule Ball. Ron says that Viktor Krum (Hermione's date) is using her and is too old for her. Hermione responds angrily, "What? What? *That's* what you think!" Ron replies, "Yeah, that's what I think." In a nearly direct quotation from the novel, Hermione says, "You know the solution then, don't you?" In a slightly longer version of Rowling's line, Hermione responds heatedly, "Next time there's a ball, pluck up the courage and ask me before somebody else does, and *not* as a last resort!" Grint, as Ron, "splutters" his answer much as Ron does in the book: "Well, that's, that's, I mean, that's just completely off the point." As the novel does, Newell's film makes it clear "that Hermione had got the point much better than Ron had."[32] Underscoring the awkwardness of the teenage crush, Newell and Kloves include several of Harry's failed attempts to communicate with Cho Chang, including his "Wangoballwime?" line, in the film relocated to the steps outside the owlery, but just as funny and touching as in the novel.[33] After Cho (Katie Leung) says "Sorry?" and Harry offers an intelligible version of his question—"d'you want to go to the ball with me?"—she is genuinely sorry when she explains that she cannot go because she's already going with someone else. The film version of *Goblet of Fire* neatly captures the heightened emotional intensity of adolescent experience.

While Newell's portrait of the teenage psyche does dramatize one of Rowling's central themes, the depiction of Cho in Yates' *Order of the Phoenix* amplifies the Potter books' partial blindness to cultural and ethnic differences. Though an intended effect of Rowling's series is a critique of bigotry, the means of her critique has some (presumably) unintended effects that undermine the anti-discrimination message. The Harry Potter novels offer a trenchant critique of racism via unsympathetic characters' mistreatment of "Mudbloods," "half-bloods," "half-breeds," and Muggles. Apart from this metaphoric engagement, the books otherwise erase race from the lived experience of minority characters: skin color and ethnicity are merely descriptors for non-white characters, not salient features of their identities. Rowling's narrative voice (usually aligned with Harry's perspective) discloses that Angelina Johnson, Lee Jordan, and Kingsley Shacklebolt are black, but they apparently face neither discrimination nor other race-based abuses of power. Cho Chang has a comparably vague relationship to her ethnicity; the novels never identify the source of her Asian ancestry. As Sarah Park points out, "Cho" and "Chang" could be either Chinese or Korean, and *both* are surnames.[34] Although identifying her only as "Asian" could be attributed to free indirect discourse (we see her through Harry's point of view), using the last name "Cho" as a first name suggests a lack of cultural knowledge on Rowling's part. Yates' film compounds the problematic representation of ethnicity by collapsing Marietta Edgecombe and Cho Chang into the same character. Although this move helps streamline the plot and solidifies Harry's break with Cho, it also means that the only Asian character in the films falls into the stereotype of the "treacherous Asian," suggesting, as Edward Said puts it, that "the Orient at bottom is something either to be feared [...] or controlled."[35] Though the movie later softens this perception by disclosing that she was forced to drink Veritaserum, having Cho instead of Marietta serve as the character who betrays the D.A. to Umbridge perpetuates some of the novels' blindness to real-world experiences of prejudice—even while both the films and the novels strive to advance Rowling's metaphoric critique of bigotry.

Wisely softening one of the book's most intense emotional effects, Yates turns down the volume of Harry's temper. The angry, moody Harry of Rowling's *Order of the Phoenix* is less angry and less moody in Yates' *Order of the Phoenix*, but the fifth film certainly retains some of his adolescent volatility. When, just after they arrive at Hogwarts, Harry shouts at Malfoy, Hermione and Ron exchange a glance that registers their concern. After Harry has challenged Seamus' skepticism and Ron stands with his friend, Harry does not thank Ron, but instead shouts at him: "I said I'm fine, Ron!" Perhaps because a "CAPS-LOCK Harry" (as some fans call the Harry Potter of the fifth book) would be even less appealing on screen, Yates and Goldenberg engineer Harry's early recognition of his short temper, and his decision not to take it out on his friends. After Luna Lovegood (Evanna Lynch) remarks that, if she were Voldemort, she would want to keep Harry isolated and alone, Harry realizes that he needs his friends. In the very next scene, in the Great Hall, he walks over to Ron, Hermione, and Ginny (who are eating), and asks, "May I join you?" Though he does not apologize, his tone is contrite—indeed, Yates nicely underplays this moment, trusting us to catch Harry's meaning without the prompting that Columbus would surely do. Harry's subsequent behavior channels his anger in more productive directions, such as Dumbledore's Army, where, in defiance of Umbridge, he teaches his fellow students the Defense Against the Dark Arts skills they are not learning in her class. In perhaps the most striking display of Harry's tumultuous emotional state, he asks Sirius whether he's "becoming bad." As discussed earlier in this chapter, Sirius offers reassurance by encouraging Harry to take a more nuanced approach toward good and bad.

Of the five films, Cuarón's symbolically dense realism most rewards multiple viewings because—like Rowling's novels—*Prisoner of Azkaban* includes so many details that it's impossible to appreciate them all the first time. The students' casual way of wearing their school uniforms and of *not* wearing them when out of class adds a realistic touch missing from the first two films (when the students wear their outfits with greater reverence). As Cuarón notes in the DVD for *Prisoner of Azkaban*, he asked the actors how their characters would wear the uniforms, and so "you will see some kids with the ties out, some with the ties all the way to here, some of them very tidy. So it's just pretty much like seeing kids walking out of school." There are more subtle ways in which his film injects a measure of realism. When the Knight Bus stops to pick up Harry, Stan Shunpike (portrayed by Lee Ingleby) delivers his lines in a perfunctory tone, reading from a script he holds in his hand: "Welcome to the Knight Bus, emergency transport for the stranded witch or wizard. My name is Stan Shunpike, and I will be your conductor for this evening." A slight change from Rowling, but having Stan read from a piece of paper underscores the fact that he is just going through the motions, doing his job. One of the assets of the Harry Potter books is that, as in Dorothy Sayers' novels, even minor characters are distinctive and seem to have a rich life history of their own. Including this detail (which is not in the book) helps Cuarón's movie grant some depth to a character who is only on screen for a few minutes.

Accompanying the psychological realism, Cuarón works in visual motifs that emphasize themes in the novel, such as time. Time is central to the third book: the Dementors revive Harry's memories of his parents; the Pensieve provides glimpses of three important trials in the past; Hermione's Time-Turner allows her to take two classes that meet at the same time; and, in Chapter 21, Hermione and Harry use it to travel three hours backwards, allowing them "to save more than one innocent life," as Dumbledore says.[36] To signal time passing, Cuarón shows seasons changing via the Whomping Willow. At the onset of autumn, the willow drops all of its leaves at once. As winter melts into spring, the willow shakes off its ice and snow, spattering the camera lens with droplets of water. In addition to figurative representations of time, Cuarón also provides iconic ones—in clocks and pendulums. Just prior to Trelawney's first Divination class, a tower clock is chiming the hour. As Harry, Ron, and Hermione walk down to their Care of Magical Creatures lesson, the same clock is chiming. Just after Professor Lupin's Defense Against the Dark Arts class, a giant pendulum swings back and forth in the hallway, behind Professor McGonagall, as Harry tries to persuade her to let him visit

Hogsmeade. Later still, after Lupin agrees to teach Harry how to fight Dementors, the camera follows an owl flying across the landscape as seasons change from autumn to winter. When the owl flies near the clock (again chiming), the camera zooms in to show Harry Potter standing behind the clock's glass face, looking out between the second hand and the minute hand, again seeing his friends go off to Hogsmeade without him. These many images emphasize time's centrality to the plot, and add a visual density that rewards repeated viewings.

A frame-by-frame analysis of Cuarón's film would be a rich and satisfying experience. That said, his *Prisoner of Azkaban* is not without the occasional misstep—such as the jabbering shrunken head on the Knight Bus. And Newell's *Goblet of Fire* has some brilliant touches, such as Ralph Fiennes' Nosferatu-like Voldemort or the emotionally intense first Defense Against the Dark Arts class with Brendon Gleeson's Mad-Eye Moody. Yates' *Order of the Phoenix* presents Imelda Staunton's pink-clad martinet, Dolores Umbridge, and weaves fascist motifs into both her regime and Fudge's—Fudge's large black-and-white banner waving high up in the Ministry of Magic echoes totalitarian propaganda, and Filch removing paintings from Hogwarts' walls recalls Nazis' attacks on art. However, of the five films, the vibrant and allusive *Prisoner of Azkaban* offers the most consistently fascinating viewing because, quite simply, there is so much to *see*. Having the Dementors cause ice to crystallize on the windows of the Hogwarts Express neatly evinces the icy mood these spectral creatures create. When Harry and Hermione enter the Shrieking Shack, Cuarón keeps dark all but the screen's very center, creating an eerie stillness as he focuses attention on the two slightly nervous teenage wizards. Early in the film, the Dursleys' several televisions, one of which Dudley continues to watch as his aunt floats away, succinctly conveys their shallowness and their consumerist values. As Harry Huan notes, Cuarón even weaves in "references to his own Mexican heritage," as when, for instance "the three teens pass the clocktower terrace en route to Hogsmeade village, [and] the sculptures surrounding the terrace fountain feature serpents and eagles that are based on a motif taken from Mexico's flag."[37] Packed with significant detail and thick with references, Cuarón's *Azkaban* offers many levels of meaning. To borrow again from Hutcheon, "translation is not a rendering of some fixed nontextual meaning to be copied or paraphrased or reproduced; rather, it is an engagement with the original text that makes us see that text in different ways."[38] Cuarón's film succeeds because it engages with Rowling's original, reinventing it and allowing viewers to see it anew.

Providing five films with (nearly) the same cast and four different directors, the Harry Potter franchise provides a unique opportunity to consider the processes of adaptation. Because the screenwriter and cast have remained mostly constant, this chapter has focused primarily on the implications of the differences in each director's vision, but there are many other profitable areas that I hope others will explore. It's worth considering the individual actors' interpretations, from the open-mouthed *Home Alone*-style scream that Columbus (director of *Home Alone*) encourages (when the trio first sees Fluffy, when Harry and Ron nearly hit the Whomping Willow, etc.), to Alan Rickman's always extraordinary Snape. As Steve Kloves has observed, Rickman "always says the lines exactly as I write them, including the ellipses. I have never met an actor who could act out ellipses, but Alan can."[39] One might also investigate how the films' music establishes mood and pace. Although much overused in Columbus' versions, John Williams' theme—a waltz in a minor key—neatly evinces Harry's basic dignity and his sadness. In the third film, which largely abandons Williams' score, a tune reminiscent of Benny Goodman's "Sing Sing Sing" imbues the Boggart lesson scene with a manic energy.

Finally, one might consider both what can and cannot be translated into film, as well as the net gains and losses that arise in any translation. As Benjamin notes in his essay on translation, "In all language and linguistic creations there remains in addition to what can be conveyed something that cannot be communicated; depending on the context in which it appears, it is something that symbolizes or something symbolized."[40] So, on the one hand, we might ask *how*, for example, a film could translate the cumulative effect of the accretion of the details in the novels. And, on the other hand, we might also ask *why* and *whether* effecting such a translation (if it were possible) would be desirable.

The Harry Potter films foreground interpretation, an activity crucial to Rowling's multi-volume mystery. Just as the characters debate the meaning of clues, the films enter into a debate on the meanings of the novels. As *Harry Potter Lexicon* founder and editor Steve Vander Ark puts it, the films are "just expensive fan fiction"[41]—that is, they are another location for creative exploration of what and how Rowling's books mean. Cautioning Harry about the "thickets of wildest guesswork" they will enter as they embark upon interpreting memories about Voldemort's past, Dumbledore admits, "I may be as woefully wrong as Humphrey Belcher, who believed the time was ripe for a cheese cauldron."[42] On the other hand, as Dumbledore says later, it is "[v]ery important" to understand these memories.[43] Viewers, tempted to judge a film on whether it agrees with their interpretation, may pronounce it either a cheese cauldron (if it does not agree) or one that truly understands (if it does agree). However, adaptations need not be divided into good and bad (or into understanding and cheesy). Successful and less successful, certainly. But there should be a wide range of opinions on the merits and demerits of the films. Thanks to their extraordinary popularity and the series' avid fans, there seems to be quite a range. As of July 31, 2007, over 3700 people had joined the Harry Potter-for-Grown-Ups' Movie listserv.[44] Discussions and essays flourish on both the *Leaky Cauldron*'s "Leaky Lounge" pages and *MuggleNet*'s "Chamber of Secrets Forums."[45] The Harry Potter films have inspired—and continue to inspire—debates about meaning and interpretation, reminding readers that each adaptation is an act of translation.

Notes

1. J. K. Rowling, *Harry Potter and the Philosopher's Stone* (London: Bloomsbury, 1997), p. 79.
2. Rowling, *Harry Potter and the Philosopher's Stone*, p. 136.
3. Rowling, *Harry Potter and the Chamber of Secrets* (London: Bloomsbury, 1998), p. 73.
4. Rowling, *Harry Potter and the Philosopher's Stone*, p. 79.
5. *Harry Potter and the Sorcerer's Stone*, dir. Chris Columbus (Warner Bros., 2001).
6. Linda Hutcheon, *A Theory of Adaptation* (New York and London: Routledge, 2006), pp. 121, 127.
7. Qtd. in Hutcheon, p. 123.
8. Gareth McClearn, "Hogwarts and All," *Guardian* October 19, 2001: Retrieved September 24, 2006. http://film.guardian.co.uk/features/featurepages/0,,576530,00.html.
9. Rowling, *Harry Potter and the Philosopher's Stone*, p. 76.
10. Rowling, *Harry Potter and the Goblet of Fire* (London: Bloomsbury, 2000), p. 394.
11. Lizo Mzimba, Conversation with J. K. Rowling and Steve Kloves, *Harry Potter and the Chamber of Secrets* DVD (Warner Home Video, 2003).
12. *Harry Potter and the Sorcerer's Stone* (Warner Bros., 2001).
13. Rosemary Johnston, "The Literary Construction of Harry Potter in Page and Screen-Based Formats," University of Sydney, April 2002, p. 9. Retrieved November 15, 2006. www.crea.uts.edu.au/downloads/harrypotter.pdf.
14. Rowling, *Harry Potter and the Order of the Phoenix* (London: Bloomsbury, 2003), p. 573.
15. Rowling, *Harry Potter and the Order of the Phoenix*, p. 271.
16. Rowling, *Harry Potter and the Order of the Phoenix*, p. 726.
17. Rowling, *Harry Potter and the Prisoner of Azkaban* (London: Bloomsbury, 1999), p. 159.
18. Rowling, *Harry Potter and the Chamber of Secrets*, p. 155.
19. Sarah Lyall, "Working a Darker Kind of Magic." *New York Times*, May 9, 2004, p. 20.
20. Harry Huan, "Sophomore Sorcery: Chris Columbus sets Sail Again for Hogwarts," *Film Journal International* 105.11 (November 2002), p. 8.
21. Rowling, *Harry Potter and the Chamber of Secrets*, p. 222.
22. Hutcheon, p. 121.
23. Jess Cagle, "The first look at Harry." *Time*, 5 November, 2001.
24. Compare with Rowling, *Harry Potter and the Goblet of Fire* (London: Bloomsbury, 2000), pp. 613–614.
25. Witherwings, "Fractured Fairy Tale: Mike Newell's Goblet of Fire," *Scribbulus* 4. Retrieved September 30, 2006 from http://www.the-leaky-cauldron.org/scribbulus/textonly.php?m=essay:204.
26. Witherwings, "Fractured Fairy Tale: Mike Newell's Goblet of Fire," *Scribbulus* 4.
27. Witherwings, "Fractured Fairy Tale: Mike Newell's Goblet of Fire," *Scribbulus* 4.
28. Hutcheon, p. 139.
29. Walter Benjamin, "The Task of the Translator," *Illuminations: Essays and Reflections*, edited by Hannah Arendt, translated by Harry Zohn (1968; New York: Schocken Books, 1985), p. 73.
30. Benjamin, *Illuminations*, p. 76.
31. Rowling, *Harry Potter and the Prisoner of Azkaban*, p. 192.
32. Rowling, *Harry Potter and the Goblet of Fire* (London: Bloomsbury, 2000), p. 376.
33. Rowling, *Harry Potter and the Goblet of Fire*, p. 346.
34. Sarah Park, conversation with Philip Nel, "International Research Society for Children's Literature: 18th Biennial Congress," Kyoto, Japan, Monday August 27, 2007, 1 p.m.
35. Edward Said, *Orientalism* (1978; New York: Vintage Books, 1979), p. 301.
36. Rowling, *Harry Potter and the Prisoner of Azkaban*, p. 288.
37. Harry Huan, "Passing the Wand: Y Tu Mama's Alfonso Cuarón Conjures a Darker Potter," *Film Journal International* 107.7 (July 2004), p. 16

38. Hutcheon, p. 16.
39. Mary McNamara, "The Sorceress' Apprentice," *Los Angeles Times*, 20 Nov. 2005. Retrieved November 21, 2005 from http://www.calendarlive.com/movies/cl-ca-kloves20nov20,0, 5765873.story?coll=cl-movies.
40. Benjamin, *Illuminations*, p, 79.
41. Steve Vander Ark, "Playing in Jo's World," *Prophecy 2007: From Hero to Legend*, Toronto, Ontario, Canada, August 3, 2007.
42. J. K. Rowling, *Harry Potter and the Half-Blood Prince* (London: Bloomsbury, 2005), p. 187.
43. Rowling, *Harry Potter and the Half-Blood Prince*, p. 203.
44. A total of 3737 people, to be precise. *Harry Potter for Grown-Ups-Movie* listserv. Retrieved July 31, 2007 from http://movies.groups.yahoo.com/group/HPFGU-Movie.
45. "The Leaky Lounge: Argent Scrim's Film Emporium," *The Leaky Cauldron*, ed. Melissa Anelli. Retrieved November 4, 2006 from http://www.leakylounge.com/index.php?showforum=51; "Chamber of Secrets: Official Forums of MuggleNet.com," *MuggleNet*, ed. Emerson Spartz. Retrieved November 4, 2006 from http://www.cosforums.com/.

Chapter Sixteen

The Migration of Media
Harry Potter in Print and Pixels[1]

ANNA GUNDER

Readers of all nationalities and cultures have unquestionably been enchanted by J. K. Rowling's words vivifying a vast, fictional world full of strange places, magical creatures, and colorful characters, and where mysterious things keep happening. However, the traditional, printed book is far from the only gateway to Harry's life and whereabouts at Hogwarts School of Witchcraft and Wizardry. Five motion pictures based on the series have been produced by Warner Brothers since 2001, with *Harry Potter and the Order of the Phoenix*, directed by David Yates and released in July 2007 being the latest instalment. Moreover, Warner Brothers licensed Electronic Arts (EA) to develop the Harry Potter computer games and from the very beginning with the first film, *Harry Potter and the Philosopher's Stone* (2001), computer games based on the series have been produced in close association with the film adaptations.[2] Unlike many other computer games produced under similar circumstances, however, the Potter games are explicitly based not only on the film adaptations of Rowling's novels but also directly on the original literary works.[3]

A game based on a popular movie and/or novel will more or less automatically be successful and make money, particularly if there is a dedicated fan community absorbing practically anything that has to do with the object of their devotion. To a significant degree this natural law of the spin-off industry explains why few Harry Potter fans seem able to resist the temptations of interactivity and the games' promises of providing the possibility of stepping into the fictional world, to "be Harry Potter" and "explore Hogwarts." Surely, the popularity of the games partly depends on aggressive marketing and faithful fans, but could it be that the Harry Potter series also are particularly well suited for ludolization, i.e., transposition into game form? Are there specific narrative and/or ludic traits in the novels that fit and support the game form and hence contribute to smooth the migration process from novel to game? Could the novels even be discussed in terms of being inspired by computer games? In the following I address these questions through an analysis of the relation between the first novel in the series, *Harry Potter and the Philosopher's Stone*, and the 2001 PC version of the computer game based on the novel.[4] Although the chapter is restricted to the examples from computer games of the first novel of the Harry Potter series, many aspects of these games also apply to the series as a whole.

The Migration of Media Forms

Texts of literary works do not stay between the covers; quite on the contrary, there is an extensive migration from the pages of the book. Literary fiction is actually an enormous narrative reserve that provides everyone from the film and computer game industries to Broadway composers and comic-strip artists with fictional worlds, characters, and plots.

Of course, media migration does not only concern literary works that leave the printed page as is the case with, for example, the Harry Potter novels. Migration goes into multiple directions (Tosca, 2001; Juul 2001b). Many films and TV series have been novelized, like *Star Wars* and the *Star Trek* series. Computer games based on or inspired by films and TV series are also common: *Star Wars* and the *Star Trek* series, *Enter the Matrix*, and the *X-files Game* are just a few examples.[5] With computer games like *Mortal Combat*, *Lara Croft: Tomb Raider*, and *Pokémon*, it is the other way around: there are films developed from these traditional games. Not surprisingly, some computer games, like *Baldur's Gate* and *Gabriel Knight II: The Beast Within*, have been novelized, moving from game to print. Another example is *Myst*, which now has three novels derived from it, all closely related to the events in the computer game.

Naturally, each medium has its own characteristics that determine what kinds of texts it can store and/or present; one cannot watch a movie in a book or read from a cassette tape.[6] All media have their limitations and possibilities and these affect the works they carry in one way or another, not only with regard to the textual elements (typographic characters, sound, images etc.) and how they are organized but also artistically (McKenzie, 1999, for example, pp. 12–17) This aspect is important to consider in analyses of single works but even more so in comparative analyses of works in different media. A work's media structure is by no means separate from its narrative and/or ludic structure. Instead, the former determines the latter, since it sets the rules and limitations for the kind of narrative and ludic effects that can be created. What is interesting to look at when comparing an adaptation to the work or works that constitute its source of inspiration are the devices and techniques, in both the media structure and narrative and/or ludic structure, that were used "to tell the story."

The traditional definition of the adjective "ludic" is "playful" (Collins, 1998). Here, the term ludic will be used to describe works or sections of works that intentionally invite the user (reader, player, listener, etc.) to solve problems that are part of the fictional world. In other words, the ludic calls for a higher degree of activity on the part of the user than the narrative does. Ludic traits are found in all kinds of works; for example, riddles and the like in novels can be regarded as ludic sequences embedded in a narrative work. Similarly, a detective story, which gives the reader the possibility of trying to figure out who is the murderer, could be characterized as ludic.[7] In computer games, the ludic aspects dominate, with the player having to figure out how to get past obstacles of various kinds and solve problems to experience the work. It should be noted that ludic works may use various navigational principles and be both ergodic (works that require the user to choose actively between alternatives to traverse the work) and nonergodic (Aarseth, 1997, pp. 1, 179). Finally, it is important to stress that describing a work or a part of a work as ludic or narrative in many cases is really a question of perspective, since reception of narrative depends on readers' perspectives. For instance, some readers of Sherlock Holmes', *A Study in Scarlet*, find great pleasure in trying to solve the mystery themselves with the help of the clues (ludic dimension), while others have no such intention but are satisfied to read how Holmes puts the pieces together (narrative dimension).

Game Elements in the Harry Potter Novels

At first, it seems that, given the textual organization and types of user activity required to experience the Harry Potter novels (which are traditional monosequential works intended to be read from the first to the last page), the series has little to do with games. On a theoretical level, however, especially game structure, visuality and pace play an important role.

Games are also a significant thematic element. Competing and participating in games is almost an everyday activity for Harry and the other students, since their actions and behavior influence how their houses fare in the House Cup. For instance, Harry and Ron win five points each for Gryffindor when they save Hermione from the mountain troll, whereas Harry, Neville, and Hermione lose a total of 150 points when they get caught helping Hagrid get rid of Norbert the dragon. Reference to competition among houses and the awarding of points continue to up through the seventh and the final book. Also, the game of Quidditch is crucial to the House Cup, since the winning house is awarded points at each match. In other words, if one is good at Quidditch, one does better in the overall game, i.e., the House Cup. In addition to these official school games, there are ongoing less formal competitions such as the one between Harry and Malfoy, where Malfoy constantly tries to upset Harry's plans and have him punished by the teachers, and the competition between Ginny and Cho for Harry's affections, and connection among the Weasley brothers.

The house system and the emphasis on house rivalry and a specific sports game are not unique features to Harry Potter, but is a defining characteristic of the English school novel genre, "literature about experiences at British private educational institutions, especially boarding schools" (Steege, 2002, p. 141). Although not the first of its kind, Tomas Hughes' *Tom Brown's School Days* (1857) is generally considered to be the genre's progenitor.[8] As David K. Steege (2002) convincingly argues, houses and a prominent sports game are not the only Harry Potter series' traits in common with the boarding school literature. In his comparative analysis of *Harry Potter and the Philosopher's Stone* and *Tom Brown's School Days*, Steege identifies similarities in a variety of aspects, from providing a moral tale to the hero's school preparations and the description of the school as a more or less isolated world (see also Smith, 2003; Iyer, 1999).

There are also significant structural parallels between Rowling's and Hughes' novels in terms of the course of events and the heroes' actions. Harry is 11 when he eagerly enters the venerable Hogwarts School of Witchcraft and Wizardry. During his first year, he makes some best friends (Ron and Hermione) while he is on bad terms with others (Draco Malfoy and his lackeys). He breaks some school rules, which he sometimes gets away with and other times gets caught and punished for. He gains popularity through being good at Quidditch and becomes the hero of his house when saving the Stone. The school principal, Professor Albus Dumbledore, is Harry's mentor and provides help when he finds it necessary. As Steege and others show, this basic structure roughly mirrors the structure of *Tom Brown's School Days* and hence echoes numerous so-called boarding school stories (Steege, 2002, pp. 143–144; Alton, 2003, pp. 149–153; Smith, 2003). Worth noting, however, is that this does not mean that the novel should be considered a conventional school story, but that it has certain key elements in common with the genre, though often transformed or altered to suit the magic world of Hogwarts— "with the added ingredient of fantasy," as Anne Hiebert Alton puts it (Alton, 2003, p. 151; cf. Steege, 2002, p. 156).

This boarding school aspect is particularly relevant when looking at games and game structure in the novel. In a study inspired by Umberto Eco's (1979) analysis of the narrative structures in Ian Fleming's James Bond series, Svedjedal (1980) examines another series, written by Swedish author Louis De Geer called the Singleton series, to show how the hierarchical structure of authorities in the traditional boarding school—and the individual's struggle for various positions within this structure—can be described as a game. This particular game is a precondition for the genre, where the new boy advances in the school hierarchy, gains acceptance, and eventually becomes a protector of younger students (and then house prefect and sometimes even a teacher). Of course, this advancement is not an end to itself, but occurs as a consequence of the protagonist being a fair person and showing true sportsmanship in fighting school villains and injustices.

Thus, boarding school life could be described as a playing field in which various positions are occupied by people who, from the protagonist's point of view (the new boy or girl in the school story), are either helpers or opponents (Greimas, 1986, pp. 172–191). This playing field of positions is also present in the Harry Potter series. Although Harry does not explicitly advance in the school hierarchy, he plays his cards honestly and well and goes from new boy to school hero and even savior. Showdowns with certain teachers and students are a crucial part in this process of development, but equally important are the friendships with other people at Hogwarts. In other words, Harry is surrounded by helpers and opponents in his struggle to manage in the new world of Hogwarts and in the new world of wizards. As early as the first chapter, the readers meet Harry's central protectors Albus Dumbledore, Hagrid, and Professor McGonagall, and they also encounter the name of Harry's worst enemy, Lord Voldemort.

There are obviously aspects of more traditional forms of game and game structure to be found in the novel. Besides the game issues already discussed, Harry and his friends also play a classical board game, namely chess, or more precisely "wizard chess," which is like traditional chess with the difference that the figures are alive (*Philosopher's Stone* 146–147). But playing chess is not always just fun, in fact, a game of wizard chess constitutes one of the obstacles that must be overcome before Harry can save the Philosopher's Stone from Voldemort. Quidditch and the Triwizard Tournament are other games that are central to the narrative.

It is also possible to see resemblances in the novel to more recent game forms and certain types of computer games, especially the adventure game. Just like the principal character of a typical adventure game who is to save a princess, find a treasure, or save a country, Harry has a mission to accomplish. The road to the ultimate task is lined with obstacles that must be cleared and problems that must be solved: leave the Dursleys, win Quidditch matches, get rid of dragons, learn new spells, find Horcruxes etc. This kind of problem-solving is accelerated in the ending chapter of each book. For example, in "Through the Trapdoor," where Harry and his friends face no less than eight obstacles before their final encounter with Lord Voldemort. They must get past (1) Neville, (2) Mrs. Norris, (3) Peeves, (4) Fluffy, and (5) the Devil's Snare, (6) catch a flying key, (7) play a game of chess, and (8) figure out a puzzle involving bottles of poison. Or, as Mary Pharr writes,

For Harry Potter, Hogwarts is a place of tests: some academic, some practical, and some moral. Many of these tests include adventure, danger, and choice—heady stuff that forces Harry to grow up or fail. [...] He must practice the skills that will let him face increasingly arduous trials.

(Pharr, 2002, pp. 58–59)

Furthermore, Hogwarts is a mysterious place full of locked doors and winding corridors. It is a place where the staircases change and what looks like a door might be just a wall:

> There were a hundred and forty-two staircases at Hogwarts: wide, sweeping ones; narrow, rickety ones; some that led somewhere different on a Friday; some with a vanishing step halfway up that you had to remember to jump. Then there were doors that wouldn't open unless you asked politely, or tickled them in exactly the right place, and doors that weren't really doors at all, but solid walls just pretending. It was also very hard to remember where anything was, because it all seemed to move around a lot. The people in the portraits kept going to visit each other and Harry was sure the coats of armour could walk.
>
> (*Philosopher's Stone* 98)

In the beginning, it is far from easy for Harry and his friends to find specific locations like classrooms, but as time goes on, parts of the castle become familiar, while other areas remain unknown.[9] It is not only the architecture and the building as such, however, that pose problems when moving around; Hogwarts is also a locus for fantastical creatures of all kinds. Some of these figures are harmless and even helpful, for example, Nearly Headless Nick and Firenzo, the centaur. Others, like Peeves, play tricks on Harry and his friends, whereas creatures such as the mountain troll and the three-headed dog Fluffy are truly dangerous.

This—the existence of fantastical creatures and the exploration of unknown places where almost anything is possible and one never knows what will happen next—are characteristics of many computer games. For example, a good part of the game *The Legend of Zelda: A Link to the Past* (2002) takes place in castles with locked doors and corridors where one has to get past various foes (monsters, ghosts, soldiers, and many other) by sneaking, running, and/or fighting. In this particular game, the imaginary figures are generally evil, while the humans are less predictable, either offering vital information at times or calling out for soldiers at others. The Harry Potter novels don't rely on interior monologues or character development to move them along. They proceed with action and choice. Many novels lack this pace, action and visuality and thus are not computer game like. Part of their appeal is this inherent screen quality.

The Computer Game *Harry Potter and the Philosopher's Stone*

The relationship between the books and computer games is even clearer when looking at one of the actual games based on the novels. The computer game *Harry Potter and the Philosopher's Stone* was first released in four platform versions in 2001.[10] Since then, games have been released based on *Chamber of*

Secrets, Prisoner of Azkaban, Goblet of Fire, and *Order of the Phoenix.* As with the film, there was close collaboration between the production team and Rowling, who helped them expand and clarify the world of Harry Potter (Goodale, 2001). The PC version of the first game is stored on a CD-ROM and comes with two thin manuals. As a matter of fact, the CD-ROM actually stores three separate games: first, there is the main game, then there is "Broomstick Practice" and "Quidditch League." The two latter, the intragames (Aarseth, Smedstad & Sunnanå, 2003, p. 49), are separate but not independent from the main game, since they only become accessible to the player when she has accomplished certain levels in the main game.[11] For example, further broomstick practice is only possible after completion of Madam Hooch's lesson at the level entitled "Broomstick Training." Hereafter, when speaking of "the game," I will be referring to the main game alone based on the first book.

The game consists of 28 levels, which the player has to go through one by one. In "Level Select" (available in "debug mode"), the levels are named and listed according to five chapters. The official description of the PC game *Harry Potter and the Philosopher's Stone* reads:

> Be Harry Potter™ in Harry Potter and the Sorcerer's Stone™. Learn to master all things magical in a world filled with wizardry, fun and danger. Attend lessons, learn and cast spells, explore Hogwarts™ and its grounds, and take flight to play Quidditch™. Interact with unforgettable characters Ron Weasley™, Hermione Granger™ and Rubeus Hagrid™. Overcome physical, mental and magical challenges to defeat the evil plans of You-Know-Who.[12]

These five sentences suggest the kind of experience the game is intended to offer and what the player will be able to do in the game world. However, it says little about the aim of the game and how it ends; what does one have to do to win? As with many similar computer games, a significant part of the gaming experience consists of conquering obstacles and completing tasks one by one as they appear. In other words, it is about figuring out how to open a door, how to get to the next floor, how to defeat foes, etc. Often, skill is crucial and the player has to learn the right technique to succeed. This is especially salient in, for example, the case of the Quidditch matches, where maneuvering the broomstick is necessary to catch the Golden Snitch. Other examples are the duel with Malfoy, the task to make the three-headed dog, Fluffy, fall asleep, and, of course, the fight with Voldemort. In general, skill is equal to knowledge of the game, timing, and dexterity with the keyboard and mouse.

The player of *Harry Potter and the Philosopher's Stone* quickly realizes that there are things that probably will matter later on or in the end of the game.

For instance, there are four main items to collect: house points, wizard cards, Bertie Bott's Every Flavor Beans, and chocolate frogs (note that these items all originate from the novel). As in the novel, Harry needs to collect house points so that the Gryffindor house will win the House Cup. But, in game reality, the number of collected points has no real significance. No matter what the number of points earned for Gryffindor, Slytherin will always be in first place over Gryffindor during the game. The more points awarded to Gryffindor, the more points the other houses get. It is only at the end when Dumbledore awards Harry 60 extra points that Gryffindor takes the lead and wins, just as in the novel. Thus, in the computer game, the House Cup competition is pre-arranged, a fixed game.

As for the wizard cards, there are total of 25, of which some are well hidden in secret areas while others are much easier to find. The twenty-fifth card, however, is different, since the player can get it only at the very end of the game when Voldemort has been defeated. What is more, to get this last card, with a picture of Harry, the player must have all of the other cards and 250 beans. In other words, the game may end somewhat unsuccessfully if the player has missed out on one or several of the cards, since that prevents her from getting the last card depicting the wizard Harry Potter. It should be noted that this remains unknown to the player until the end.

Bertie Bott's beans are ubiquitous in the game and the player learns early on that it is a good idea to collect as many as possible. At times, they help in the collection of wizard cards, since Fred and George trade cards for beans, but the other things they can be used for are unknown to the player during the game. She does not know, for instance, that 250 of them are required to get the last wizard card. This has little significance, however, and most players tend to collect all the beans they can find just to be on the safe side and to be prepared when and if beans are needed later on. Not knowing the rules of the game is more like what Harry and friends face.

Finally, the chocolate frogs give Harry new stamina when he is low on strength and help him hold out longer before fainting when hit, for example, by vicious spells. If the player is unsuccessful, for example, when Harry has to fight a foe or jump over a chasm, Harry faints and the game is resumed from where it was last saved. Apart from the automatic saving in shifts between levels, the game can only be saved at certain saving spots. These appear in the game world in the form of a floating book, the "Save game book," which mostly turns up in relation to more difficult tasks. In this way, the player does not have to replay an entire level but only a part of it, from the last "Save game book." In the books, by contrast, help comes heavily from friends and connections and is not at all skill based nor a lone enterprise.

In "Voldemort," which is the final level of the game, Harry has to defeat the evil wizard by casting spells on him while avoiding the green counter-spells. When Harry has won the battle, the end sequence starts showing Harry in bed, with Dumbledore sitting by his side. This end sequence, which consists of a series of pictures with captions and looks similar to the intro sequence, also depicts Ron giving Harry a wizard card and the feast in the Great Hall with Harry's smiling face and the caption: "It was the best evening of Harry's life. Better than winning at Quidditch or Christmas, or knocking out mountain trolls. He would never, ever forget tonight." At the very end of the game, Fred and George reveal how they intended to use their bean collection: they have it rain over Professor Snape, an incident that has no correspondence in the novel and would likely not to have been included if Snape's heroics had been revealed yet. Also, it might be mentioned, the circular movement in the novel, with the students returning to the real, domestic, non-magic world, is absent in the game, which ends in the Great Hall at Hogwarts.

Harry Potter and the Philosopher's Stone shares certain traits with computer games referred to as *adventure games*. What characterizes this type of game genre is, in short, that the player explores a fictional world while solving various puzzles (Juul, 2001a, pp. 10, 12; Aarseth, 1997, pp. 100–101).[13] A more detailed definition has been proposed by Mark J. P. Wolf (2001), who describes the adventure game genre thus:

> Games which are set in a "world" usually made up of multiple con-nected rooms, locations, or screens, involving an objective which is more complex than simply catching, shooting, capturing, or escaping, although completion of the objective may involve several or all of these. Objectives usually must be completed in several steps, for example, finding keys and unlocking doors to other areas to retrieve objects needed elsewhere in the game. Characters are usually able to carry objects such as weapons, keys, tools, and so on.
>
> (p. 118)[14]

The early adventure games were text based, originating from William Crowther and Don Woods' *Adventure* (1976), but in the mid-1980s, the graphical interface made its appearance in the game world and by the end of the decade, text-based games were no longer being published.[15] Examples of well-known adventure games are *Zork* (a text-based trilogy, 1981, 1982), *Myst* (Cyan, 1993) *Gabriel Knight 3—Blood of the Sacred, Blood of the Damned* (Sierra, 2000), and *Grim Fandango* (Lucas Arts, 1998). Searching the corri-dors and rooms at Hogwarts and walking around in the garden looking for secret areas are examples of adventure game elements in the game *Harry Potter and the Philosopher's Stone*.

The game has traits of other genres as well. Quidditch and the "Quidditch League," which in themselves are games, function in different ways compared to the main game and cannot be categorized as adventure games. Thus, to a certain extent, the *Harry Potter and the Philosopher's Stone* game resembles games that are "adaptations of existing sports or variations of them" (Wolf, 2001, p. 132), that is, so-called sports games. Of course, the fact that Quidditch is a fictitious game makes it a special case. In essence, however, these Quidditch matches simply consist of Harry chasing the Golden Snitch while avoiding Bludgers and the other players, and there is very little difference at the level of "Winged Keys," where Harry is supposed to catch a key while flying on his broomstick. This means that the Quidditch sections can hardly be described as sports games.[16] Instead, they have certain traits of action games, which according to Jesper Juul have the following characteristics:

> A player controls an object/an actor against some enemies; a score is kept; the game is real-time and requires fast reflexes; the player has a fixed amount of lives (typically three); the game is based on successive levels of increasing difficulty; the game (or just the title) places the player's action as part of a minimal narrative.
>
> (2001a, p. 8)

In recent years, a genre has formed that includes hybrids between action and adventure games, the so-called action-adventure games. The genre is a broad one, comprising both games with a strong action bias (like the first person shooters *Half-Life* and *Star Trek: Voyager Elite Force*) and games with a more balanced mix of action and adventure (such as *Resident Evil 2*, *Silent Hill*, and the series *Alone in the Dark*) (Luban, 2002). In fact, *Harry Potter and the Philosopher's Stone* is often described as belonging to the genre of action-adventure games (of the second type).[17] A more fine-tuned genre description of the game, however, is provided by Randi Sluganski at the site *Just Adventure*:

> *Harry Potter and the Sorcerer's Stone* is not an adventure game in the purest sense of the term. There are no inventory items to be used to solve puzzles and the only point-and-clicking involved is when using your wand to cast a spell. There is though plenty of "adventuring" as Hogwarts School of Witchcraft and Wizardry must be searched from top to bottom for secret passages and clues to solve the mystery. So is it an action game then? Not really even though there are jumping puzzles, spell casting and sequences that involve racing your Nimbus 2000 against Draco Malfoy. Maybe it is a sports game since you must master the Quidditch position of Seeker and hunt down the Golden Snitch. Nope—sorry. Instead, *Harry Potter and the Sorcerer's Stone* is a conglomeration of all of these genres.
>
> (*Just Adventure*)

This brings to mind the novel *Harry Potter and the Philosopher's Stone*, which, has traits of several genres (see Alton chapter in this book).

Suspense and Curiosity

In fictional works of all kinds, there is generally a narrative drive that compels the user to continue reading a novel, watching a film, listening to an audio book, etc. Basically, this narrative drive lies in arousing the user's interest in the unfolding discourse and what it will disclose. In other words, the user's interest is directed toward untold events. From a chronological point of view, however, these may be future events answering the question "What next?" or past events addressing the question "Why?" In traditional narratology, the established terms for these narrative drives are *suspense* (future-oriented) and *curiosity* (past-oriented), both of which involve events in their chronological rather than narrative order (i.e., story level, not discourse level). Another important narrative device is the *surprise*, which, as the name indicates, is an unexpected event of some kind (for an exhaustive exposition of the concepts of suspense and curiosity, see Svedjedal, 2000, chapter 2).

Naturally, the novel *Harry Potter and the Philosopher's Stone* uses these traditional strategies to maintain the reader's interest and make her read to the end. The principal questions are: will Harry be able to leave the Dursleys? What will it be like at Hogwarts? Will Harry make new friends at Hogwarts and will he keep up with the other students in his class? Does Harry have what it takes to become a wizard—is he really a wizard? Who are Harry's friends and who are his enemies? Will he be able to stand up to his enemies? What strange things are going on at Hogwarts? Will Gryffindor win the House Cup? Also, Harry's past and his parents are important questions: what were his parents like and why were they killed?

In addition to these main issues that the reader wants to know more about, each chapter uses this method to create interest in its events. For example, in the chapter, "Norbert the Norwegian Ridgeback," the readers wonder why Hagrid is reading about dragons (curiosity) and whether Harry and Hermione will manage to get rid of Norbert (suspense). They are surprised when, for example, Malfoy is suddenly at the window or when Professor McGonagall appears in the corridor (surprise). In the novel series as a whole, suspense, curiosity, and surprise create an effective and tight narrative pattern that quickly engages the reader and keeps her interest in a firm grip until the last page. Also, as a consequence of the work being mainly scenic, the reader's experiences often appear to coincide with the characters' feelings; like the reader, Harry, Ron, and Hermione wonder about Hagrid's or Sirius' whereabouts and they are taken by surprise when people show up unexpectedly.

Similarly, the driving force of the computer games lies in the effects of suspense, curiosity, and surprise. A crucial difference is that in mainly ergodic works, including a computer game like *Harry Potter and the Philosopher's*

Stone, these effects apply primarily to the user's activity. Instead of reading about problem-solving, lessons in magic, and close encounters with trolls, the player herself is supposed to solve problems, take lessons, and fight trolls. This means that, unlike the reader of the novel who wonders if Harry and Hermione will manage to sneak up to the top of the tower, the players of the game ask themselves, "Will *I* manage to sneak up to the top of the tower with Norbert?" Many of the main questions of the novel are also found in the game, which is quite natural considering the similarities of events, actions, characters, and setting. What will it be like at Hogwarts? Will Harry be able to win the fights against his enemies? Who are Harry's friends and enemies? What is the mystery? Will Gryffindor win the House Cup?

A crucial difference, however, lies precisely in what was just described: in the game, Harry is often a player character directed by the actual player, which makes her feel more present in the fictional world and responsible for what happens there. If, for instance, Harry fails to open a door or defeat a foe, it is because of the player and not the fictitious character Harry. Worth taking into account here is also the fact that the dignity of the questions above depends to a great deal on the player's acquaintance with the novel (or another work inspired by it). A player who has read the novel before playing the game has different expectations about what will happen at Hogwarts than a player who only plays the game.

As already mentioned, there are several main novelistic elements that are not accounted for in the game. Of the principal questions in the novel, the followings are not addressed in the game: will Harry be able to leave the Dursleys? Will Harry make new friends at Hogwarts and will he keep up with the other students in his class? Does Harry have what it takes to become a wizard—is he really a wizard? Last but not least is the question of what Harry's parents were like and why they were killed.

There are principally two explanations as to why these questions have been left out of the game. First, the main reason is simply that they are described and function in chapters of the novel that are ignored in the game, typically, Harry leaving the Dursleys. Second, questions that have to do with Harry's personal development and his past have either been left out or are treated only superficially in the game. No player wonders if Harry will make new friends at Hogwarts or if he will learn about his past. Similarly, there are no uncertainties as to whether Harry will become a wizard, since Harry pretty much begins brandishing a magic wand right away.

A problem and its solution, or, to use Espen Aarseth's terms, *aporia* and *epiphany* (Aarseth, 1997, 1999), is a fundamental figure in adventure games, where the aporia is "local and tangible, usually a concrete, localized puzzle whose solution eludes us" (Aarseth, 1997, p. 124) while the epiphany is "the sudden revelation that replaces the aporia" (p. 91). In *Harry Potter and the Philosopher's Stone* and other games of the kind, the alternation between aporia and epiphany is a ludic drive that motivates the player to continue playing the game. Having managed to escape the troll, for example, the player is eager to take on the next challenge. This becomes obvious when considering how hard it is to stop playing once you have started. If you're stuck in aporia, you want epiphany before quitting, but then, when epiphany is obtained, you have to continue to the next aporia "just to see what it's like," and before you know it, you're craving for another epiphany: "I'll just do one more." In essence, the player constantly lacks information, wondering, when facing aporia, how to accomplish epiphany and, when facing epiphany, what the next aporia consists of and what it will be like.

In the game, suspense also works on a different level due to this alternation between aporia and epiphany. Furthermore, the player may wonder why certain things have to be done or why they happen. "Why do you collect wizard cards?" "How important is the number of house points collected?" and "Why does Hagrid give you a flute?" are questions that arouse the player's curiosity. Curiosity also comes into play when the player fails to solve a puzzle and has to try again: "Why did I faint?" "What did I do wrong?" Surprise is an equally important effect of the game when, for example, doxys attack you out of the blue and gnomes suddenly come running toward you. As in the novel, suspense, curiosity, and surprise are intertwined and work closely together: when entering the first cave in "Fireseed Caves," the player asks herself what will happen here (suspense), a doxy attacks (surprise), and Harry faints (curiosity: what did I do wrong?).

So, although dissimilar in many ways, the novel *Harry Potter and the Philosopher's Stone* and the computer game of the same title function very similarly when it comes to capturing the user's interest and maintaining it. The user effects of suspense, curiosity, and surprise are effective tools successfully applied by both works. Worth mentioning is that the effect of these effects, so to speak, varies depending on the user's acquaintance with the work. For obvious reasons, the surprising effect of the attacking doxy in the example above will peak the first time and then, provided that the section is played more than once, diminish as the player's familiarity with the section increases. Or, to use Torben Grodal's words, the surprise will be transformed into a "suspense-like coping anticipation" (pp. 149). Of course, the same phenomenon occurs in novels—the second time around the reader knows when the "unsuspected" visitor will arrive, and the surprise is transformed into, if you will, suspense-like anticipation.

Finally, players may be eager not only to give their own skills a trial over and over again, but many of them take an interest in the game's technical design (the graphics, sound, etc.) and make comparisons with other computer games. In computer games that are adaptations, like the one analyzed here, we might suspect that comparisons with other works that have the same source of inspiration would also be common. In the case of *Harry Potter and the Philosopher's Stone*, the players of the game are often readers of the novel as well as viewers of the film. Hence, they compare the different works more or less automatically. Someone who reads the novel first may, for instance, look at how passages of the novel have been adopted into the film and the game. This may give rise to what could be called transmedial expectancy, when anticipation of what something is like in another media form functions as a driving force and entices the reader also to become a listener, player, and/or viewer.

The computer games based on the Harry Potter series constitute an intrinsic part of the Harry Potter phenomenon with millions of players all over the world. The games contribute to the overall experience of Harry Potter's world and adventures—for many people "being" Harry Potter or one of the other characters and exploring Hogwarts through completing tasks and overcoming obstacles is as important as reading the novels and watching the films. Early on in the series when Dudley gets a new computer and 16 computer games for his birthday Harry secretly hopes to "have a go" on the computer, but he never gets the chance (*Philosopher's Stone* 20–22). Instead of playing and hence exploring the virtual worlds of the computer games with their mysteries, dangers, and odd creatures and characters, Harry soon finds himself in the wizard world, in an environment and among people that, just like in most computer games, are quite different from what we are normally used to. In a way you could even say that Harry is living, not playing, a game when facing real adventures, puzzles, and dangerous situations. As described above this world and the things happening there in many ways recall aspects typical of certain types of computer games, which, in combination with stylistic and narrative traits such as a strong protagonist, scenic narration, spatial awareness, visualty, and high pace, suggest that the novels have been inspired by the modern mediascape they are such an important part of.

Notes

1. This chapter expands the arguments developed in my article "Harry Ludens: Harry Potter and the Philosopher's Stone as a Novel and Computer Game" (Gunder, 2004a), which constitutes a part of my thesis: "Hyperworks: On Digital Literature and Computer Games" (Gunder, 2004b).
2. In this chapter, the term "computer game" denotes all electronic games using computers in a wide sense, i.e., not only games played on personal computers but also so-called console games, video games, and arcade games. (cf. Juul, 2001a, p. 8.)
3. When Electronic Arts announced that it had obtained the rights from Warner Brothers to develop the computer games, it was clearly stated that the games would be based on both the novels and the films:

    Electronic Arts [...] said it will pay Warner Bros. for a license to develop and market games based on the first four books in the seven-part series written by British author J. K. Rowling. [...] Electronic Arts said it also will base its games on the film that Warner Bros. plans to release in 2001, as well as subsequent films distributed during the tenure of the agreement.

    (*Wall Street Journal* 2000, p. A.4)

Naturally, there are obvious and striking resemblances between the *Harry Potter and the Philosopher's Stone* game and film. The present discussion, however, primarily concerns the relation between the novels and the games.

4. The novel was published in the U.S. as *Harry Potter and the Sorcerer's Stone* (1998). The game, the novel, and the film that I refer to are all entitled *Harry Potter and the Philosopher's Stone*, but the American title appears in a few quotes. For a discussion of the British and the American versions of the novels, see Philip Nel (2002).

5. Of course, these works have been transposed to other media forms as well; *Star Wars*, for example, has conquered practically the entire media sphere, with everything from dolls and posters to printed screenplays, radio dramatizations, and radio dramatization book adaptations.

6. All man-made products can be seen as systems of signs. All these sign systems (consisting, to mention only a few examples, of alphanumeric characters, sound, still pictures, and moving pictures) can be considered texts that present works. Thus, by "text," I refer not only to texts consisting of typographic characters but also to computer games, web pages, films, etc. (Gunder, 2004b, pp. 166–167.)

7. Cf. Marie-Laure Ryan's (2001) discussion of games in literature and literary theory (pp. 176–191). In its widest sense, the understanding of play and game in traditional literature applies to linguistic style, figures, form, etc. (see, for example Burke, 1994 and Motte, 1995).

8. Actually, Hughes' work was preceded by at least 60 school stories (Kirkpatrick, 2000, pp. 1–2, 189; Gathorne-Hardy, 1977, pp. 77–78, 211; Reed, 1964, pp. 17, 26).

9. As Julia Eccleshare notes, the special character of the Hogwarts building gives Rowling great flexibility and the possibility to "somewhat indiscriminately" add new dimensions (such as secret passages, hidden chambers, etc.) whenever the plots demand it (Eccleshare, 2002, p. 56).

10. The versions differ as a consequence of the developers wanting each version to make maximum use of its technology (Gibbon, 2001). The four platforms are: PC, Play Station One, Game Boy Color, and Game Boy Advance. It should be noted that the 2001 game was ported to the Mac in 2002. Moreover, in 2003 a new version of the game, quite different from the 2001 versions, was released for Nintendo GameCube, Sony PlayStation 2, and Microsoft Xbox.

11. For purely practical reasons, the player, the user, and the reader will all be referred to as "she" in the following.

12. Presentation on EA Games website downloaded in April 2004 from Harry Potter, http://hpgames.ea.com/main.html. The webpage is no longer available online but the presentation is similar to the one on the case of the game.

13. It should also be mentioned that adventure games, especially if they are text based, also sort under the notion of "interactive fiction." (see Aarseth, 1997, p. 48; Juul, 2001a, pp. 10–12).

14. It should be noted that Wolf distinguishes between the adventure game genre and the puzzle game genre, and that he would place *Harry Potter and the Philosopher's Stone* in both of these, as well as in what he calls the adaptation genre (Wolf, 2001, pp. 115, 116, 129).

15. It is important to remember that although they no longer exist in the commercial arena, the text-based games live on in a substantial subculture (Juul, 2001a, p. 11). For an exhaustive history of the adventure game genre, see, for example, Aarseth, 1997, pp. 97–111.

16. A separate computer game entirely devoted to the sport of Quidditch, *Harry Potter: Quidditch World Cup*, was released in 2003. This game, which has both single player competition and multiplayer competition where "players compete head-to-head," is generally categorized as a sports game: "Take Flight and Compete for the Cup in *Harry Potter: Quidditch World Cup* Game from EA" (EA Games Press Release 2003).

17. For example, the game site *Mobygames—Harry Potter and the Sorcerer's Stone*, classify the game as action/adventure.

References

Aarseth, E. "Aporia and Epiphany in *Doom* and *The Speaking Clock*: The Temporality of Ergodic Art." *Cyberspace Textuality: Computer Technology and Literary Theory*. Ed. M-L. Ryan. Bloomington & Indianapolis, IN: Indiana University Press, 1999. 31–41.

———. *Cybertext: Perspectives on Ergodic Literature*. Baltimore, MD & London: The Johns Hopkins University Press, 1997.

———. S. M. Smedstad and L. Sunnanå. "A Multi-Dimensional Typology of Games." *Level Up. Digital Games Research Conference*. Eds. M. Copier and J. Raessens. November 4–6, 2003, Utrecht University. Utrecht: Faculty of Arts, Utrecht University. 48–53.

Alton, A. H. "Generic Fusion and the Mosaic of *Harry Potter*." In *Critical Perspectives on Harry Potter*. Ed. E. Heilman. New York & London: RoutledgeFalmer, 2003. 141–162.

Burke, R. E. *The Games of Poetics: Ludic Criticism and Postmodern Fiction*. American University Studies, Series III Comparative Literature vol. 47. New York: Peter Lang, 1994.

Collins English Dictionary, 4th edn. "Ludic." London: HarperCollins, 1998.

Doyle, A. C. *The Oxford Sherlock Holmes: A Study in Scarlet*. Oxford: Oxford University Press, 1993.

EA Games Press Release April 29, 2003. "Take Flight and Compete for the Cup in *Harry Potter: Quidditch World Cup* Game from EA." Retrieved November 2007, from http://info.ea.com/news/pr/pr310.doc.

Eccleshare, Julia, *A Guide to the Harry Potter Novels*, Contemporary Classics of Children's Literature (London & New York: Continuum, 2002).

Eco, U. *The Role of the Reader: Explorations in the Semiotics of Texts*. Advances in Semiotics. Bloomington, Indiana University Press, 1979.

Gathorne-Hardy, J. *The Old School Tie: The Phenomenon of the English Public School*. New York: The Viking Press, 1977.

Gibbon, D. "Potter Game Targets Youngsters." *BBC News*, November 16, 2001. Retrieved November 2007, from http://bbc.co.uk/1/hi/entertainment/reviews/1658677.stm.

Goodale, G. "To be Harry and Live in his World." *Christian Science Monitor* 93, 140 (June 14, 2001). Retrieved November 2007, from www.csmonitor.com/2001/0614/ p16s1.html.

Greimas, A. J. *Sémantique structurale: Recherche de méthode*. Formes sémiotiques. Paris: Presses Universitaires de France, 1986.

Grodal, T. "Stories for Eye, Ear, and Muscles: Video Games, Media, and Embodied Experiences." *The Video Game Theory Reader*. Eds. M. J. P. Wolf & B. Perron. New York & London: Routledge, 2003. 129–155.

Gunder, A. "Harry Ludens: *Harry Potter and the Philosopher's Stone* as a Novel and Computer Game." *Human IT* 7:2 (2004a): 1–137. Retrieved November 2007, from www.hb.se/bhs/ith/2-7/ag.pdf.

———. "Hyperworks: On Digital Literature and Computer Games." Publications from the Section for the Sociology of Literature at the Department of Literature, Uppsala University, 48. Dissertation, Uppsala University. Uppsala, 2004b.

Harry Potter and the Philosopher's Stone. DVD, Warner Brothers. 2001.

Harry Potter and the Philosopher's Stone. KnowWonder Digital Mediaworks, Electronic Arts. 2001.

Hughes, T. *Tom Brown's School Days*. Leipzig: Bernhard Tauchnitz, 1858 (first publ. 1857).

Iyer, P. "The Playing Fields of Hogwarts." *New York Times Book Review*. October 10, 1999: 39.

Just Adventure/Review: Harry Potter. Retrieved November 2007, from www.justadventure.com/reviews/HarryPotter/HarryPotter.shtm.

Juul, J. "A Clash between Game and Narrative: A Thesis on Computer Games and Interactive Fiction." Institute of Nordic Language and Literature. University of Copenhagen, 2001a.

———. "Games Telling Stories? A Brief Note on Games and Narratives." *Game Studies* 1:1 (2001b). Retrieved November 2007, from www.gamestudies.org/0101/juul-gts.

Kirkpatrick, R. J. *The Encyclopaedia of School Stories. 2, The Encyclopedia of Boys' School Stories*. Aldershot: Ashgate, 2000.

The Legend of Zelda: A Link to the Past. Flagship, Nintendo. 2002.

Luban, P. "Designing and Integrating Puzzles in Action-Adventure Games." *Gamasutra*. December 6, 2002. Retrieved November 2007, from www.gamasutra.com/features/20021206/luban_01.htm.

McKenzie, D. F. *Bibliography and the Sociology of Texts.* Cambridge: Cambridge University Press, 1999.

Mobygames—Harry Potter and the Sorcerer's Stone. Retrieved November 2007, from www.mobygames.com/game/sheet/gameId,5416/.

Motte, W. F. *Playtexts: Ludics in Contemporary Literature.* Stages vol. 3. Lincoln, NE & London: University of Nebraska Press, 1995.

Nel, P. "You say 'Jelly,' I say 'Jell-O'? Harry Potter and the Transfiguration of Language." *The Ivory Tower and Harry Potter: Perspectives on a Literary Phenomenon.* Ed. L. A. Whited. Columbia, MO & London: University of Missouri Press, 2002. 261–284.

Pharr, M. "In Medias Res, Harry Potter as Hero-in-Progress." *The Ivory Tower and Harry Potter: Perspectives on a Literary Phenomenon.* Ed. L. A. Whited. Columbia, MO & London: University of Missouri Press, 2002. 53–66.

Reed, J. R. *Old School Ties: The Public Schools in British Literature.* New York: Syracuse University Press, 1964.

Rowling, J. K. *Harry Potter and the Philosopher's Stone.* London: Bloomsbury, 1997.

Ryan, M-L. *Narrative as Virtual Reality: Immersion and Interactivity in Literature and Electronic Media.* Parallax: Re-visions of Culture and Society. Baltimore, MD & London: Johns Hopkins University Press, 2001.

Smith, K. M. "Harry Potter's Schooldays: J. K. Rowling and the British Boarding School Novel," *Reading Harry Potter: Critical Essays.* Contributions to the Study of Popular Culture 78. Ed. G. L. Anatol. Westport, CT: Praeger, 2003. 69–87.

Steege, D. K. "Harry Potter, Tom Brown, and the British School Story: Lost in Transit?" *The Ivory Tower and Harry Potter: Perspectives on a Literary Phenomenon.* Ed. L. A. Whited. Columbia, MO & London: University of Missouri Press, 2002. 140–156.

Svedjedal, J. *The Literary Web: Literature and Publishing in the Age of Digital Production. A Study in the Sociology of Literature.* Acta Bibliothecæ Regiæ Stockholmiensis, 62. Publications from the Section for the Sociology of Literature at the Department of Literature, Uppsala University, 42. Stockholm: Kungl. Biblioteket, 2000.

——. *Spela spelet. Om Louis De Geers Singletonböcker.* Litteratur och samhälle. Meddelande från Avd. för litteratursociologi vid Litteraturvetenskapliga institutionen i Uppsala 16:3 (1980).

Tosca, S. P. "Role-playing in Multiplayer Environments: *Vampire: The Masquerade. Redemption.*" Presentation at the conference "Computer Games & Digital Textualities," IT University of Copenhagen, March 2001. Retrieved November 2007, from www.it-c.dk/people/tosca/multiplayer.html.

Wall Street Journal (Eastern edition). "Electronic Arts Gets Rights to Develop Harry Potter Games." August 11, 2000: p. A.4.

Wolf, M. J. P. "Genre and the Video Game." *The Medium of the Video Game.* Ed. M. J. P. Wolf. Austin, TX: University of Texas Press, 2001. 113–134.

Chapter Seventeen

Writing Harry's World
Children Co-authoring Hogwarts

ERNEST L. BOND AND NANCY L. MICHELSON

You should turn up the volume when you read.

Joe DeGeorge of *Harry and the Potters*

When J. K. Rowling made the announcement during an interview on October 19, 2007 that Dumbledore was gay, the Internet erupted with activity. Fans posted to cyberspace on forums, blogs, and vlogs, some wanting to give away their books, others praising Rowling for outing a prominent character. Scholars on the childlit listserv commenced a four-day passionate discussion about authorial intent and other implications of the announcement. *The Leaky Cauldron* website held a blog interview with GLAAD (the Gay and Lesbian Alliance Against Defamation). The wizard rock band Justin Finch-Fletchley & The Sugar Quills posted a new song "Dumbledore is Gay" on *MySpace*. Dozens of fans were inspired to write new works of fan fiction about Dumbledore and Grindelwald. Though this announcement was a rather big incentive for new riffs on the Harry Potter storylines, it is actually indicative of the way popular fictional narratives might be understood in the age of Web 2.0: as ever expanding networks of story.

In the first edition of this book (2003), this chapter explored the theoretical underpinnings for the participatory authoring of literary worlds. We then offered some examples of readers writing in response to the Harry Potter series. Although Rowling's series has now reached its conclusion, the Harry Potter stories are obviously still inspiring young people to create stories set in the world of Hogwarts. Fans of the series are actively creating and extending histories, characters, and storylines, which arise from the series but then take on their own lives.

In this chapter, we utilize Rebecca Tushnet's definition of fan fiction: "any kind of [written] creativity that is based on an identifiable segment of popular culture ... and is not produced as 'professional' writing" (1997, p. 651). According to Henry Jenkins (1992), fan fiction is merely a contemporary version of the age-old human desire to tell stories. Originally enacted as a tradition of orally sharing experiences valued by members of a culture, retellings changed over time, as each storyteller added personal touches to the existing narrative. Thus, narrative might be viewed as a way for individuals to find a personal niche in experience shared with other members of their society. Jenkins asserts that today, our common narratives no longer originate with the lived experience of the members of a society; our shared heroes and villains and their challenges and victories are primarily created and distributed by publishing houses and production studios. Technological development has gradually transformed the shared experience of story into a producer–receiver dynamic. With the space between storyteller and story recipient thus growing increasingly more distant, it is not surprising that story recipients seek greater agency for their own participation in the story.

Although fan fiction has sprung from other popular narratives over the past several decades, the volume and scope of Harry Potter fan fiction is unprecedented. In particular, the Harry Potter books have inspired many youth and young adults actively to create and extend characters and storylines from the world of Hogwarts. In the original chapter we looked through a lens that included these foundational points:

- literacy is a constructivist process of meaning-making,
- reading and writing are intricately connected processes,
- technology mandates an expansion of the constructs of text, reading, and even literacy.

In this revisiting of the chapter we borrow from several other lines of investigation into the concept of story. First, from Bakhtin (1982) we have the concept that in any narrative there are echoes of and inferences to other storylines. Second, from cognitive science we borrow the concept that blended stories often lead to a cascading interconnected network of story (Turner 2003). Finally, from narrative theory we take the idea that this network of connections (giving events coherence, motivation, closure, and intelligibility) reconstructed by the reader, demonstrates a transmedial existence (Ryan 2007b).

It is generally accepted among reading theorists that the act of reading is constructivist: meaning unfolds as a reader draws upon personal knowledge and experience to guide developing understanding of the text being read. Langer (1991) describes the reader's envisionment of a text, (as opposed to understanding) as "an act of becoming" (p. 5). While understanding implies a single, static response to text, envisionment is a dynamic process in which meaning and reaction change as the reader progresses through a text. Thus, according to Langer, readers may be "out and stepping into an envisionment" (p. 6), as they use their own existing knowledge and the surface features of the text to enter the narrative world. A reader is "in and moving through an envisionment" (p. 6) when prior knowledge and the emerging envisionment involves greater immersion in the deep structures of the text. "Stepping back and rethinking what one knows" (p. 6) occurs when the reader reflects on what has been read, in order to consider how prior understandings might have changed as a result of the reading experience. Finally, when a reader is "stepping out and objectifying the experience" (p. 7) s/he is reacting to what has been read, or even the experience of reading itself.

Terry Rogers and her colleagues build on Iser's (1978) conception of the indeterminate nature of literary works, asserting that interpretation is not a static activity; rather, it involves ongoing dialogue and constantly evolving interactions (Rogers, O'Neil, & Jasinski, 1995). Unfortunately, studies of adolescent and pre-adolescent text constructions in school settings have revealed that the reading of text often occurs as a discrete act; indeed, Langer (1993) found that of her four stances, adolescent readers rarely took the third stance—applying their envisionment to experience outside the text—under study. Rather than taking advantage of the potential for expanding meaning development, for young readers in school situations, textual study tends to establish an endgame: the purpose of envisioning the text often remains rooted in that text. Once the reading is complete, the envisionment ends abruptly. The reader's experience of the text often remains encapsulated, largely isolated from other meaning-making in the readers' lives.

By contrast, McArdle (2003) argues that a natural response for readers is to wonder when they read—about character motivations and background, or what would have happened if the plot had moved in a different direction. Fan fiction allows such internal wondering to find external form. Cadernos (retrieved November 1, 2007) recognizes fan fiction writing as a form of theorizing about the narrative gaps that exist in any story. The appeal for fan fiction writers is their ability to appropriate the story and its characters for their own purposes, filling in the narrative gaps they find according to their personal preferences for character relationships and plot. Although some view such appropriation as negative (the popular novelist Anne Rice, for example, is vehemently opposed to any fan fiction spin-offs from her work), Jenkins (1992) might argue that the phenomenon represents an electronic return to not only the oral tradition, but also to the historical print tradition of adapting history and folklore with new form—the most obvious example being the work of Shakespeare.

The popularity of the Harry Potter series has shifted reading for many young readers from the encapsulated textual experiences of their classrooms to the more personally connected reading experience of an envisionment.

Because children and adolescents are reading these texts primarily outside of the classroom, they are establishing their own envisionments. Facilitated by the increasing accessibility of the Internet, these young readers-turned-authors have been able to co-construct a web of meaning-making as they find a wide audience for their writings. How ironic, given the trend for techno-logical advances to increase the distance between story-teller and story-recipient! We would argue that the Internet has expanded available modes of response: when the first edition of this book was published, most Harry Potter fan fiction was narrative. In the few short years since then, new technologies have emerged, promoting the addition of blogs, vlogs, song fic, video trailers, RPGs, and various combinations of the above.

However, the expanding influence of technology in modern society has not been universally viewed as a positive influence on literacy. Carter (2000) expresses the fears felt by many book-lovers that traditional print will eventu-ally be displaced, and indeed, disappear altogether, when she laments the dis-appearance—sometimes gradual, sometimes not so gradual—of books from school media centers. She finds it problematic that this shift signals a growing emphasis on children's reading of informational text, at the expense of their reading of literature. Citing the empowerment that innumerable authors—Richard Wright and Annie Dillard, for example—found in their early reading of literature, as they made connections between themselves and the characters and situations they encountered. Carter, echoing Jenkins, sees an increasing need for children to find such personal connections. This is especially import-ant, she argues, in an era of "virtual friends; e-commerce… and family dynamics … [that seem] more real on television talk shows than in their own kitchens" (p. 19). For Carter, an essential value of literature in a technological society is the opportunity that story provides for children to recognize the "connections between individuals and society" (p. 19)—the same connections experienced in the early oral tradition.

Bishop (2000) also champions literature as a significant foundation for the development of values, since literature encodes a society's history and belief systems, and provides a source of hope and comfort. Literary narrative is seen by Bishop, Carter, and many others as an important form of text, for its role in the reader's constantly shifting understandings of self and the world (Bruner, 1986). Indeed, Bronwyn Davies (1993) has suggested that we not only read and write storylines, but also live them. Both fictional texts and lived story-lines allow us to envision possibilities for what we may become. Our story-lines are socially constructed entities, which, in turn, inspire the types of fictions we create for and about ourselves. They suggest possibilities for what we may become, and offer us cultural storylines that guide our presentation of self. Readers of literature vicariously experience dilemmas that allow them to make judgments, test the results of decisions, and imagine alternatives, and in doing so, they prepare themselves to respond to moral issues.

When the first Harry Potter book was published, fan fiction as an online experience was still in its infancy. Today it takes hours of investigating to begin to grasp the extent of the variations of storyline being produced. There are hundreds of thousands of pieces of fan fiction, with multiple genres of story from drama to horror to slash. Some of these stories take place in the times and places found in the books; others are set in the past and follow the Founders of Hogwarts, or in a future in which Harry is an adult. There are now sites that are devoted to fan fiction entirely about a single character, and other sites that focus on romantic pairings including both the ones you might expect (GinnyPotter.com for example specializes in stories that emphasize the Ginny/Harry relationship), and ones that seem farfetched but are nonetheless quite popular (such as the pairing of Draco and Hermione).

The most popular piece of fan fiction on the *Harry Potter Fan Fiction* website, at the time of this writing, was a novel called *Daddy* by blondebouncingferret (retrieved November 1, 2007). This story takes place a few years after Harry and friends have graduated from Hogwarts. It turns out that Ron and Hermione had a major goodbye celebration the night before Ron left to go and train as an Auror. Two years pass by before Ron and Harry return on vacation (Ron with a new girlfriend) only to find out that there were some major changes while they were gone.

"So what's been going on here since we left? Anything interesting?" Ron asked, taking in his surroundings, glad to be home.

"Well actually—" Hermione began.

"Harry!"

Ginny almost ran down the stairs. Her activity for the day was to keep the lounge free of anyone but her brother and Hermione, so her friend could, without interruption, break the news to Ron that he was a dad. "I think I hear mum calling, let's go into the kitchen," she said, hurrying over to his chair.

"I didn't hear anything," Harry said, looking through the kitchen door, where Molly was currently fiddling with something on the counter.

"Well I have great hearing, much like a Niffler," Ginny said.

"It's okay Ginny, he can stay, I don't mind," Hermione said softly. Ginny breathed in deeply and sat on the edge of the sofa.

"What's going on?" Ron asked, feeling as though the girls were keeping something from him. They looked guilty and a little scared. What had they done?

"I have something to tell you, Ron ... what I mean is, show you ... you should know," Hermione mumbled. She had been practicing this speech for weeks, why couldn't she get the words out right? It wasn't like her to forget what she studied.

"Just spit it out!" Ron said, his face red with exasperation.

"Marmee?"

Everyone froze.

From the open den door came a wobbling Hannah, carrying her toy cow, Buttercup, by his leg. "Hungy! Marmee, hungy!" she cried, rubbing her little stomach.

"Oh, Bear," Hermione whispered softly. Oh no, no, no, no. This wasn't supposed to happen this way! "Grandma is making you some nice milk," Hermione said, her face as red the bow around Buttercup's neck. "Aunt Ginny will take you when it's ready."

Hannah smiled and planted herself down on the carpet, looking up at the two strange men. One with sheet-white face, the other with a mixture between green and white.

"That counts as something interesting," Harry said, removing his glasses to clean them. He replaced them on his face and then, upon realizing [sic] that the child—Hermione's child—had a mop of bushy red hair and a nose full of freckles, looked straight at Ron, open-mouthed.

Ron looked hurt. Deeply hurt that Hermione was a mother. How long had it been before she found someone new? Feeling as though his insides had exploded, he said painfully, "You ... you had a baby."

"Moooooooooo!" Hannah squealed, giggling loudly as she pulled at Buttercups ears.

The room was silent. Harry suddenly jumped up and turned to Ginny. "You're right! I *can* hear your mum calling us!"

Ginny, relieved that she could leave the room, jumped up also. The pair left silently, but rapidly, Ginny whispering that she would tell him everything in the kitchen.

Once they were alone, Hermione looked at Ron, her eyes feeling teary at the sight of Ron's hurt expression. "I did," she verified. Hermione's gaze fell onto her young daughter and she stroked back the bushy curls found there.

"When did this ... why did this ... I mean ... where's the father?" Ron asked, not sure which questions out of the hundreds that he had to ask first. And yet, looking at the little girl, he had a good idea of the answer. He felt his stomach flip over.

"I'm looking at him," Hermione said, staring Ron in the eye, trying not to blink.

Of course this particular story is not Rowling's ... but it is easy for many readers of the series to enjoy the twists of this new storyline. When the literature a person has read is consciously used as a model, it provides the reader with a sense of narrative and allows her to internalize story structures and conventions. The reader in effect apprentices the writer's craft. Narratives familiarize the reader with style and voice, allow them to gain familiarity with character possibilities, and provide schemata for story creation.

The authors of fan fiction often write about characters and themes that are not developed in the books themselves; the plot threads and fictional possibilities found in fan fiction riff off of what is given in Rowling's works. Writers on these sites also benefit from reviews by their peers but in contrast to early fan fiction sites, newer sites tend to be password protected and the fiction rated for appropriateness. Another thing that is new is that many of the sites now have writing workshop/editing guidelines and advice pages to guide readers in writing fan fiction. A complex transactional process occurs in which each borrowing is echoed within a cumulative response to a variety of previous readings and experiences. Online fiction has the added potential of allowing students to dialogue with peers about the writing—creating a virtual writing workshop atmosphere. Some of the fan fiction on the *Harry Potter Fan Fiction* website have been reviewed and rewritten literally hundreds of times.

The gaps that fan fiction writers find in existing narratives (Cadernos, retrieved November 1, 2007) allow these readers to test stories' cultural guidelines. When readers do not see themselves represented in an original text, fan fiction provides for them a venue for social comment or criticism, particularly for persons who feel marginalized in their society (McArdle, 2003). Slash, a form of fan fiction that explores the erotic and generally homosexual possibilities of characters, is not necessarily designed to be sensational in nature; rather, many of these works represent thoughtful explorations of the complexities of same-gender relationships (Ashi, 2007). The pairing of Grindelwald and Dumbledore, while not common, had already appeared on the Internet before Rowlings outed them. For example, the blog "For Fans of Grindelwald and Dumbledore" has been a source for stories, art, and discussion about the pair since July 23, 2007.

In schools, Internet technology tends to be used simply to gather and share information, rather than to foster aesthetic and ethical sensibility. However, there is no reason why this needs to be the case. Some scholars have an optimistic vision of the power of technology to enhance literacies and address existing societal problems. Rogers et al. (2000), for example, find technology to have a potentially transformative function that could level the playing field for children. Young people whose cultural histories are influenced by literacies such as storytelling or the visual arts, may find that technology, with its emphasis on diverse modes of communication, can actually encompass and extend their language and story experiences.

Andrea Pinkney (2000) believes in the power of the Internet to break down cultural barriers because it can connect people of all walks of life throughout the world. Pinkney believes that people will more easily come to understand those who are different from themselves as the faceless interactions that occur on the Internet remove many cultural markers that allow prejudices that interfere with our ability to communicate. Pinkney observes, "When I go on-line ... [n]o one makes assumptions based on my skin color, or the way I speak, or on my clothing" (p. 48). Rogers et al. (2000) and Pinkney (2000) then find that technology may have the potential to provide children with wider opportunities to make, and even extend, their personal connections. Rogers and her colleagues (2000) envision the Internet's role in providing the means to support "interactive, dialogic and collaborative models of learning" (p. 80).

It appears, then, that adult literacy experts are engaged in an active dialogue about the intersections between literature and the information super-highway. Meanwhile, young readers appear to have forged their own paths through the mire, finding ways to link their experiences with the characters and situations from the series, in formats that allow them also to connect with other readers of Harry Potter. A number of sites exist on the World Wide Web that extend the fictional world through narrative, visual images, and role playing games.

Young authors of fan fiction, clearly have taken a constructivist approach to their reading. Their work signifies a breakdown of the borders that as adults, many of us have accepted as natural. In fact, the abundance of child-authored literature on the World Wide Web takes the concept of expanded literacies a step farther than the envisionments of most literary theorists. Until recent years it could be argued that there was no real "children's literature"—published narratives written by young people for young people. However, Internet browsing and publishing software have made this genre a reality. Many of these narratives are even edited and peer reviewed. The sites are constantly being updated by their young webmasters, who show tremendous commitment to their work. As we have returned to these sites over the past few years, we have seen an amazing variety of new work, and an increasing number of site features.

In the past, one excellent project involving a number of young authors who were reading, writing, and extending the world of Harry Potter was the *Daily Prophet* (Malfoy & McGonagall, pseudonyms, retrieved November 21, 2001). Based on Rowling's newspaper of the wizards and witches, these web-writings dissolved the boundaries between informational and literary text. The site took on the format of an online newspaper, but the articles display the imaginative realms of its authors: news items inspired by events in our Muggle world are combined with fan fiction columns on sports (Quidditch), events, such as a robbery at Gringotts, and advice (p. 1). An ongoing feature focused on "magical creatures" (p. 1), some of which are mentioned in the series, others of which are pulled from fantasy, folklore, or imagination.

Some of these articles take elements from Rowling's storylines and extend them in interesting directions. For example, the news article, "Muggle Magic," describes an attack by Voldemort on the Dursleys while Harry is away visiting the Weasleys:

> Mr. Dursley went down the stairs screaming for the man to go away. "We'll not have any of your kind here! I forbid you to come into this house!"
>
> Of course He-Who-Must-Not-Be-named would not heed the words of a Muggle, especially one as Mugglish as was Mr. Dursley. You-Know-Who entered the Dursley home demanding that they "hand over Harry Potter, or die a very painful death!"
>
> "You would be a friend of his," muttered Mr. Dursley.
>
> Meanwhile, Mrs. Dursley who was still wiping potatoes out of her hair sat cowering behind her great lump of a son on the stairs. She suddenly stood up, "Take him, we don't want him. We've never wanted him. If it weren't for my stupid sister Lily dying, I would have a normal life."
>
> When the name Lily was mentioned, You-Know-Who turned his attention to her. "So, you are Lily Potter's sister, are you?"
>
> As his mother stood frozen in fear, Dudley finally managed to heave himself up the rest of the stairs and squeeze through the door to his bedroom. He-Who-Must-Not-Be-Named slowly pointed his wand at Mrs. Dursley. Mr. Dursley knew that this wasn't going to be good, so he ran towards his wife. Unfortunately for Mr. Dursley, You-Know-Who was faster. He spun around and leveled his wand at Mr. Dursley, saying "Imperio," in a bored tone. Mr. Dursley fell to the floor in mid-stride and began counting his toes in a delighted manner.
>
> In a moment of utter panic, Petunia Dursley began to glow a sickly shade of yellow. He-Who-Must-Not-Be-Named turned back towards her, and his mouth dropped open in astonishment. The yellow light grew brighter as it slowly spread from her body to the stairs. You-Know-Who, the most evil wizard in the world, backed away from the light as he recognized one of the most ancient charms of protection in the wizarding world.
>
> ("Classic Prophetonian: Muggle Magic," para. 2)

Under pressure Harry's aunt (much to her dismay) displays some powerful magical ability. Knowing the Dursleys from Rowling's narratives, readers will recognize this as poetic justice of sorts and likely much more painful for the Dursleys than a simple death at the hands of He-Who-Must-Not-Be-Named. This turn of events also opens up a range of possible new storylines. The use of language in this writing also illustrates intertextuality as described by Barthes (1977):

> The text is a tissue of quotations drawn from the innumerable centers of culture ... the writer can only imitate a gesture that is always interior, never original. His only power is to mix writings, to counter the ones with the others, in such a way as never to rest on any one of them.
>
> (pp. 146–147)

One possibility that the technology allows for is the seamless versioning of text. Not only is there no longer necessarily one fixed narrative but the reader can also with a click choose a different pathway or can even write her own ending.

While most fan fiction is like the above adolescent-authored third-person narratives, in which the authors are the storytellers, some young web authors inspired by the Harry Potter series have found ways actually to invite their readers and co-authors more intimately into the world of Hogwarts through freeform online Role Playing Games. What RPGs do is systemize the inevitable creative interplay. *Hogwarts Extreme* (retrieved November 6, 2007) is one of the largest of these sites. Fans come here to interact and to role-play. The participants also collaborate to create a newspaper, classes, forums, even a stock exchange. Another popular RPG called *Hogwarts Live* (retrieved November 6, 2007) takes place in a futuristic world where Harry Potter is remembered as a legend. You purchase the items you need, battle fantastic beasts and evil professors, duel with other students ... Each role player has her own adventure. However, like all role playing games, these online RPGs create new storylines that live only fleetingly and only for the individual engaged in that particular game ... but they also have with them storyline features that are retained on site. Newspaper articles, fan art, and maps all add to the larger narrative about Hogwarts.

Many fans have utilized the capabilities of computer technology to expand literacy beyond print through the creation of fan art. One of the most versatile fan artists is Tealine Raintree. Most of the art posted on her site *Tealine's Harry Potter Headquarters* was drawn when she was a teen. One of these works done in two panels is an amazing picture of Harry taking off to fight Voldemort (retrieved November 6, 2007). Harry is in a small boat screaming "Go Back, You Guys! I'm going to fight Voldemort alone." In the second panel we see Ron and Hermione following him into the water. Ron says "Of course you are." And Hermione adds "And we're going with you!" This is of course actually an intertextual reference to a scene between Frodo and Sam in *The Lord of the Rings*. This blending of the two narratives beautifully high-lights some of the connections between these two fantasies.

One of the most popular trends, which did not exist when the first edition of this volume was published, is the inclusion of banners to accompany fan fiction. These banners include original art and images from the movies mixed together to create mood and to fit the theme of the story being told. Interestingly, it is often someone other than the author who creates the banner. Certain fans have a reputation as bannermakers. These artists interpret the author's fan fiction and attempt to draw out the mood and major themes. For example in the banner "Harry Potter and the Mysteries Unveiled" (retrieved November 6, 2007), the artist, Alora, has used a selection of clips—Harry and Ginny at the center, strange tomb-like statuary, and bleak unidentifiable locations—linked together, all depicted in sepia tones to reflect the mysterious yet romantic adventures entangling Harry and Ginny in the story of the same name written by morgana67. On its own, an image like a banner might simply evoke story, rather than exist as a narrative ... but when connected to the grand narrative of Harry Potter, the images evoke stories in the mind that reflect and impact the ongoing storylines.

Fans of all ages are creating art, comics, and other graphics that expand the visual storylines. Artist Dave Roman has created a Ron Weasley Fanzine that is a brilliant read. This fanzine written in the voice of Ron makes fun of itself while at the same time demonstrating a depth of knowledge about the series and a regard for the fandom. In introducing the fanzine he writes:

Hi, my name is Ron Weasley.

You might know me as Harry Potter's best chum or through one of my MANY siblings. But what you may not know is that I'm simply mad about comics! So now thanks to some of my muggle friends I get to be the star! I hope you enjoy them! And maybe you can draw your own (Harry says you don't need magic—just a pencil and paper! – Brilliant!)

– Ron.

(retrieved November 6, 2007)

Fan fiction requires the presence of an external canon, obviously—without it, you're not writing fan fiction, you're just writing fiction. The canon seems, at the very least, to provide a wealth of potential stories and themes to riff off, and additionally grants legitimacy and attracts an audience to the derived works that an original work might not have. But if you riff too far, or outright contradict something that the original work has established, you risk losing that. That is part of the reason why the majority of fan fiction stays close in voice and logic to the original Harry Potter storylines.

Fans have certainly explored the diverse modes of communication envisioned by Rogers et al. (2000). Yet early fan efforts to create, recreate, and co-create storylines met with some resistance from Warner Brothers. Claire Field who ran a site called "The Boy Who Lived" was at the center of a demand by Warner Brothers that owners of fan sites give up their Harry Potter domain names. Claire and others refused to do so. They received strong support from Alistair Alexander, creator of the *PotterWar*, a site that provided information about the legal issues faced by online fansites. Another site, *The Daily Prophet*, formed an organization called DADA (Defense Against the Dark Arts), which initiated a boycott and other actions in support of fans being threatened by Warner Brothers. Since 2001, for the most part a comfortable détente has existed between publishers, Warner Brothers, and fans. Many young site creators began posting disclaimer statements on their sites, acknowledging that they have not created trademark Harry Potter characters, and Warner Brothers learned that at least with popular fandoms, talking with the fans will achieve more than threats. The fact that Rowling herself has expressed pleasure with the idea of fan fiction gives these writers even more credibility (though Rowling and Scholastic did sue to stop Michigan based RDR Books from publishing a print version of online *The Harry Potter Lexicon* (Associated Press, 2007)).

On many sites, blogs and podcasts are now being used to further communication about Harry Potter. One of the most frequented blogs is found on *The Leaky Cauldron*. As for podcasts, there are two that have played a huge role in connecting fandom to all issues Harry Potter: *Pottercast* and *Muggle-Cast*. A podcast is basically a radio show that can be listened to at any time using iTunes or other software. Some of the most popular podcasts discuss issues arising from the books and updates on movies, but even with these informational-type discussions they often go into character and enter into the fictional world. What's more, fans of these shows respond in writing, audio, and video. Another new development is the podcasting of fan fiction on the *Harry Potter Fanfiction* website. As of March 2007, many of the favorite works of fan fiction can be downloaded and listened to directly as streamed audio on a computer.

Online audio has definitely impacted the ways in which fans interact with the expanding world of Harry Potter. The term 'songfic' is used to refer to fan fiction written to accompany an existing song, original lyrics that are connected to the Harry Potter world, or even fiction in which a character listening to a particular song becomes part of the narrative. Sometimes other media intersect with the songfic concept. One vlog now known as "Hank's Harry Potter Video" hit number one on *YouTube* for several days. Hank Green is the brother of young adult author John Green. The two brothers have embarked on a year-long project called *Brotherhood 2.0*, during which time they only communicate via video blogs or vlogs. Hank's cool-nerd-rant-song written in anticipation of the final book, and sung accompanied by simple guitar strumming includes the following lines:

> Accio deathly hallows I'm getting kinda petrified
> What would Ron do if Hermione died
> Or if Voldemort killed Hedwig just for yucks
> I have no confidence in theories about the half blood prince

And what if Harry's brain is a horcrux
Holy crap that would frikkin suck

But mostly I'm just feelin' sad
I know this could end real bad but
I wish it didn't have to end at all
Yeah I wish it didn't have to end at all
Cause I couldn't care more about Harry Potter
If Hogwarts was my Alma Mater....
(retrieved November 6, 2007)

Although humor is definitely part of the hook for this song, Hank's predictions demonstrate a good knowledge of the storyline, and he deftly captures the fear that the grand Potter narrative might end with the series.

Another video/music intersection that really stretches understandings of the narrative worlds of Harry Potter is the music video trailer. The majority of these videos are created as trailers for existing works of fan fiction. Playlists of these trailers are listed on *Youtube*. One need only watch "Silent Screams: A Harry Potter Fanfic Trailer" by Lindzie914 (retrieved November 6, 2007) or "Yellow Charm, Green Indifference" by Phoenixproductions05 (retrieved November 6, 2007) to see the level of multimedia storytelling that goes into these trailers and the care the producers take to connect with the immediate work of fiction. The fan fiction "Silent Screams," which takes place during sixth year, focuses on Hermione and how the dark side attempts to seduce her. In the trailer, most of the images are from the Harry Potter movies with some mixed in from Angel. Many of the voice-overs are from various Kate Winslet films. The moody background music is a song by Breaking Benjamin. As Lindzie914 says in her "About the video" disclaimer: "I don't own any of it, I just own the story line." It sounds chaotic, but put together, the images and audio create an eerie seductiveness that viewers of the trailer have responded to well. "Yellow Charm, Green Indifference," which retells the fan fiction of the same name by High-Voltage (retrieved November 6, 2007) is one of many stories about the Founders of Hogwarts. The trailer uses footage from *King Arthur*, *Tristan and Isolde*, and *Pride and Prejudice* ... but put together so well that they might easily be from the same movie. After reading the casting sheet, it is fairly easy to follow the relationships that are evoked between the various characters.

One of the most interesting concepts to arise from fandom is Wizard Rock or Wrockers. There are currently over 200 bands that write and play music connected to the fictional world of Harry Potter. What makes this phenomenon especially interesting is that the bands take on the persona and voice of a character(s) from the series. The Moaning Myrtles for example sing about being dead and stuck in a toilet, and having a crush on Harry who will never kiss her (cause his lips would pass right through her).

Wizard Rock dates from at least 2002 when Harry and the Potters hit the scene with songs such as "Save Ginny Weasley":

Are you scared to walk through the hallways?
Are you worried that the spiders run away?

Are you petrified
Of being petrified?
Are we going to have to save the school again?
We've got to save Ginny Weasley from the Basilisk
We've got to save the school from that unseen horror
We've got to save Ginny Weasley from the Basilisk
We've got to save the school again
(retrieved November 6, 2007)

Today groups with names like Draco and the Malfoys, The Whomping Willows, and Siriusly Black (wizard rap) sing about scenarios from the books, as well as extensions and possibilities as diverse as any that might be found in fan fiction. The musical stylings are all over the spectrum from rap, to rock, to folk, and indie. Some of the musicians are older (in their twenties) and a few tweens have been inspired to start their own bands, but most seem to be around college age—people who were young teens when *Harry Potter and the Sorcerer's Stone* was first published. In general, the movement is made up of readers who have never written music nor been in a band before but are now inspired. Matt, lead singer of The Whomping Willows says, "The beauty of Wizard Rock is that for many of the bands, it's nothing more than a learning experience" (Leib, 2007). There is a level of satire involved: wrockers often make fun of what they are doing, but many of the lyrics are insightful and they inspire a read-and-rock aesthetic (Carroll, 2005).

The Hermione Crookshanks Experience sings a very clever song called "Bonjour Fleur." The song is in the voice and temperament of Hermione and though not something that happens in the book, it is certainly easy to imagine Hermione feeling this way.

Hello Fleur
How are you doing today?
I've got something I need to say.
And I don't mean to condescend
But I'll say it in a way you can comprehend.
Bonjour Fleur
Comment allez-vous?   (How are you?)
Je suis très fatiguè   (I am very tired)
Avec vous, avec vous.   (With you, with you)

Vous êtes bête. (You are stupid)
Je vous déteste. (I hate you)
Je vous déteste.
Oui, c'est vrai (Yes, it's true)
Alors, si vous plait, (So, if you please)
Allez. Partez. Allez. Allez. (Go, leave. Go. Go)
Maintenant, (Now)
C'est le temps (it's time)
Pour au revoir. (for good-bye)
Alors au revoir, Fleur, au revoir. (So good-bye, Fleur, good-bye).
(retrieved November 6, 2007)

The idea that Hermione would learn French in order to tell Fleur off in her own language (even if she would only do it in her head) seems very much in character.

Sometimes the bands delve into more complicated emotions. Not everything that wizard rockers sing about is directly from the books or movies. The Parselmouths, are a good example of a character type that might be easy to imagine as female Slytherins. In "Oh Dumbledore" The Parselmouths respond to the death of Dumbledore:

Oh, Dumbledore, he's gone now
And school will not be the same

Our world's turned upside-down now
'Cause our Headmaster has been slain
Oh, Dumbledore, this is crazy
I'm sure the Dark Lord is thrilled
I'm feeling a little mixed up
Over how your blood has been spilled
(retrieved November 6, 2007)

These young women are spoiled bullies, rather superficial and air-headed—they are not based on any particular person but rather on the general idea of Slytherin girls who are perhaps not totally evil.

These bands play at Yule Balls, bookstores, and libraries. They are recording their music, shooting videos, and touring. Many of the bands make their music available on myspace.com but they also sell their own CDs. There is now also a "Wizard Rock CD of the Month Club," each of which includes a variety of new songs. One of the best sites for finding out what's happening on the Wizard Rock scene is *Wizrocklopedia*. Another website, *Realwizardrock*, provides lyrics to songs by most of the popular Wizard rockers.

It is widely believed that people learn effectively by becoming agents in their own learning. Participatory literacy, in its broadest sense, describes the multiple ways readers take ownership of reading and writing to construct meanings situated within their own socio-cultural characteristics (Fingeret, 1989). We have argued in this chapter that reading, writing, and other responses to text are socio-constructivist processes in which learners interact to create worlds of meaning that incorporate a text, personal context, and prior knowledge (Kucer, 1985). Ways of seeing self and the world are co-constructed as people insert themselves and others into various storylines. Lived experience conditions and informs a person's inscription of self into the fictions encountered. These everyday discourses and practices are implicit and embedded in everyday social worlds, talk, and texts that children encounter. The possibilities children might adopt are defined by the available discourses through which their individual personality and their social worlds are constituted. Where technology might best contribute to this constructive process is by providing an arena for publication of and communication about student narratives that take advantage of the potentials of hypertext.

Seymour Papert (1993) has posited that technology offers incentives to learning that are not present in schools. He contrasts the extraordinary cognitive growth of pre-schoolers, who learn through self-directed experiments with their environment, with the resistant behaviors of the same children when they enter a classroom where encounters with real-world events are mediated by print. He questions the desirability of creating literate students, when only "the literal sense of literacy" (p. 11) is what is meant. Papert, evokes Shirley Brice Heath, advocating that literacy be defined instead, as "ways of knowing" (p. 10). Only when young people can use their knowledge of what Papert calls "letteracy" (p. 11) to transform themselves and their sense of the world around them, do they become truly literate.

This is exactly what is happening among the growing number of young authors on the web. Their work displays control over a variety of textual forms. They can use voice in an effective and flexible manner. They do not limit themselves to print as a means of expression, but also use art and multimedia as legitimate expressions of ideas. These young authors are engaging in activity that would be viewed by many educational practitioners as optimal for their growth as learners. Papert (1993) cites the recommendations from some key educational theorists that inform teachers today:

- that children learn better if learning is part of lived experience (John Dewey, 1934);
- that children learn better if they are truly in charge of their own learning processes (Paulo Freire, 1973);
- that conversation plays a crucial role in learning (Lev Vygotsky, 1962)

While the websites discussed demonstrate all of these ideas in practice to a certain extent, the most crucial point is that the use of technology is not detracting from literature in these instances; in fact, these online interactions enhance reading and help young adults build envisionments of literature. In visiting these sites, young people continuously come into contact with intersecting storylines, which will affect their understandings of the narratives and of self. The young Harry Potter fan fiction writers have clearly been able to "see the intersection between themselves as fictions (albeit intensely experienced fictions) and the fictions of their culture; which are constantly being (re)spoken, (re)written, and (re)lived" (Davies, 1993, p. 2). That these are by and large not related to school activities and tend to be child initiated is a wonderful statement on the motivation *story* can provide for writing.

References

Alexander, A. *Potterwar*. Retrieved November 21, 2001 from http://www.potterwar.orguk/home/index.html.

(Anonymous), K. Harry Potter fan fiction. Retrieved November 21, 2001 from http://wwwgeocities.com/kim_2000rl/KimFanfic.html.

Ashi. "Mmm ... Slash. Also, Fanfiction and Authority." *Flight Papers*. July 10, 2007. Retrieved November 6, 2007 from http://www.flightpapers.org/?p=14.

Associated Press (2007, October 31). J.K. Rowling sues to stop "Harry Potter Lexicon" *MSNBC*. Retrieved January 7, 2008 from http://www.msnbc.msn.com/id/21568449/.

Bakhtin, M. (1982). *The dialogic imagination: Four essays*. Texas: University of Texas Press.

Barthes, R. (1977). "Introduction to the structural analysis of narrative," in Roland Barthes (ed.), *Image Music Text*, trans. S. Heath, New York: Hill and Wang, 142–148.

Bishop, R. S. (2000). Why literature? *New Advocate, 13*(1), 73–76.

Bruner, J. (1986). *Actual minds, possible worlds*. Cambridge, MA: Harvard University Press.

Cadernos, I. *Roswell*, textual gaps and fans' subversive response. Retrieved November 1, 2007 from http://www.cadernos.ufsc.br/download/7/doc/Isabella_Cadernos7.doc.

Carroll, Larry. "Harry Ramone? Iggy Voldemort? Band splices punk with Potter: Boston's Harry and the Potters tour libraries, bookstores." Sept 8 2005. Retrieved November 6, 2007 www.mtv.com/news/articles.1509166/20609081d-O.jhtml.

Carter, B. (2000). Literature in the information age. *New Advocate, 13*(1), 17–22.

Davies, B. (1993). *Shards of glass: Children's reading and writing beyond gendered identities*. Cresskill, NJ: Hampton Press.

Dewey, J. (1934). *Art as experience*. Carbondale, IL: Southern Illinois University Press.

Field, C. *The boy who lived*. Retrieved November 21, 2001 from http://harrypotterguide.co.uk/.

Fingeret, H. A. (1989). The social and historical context of participatory literacy education. *New Directions for Continuing Education, 42*, 5–15.

Freire, P. (1973). *Pedagogy of the oppressed*. New York: Seabury Press, Inc.

Iser, W. (1978). *The act of reading: A theory of aesthetic response*. Baltimore, MD: John's Hopkins University Press.

Jenkins, H. (1992). *Textual poachers: Television fans and participatory culture*. London and New York: Routledge.

Kucer, S. L. (1985). The making of meaning: Reading and writing as parallel processes. *Written Communication, 2*(3), 317–336.

Langer, J. A. (1991). *Literary understanding and literature instruction* (Report Series 2.11). Albany, NY: Center for the Learning and Teaching of Literature.

Langer, J. A. (1993). *Approaches toward meaning in low- and high-rated readers* (Report Series 2.20). Albany, NY: Center for the Learning and Teaching of Literature.

Leib, Matt. "Wailing Wizards. Only the 'Harry Potter' series could start its own music genre." Issue date: October 18, 2007. *The Daily Northwestern*. Retrieved November 6, 2007 from http://media.www.daily.northwestern.com/media/storage/paper853/news/2007/10/18/Play/Wailing.wizard-3040.

McCardle, M. (2003). Fan fiction, fandom, and fanfare: What's all the fuss? *Boston University Journal of Science and Technology Law, 9*, 433–470.

Malfoy (pseud.), L., & McGonagall (pseud. for Heather Lauver), M. *The daily prophet*. Retrieved November 21, 2001 from http://www.dprophet.com.

Papert, S. (1993). *The children's machine: Rethinking school in the age of the computer*. New York: HarperCollins.

Pinkney, A. S. (2000). Books and megabytes: Good friends in the information age. *New Advocate*, *13*(1), 43–48.

Raintree, T. *Tealine's Harry Potter page*. Retrieved November 6, 2007 from http://tearain.tripod.com/hp/.

Raintree, T. *Harry goes it alone*. Retrieved November 6, 2007 from http://img.photobucket.com/albums/v241/ twirlynoodle/lotrgagc.jpg.

Rogers, T. (1991). Students as literary critics: The interpretive experiences, beliefs and processes of ninth-grade students. *Journal of Reading Behavior, 23*(4), 391–423.

Rogers, T., O'Neil, C., & Jasinski, J. (1995). Transforming texts: Intelligences in action. *English Journal, 84*(8), 41–45.

Rogers, T., Tyson, C., Enciso, P., Marshall, E., Jenkins, C., Brown, J., Core, E., Cordova, C., Youngsteadt-Parish, D., & Robinson, D. (2000). Technology, media and the book: Blurring genres and expanding the reach of children's literature. *New Advocate, 13*(1), 79–83.

Ryan, M. (2007a). "Narrative," in Herman, D., John, M., & Ryan, M-L, (eds.), *Routledge Encyclopedia of Narrative*. London: Routledge.

Ryan, M. (2007b). "Media and Narrative," in Herman, D., John, M., & Ryan, M-L, (eds.), *Routledge Encyclopedia of Narrative*. London: Routledge.

Turner, M. (2003). "Double-scope stories" In David Herman (ed.), *Narrative Theory and the Cognitive Sciences* (pp. 117–142). Stanford: *CSLI*.

Tushnet, R. (1997). Using law and identity to script cultural production: Legal fictions: copyright, fan fiction, and a new common law. *Loyola of Los Angeles Entertainment Law Journal, 17*, 651–655.

Vineyard, J. "Groups like Draco and the Malfoys, Whomping Willows are even trying to save the world like Harry with charity efforts." June 6, 2007. Retrieved November 6, 2007 from http://www.mtv.com/news/srticles/1561855/20070606/id_o.jhtml.

Vygotsky, L. (1962). *Thinking and speech*. Cambridge, MA: MIT Press.

Other Resources

Websites

- Ginny Potter.com: www.ginnypotter.com/phpnuke/index.php
- Harry and the Potters: www.eskimolabs.com/hp/
- Harry Potter Fanfiction site: www.harrypotterfanfiction.com/
- The Leaky Cauldron: www.the-leaky-cauldron.org/
- Real Wizard Rock by Tess: http://realwizardrock.com/
- Wizrocklopedia: www.wizrocklopedia.com/

Blogs and Podcasts

- "For Fans of Grindelwald and Dumbledore": http://community.livejournal.com/hpannuitcoeptis/
- MuggleCast: www.mugglenet.com/mugglecast/
- Pottercast: http://pottercast.the-leaky-cauldron.org/

Fan Fiction

- "Daddy" by blondebouncingferret. Retrieved November 21, 2001 from http://fanfiction.mugglenet.com/viewstory.php?sid=8532
- "Eclipse of the Sky" by Firefawn. Retrieved November 21, 2001 from www.harrypotterfanfiction.com/viewstory.php?psid=69102
- "Yellow Charm, Green Indifference" by HighVoltage. Retrieved November 21, 2001 from http://www.fictionalley.org/authors/highvoltage/YCGI01a.html

Fanart

- Alora. "Harry Potter and the Mysteries Unveiled." Retrieved November 6, 2007 from www.harrypotterfanfiction.com/viewstory.php?psid=217675
- Raintree, T. "Harry goes it alone." Retrieved November 21, 2001 from http://img.photobucket.com/albums/v241/twirlynoodle/lotrgagc.jpg
- The Ron Weasley Fanzine! Retrieved November 6, 2001 from www.yaytime.com/roncomics.html

Songs

- "Bonjour Fleur" from *How to Write with a Feather* by The Hermione Crookshanks Experience (Kristine). Retrieved November 21, 2001 from www.myspace.com/hermionecrookshanks
- "Dumbledore is Gay" by Justin Finch-Fletchley & The Sugar Quills. Retrieved November 21, 2001 from www.myspace.com/justinfinchfletchley
- Harry and the Potters. Retrieved November 21, 2001 from www.myspace.com/harryandthepotters
- "Oh Dumbledore" from *Illegal Love Potion* by The Parselmouths (Brittany Vahlberg and Kristina Horner). Retrieved November 21, 2001 from www.myspace.com/theparselmouths
- "Save Ginny Weasley" from *Harry and the Potters* by Harry and the Potters (Joe DeGeorge and Paul DeGeorge). Retrieved November 21, 2001 from www.myspace.com/harryandthepotters

Vlogs and Video

- "Hank's Harry Potter Video" July 18, 2007. Retrieved November 21, 2001 from www.youtube.com/watch?v=CvvFiZyEyTA
- Homemade videos: www.veritaserum.com/vtmmedia/fanmade/
- "Silent Screams: A Harry Potter Fanfic Trailer" by Lindsay. Retrieved November 21, 2001 from www.youtube.com/watch?v=RYj1E9Rx9xo
- "Yellow Charm, Green Indifference" (Founders Fanfic) Trailer Phoenixproductions05. Retrieved November 21, 2001 from www.youtube.com/watch?v=sbUyiALD-HIo

RPGs

- Hogwarts Extreme: http://www.hexrpg.com/
- Hogwarts Live: http://www.hogwartslive.com/

Chapter Eighteen

Pottermania
Good, Clean Fun or Cultural Hegemony?

TAMMY TURNER-VORBECK

Muggle mania swept the country yesterday as *Harry Potter* fans queued for hours in atrocious weather conditions outside bookstores before the release of the series' seventh and final book

(*Irish Independent*, July 21, 2007)

This last summer, while away on vacation and collecting my thoughts in order to write an updated version of my original book chapter for the second edition of *Critical Perspectives on Harry Potter*, I awoke at my bed and breakfast outside of Dublin, Ireland to the above newspaper headline (Riegel and McDonagh, 2007) and was instantly reminded of why the work in this new collection would be so important. I knew that the seventh Harry Potter book was due to arrive on bookstore shelves, but as an American, had not anticipated being faced so squarely with the frenzy overseas. It began with the newspaper over tea in the common area of the inn but as I ventured into Dublin, I was soon aware that the day was going to be indelibly marked by Pottermania. The bookstores of Dublin overflowed into the streets, spilling out the hundreds of humans, many of them costumed, awaiting their copy of the "last book" and the various figurines and related merchandise available for point-of-purchase sale. The traffic patterns of Dublin, which I had already become accustomed to in just a few days' time, were significantly compromised and the city had the air of a party taking place. The mania continued throughout the day and followed me into the train station as I prepared to depart on a journey to the city of Cork. The train station at Dublin had a small bookstore and it too was bustling with people vying to buy their copies of the book, several of whom I am quite sure gave up their places on the scheduled trains to stay in line! Upon my arrival in Cork, I was greeted by a handful of enterprising people who had bought several dozen copies of the book early in the morning, stacked them high in cardboard boxes, and were selling them to eager tourists from all over the world at prices far greater than the original cover price of the books. The evening's news back in Dublin was full of stories about the day's Pottermania and news coverage continued through the next week.

It was a bit of serendipity that allowed my summer vacation in Ireland to overlap with the release of Rowling's seventh and final Harry Potter book and it gave me an increased sense of importance of the need to examine critically this cultural phenomenon, which has certainly expanded since the first edition of *Critical Perspectives on Harry Potter* was released back in 2003. In this updated chapter, my original arguments remain cogent and in place, although I have endeavored to bring them up to date with the work of others who have added to the conversation since the first writing was completed. The section I wrote on social normative messages found in these texts has been removed since the other authors in this updated book pursue such analysis in depth. As a new edition, this collection represents a renewed and continuing effort to examine and illuminate the phenomenon that we are witnessing worldwide and of which several generations will undoubtedly feel the impact, Pottermania.

A Neo-Marxist Perspective on the Media

Although long criticized for its overly deterministic and reductionist emphasis, Marxism is nonetheless able to lend its central tenets for a useful critical examination of societal and cultural phenomenon. Marxist critical theory can be effectively employed to analyze Pottermania, and explore the significance of its impact upon our culture and our society because it "draws our attention to the issue of political and economic interests in the mass media and highlights social inequalities in media representations" (Chandler, 2001, p. 14). A central tenet of Neo-Marxism is that "Cultures are structured in ways that enable the dominant group holding power to have the maximum control with the minimum of conflict" (Lye, 1997, p. 1). This applies directly to the phenomenon of Pottermania, as we witness corporations imprinting upon and manipulating children and child culture through Pottermania; yet, we do not perceive this as anything unusual or threatening. In fact, by contrast, we embrace it. This is significant when we accept the premise that our ideas of the way things are and how the world should (and does) work are generally taught for the legitimization of the current order of society. Cultural values and practices are constructed to appear normal and natural, rendering them beyond our question. In this sense, Pottermania allows the Harry Potter books and related products to be seen as good, clean, capitalist fun rather than something possibly sinister and in need of perlustration.

It is important to realize that childhood and child culture, specifically, represent prime opportunities for exercising such ideological control. This control is not always a matter of groups deliberately planning to oppress people or alter their consciousness (although this can happen) but occurs as dominant institutions in society work to use values, conceptions of the world, and symbol systems to legitimize the current order (Lye, 1997). Woodson (1999) states:

> Children are a prerequisite for cultural reproduction over time and childhood literally exists as the site of enculturation. Adults and social institutions are invested in ascribing meaning onto and into childhood in order to maintain social order and the socialization of children negotiates not only behavior patterns but also identity formation.
>
> (p. 3)

Inasmuch, diligent awareness and governance over what takes place at this "site of enculturation" seems paramount, yet, simply does not occur when cultural phenomena such as Pottermania are uncritically received and viewed as part of the natural landscape of childhood. As Chandler (2001) describes,

> The subject (viewer, listener, reader) is constituted by the text and the power of the mass media resides in its ability to "position" the subject in such a way that their representations are taken to be reflections of everyday reality.
>
> (p. 7)

My argument is that Pottermania *can* and *should* be examined through this sort of Neo-Marxist lens to consider the political and social functions of these mass media texts, beginning with an understanding of the commodification of child culture and childhood.

The Commodification of Child Culture and Childhood

Corporate consumerism is increasingly targeting child culture and childhood itself is now subject to commodification. Schor (2006) explains this process, "The commodification of childhood refers to a process in which the cultural category of childhood is itself produced for the purpose of being sold" (p. 90). She extends this concept by explaining the role of those who market and advertise to children in what industry insiders refer to as *kidspace,*

> These industry professionals have become increasingly influential in the social, cultural, and economic construction of childhood. They affect children's sense of identity and self, as well as their values, behaviors, relationships with others and daily activities. They help shape the normative vision of childhood that is held by both children and adults. In this sense, they are creating, transforming, and packaging childhood

as a productive cultural concept that they then sell to the companies who make the actual products that children buy.

(p. 90)

In this process, there are two troubling things at work. The first is that what constitutes childhood (for both adults and children) is envisioned, represented, and subsequently marketed to the public, through mass media channels, by corporations motivated by the sale of their products rather than arising from the authenticity of our lives. This is the process of the commodification of childhood and child culture, a sort of cultural anti-trust, if you will, the result of which is the carefully orchestrated manipulation of identity and desires in order to produce the obedient child shoppers of today and the consummate consumers of the future.

Contemporary elements of child culture such as television, movies, and computer games were created in the age of late capitalism and have always been closely associated with and reliant upon marketing tactics such as print advertising and commercials in the electronic media. Recently, however, the traditional elements of child culture such as children's literature, imaginative play, toys, art, and music have been increasingly infiltrated and manipulated through the skillfully crafted images and products of marketing and media giants, a prime example of which is the Disney Corporation. As Giroux (2004) suggests, "Disney's all-encompassing reach into the spheres of economics, consumption, and culture suggests that we analyze Disney within a range of relations of power." Pottermania, generated by another corporate giant (Time Warner), has reached a level of cultural phenomenon such that it deserves similar consideration to Disney. Like Disney, one need only stroll through the aisles of any large department store to find evidence of Pottermania's impending legacy on the images of childhood.

In their book *Kinderculture: The Corporate Construction of Childhood*, Steinberg and Kincheloe (2004) critique the corporate construction of childhood and state:

Using fantasy and desire, corporate functionaries have created a perspective on late-twentieth-century culture that melds with business ideologies and free-market values. The worldviews produced by corporate advertisers to some degree always let children know that the most exciting things life can provide are produced by your friends in corporate America. The economics lesson is powerful when it is repeated hundreds of thousands of times.

(p. 16)

Kapur (2003) states that, "We hope that from the site of childhood, we can critique the inequities and injustices of this world and imagine a different one.

However, aggressive marketing to children to bring them into the market as consumers blurs that boundary" (p. 2).

Should it be alarming that a fundamental element of childhood such as the pleasure of reading a good book is now targeted by those who seek to shape the collective imagination of an identifiable demographic buying unit en masse? The Harry Potter phenomenon, or Pottermania, presents a focal point through which to consider this and related questions. The fact that the Harry Potter books and their associated paraphernalia are cultural products created and produced by adults for consumption by children is clear. These cultural products and elements of child culture contain powerful messages of what constitutes social and cultural normalcy and they, therefore, call for continuing, ongoing critique; and when children's identities and child culture are used as the means to the end of creating the consummate future consumer, one must begin to question seriously the proclaimed innocuousness of Pottermania. Henry Giroux warns in his book *Stealing Innocence* that "as culture becomes increasingly commercialized, the only type of citizenship that adult society offers to children is that of consumerism" (2000, p. 19). This notion holds significant implications not only for relationships between adults and children, but, also, for the future of our society as a whole.

Complicating all of this is the fact that children today are living in a postmodern world, which facilitates corporate consumerism's full frontal attack on child culture. Strinati (1993) describes postmodernism as the breakdown of the distinction between culture and society. The idea is that popular cultural signs and media images increasingly dominate our sense of reality and the way we define ourselves and the world around us (p. 360). Kellner (1998) argues that child culture's traditional artifacts are being replaced and manipulated by media culture artifacts. He is concerned that:

A commercially produced and dominated youth culture has replaced traditional artifacts of children's culture. In this media youth culture, popular music, television, film, and video and computer games create new idols, aspirations, and artifacts that profoundly influence the thought and behavior of contemporary youth.

(p. 85)

Our postmodern children are living in a state of what Baudrillard (1983) calls *hyperreality* where simulation and appearance come to be more "real" and meaningful to children than substance and reality. Children are continually bombarded with information and supersaturated by the media. Disney is a classic representation of corporate consumerism meets postmodern world. Giroux writes that Baudrillard "has captured the scope and power of Disney's influence by arguing that Disneyland is more 'real' than fantasy because it now provides an image upon which America constructs itself" (1998, p. 55).

But what *is* the significance of corporate consumerism's targeting of child culture when children today are living in a postmodern hyperreality and how is it accomplished?

Commodity Fetishism

The infringement of consumerism on child culture is particularly evident in the mass marketing of the Harry Potter products. Far beyond the seven Harry Potter books currently published, we now have the collection of Harry Potter movies from Warner Brothers (of Time Warner), which are also available on DVD for private use and ownership. These wildly successful movies have been worldwide box-office smashes. Available for sale are myriad items, over 400 and too numerous to detail here, but which include items such as the Harry Potter I-POD, leather miniature trunks customized to hold the seven book collection under lock and key, movie poster books, movie soundtracks, wall calendars, postcard books, sticker books, guidebooks to the world of Harry Potter, Harry Potter UNO card games, carrying cases, glow in the dark puzzles, board games, video games, magic sets, books of spells, Hogwarts House Watches, a Golden Snitch puzzle, Harry Potter boxer shorts, Harry Potter action figures, Bertie Bott's Every Flavor Beans, the textbooks which the character of Harry Potter used in the Harry Potter books and movies, and even a full-sized Harry Potter leather embossed trunk to "store books, clothes, and more," not to mention several dozens of websites on which to compare notes and trade items with other fans. Kapur (2003) explains this confounded expression of ideas from books emerging as products,

> As in commercials, one of the most exciting human activities *Harry Potter* presents is shopping. Aspiring wizards and witches press their noses into a show window, eyeing with longing the latest branded broomstick, Nimbus 2000, on display. Accompanied by a sigh from desiring children, the camera pans in the style of TV commercials to reveal the broomstick's brand name in the show window, and it does the same kind of pan later when Harry receives the broomstick as a gift for Christmas. Like other children's candy on store shelves today, Bertie Bott's Every Flavor Beans comes in a "variety of disgusting flavors" and like the promotional toys that make children eat at McDonalds, chocolate frogs in the wizard world are bought to get the holographic cards they come with.
>
> (p. 3)

The proliferation of these items is a blatant exploitation of the genuine excitement for children's literature that stems from children's true interests. In the effort to create more profits for its shareholders, conglomerates such as Time Warner, which holds distribution rights to Harry Potter products, supersaturate the marketplace with every conceivable spin-off product. In addition to the products themselves, these media giants use their distribution channels, which they also own and operate, to supersaturate the media with advertisements and news stories for their products. For example, when Warner Brother's studios makes an investment, as it did by purchasing the movie rights for Harry Potter, it can then turn to its sister companies within the same organization to help insure the movie's profitability. They can make a short article run in the widely respected periodical, *Time* magazine, describing the "phenomena" of Harry Potter and how the children in the UK are frenzied over the books. Then, AOL's CNN news subsidiary begins making headlines about the "phenomena." Shortly after the "phenomena" makes headlines, Pottermania is scheduled for a special interest segment in prime-time news on CNN and also on CNN Classroom, bringing the "phenomena" directly to the children in schools. Perhaps AOL's *People* magazine also concurrently runs a biography on J. K. Rowling. *Fortune* and *Money* magazines could also be called upon for support as they are all controlled by the same mega-corporation, Time Warner. Once the "phenomena" takes root, Time Warner has vast advertising capabilities within its own reach. Commercial advertising begins on its own TBS Superstation, TNT, and the Cartoon Network. In all, Time Warner boasts access in one form or another to over 100 million U.S. households. It creates and then supports the phenomena of Pottermania. Kapur (2006) explains it this way,

> It would be hard to find a child in the US who has not heard of *Harry Potter*, even if they decided not to see the film or read the book, unless like Rip Van Winkle, they had been asleep since 1998 when the book was first optioned by AOL-Warner to be made into a movie. Since then, the AOL-Warner machine made sure that the Harry Potter brand was sold through its own subsidiaries, such as its television channels, WB, Cartoon Network, and CNN, and its magazines including *Time*, *Entertainment Weekly*, and *People*. Potter was also brought to your home and the mall nearest you through AOL-Warner's deals with other businesses. Some of these were: Mattel who put out the toys; Tiger Electronics who produced alarm clocks with talking portraits, a Trivia game, a board game, costumes, and puzzles; Scholastic Paperbacks who came out with Harry Potter journals, stationery kit, and even Hogwarts crests; and Electronic Arts Inc. who produced computer and video games.

This is an example of the business model concept of vertical integration where mega-corporations control the entire process of distribution. By using its vast enterprise to *infuse* popular culture with Pottermania, the conglomerate then controls every commercial aspect of Pottermania and they, therefore, "own" a significant segment of popular culture. The insidious nature of all of this is that these corporations not only own a segment of popular culture through their control of the commodity, they also *created the fetishism*, the need, the desire, and the very market for that commodity! While these books have many merits, children and literature critics alike have identified other series that are at least as compelling for imagination but not for creating spin-off products.

Such commodity fetishism is even modeled in the Harry Potter books themselves as the children characters long to purchase particular items such as specific kinds of brooms and trading cards, for example. Waetjen and Gibson (2007) state that, "The current explosion of Potter-inspired merchandise is, to be sure, a textbook case in the commodification of children's culture" (p. 4) and in an effort to "impose unity onto production, licensing, and marketing activities," Time Warner has created a

> singular focus on the object-collecting Harry, the Harry who possesses an impressive array of magical gadgets and treats—none of which fail to deliver on their promises, as advertised. AOL Time Warner's Harry, in other words, is the ideal consumer.
>
> (p. 17)

The fundamental implication at work here is that there needs be nothing aesthetically valuable or unique about that upon which an imposed phenomena is generated. Is it something special about the Harry Potter books that has caused such a sensation or is the sensation artificially manufactured and simply centered around them? An understanding of commodity fetishism supports the latter position. If the Harry Potter books were, indeed, worthy of such widespread adulation, then the support for them would have naturally risen up from the readers rather than being pushed down upon them by mass media marketing.

Corporate consumerism's mass marketing of manufactured cultural products does not simply represent its infringement upon and control over the objects of child culture; it is also exercising control over the imaginations of children. When children are no longer able to sit with a book and create its images, sounds, voices, smells, and sensations from their own act of reading, they have been robbed of the free use of their own minds. Take the example of a third grader who, back at the beginning of Pottermania, had seen all of the media hype for the original Harry Potter movie, *Harry Potter and the Sorcerer's Stone* (2001), on television and in print advertisements along with the related products brought to school by her classmates. She considered herself deprived, as she was one of the last students in her class who had still not seen the original Harry Potter movie. She pleaded with her parents to go and see the movie and after doing so, decided to buy the first Harry Potter book in the series. She sat down to read the book with the images from the advertising, the commercials, the movie, and the product spin-offs all swirling around in her mind, creating even more anticipation. She then emerged within 30 minutes from her bedroom to announce to her parents that the book was nothing like she expected and she was bored with it. It was just a book, after all. This is the story of my own daughter, who was eight years old at the time of the release of the first Harry Potter film.

What is the moral of this story? Once a cultural phenomenon such as Pottermania takes hold, the majority of children are destined to find their first exposure not to the authentic elements of child culture (in this case, the Harry Potter books themselves). Rather, their first experience is often with the marketing spin-offs, which represent corporate America's interpretation of the real thing. In this respect, children's imaginations are certainly being severely limited. As adults, the parents, teachers, guardians, and neighbors of our children, we have a responsibility to be aware of this phenomenon, but what can be done about it?

Human Agency and Resistance

Our awareness of the commodification of childhood and the preponderance of commodity fetishism is important and potentially empowering, but it is also tricky. Schor (2006) states that,

> On the one hand, kids are increasingly constituted as a market of *empowered subjects*: they have money, exert influence, and navigate consumer culture on their own. Marketers argue that we should treat them as functionally equivalent to adults in the liberal discourse of laissez-faire consumer policy, that is, as rational, knowing subjects who can act in their own long-term interest. At the same time, these same people are constructing children as marketable objects, dissected and classified, and then served up to client companies. This knowledge enhances the power of those client companies to affect children's everyday lives, by making their products and experiences ever more irresistible. Together, marketers and manufacturers are creating a powerful experience of commodified childhood.
>
> (p. 101)

Because "a new relationship between child consumers and the people who make a living from them" is evolving (p. 101), we are uniquely poised to intercede.

Most scholars of child culture believe that children are *participants* in their own cultural production and expression. Similarly, they contend that the ways in which children interpret media are subject to their daily life experiences and environment. Hall (1982) argues that the media *appear* to reflect reality when in fact, *they construct it.* This supports the idea that the mass media tend to serve the interests of the ruling class but it also supports the idea that the mass media is a field of ideological struggle. The questions we are faced with here at the intersection of imposition and resistance are crucial to tilting the power differential back to the public's favor: how much struggle is possible when we are confronted with a capitalist marketing machine that seduces its public through normative messages consisting of comfortable, familiar images and the appearance of "good, clean fun"? Is it realistic to believe that child culture can be a place of ideological struggle in the face of commodity fetishism?

Strictly examining the ways in which humans are acted upon by such cultural hegemonic structures leaves out a vital element of the equation, *human agency*. Foucault's examination of the linkage between power and knowledge yields a useful conception of power where corporate consumerism's creation and manufacture of Pottermania is understood as extremely difficult to identify because "a relationship of power is that mode of action which does not act directly and immediately on others. Instead it acts upon their actions" (Foucault, 1983, p. 229).

Acknowledging the insidious way in which power works, critical theorists such as Bourdieu (1990) and Willis (1981), among others, have attempted to link agency and structure in a meaningful way. Bourdieu (1990), considering the question of the opposition between objectivism and subjectivism, states that a strictly structuralist Marxist view creates an "absurd opposition between individual and society" (p. 31). This shift in perspective Aronowitz and Giroux (1993) state that "resistance theorists have developed a framework and method of inquiry that restores the critical notion of agency" (p. 67). The focus on how power and hegemony create subordinate social classes as seen through a structuralist perspective is tempered through resistance theory to "restore a degree of agency and innovation to the cultures of these groups" (p. 68). These theories of resistance, with their emphasis on human agency, create the necessary space for us to theorize how we *talk back* to the social normative messages we constantly and consistently receive through corporate consumerism. How might this resistance occur? What tools do we have at our disposal? Where do we begin?

Talking Back to Pottermania

The tendency of late capitalism is that human thinking becomes mechanized as the mind begins to correspond to a machine. In this way, the human mind becomes a segmented and degraded instrument that has lost its capacity for aesthetic creation and critical thought, "especially its ability to imagine another way of life" (Aronowitz, 1992, p. 80). What, then, are the possibilities for resistance? To create room for resistance, awareness must be raised and critical thought must be fostered. In order to achieve this, *space must be created in between the imposed phenomena and the people from whom the phenomena allegedly arose.* There are obvious fronts on which to fight this particular battle: literary criticism and critical literacy. It is within literary criticism that the true, aesthetic value of children's books can be critically considered and it is within the view of the media as a site for ideological struggle that hope lies for the possibility of resistance to the ravages of Pottermania on child culture.

When considering the huge success of Pottermania, critical questions should come to mind, "What is special about the Harry Potter books?" and "Are they deserving of such a heralded place in our culture?" John Pennington (2002) warns that "the series is fundamentally failed fantasy" (p. 79). Jack Zipes (2001) uses a Marxist critical theory perspective to examine children's literature and he warns that "Phenomena such as the Harry Potter books are driven by commodity consumption that at the same time sets the parameters of reading and aesthetic taste" and that "What appears as something phenomenal turns or is turned into its opposite through a process of homogenization: the phenomenal thing or occurrence must become a conventional commodity that can be grasped or consumed to fit our cultural expectations" (p. 172). Zipes further argues that the Harry Potter series is not a reinvention and reinvigoration of the fantasy genre but rather a less than admirable example of what good fantasy writing can be. He also warns, like authors of other chapters in this book, that the Harry Potter books validate socially questionable practices such as sexism. The fact that the Harry Potter books are able to be critically examined and determined, at least by some, to be aesthetically "failed fantasy" containing unsavory social normative messages supports the argument that perhaps these books are not innocuous, "good, clean fun" and that the implications of the cultural phenomenon surrounding these books needs to be further scrutinized.

Beyond the inquiry into the aesthetic value of popular children's literature and the social messages found within popular books, we can urge the creation of a media literate public, consisting of both adults and children. "Talking back" to Pottermania is crucial as it represents a chance for resistance against the corporate mass marketing machines that have come to dictate what constitutes popular culture. McLaren *et al.* (1995) emphasize that developing a critical understanding of the media is crucial for teachers, parents, and children and that understanding needs to go beyond interpreting the meaning found in media messages. Media literacy refers to the ability of individuals to reflect upon and analyze their own consumption of media and how they are subtly influenced by media messages.

An ever broader form of emancipatory literacy is critical literacy, which focuses upon the relationship of knowledge and the distribution of power, through the creation of a critically literate public. It has grown out of the work of Freire (1970, 1998a, 1998b) who called for "reading the world" in order to facilitate human liberation and has been embraced and expanded by several theorists such as Stanley Aronowitz, Henry Giroux, Joanathan Kozol, and Ira Shor, among others. This perspective defines literacy as the ability to comprehend and resist the social relations of oppression. Aronowitz and Giroux describe their conception of critical literacy, which

> would make clear the connection between knowledge and power. It would present knowledge as a social construction linked to norms and values, and it would demonstrate modes of critique that illuminate how, in some cases, knowledge serves very specific economic, political, and social interests.... Thus, critical literacy is linked to notions of self- and social empowerment as well as to the processes of democratization. In the most general sense, critical literacy means helping students, teachers, and others learn how to read the world and their lives critically and relatedly; it means developing a deeper understanding of know-ledge gets produced, sustained, and legitimated; and most importantly, it points to forms of social action and collective struggle.
>
> (1993, p. 127)

This kind of critical thinking is capable of fostering the necessary space between the people and their real artifacts of culture. The authors of these chapters hope that this book, like the edition before it, can help readers to do just that.

References

Aronowitz, S. (1992). *The politics of identity*. New York: Routledge.

Aronowitz, S., & Giroux, H. (1993). *Education still under siege* (2nd edn.). Westport, CT: Bergin & Garvey.

Baudrillard, J. (1983). *Simulations* (Trans. N. Dufresne). New York: Semiotext(e).

Bourdieu, P. (1990). *In other words: Essays toward a reflexive sociology*. Cambridge, MA: Polity Press.

Chandler, D. (2001). Marxist media theory. Retrieved March 25, 2008, from http:www.aber.ac.uk/media/Documents/Marxism/marxism13.html.

Foucault, M. (1983). The subject and power. In H. Dreyfus and P. Rabinow (eds.), *Michael Foucault: Beyond hermeneutics and structuralism* (pp. 208–226). Chicago, IL: University of Chicago Press.

Freire, P. (1970). *Pedagogy of the oppressed*. New York: Continuum.

Freire, P. (1998a). Pedagogy of freedom: Ethics, democracy and civic courage. Lanham, MD: Rowman & Littlefield.

Freire, P. (1998b). *Teachers as cultural workers*. Boulder, CO: Westview Press.

Giroux, H. (1983). *Theory and resistance in education: A pedagogy for the opposition*. South Hadley, MA: Bergin & Garvey.

Giroux, H. (2000). *Stealing innocence*. New York: St. Martin's Press.

Giroux, H. (2004). Are Disney movies good for your kids? In S. R. Steinberg & J. L. Kincheloe (eds.), *Kinderculture: The corporate construction of childhood* (pp. 164–180) (2nd edn.). Boulder, CO: Westview Press.

Hall, S. (1982). The rediscovery of "ideology": Return of the repressed in media studies. In M. Gurevitch, T. Bennett, J. Curran, & J. Woollacott (eds.), *Culture, society and the media* (pp. 56–90). London: Methuen.

Heyman, D. (Producer), & Columbus, C. (Director). (2001). *Harry Potter and the sorcerer's stone.* [Film]. (Available from Warner Brothers, 4000 Warner Boulevard, Burbank, CA 91522).

Kapur, J. (2003). Free market, branded imagination: Harry Potter and the commercialization of children's culture, *Jump Cut: A Review of Contemporary Media, 46.*

Kapur, J. (2006). Rehearsals for war: Capitalism and the transformation of children into consumers. *Socialism and Democracy, 21*(2).

Kellner, D. (1998). Beavis and Butt-Head: No future for postmodern youth. In S. R. Steinberg & J. L. Kincheloe (eds.), *Kinderculture: The corporate construction of childhood* (pp. 85–102). Boulder, CO: Westview Press.

Lye, J. (1997). Ideology: A brief guide. Retrieved March 25, 2008, from http:www.brocku.ca/English/jlye/ideology.html.

McLaren, P., R. Hammer, D. Sholle, & S. Reilly. (1995). *Rethinking media literacy: A critical pedagogy of representation.* New York: Peter Lang.

Pennington, J. (2002). From Elfland to Hogwarts, or the aesthetic trouble with Harry Potter. *Lion and the Unicorn, 26*(1), 78–97.

Riegel, R., & McDonagh, P. (2007, July 21). They're under Harry's spell. *Irish Independent,* pp. A2–3.

Schor, J. (2006). The commodification of childhood: Tales from the advertising front lines. In S. Pfohl, A. Van Wagenen, P. Arend, A. Brooks, & D. Leckenby (eds.), *Culture, Power, and History* (pp. 89–101). Leiden, The Netherlands: Brill Academic Publishers.

Steinberg, S. R. & Kincheloe, J. L. (2004). Introduction: No more secrets—kinderculture, information saturation, and the postmodern childhood. In S. R. Steinberg & J. L. Kincheloe (eds.), *Kinderculture: The corporate construction of childhood* (pp. 1–47) (2nd edn.). Boulder, CO: Westview Press.

Strinati, D. (1993). The big nothing? Contemporary culture and the emergence of postmodernism. *Innovation: The European Journal of Social Sciences, 6*(3), 359–375.

Waetjen, J.. & Gibson, T. (2007). Harry Potter and the commodity fetish: Activating corporate readings in the journey from text to commercial intertext. *Communication and Critical/Cultural Studies, 4*(1), 3–26.

Willis, P. (1981). Cultural production is different from social reproduction is different from reproduction. *Interchange, 12*(2), 48–67.

Woodson, S. E. (1999). Mapping the cultural geography of childhood or, performing monstrous children. *Journal of American Culture, 22*(4), 31–44.

Zipes, J. (2001). *Sticks and stones: The troublesome success of children's literature from Slovenly Peter to Harry Potter.* New York: Routledge.

Contributors

Anne Hiebert Alton is a Professor of English at Central Michigan University, where she teaches courses in Children's and Victorian Literature. Her recent publications include works on Arthur Rackham, Roch Carrier and Sheldon Cohen, and Children's Fantasy, along with a scholarly edition of *Little Women*. She is currently editing a new edition of *Peter Pan* for Broadview Press.

Peter Appelbaum is Coordinator of Mathematics Education and Curriculum Studies Programs and Director-at-Large of General Education at Arcadia University, where he also directs the sTRANGELY fAMILIAR mUSIC gROUP. The Sorting Hat on Facebook placed him in Ravenclaw. Dr. Appelbaum's recent books include: *Children's Books for Grown-up Teachers: Reading and Writing Curriculum Theory*; *Multicultural and Diversity Education*; and *Embracing Mathematics: On Becoming a Teacher and Changing with Mathematics*.

Kate Behr is a Professor of English and Director of the Honors Program at Concordia College, Bronxville, NY. She is the author of *Representations of Men in the English Gothic Novel* (2002). Her research interests include stereotypes in popular fiction (eighteenth century to present day), William Henry Ireland, and, of course, Harry Potter.

Megan L. Birch is an Assistant Professor in the English Department at Plymouth State University, where she teaches students in their English Education option, as well as students who take general education courses through the English Department. Megan's research interests include curriculum studies, multicultural education, and teacher education. Megan's soon to be completed dissertation examines the spaces and places in which pre-service English teachers learn about diversity, and how these places position students to think about diversity and become multicultural educators.

Ernest L. Bond is an Associate Professor and Coordinator of the Elementary Education Program at Salisbury University. He is co-author of *Interactive Assessment: Teachers, Parents and Students as Partners* (Christopher-Gordon) and author of the forthcoming *Literature and the Young Adult Reader* (Merrill). His work has appeared in the *Journal of Children's Literature, School Library Journal,* and *Bookbird.*

Marc Bousquet is an Associate Professor of English at Santa Clara University, where he teaches courses in radical U.S. culture, internet studies, and writing with new media. His most recent book is *How The University Works: Higher Education and the Low-Wage Nation* (New York University Press). He serves on the A.A.U.P. National Council.

Peter Ciaccio, of Italian and Northern Irish origins, was born in Belfast in 1975 and raised in Rome. In 2004 he mastered in Divinity at the Waldensian Faculty of Theology in Rome, with a Thesis on "Pastoral Models in Cinema: The Example of Ingmar Bergman." He served between 1999 and 2003 as European vice-chairperson of the World Student Christian Federation. His main interest is the relationship between Popular Culture (mainly cinema) and Theology. He is co-founder and chairperson of the Protestant Cinema Association "Roberto Sbaffi." Currently he serves as a Methodist minister in Forano and Terni (Central Italy).

Peter Dendle is an Associate Professor of English at Pennsylvania State University, Mont Alto. His primary field is medieval literature, folklore, and popular religion, but he has worked more broadly on the monstrous in a number of historical and literary contexts. He has published on cryptozoology, the devil and demonology, zombie movies, and other monstrosities in two books (*Satan Unbound: The Devil in Old English Narrative Literature* and *The Zombie Movie Encyclopedia*) and in journals such as *Folklore, English Studies,* and *Journal of the Fantastic in the Arts.*

Trevor Donaldson graduated from Michigan State University with a B.A. degree in English in 2007 where he served on the editorial board of the Red Cedar Review. He is currently living in Colorado and will focus on traveling and writing before exploring graduate school.

Anna Gunder is a researcher in literature at the Nobel Museum in Stockholm where she is currently working on a research project entitled "The Nobel Effect: The Consequences of the Nobel Prize in Literature for the Literary Culture 1950–2005." She wrote her Ph.D. thesis, "Hyperworks: On Digital Literature and Computer Games" (2004) within the research project "IT, Narrative Fiction and the Literary System" run by the Section for Sociology of Literature at the Department of Literature, Uppsala University.

Elizabeth E. Heilman is an Associate Professor in the Department of Teacher Education at Michigan State University and has served in leadership roles in social studies and curriculum studies both nationally and at Purdue and Michigan State University. She is the author or editor of six books and more than 35 book chapters and articles. Her work explores how social and political imaginations are shaped and how various philosophies, research traditions, and educational policies influence democracy, social justice, and critical democratic and global education.

John Kornfeld is a Professor in the School of Education at Sonoma State University. His research in curriculum, children's literature, school/university collaboration, and the politics of schooling has been published in such journals as *Theory into Practice, Teacher Education Quarterly,* and *Theory and Research in Social Education.* His recent publications include "Framing the Conversation: Social Studies Education and the Neoconservative Agenda" in *Social Studies,* and "Caught in the Current: A Self-Study of State-Mandated Compliance in a Teacher Education Program" in *Teachers College Record.*

Nancy L. Michelson is an Associate Professor in the Department of Education Specialties at Salisbury University in Salisbury, Maryland. Her professional interest is in the area of striving readers, and she is a co-author of "Literature-based Curricula in High Poverty Schools," in *The First R: Every Child's Right to Read* (Teachers College Press) and of a case study in *Teachers Taking Action: A Comprehensive Guide to Teacher Research* (International Reading Association).

Alice Mills is an Associate Professor of literature and children's literature at the University of Ballarat in Australia. Her most recent book is *Stuckness in the Fiction of Mervyn Peake* (2005).

Philip Nel is an Associate Professor of English and Director of the graduate Program in Children's Literature at Kansas State University. He is the author of *The Annotated Cat: Under the Hats of Seuss and His Cats* (2007), *Dr. Seuss: American Icon* (2004), *The Avant-Garde and American Postmodernity: Small Incisive Shocks* (2002), *J. K. Rowling's Harry Potter Novels: A Reader's Guide* (2001), and the forthcoming *Tales for Little Rebels: A Collection of Radical Children's Literature* (2008, co-edited with Julia Mickenberg). Currently, Phil is writing a biography of Crockett Johnson and Ruth Krauss.

Maria Nikolajeva is a Professor of Education at the University of Cambridge, UK. She is the author and editor of several books on children's literature, among them *Children's Literature Comes of Age: Toward the New Aesthetic* (1996), and *From Mythic to Linear: Time in Children's Literature* (2000).

Taija Piippo is a recent English Philology graduate from Tampere University in Finland. Piippo is currently working as a technical writer for Lionbridge. Her chapter is based on the Master's thesis she wrote for Tampere University entitled "The Effect of Desire on Identity in the Harry Potter novels. Gilles Deleuze and Félix Guattari Against Psychoanalysis."

Laurie Prothro is a school library consultant and children's librarian in Sonoma County, California. She specializes in collection development and young adult literature. Her most recent publication with John Kornfeld, entitled "Envisioning Possibility: Schooling and Student Agency in Children's and Young Adult Literature," was published in *Children's Literature in Education*.

Heather L. Servaty-Seib is a counseling psychologist and Associate Professor of Educational Studies at Purdue University. She teaches in the area of counseling and development and maintains a small private practice counseling children, adolescents, and adults struggling with loss issues. Her research and clinical interests are in the areas of adolescent bereavement, support for the bereaved, and using the concept of loss in a broad manner to better understand difficult life experiences. Servaty-Seib is first Vice President of A.D.E.C., book review editor of Omega, and co-editor of upcoming Jossey-Bass text entitled "Assisting Bereaved College Students."

Nicholas Sheltrown, Ph.D., is a Performance/Technology Specialist at Grand Valley State University and an adjunct instructor at Michigan State University. His research focuses on critical social and political theory, and technology and education. His major current project is a book "Follow the Link: Critical Narratives on the Internet."

Deborah J. Taub is an Associate Professor of Higher Education at the University of North Carolina at Greensboro. Her research interests include the psychosocial development of college students, the impact of parents on students' development, and graduate students in student affairs. She is Past Chair of A.C.P.A.'s Commission on Professional Preparation, a member of the editorial board of the Journal of College and University Student Housing, Project Director of the ALIVE @ Purdue Campus Suicide Prevention Program, and co-editor of the upcoming Jossey-Bass New Directions for Student Services volume, "Assisting Bereaved College Students."

Tammy Turner-Vorbeck, Ph.D., is a visiting Professor of Education at Wabash College whose focus includes multiculturalism/diversity, curriculum theory, and sociology of teaching. Her research explores relationships among schooling, culture, and identity, particularly family structure diversity and equity issues. Her work has appeared in *Curriculum Inquiry* and *Multicultural Education*, and she is the author of many book chapters. Her new edited book, *Other Kinds of Families: Embracing Diversity in Schools* (co-edited with Monica Miller Marsh), is newly available from Teachers College Press.

Index